Lecture Notes in Computer Science 11952

More information about this series at http://www.springer.com/series/7410

Deepak Garg · N. V. Narendra Kumar ·
Rudrapatna K. Shyamasundar (Eds.)

Information Systems Security

15th International Conference, ICISS 2019
Hyderabad, India, December 16–20, 2019
Proceedings

 Springer

Editors
Deepak Garg (iD)
Max Planck Institute for Software Systems
Kaiserslautern and Saarbrücken, Germany

N. V. Narendra Kumar
Institute for Development and Research
in Banking Technology
Hyderabad, India

Rudrapatna K. Shyamasundar (iD)
Indian Institute of Technology Bombay
Mumbai, India

ISSN 0302-9743 ISSN 1611-3349 (electronic)
Lecture Notes in Computer Science
ISBN 978-3-030-36944-6 ISBN 978-3-030-36945-3 (eBook)
https://doi.org/10.1007/978-3-030-36945-3

LNCS Sublibrary: SL4 – Security and Cryptology

This Springer imprint is published by the registered company Springer Nature Switzerland AG
The registered company address is: Gewerbestrasse 11, 6330 Cham, Switzerland

Preface

On behalf of the entire Organizing Committee, we welcome you to the 15th International Conference on Information Systems Security (ICISS 2019).

ICISS is a selective venue for disseminating scientific results related to the theory and practice of security. In recent years, the acceptance rate of the submitted papers has been around 30%. This year, 17 papers were accepted from 63 submissions (an acceptance rate of less than 27%). Of the accepted papers, 13 are regular full-length papers reporting mature work, and 4 are shorter work-in-progress papers. Most papers received three or four reviews largely carried out by the Program Committee. In some cases, external experts provided reviews. A few papers were rejected based on only two reviews when it was clear that the papers could not be accepted.

In addition to the accepted papers, the conference program also featured four invited talks by eminent speakers working in different sub-areas of security. The invited speakers, in alphabetical order of last names, were Karthikeyan Bhargavan (Inria), Krishna Gummadi (MPI-SWS), Manoj Prabhakaran (IIT-Bombay), and Reza Shokri (NUS). We hope that you found the entire program engaging, educational, and helpful to your own research.

Many people contributed substantially to the organization of ICISS 2019. Program Committee (PC) members provided careful reviews and helped select the conference program. Several tutorials were affiliated with ICISS 2019, and their organizers put in a tremendous amount of effort making the tutorials interesting and accessible. The Steering Committee provided valuable inputs on PC selection and advertising. Numerous people at IDRBT provided logistical support in organizing the conference and its website. We would specifically like to mention the administrative section, the publications office, the program office, and the faculty members. The IDRBT management, led by Director A. S. Ramasastri, kindly agreed to host the conference and extended a generous amount of funding, including the institution of the Best Practice Paper Award, which was awarded at the conference for the first time this year and will continue to be presented at future ICISS conferences. We would also like to acknowledge the generous contributions of our platinum sponsors the National Payments Corporation of India (NPCI) and the State Bank of India (SBI), our silver sponsor Thales, and others who confirmed their sponsorship after this writing. Springer and its staff handled all the copyediting and the production of the proceedings. Finally, a conference succeeds primarily due to the active participation of its community year after year, so we extend a very warm thanks to all of you for participating!

We hope you had an excellent and productive time at ICISS 2019 and in the city of Hyderabad, and hope to see you again at next year's ICISS.

October 2019

Deepak Garg
N. V. Narendra Kumar
R. K. Shyamasundar

Organization

General Chair

R. K. Shyamasundar   IIT Bombay, India

Program Committee Chairs

Deepak Garg   MPI-SWS, Germany
N. V. Narendra Kumar   IDRBT, India

Workshop Chairs

Abhishek Kumar Thakur   IDRBT, India
Kannan Srinathan   IIIT Hyderabad, India

Tutorial Chairs

Basant Rajan   Coriolis Technologies, India
Vishwas Patil   IIT Bombay, India

Local Organizing Committee

S. Rashmi Dev (Chair)   IDRBT, India
Vijay Belurgikar   IDRBT, India
K. Dharmender   IDRBT, India
Mrudula Petluri   IDRBT, India
Abhishek K. Thakur   IDRBT, India
N. V. Narendra Kumar   IDRBT, India

Steering Committee

Aditya Bagchi   ISI Kolkata, India
Venu Govindaraju   SUNY Buffalo, USA
Sushil Jajodia   George Mason University, USA
Somesh Jha   University of Wisconsin-Madison, USA
Arun Kumar Majumdar   IIT Kharagpur, India
Chandan Mazumdar   Jadavpur University, India
Atul Prakash   University of Michigan, USA
A. S. Ramasastri   IDRBT, India
Pierangela Samarati   University of Milan, Italy
R. K. Shyamasundar   IIT Bombay, India

Program Committee

Adwait Nadkarni	College of William & Mary, USA
Aniket Kate	Purdue University, USA
Arunesh Sinha	University of Michigan, USA
Atul Prakash	University of Michigan, USA
Basant Rajan	Coriolis Technologies, India
Bharath Kumar Samanthula	Montclair State University, USA
Bimal Roy	ISI Kolkata, India
Biswabandan Panda	IIT Kanpur, India
Bogdan Carbunar	Florida International University, USA
Boxiang Dong	Montclair State University, USA
Bruno Crispo	University of Trento, Italy
Chandan Mazumdar	Jadavpur University, India
Chester Rebeiro	IIT Madras, India
Debdeep Mukhopadhyay	IIT Kharagpur, India
Donghoon Chang	IIIT Delhi, India
Eric Filiol	ESIEA, France
Frederic Cuppens	IMT Atlantique, France
Gopinath Kanchi	IISc, India
Kannan Srinathan	IIIT Hyderabad, India
Laszlo Szekeres	Google Inc., USA
Lorenzo Cavallaro	King's College London, UK
Lorenzo DeCarli	Worcester Polytechnic Institute, USA
Luigi Logrippo	Université du Québec en Outaouais (UQO), Canada
Mahavir Jhawar	Ashoka University, India
Mohan Dhawan	IBM Research India, India
Oana Goga	CNRS, France
Omar Chowdhury	University of Iowa, USA
Peng Liu	Pennsylvania State University, USA
Pierangela Samarati	University of Milan, Italy
Pratyusa Manadhata	Micro Focus, USA
Rajesh Pillai	DRDO, India
Ramanujam R.	IMSc, India
Sabrina De Capitani di Vimercati	University of Milan, Italy
Sanjay Rawat	Vrije Universiteit Amsterdam, The Netherlands
Sanjit Chatterjee	IISc, India
Scott Stoller	Stony Brook University, USA
Sekar R.	Stony Brook University, USA
Shweta Shinde	University of California Berkeley, USA
Siddharth Garg	New York University, USA
Silvio Ranise	Fondazione Bruno Kessler, Italy
Stefano Zanero	Politecnico di Milano, Italy
Venkatakrishnan V. N.	University of Illinois, USA
Vijay Ganesh	University of Waterloo, Canada

Vishwas Patil   IIT Bombay, India
Yanick Fratantonio   Eurecom, France

Additional Reviewers

Maria Isabel Mera
Stefano Berlato

Abstracts of Invited Talks

Secure Messaging: Towards Verified Standards and High Assurance Implementations

Karthikeyan Bhargavan

Inria, France

Abstract. Modern messaging applications like WhatsApp and Skype rely on sophisticated cryptographic protocols to provide end-to-end security against powerful adversaries. These protocols are hard to get right, and harder still to implement correctly. Any logical flaw or cryptographic weakness in the design of a protocol, or any software bug in its implementation may lead to an attack that completely break its expected security guarantees. I advocate for the use of formal modeling and software verification to build verified messaging protocols with high assurance implementations. I will illustrate this proposed methodology using examples taken from the Signal protocol, which is used in a number of popular messengers, as well as new protocols proposed by the IETF Messaging Layer Security working group.

Trusting Machine Learning: Privacy, Robustness, and Interpretability Challenges

Reza Shokri

National University of Singapore, Singapore

Abstract. Machine learning algorithms have shown an unprecedented predictive power for many complex learning tasks. As they are increasingly being deployed in large scale critical applications for processing various types of data, new questions related to their trustworthiness would arise. Can machine learning algorithms be trusted to have access to individuals' sensitive data? Can they be robust against noisy or adversarially perturbed data? Can we reliably interpret their learning process, and explain their predictions? In this talk, I will go over the challenges of building trustworthy machine learning algorithms in centralized and distributed (federated) settings, and will discuss the inter-relation between privacy, robustness, and interpretability.

Privacy, Fairness, Transparency, and Abuse of Targeted Advertising on Social Media

Krishna Gummadi

Max Planck Institute for Software Systems (MPI-SWS), Germany

Abstract. All popular social media sites like Facebook, Twitter, and Pinterest are funded by advertising, and the detailed user data that these sites collect about their users make them attractive platforms for advertisers. In this talk, I will first present an overview of how social media sites enable advertisers to target their users. Next, I will pose and attempt to answer the following four high-level questions related to privacy, fairness, transparency, and abuse of social media advertising today.

1. Privacy threats: what personal information about users are the sites leaking to advertisers to enable targeted ads?
2. Fairness: can an advertiser target users in a discriminatory manner? If so, how can we detect and prevent discriminatory advertising?
3. Transparency: can users learn what personal data about them is being used when they are targeted with an ad?
4. Abuse: can malicious advertisers exploit personal data of users to increase societal discord?

An Introduction to the CellTree Paradigm

Manoj Prabhakaran

IIT Bombay

Abstract. This note is a brief introduction to CellTree, a new architecture for distributed data repositories, drawing liberally from our article which introduces the concept in greater detail.

A CellTree allows data to be stored in largely independent, and highly programmable *cells*, which are "*assimilated*" into a tree structure. The data in the cells are allowed to change over time, subject to each cell's own policies; a cell's policies also govern how the policies themselves can evolve. A design goal of the architecture is to let a CellTree evolve organically over time, and adapt itself to multiple applications. Different parts of the tree may be maintained by different sets of parties and the core mechanisms used for maintaining the tree can also vary across the tree and over time.

We outline the architecture of a CellTree, along with provable guarantees of liveness, correctness and consistency that can be achieved in a typical instantiation of the architecture. These properties can be guaranteed for individual cells that satisfy requisite trust assumptions, even if these assumptions don't hold for other cells in the tree. We also discuss several features of a CellTree that can be exploited by applications. Finally, we briefly outline a sample application that can be built upon the CellTree, leveraging its many features.

Contents

Cryptography

Online Social Networks

Images and Cryptography

Miscellaneous Mix

Smart Contracts

A Transparent and Privacy-Aware Approach Using Smart Contracts for Car Insurance Reward Programs

Lucas M. Palma$^{(\boxtimes)}$, Fernanda O. Gomes, Martín Vigil, and Jean E. Martina

Federal University of Santa Catarina, Florianópolis, Brazil
{lucas.palma,fernanda.gomes}@posgrad.ufsc.br,
{martin.vigil,jean.martina}@ufsc.br

Abstract. Car insurance companies worldwide have launched reward programs that provide benefits (e.g., cash-back) to good drivers. However, two issues may arise from these programs. First, drivers cannot easily verify whether their insurer is properly following the program rules upon computing their rewards. The second issue is that privacy can be violated when sensing data is collected from policyholders' cars to identify whether they are good drivers. This paper proposes a smart contract-based solution that trades off user privacy for reward transparency. A smart contract computes rewards based on sensing data policyholders provide to the Ethereum blockchain. To preserve privacy, a policyholder can (i) select what sensing data is sent to the blockchain, (ii) use distinct pseudonyms to hide his or her real identity, (iii) choose what accuracy sensing data has, and (iv) verify whether his or her sensing data allows him or her to remain indistinguishable from other drivers whose data has been already disclosed in the blockchain.

Keywords: Blockchain · Smart contracts · Privacy · Car insurance

1 Introduction

Since the early 2000s, car insurance companies have offered discount programs to bring more awareness to their customers about driving behavior [45]. These programs reward *good* drivers by giving discounts on insurance premiums. Insurers usually refer to good drivers as those who respect traffic rules. Moreover, good drivers can be identified by lacking aggressive driving behavior, such as excessive speeding, improper following, erratic lanes changing, and making improper turns [20]. To allow an insurance company to decide whether drivers are good, onboard sensing devices have been installed in cars to collect data such as wheel angle, brake status, acceleration status, vehicle speed, and spatial coordinates [14,17,19,24]. Examples of such devices are GPS and CAN-bus sensors.

A usual problem is that the way insurers calculate premiums may not be transparent to customers [27,29]. One can expect a similar issue when it comes

© Springer Nature Switzerland AG 2019
D. Garg et al. (Eds.): ICISS 2019, LNCS 11952, pp. 3–20, 2019.
https://doi.org/10.1007/978-3-030-36945-3_1

to computing discounts or rewards using sensor data collected from cars. More precisely, a policyholder is likely to find hard to verify whether insurers are offering the proper discount they are supposed to offer based on his or her driving data. Since this verification can be hard for customers, insurance companies could easily advertise a reward program to attract new customers but not follow their program rules in practice. Moreover, insurers can tamper with data received from customers' car sensors to manipulate the discounts offered to their clients.

A further issue that arises from feeding cars sensor data into rewards programs is violating customers' privacy. Besides, the disclosure of this data runs into privacy problems due to the fact that location and personal data allow intrusive inferences, which may reveal habits, social behavior, religious and sexual preferences of individuals [1]. If malicious people have access to this data, stalking can be facilitated, as well as operational support for committing crimes, leading to a threat to the safety of people [13].

To address such issues, the insurance industry has been moving towards the blockchain technology. This was first devised to realize the so-called Bitcoin cryptocurrency [26] but has been recently applied in many areas. For instance, medicine [32, 33] and internet of things [6, 11].

A blockchain is a chain of blocks where each block but the first is cryptographically chained to the previous block. On the top of a blockchain and a peer-to-peer network, a distributed ledger can be built as follows. Blocks are used to compute the next state of the ledger. More precisely, for every two consecutive, distinct states of the ledger, there is a block containing the difference between the states. As such, one can compute the current state of the ledger by transversing the blockchain and computing the updates every block provides.

The ledger is often used to keep track of the balance of cryptocurrency accounts, for example, in Bitcoin [26]. Accounts are usually identified and controlled with the help of public-key cryptography. Every account is identified by a public key. The corresponding private key allows the account owner to issue a transaction moving funds from his or her account to another account. We refer to such a public-private key pair as *wallet*. For privacy reasons, a user is encouraged to create a new account and wallet for each transaction to be received in order to make it harder to link multiple transactions to the same user. To help users to do so, *hierarchical deterministic wallets* (HD wallets) have been proposed [44].

Note please that transactions change accounts state. Correspondingly, the distributed ledger should have its current state updated by creating a new block. Peers that keep a copy of the blockchain reach consensus on what the next block is as follows:

- Peers broadcast transactions on the peer-to-peer network;
- A subset of the peers usually called miners confirms these transactions. More precisely, on a regular basis a miner is selected to validate a set of transactions (e.g., to check that the signature on a transaction is valid) and pack this set to a new block;
- The miner chains the new block to the last block in his or her local copy of the blockchain;

- He or she then adds the new block to his or her blockchain, and propagates the new block in the network;
- The remaining miners learn the new block and add it to their local copy of the blockchain if the block is properly chained to their last block and contains only valid transactions;
- The miner selected to broadcast a new, correct block is often rewarded with new coins or transaction fees.

Because of conflicting transactions or propagation delays, peers may differ in their blockchain copy. As a rule of thumb, peers solve such differences by accepting the copy that contains the longest blockchain. Thus, the transactions in the blockchain are secure, trusted, immutable, and auditable [38].

A further advance in blockchain technologies is smart contracts [36]. A smart contract is a script comprising procedures and optionally a state. These scripts are stored in the blockchain. Whenever a transaction addresses a procedure contained in a smart contract, miners execute this procedure and agree on the outcome. The internal state of smart contracts can change when miners run their procedures. Every state from the initial state to the current state is stored in the blockchain.

Blockchains and smart contracts have been used to improve processes stakeholders in the insurance market carry out. For example, to buy insurance [30], change policies [22], and securely store logs [15]. However, to the best of our knowledge, we are the first to propose a smart contract-based solution that trades transparency for privacy when it comes to compute insurance premium discounts. More precisely, we propose that insurance company provide smart contracts to transparently compute premium discounts from driving data policyholders. Sensors installed in policyholders' cars collect such data and an additional, programmable device helps policyholder to prepare and store sensing data in the blockchain. As to privacy, the five approaches are used. First, the programmable device allows the policyholder to select a subset of the sensing data to be stored to the blockchain. Second, the programmable device allows the policyholder to generalize his or her sensing data by using the so-called *(k, δ)-anonymity*, so that his or her sensing data is similar to other policyholders' data stored in the blockchain. Third, to send the selected data to the blockchain, the programmable device uses HD wallets to keep the policyholder's identity secret and to prevent every two transactions containing sensing data from being linked to the same policyholder. Fourth, the policyholder can provide a subset of the stored data as input to the smart contract upon requesting his or her reward to be computed. The less suppressed or generalized the input data has been, the more accurately the smart contract can compute the reward, but the narrower the privacy protection. Furthermore, to redeem his or her discount, the policyholder personally demonstrates to the insurer company that he or she is the origin of the data used as input to the smart contract. This process is off-chain and the policyholder's identity is not disclosed in the blockchain.

The remaining of this manuscript is organized as follows. Section 2 provides the background needed for this work. Section 3 outlines our proposal and Sect. 4

presents the prototypical implementation. Section 5 discusses the proposed solution and Sect. 6 compares it to the literature. In Sect. 7 we draw our conclusions and plan future work.

2   Background

This section presents the basic concepts on which our proposal is built.

2.1   Cryptographic Hash Functions and Digital Signatures Schemes

A cryptographic hash function H is a map from the set $\{0,1\}^*$ of binary strings of arbitrary length to the set $\{0,1\}^k$ of k-bit strings [16]. We refer to an element of the set $\{0,1\}^k$ as a *hash*. We assume H is *collision resistant*. More precisely, finding distinct $x, x' \in \{0,1\}^*$ such that $H(x) = H(x')$ is computationally infeasible. This allows us to use H to securely verify that a piece of data $m \in \{0,1\}^*$ has not been changed (i.e., integrity) as follows. First, compute a hash $y = H(m)$ and store it at a safe place. Later, to check that m has not been changed, compute a new hash $y' = H(m)$ and verify that y' equals y. An example of a cryptographic hash function is Keccak-256 [40], where $k = 256$.

A digital signature scheme consists of three algorithms. The first algorithm generates a public-private key pair. The second algorithm receives the private key and a message as input and computes a signature on the message. The third algorithm receives the message, signature, and public key as input and decides whether the signature is valid. A valid signature shows that the message has not been changed (integrity) and has been signed by who holds the private key (authenticity). A choice for a digital signature scheme is ECDSA [16].

2.2   Blockchain and Smart Contracts

The concept of blockchain was introduced by Satoshi Nakamoto as a building block for the so-called Bitcoin cryptocurrency [26]. A blockchain is a sequence of linked blocks as illustrated in Fig. 1. A block is a container that stores arbitrary pieces of data. For example, a message describing a transfer of some Bitcoins between two individuals. Moreover, when blocks other than the first are created, they must include a pointer to the previous block. This pointer is realized as a hash calculated from the previous block. Please note that the integrity of every block but the most recent is guaranteed by its hash stored in the next block.

The blockchain is grown in a decentralized way. More precisely, no central party is trusted to grow the blockchain. Instead, a peer-to-peer network of participants jointly maintains the blockchain. Every participant keeps a replica of the blockchain and engages a consensus protocol to agree on what the next block to be created is. To tackle issues commonly found in a distributed system (e.g., Sybil attacks [9]) participants should demonstrate they have spent some computational effort to be able to propose the next block. To pay participants for such an effort and incentivize them to collaborate properly, monetary rewards apply.

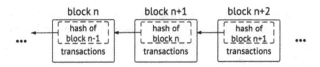

Fig. 1. The blockchain structure [7].

This consensus protocol together with hash links between consecutive blocks allows a blockchain to be an immutable, trustless database.

Szabo [36] proposed the idea of smart contracts to formalize and secure agreements between parties over a network. The author proposed clauses of a contract to be translated to programmable scripts that can be executed without the interference of a third party. However, the idea has become realizable when the blockchain technology matured. Platforms such as Ethereum [43] implement the idea presented by Szabo using programming languages. In this way, one can translate the clauses of a contract to a piece of code. Any node in the network can broadcast a transaction instantiating a smart contract. Upon request, nodes execute instantiated smart contracts and come to consensus about the execution results.

2.3   Anonymity and Pseudonymity

Privacy can be defined as the option that a person has in limiting access to their personal information [34]. Anonymity is considered a state of privacy [42]. To Warekar and Patil [41] the central idea of anonymization is to ensure that a person cannot be identified, reached and tracked [41]. To guarantee anonymity of a subject, a set of subjects with potentially the same attributes is necessary. Pseudonymity can be regarded as "means to process personal data in such a manner that the personal data can no longer be attributed to a specific subject without the use of additional information" [12]. Note please that, in contrast to anonymity, pseudonymity is lost if such additional information is publicly available. Next, we will explain how to achieve the anonymity in trajectories and pseudonymity on the data published on the blockchain.

According to Monreale et al. [25], a trajectory is a discrete sequence of points. A point is a tuple that contains spatial coordinates and a timestamp [4]. A segment of the trajectory is considered a sub-trajectory. The disclosure of trajectory data runs into privacy problems since location and personal data allows intrusive inferences, which may reveal habits, social behavior, religious, and sexual preferences of individuals [1]. In this work, we are dealing with personal trajectory data and a user can choose when to publish it to insurance companies for them to classify him or her as a good or bad driver.

In order to achieve anonymity on trajectories, one of the most used techniques in the literature is k-anonymity. This method of anonymization makes a data item indistinguishable from at least $k - 1$ others that have the same quasi-identifiable attributes, making the chance of re-identification of an individual reduced to $1/k$ [35]. The techniques most used to achieve the k-anonymity in a data set are generalization and suppression [13]. Generalization overrides attribute values by more generic values. Suppression is a technique that excludes attribute values from the data set.

One example of the application of k-anonymity on trajectories is the so-called Never Walk Alone ($\mathcal{NWA}$) approach [1]. It takes advantage of the inherent uncertainty of the location of a moving object and introduced the concept of *(k, δ)-anonymity*. In this approach, the location of an object at a given moment is not a space-time point, but a circle of radius $\delta/2$. The object can be anywhere within this area. To achieve k-anonymity, first the authors propose to generalize the trajectories by assigning each of them to a group of at least k other trajectories that are entirely located within the same cylinder (area of uncertainty) of radius $\delta/2$ in order to be published, otherwise they are suppressed, as can be seen in Fig. 2.

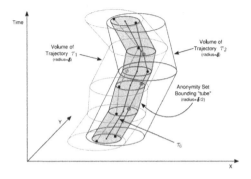

Fig. 2. Example of an anonymity set with $(2, \delta)$-anonymity [1]

As to guaranteeing pseudonymity to data published in a blockchain, one can replace real names by pseudonyms. Blockchains such as Ethereum do so by using public keys as pseudonyms.

3   Proposal

This section presents our smart contract-based solution for insurance rewards programs as follows. We start by providing an overview of the solution in 3. Section 3.2 describes how we address privacy in our proposal. Section 3.3 details the protocol used in our solution.

3.1   Overview

We start by introducing the types of entities and objects involved in our proposal. Namely, car drivers, insurers, onboard car hardware, and smart contracts.

Car drivers are policyholders of insurance companies. Drivers have two types of onboard hardware installed in their cars. The first type is the CAN-Bus sensors. For example, sensors like Positioning System (GPS), acceleration, speed, steering wheel angle, and brake status. The second type of hardware is a programmable device (e.g., an Arduino) which stores data from sensors. It is needed because such sensors are shipped with limited storage. Moreover, drivers use this programmable device to send sensing data to smart contracts. We assume both types of hardware are tamper-proof. That is, policyholders should not be able to manipulate sensing data. Smart contracts are deployed in a public network of the Ethereum blockchain by insurers to compute rewards to their customers as part of a reward program. The reason we select this public blockchain is to expose a reward program to public scrutiny, thereby allowing anyone to check program rules as well as to compare distinct rewards programs. Figure 3 illustrates the introduced entities and objects.

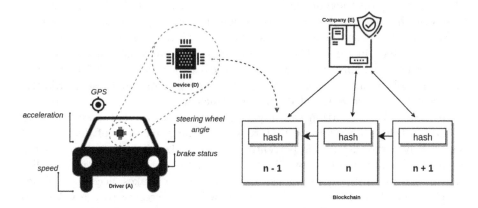

Fig. 3. Entities and objects involved in our proposal.

The interaction among policyholders, smart contracts, and insurers occurs in three phases. In the first and second phases, policyholders interact with the smart contract without revealing their real identities. More precisely, in the first phase, policyholders send data collected from their cars to a smart contract on a regular basis. For example, they send sensing data after every journey they finished.

In the second phase, a policyholder can ask the smart contract to compute his or her reward. The smart contract computes the reward based on the sensing data the policyholder sent in the first phase and on the rewarding rules the insurer has provided. The computed reward is ready to be redeemed by the policyholder.

In the third phase, the policyholder can redeem his or her reward. In contrast to the previous phases, the third phase is carried out off-chain (i.e., outside the blockchain) as follows. The policyholder should personally visit the insurance company to authenticate him or herself and claim his or her reward. Then, the insurer verifies that he or she is an eligible customer for the reward program and that he or she can redeem the reward claimed. If the verification succeeds, the employee pays the reward to the policyholder. The policyholder's real identity is not disclosed in the blockchain.

3.2   Privacy Measures

This section details the privacy measures we adopt in our solution. Namely, we adopt suppression, generalization, a method based on k-anonymity, and pseudonymity (see Sect. 2.3). Next, we explain how we apply these techniques in the phases presented earlier.

In the first phase, we allow the policyholder to select what sensing data he or she wants to send to the blockchain. By doing that, the user can suppress information by choosing when turn on and off the programmable device. Then, when the device is turned on the data starts to be collected. At this moment, we generalize the sensitive data that has been collected, e.g., we create time ranges for the timestamp and delete the last digits of the coordinates. It can be seen in the flow chart in Fig. 4. The generalization guarantees data privacy against the insurance company, which will have access to the data needed to identify the policyholder only in phase three. The more generalized these attributes, the greater the percentage of distorting, which will impact negatively on the reward. Since the distortion can impact the quality of the data, we also send to the blockchain an attribute that represents the percentage of distortion of the sensitive attributes. This percentage will be taken into account when the reward is evaluated in phase two. It is important to say that when we generalize the timestamp of the points, we can calculate neither brakes, acceleration, nor vehicle speed. In order to get this data, it will be necessary to use CAN-Bus or other vehicle sensors. With this mechanism, we only consider the trajectory data needed to learn where and when the user has been.

Also, in phase one, we create to the customers an extra privacy layer on the smart contract. This step is executed when the device sends the data to the blockchain and was partially based on ($\mathcal{NWA}$) method [1]. The programmable device installed on the vehicle sends the driver's data and three more values to the smart contract. The first value is the percentage of distortion of the attributes, that will be only used on the evaluation. The second, that we will call as k, represents the minimum quantity of sub-trajectories on the blockchain that are similar to the sub-trajectory sent as parameter. The second value, that we will call as r, represents a radius distance. Each point of the sub-trajectory will be represented as a circle of radius r. It will form a cylinder, instead of having a sequence of points we will have a sequence of circles. All the sub-trajectories of the blockchain that are within this circle are considered similar to the sub-trajectory send by as parameter. If the quantity of similar sub-trajectories found is greater than k, then the smart contract can publish this data on the blockchain. Even if there are no k similar trajectories, the device asks for the user if he or she still wants to send it anyway, otherwise, the data is discarded, as we can see in Fig. 4.

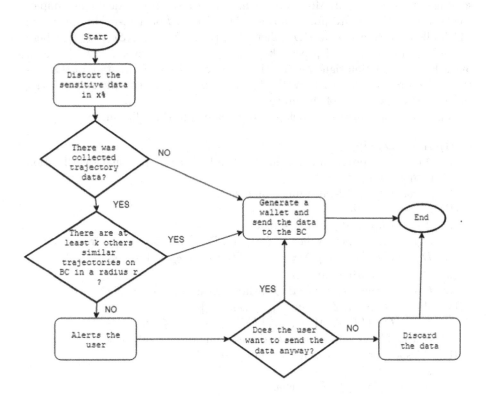

Fig. 4. Privacy process represented by a flow chart

The k, and k, values are set by the policyholder. So, he or she can choose the desired privacy level. By taking this measure it becomes more difficult to link a trajectory to an individual as there are more people with similar trajectories in the blockchain. The first sub-trajectories added to the blockchain will need to be included without this verification. The application of this approach, which is similar to k-anonymity, guarantees a certain level of data privacy since the data is added in plain-text.

In the second phase, distinct pseudonyms (addresses) are used to send data to the blockchain without revealing the policyholder's identity.. We do this by using a distinct wallet (then, a new address), it means a different key pair to sign each transaction. When the addresses are used more than once, it allows the easier re-identification of the true identity of the owner of the address.

3.3   Protocol

This section presents a protocol describing the interactions among participants and considering the above privacy measures.

We start by fixing the protocol notation. Let E be an insurer, A a driver insured by E, D the programmable device that receives and stores CAN-Bus sensing data from A's car. Moreover, we have C as a smart contract which implements insurer E's reward program rules. Also, let $seed$ be a 12-world mnemonic which allows to compute an HD wallet $W = \{(\mathcal{S}_{k_1}, \mathcal{P}_{k_1}), \ldots, (\mathcal{S}_{k_n}, \mathcal{P}_{k_n})\}$, where $\mathcal{S}_k$ and $\mathcal{P}_k$ are public and private keys, respectively. We refer to $\{T()\}_{\mathcal{S}_k}$ as a blockchain transaction signed with private key $\mathcal{S}_k$. We label the steps of the protocol with numbers from I to VIII. We use letters to identify the subactivities carried out in each step of the protocol.

The protocol is presented below and explained in the following.

(I) $A \longrightarrow D : pin_A$
(a) A resets the programmable device D and sets a new personal identification number pin_A.
(b) D generates a 12-word mnemonic $seed_A$.
(II) $D \longrightarrow A : seed_A$
(a) A backs up $seed_A$ at a safe place.
(b) D generates a new wallet $W = \{(\mathcal{S}_{k_1}, \mathcal{P}_{k_1}), \ldots, (\mathcal{S}_{k_n}, \mathcal{P}_{k_n})\}$ from $seed_A$.
(III) $D \longrightarrow C : \{\{T(entry_1)\}_{\mathcal{S}_{k_1}}, \ldots, \{T(entry_j)\}_{\mathcal{S}_{k_j}}\}, 1 \leq j < n$
(a) D selects sensing data $entry$
(b) D signs transaction $T(entry)$ using a fresh private key $\mathcal{S}_k$.
(IV) $A \longrightarrow D : pin_A, Z \subseteq \{entry_1, \ldots, entry_j\}$
(V) $D \longrightarrow C : \{\{T(\mathcal{P}_{k_n})\}_{\mathcal{S}_{k_1}}, \ldots, \{T(\mathcal{P}_{k_n})\}_{\mathcal{S}_{k_i}}\}, 1 \leq i \leq j$
(a) D asks C to compute a reward based on subset Z of the sent entries.
(b) C issues a reward token I to public key $\mathcal{P}_{k_n}$
(VI) $A \longrightarrow E : \{I\}_{\mathcal{S}_{k_n}}$
(a) A sends $\{I\}_{\mathcal{S}_{k_n}}$ to E off-chain.
(b) E pays the reward I to A.
(VII) $A \longrightarrow C : \{ok\}_{\mathcal{S}_{k_n}}$
(VIII) $E \longrightarrow C : \{ok\}_{\mathcal{S}_{k_E}}$
(a) C marks reward I as redeemed.
(b) C marks subset Z as deprecated.

In steps (I)–(II), driver A sets up programmable device D. After that, D is ready to collect a set of data from A's car and upload it to smart contract C in the form of signed blockchain transactions. Moreover, the driver can optionally set values for the k and r parameters presented in Sect. 3.2.

In step (III) driver A uploads disjoint sets $entry_1$ to $entry_j$ of sensing data to smart contract C. For every set to be sent, a distinct transaction signed using a different key $\mathcal{S}_k$ is created. Once a transaction containing set $entry$ has been confirmed in the blockchain, $entry$ should not be uploaded again.

Driver A takes steps (IV)–(V) when he or she wants smart contract C to compute his or her reward. In (IV), A selects a subset Z of sets $entry_1, \ldots, entry_j$ containing the sensing data he or she has uploaded to C. Note please that A can rule out any uploaded set for privacy reasons. In (V), driver A demonstrates that he or she controls the private keys used to upload every $entry \in Z$ and that he or she is the owner of public key $\mathcal{P}_{k_n}$ to redeem the reward to be computed from Z. Smart contract C grants a reward token I to public key $\mathcal{P}_{k_n}$.

Driver A and insurer E perform step (VI) outside the blockchain so that A's real identity is not disclosed in the blockchain. Driver A claims his or her reward by proving he or she is the owner of the public key $\mathcal{P}_{k_n}$. More precisely, he or she presents a valid signature $\{I\}_{\mathcal{S}_{k_n}}$ on token I using private key $\mathcal{S}_{k_n}$. If the presented signature is valid and A is a policyholder participating in the reward program, E pays A the claimed reward.

Steps (VII)–(VIII) prevent a token reward from being redeemed again. The steps also avoid that insurer E marks a reward token as redeemed without having paid it to some policyholder. Moreover, by labeling sensing data with *deprecated* insurers prevent policyholders from reusing such data for claiming further rewards.

4   Prototype

This section describes the prototypical implementation of our proposal. More precisely, we present the main structures, variables, and functions presented in a smart contract written in the Solidity language [10]. The complete prototype code can be found at https://pastebin.com/Vu336Src.

The main smart contract is called *Storage*. It works as a basic framework which insurers can use to write their contracts implementing their reward programs. More precisely, the contract provides standardized structures, variables, and functions needed to store sensing data but intentionally leaves function *evaluate* blank. This function is to compute rewards. Insurers should extend this contract overwriting *evaluate* according to their reward program rules. As such, the contract should not be deployed in the Ethereum blockchain and is marked as *abstract*.

We now highlight the main implementations of contract *Storage* (see Code 1.1).

The smart contract has four functions: *store, linkto, update* and *evaluate*. Function *store* allows a driver to store sensing data from his or her car in the blockchain (see Sect. 3.3, step (III)). Function *linkto* refers to step (V) of the protocol. In line 26, we define the *update* function that is executed as the last agreement between the policyholder and the insurer. More precisely, in this function both entities confirm that the reward has been redeemed and the sensing data has been consumed. Please note that function *evaluate* is marked as abstract and has no body. In this way, every contract that extends *Storage* should provide a body to *evaluate* implementing the rules of a reward program.

```
1    contract Storage {
2        struct Data {
3            uint8 size;
4            uint8[] code;
5            int256[] data;
6            uint8 valid;
7        }
8
```

```
9     enum Codes {SPD, ACC, BRE}
10
11    address owner;
12    mapping (address => Data) public entry;
13    mapping (address => address[]) link;
14    mapping (address => uint8) token;
15
16    constructor () public {}
17
18    function store(uint8 s, uint8[] c, int256[] d) public {
19        entry[msg.sender] = Data({size:s, code:c, data:d, valid:2});
20    }
21
22    function linkto(address addr) public {
23        link[addr].push(msg.sender);
24    }
25
26    function update(address addr) public {
27        if(msg.sender == owner && entry[addr].valid >= 1)
28            entry[addr].valid -= 1;
29        else if(entry[addr].valid >= 1)
30            entry[addr].valid -=1;
31        if(entry[addr].valid == 0)
32            token[addr] = 0;
33    }
34
35    function evaluate() public;
36 }
```

Code 1.1. Smart contract to store the driver's data.

4.1   Costs

In this section, we estimate the costs of running our solution in the Ethereum public network. More precisely, we approximate the costs of storing driving data and computing rewards. Costs are provided in terms of gas (Ethereum price unit) and are to be covered by policyholders.

We start by estimating the cost of storing data in the blockchain. We take into account the worst-case when a policyholder wants to store every piece of data collected from his or her car's sensors. The formula below can be used to compute the costs of storing data. The parameters of this formula are message size (ms), sampling rate (sr), the standard cost to store a message of 256 bits in the blockchain (20,000 gas) and the transaction cost (21,000 gas). For more information about gas prices, we refer the reader to Appendix G, in the Ethereum yellow paper [43].

$$(\lceil \frac{ms * sr}{256} \rceil * 20.000) + 21.000$$

To conduct this estimation, we use the following real-world information. We consider the American average driving time of 50.6 min per day [37]. Yet, we consider the sampling rate sr to be 1 CAN-Bus message for every 10 seconds and message size ms to be 126 bits long as defined in the J1939 protocol [18].

In this way, the storage cost for an average American driver is 3,021,000 gas per day. As of the time of writing, this amount of gas is $1.42 worth. In one year, the driver would have to pay $518.30 to store his or her data in the blockchain.

As to the insurer costs to read these data on the time of the driver's data evaluation. We simply replace storage cost (sc) by reading cost (rc) of 9,000 gas. In this way, the cost to read one day of driver's data is 1,709,850 gas or $0.80. Therefore, the insurer would have to pay $292.00 per year.

5   Discussion

We now discuss privacy and costs with respect to our proposal. The level of privacy of our solution depends on design and policyholder choices. Let us start with design choices. Recall please that a policyholder uses distinct public keys rather than his or her identities whenever he or she uploads sensing data to the blockchain. By doing so, uploaded sensing data sets are pseudonymized. Nonetheless, pseudonymization is lost in relation to the insurance company and the trajectories can be linked to a single public key when the policyholder asks a smart contract to compute his or her reward by providing the public key to claim the reward (see Sect. 3.3, step (V)). This issue can be solved by dropping step (V). However, a policyholder will need to demonstrate personally that he or she controls a subset of the private keys he or she used to upload the sensing data. Therefore, the policyholder has the option to not prove the ownership of all their data stored in the blockchain. Therefore, the solution to this issue trades off privacy for usability.

We now turn to policyholders' choices. We took some precautions related to privacy in order to protect the policyholder's data. Related to the generalization of the trajectory data, the user needs to be aware that the more the generalization, the worst the quality of the data. On the other hand, the lack of generalization can compromise the user's privacy. So, the idea is to find a middle ground between the generalization and the quality of the data. Basically, if the data is very generalized, it has a high level of privacy but loses its value and quality, making the reward low since it becomes harder to evaluate the driver with this low-quality data. When the policyholder asks a reward to the insurer, if the policyholders find a middle ground between the generalization and privacy it can guarantee that the insurer will not know exactly their location but at the same time will have enough information to evaluate the policyholder.

A further choice regards the variables k and r in the anonymization of trajectories. The policyholder should be also aware that a low value of k makes re-identification easier since few people have similar trajectories. The value of r also impacts privacy. The higher the r the higher the chances of finding similar trajectories within this radius. However, these trajectories may not be so similar due to the large area being considered. Therefore, one should pick a value for r such that it covers the closest areas where the policyholder and further people take similar paths. One open problem is to find the ideal values for those two attributes since it is not an easy task for the user to find it by him or herself.

As to the costs of running our solution in the public Ethereum network, the average reward given to the driver must be greather than the annual cost of storing his or her data in the blockchain. A similar assessment must be made by the insurer. Therefore, a different blockchain platform could be used. For instance, the Hyperledger permissioned blockchain [5], where transaction fees do not apply.

6   Related Work

There are distinct blockchain-based solutions for the insurance market. They apply to car insurance, cyber insurance (i.e., insurance against cyber threats), and general insurance. Their common goals are to automate and prevent fraud in the insurance process. Next, we first introduce these solutions and then compare them to our work.

Raikwar et al. [30] propose a solution for general insurance use cases (e.g., client registration, policy assignment, paying a premium, claim submission, and processing refunds). The goal is to prevent customers from falsely accusing the insurer of offering some service and to hold insurer accountable for the provided service. To this end, the customer and insurer interact through a smart contract in a permissioned Hyperledger network. Claim verifications are off-chain and interactions are logged in an external database, making the user to trust this database is secure.

WISChain [15] is a blockchain-based solution devised to cyber insurances. The goal is to avoid fraud with respect to claim evidence. Customers are individuals whose authentication data may be leaked from online password managers and commercial websites which may be hacked. In this proposal, the insurance companies select policies and pay premiums via smart contracts. The policyholders send authentication or firewall logs to a third party, who also is trusted to solve claims. The hash of these logs is also written in a blockchain.

A further solution to be used for cyber insurance is BlockCIS [23]. The objective of that work is to allow to assess customer risk and premium value online and transparently. Moreover, BlockCIS records data that can be used to process claims in the blockchain. They propose to combine private channels, selective disclosure of data, and homomorphic encryption to achieve confidentiality and privacy. However, such a solution seems not to be feasible yet. More precisely, premiums are often computed based on simple formulas, e.g., flat rates, or weighted sums [31]. The problem is that homomorphic encryption supports either addition or multiplication [28], so for the metrics that need to use both it will be necessary to use fully homomorphic encryption (FHE). However, FHE approaches have a lot to improve in order to be practical, since they are extremely expensive for real-life systems. For example, the computational cost of such an approach can be prohibitive for several scenarios [2,21].

Vehicle insurers can also use the help of blockchains [3,8,22,39]. Bader et al. [3] propose an Ethereum-based solution to reduce costs and improve transparency when dealing with claims. More precisely, smart contracts allow customers to fill a claim and check their status. Data from drivers' car is collected from tamper-proof sensors, encrypted using AES encryption, and stored in the blockchain. Because of sensor's data is encrypted, smart contracts do not process claims. This is why claim processing occurs off-chain.

Lamberti et al. [22] present a system for vehicle insurance that uses Ethereum smart contracts, mobile apps and sensors data. The work aims to enable customers to buy and change insurance policies and fill a claim on-chain. The smart contract stores the history of changes in the a insurance policy coverage. The electronic device is used to enable automatic changes in the coverage based on the vehicle's location and the number of passengers on board. The location and safety belt connection data are saved periodically on the company's database raising trust and privacy concerns. Pictures are taken and sent to the insurance company to fill the claim. Also, a hash of the picture is recorded in the blockchain in order to guarantee immutability.

Dorri et al. [8] propose a blockchain-based architecture to protect the privacy of users and to increase the security of the vehicular ecosystem. They collect data through sensors and authenticate them on the blockchain. The privacy of the users is guaranteed by using changeable public keys. The authors provide an example of use case for automotive services by providing a secure and trustworthy mechanism but with a lack of transparency. In their work, the user cannot know how the data is used after being decrypted since some processes are executed off-chain.

Vahdati et al. [39] propose a framework for insurance based on IoT and blockchain. This framework allows assessing customer risk and computing premiums online and transparently. The authors show an example for vehicle insurance. In this study, each user and vehicle has an identifier, and their information is saved as plaintext on the blockchain with no privacy protection.

Our proposal differs from the related work in transparently computing rewards to drivers with the help of smart contracts and privacy measures. These measures include suppression, generalization, k-anonymity, and pseudonymity. We make all data analysis on-chain, making this process as transparent as possible.

7   Conclusion

In this paper, we proposed a smart contract-based, privacy-aware solution to transparently compute rewards to drivers that participate in reward programs offered by car insurance companies. A smart contract computes rewards based on sensing data policyholders provide in the Ethereum Blockchain. To preserve privacy, we propose the use of: (i) distinct pseudonyms to hide real identities in the blockchain, (ii) suppression to allow policyholders to select what sensing data is sent to the blockchain, (iii) generalization of sensitive data and k-anonymity to verify whether user's sensing data allows him or her to remain indistinguishable from other drivers whose data has been already disclosed in the blockchain. We evaluated our work by analyzing costs and bring some discussion.

As future work, we plan to the use of real data collected from sensors to perform a more precise evaluation of the costs and privacy choices. We also want to develop a procedure that enables the updating of the driver's data evaluation metric, in a dynamic way, in the same instance of the smart contract. The update should be transparent and does not affect running evaluations. With this new feature, the companies could use the same contract instead of deploying a new one for each rule change.

Acknowledgments. This study was financed in part by the Coordenação de Aperfeiçoamento de Pessoal de Nível Superior - Brasil (CAPES) - Finance Code 001.

References

1. Abul, O., Bonchi, F., Nanni, M.: Never walk alone: uncertainty for anonymity in moving objects databases. In: 2008 IEEE 24th International Conference on Data Engineering, ICDE 2008, pp. 376–385. IEEE (2008)
2. Acar, A., Aksu, H., Uluagac, A.S., Conti, M.: A survey on homomorphic encryption schemes: theory and implementation. ACM Comput. Surv. (CSUR) **51**(4), 79 (2018)
3. Bader, L., Bürger, J.C., Matzutt, R., Wehrle, K.: Smart contract-based car insurance policies. In: 2018 IEEE Globecom Workshops (GC Wkshps) (2018)
4. Bogorny, V., Renso, C., Aquino, A.R., Lucca Siqueira, F., Alvares, L.O.: Constant-a conceptual data model for semantic trajectories of moving objects. Trans. GIS **18**(1), 66–88 (2014)
5. Cachin, C.: Architecture of the hyperledger blockchain fabric. In: Workshop on distributed cryptocurrencies and consensus ledgers, vol. 310 (2016)
6. Cha, S., Chen, J., Su, C., Yeh, K.: A blockchain connected gateway for ble-based devices in the internet of things. IEEE Access **6**, 24639–24649 (2018). https://doi. org/10.1109/ACCESS.2018.2799942
7. Christidis, K., Devetsikiotis, M.: Blockchains and smart contracts for the internet of things. IEEE Access **4**, 2292–2303 (2016)
8. Dorri, A., Steger, M., Kanhere, S.S., Jurdak, R.: Blockchain: a distributed solution to automotive security and privacy. IEEE Commun. Mag. **55**(12), 119–125 (2017)
9. Douceur, J.R.: The sybil attack. In: Druschel, P., Kaashoek, F., Rowstron, A. (eds.) IPTPS 2002. LNCS, vol. 2429, pp. 251–260. Springer, Heidelberg (2002). https:// doi.org/10.1007/3-540-45748-8_24
10. Ethereum Foundation: Solidity (2019). https://solidity.readthedocs.io/en/ develop/. Accessed 4 Apr 2019
11. Florea, B.C.: Blockchain and internet of things data provider for smart applications. In: 2018 7th Mediterranean Conference on Embedded Computing (MECO), pp. 1–4, June 2018. https://doi.org/10.1109/MECO.2018.8406041
12. GDPR, E.: The eu general data protection regulation (gdpr) is the most important change in data privacy regulation in 20 years (2018). https://eugdpr.org/
13. Gomes, F.O., Silva, D.S., Agostinho, B.M., Martina, J.E.: Privacy preserving on trajectories created by wi-fi connections in a university campus. In: 2018 IEEE International Conference on Intelligence and Security Informatics (ISI), pp. 181–186. IEEE (2018)
14. Grengs, J., Wang, X., Kostyniuk, L.: Using GPS data to understand driving behavior. J. Urban Technol. **15**(2), 33–53 (2008)
15. Guo, Y., et al.: Wischain: An online insurance system based on blockchain and denglu1 for web identity security. In: 2018 1st IEEE International Conference on Hot Information-Centric Networking (HotICN), pp. 242–243. IEEE (2018)

16. Hoffstein, J., Pipher, J.C., Silverman, J.H., Silverman, J.H.: An Introduction to Mathematical Cryptography, vol. 1. Springer, Heidelberg (2008)
17. Hu, X., An, S., Wang, J.: Taxi driver's operation behavior and passengers' demand analysis based on GPS data. J. Adv. Transp. **2018** (2018)
18. SAE International: Serial control and communications heavy duty vehicle network - top level document j1939_201206 (2012)
19. Jain, J.J., Busso, C.: Analysis of driver behaviors during common tasks using frontal video camera and can-bus information. In: 2011 IEEE International Conference on Multimedia and Expo, pp. 1–6. IEEE (2011)
20. Johnson, D.A., Trivedi, M.M.: Driving style recognition using a smartphone as a sensor platform. In: 2011 14th International IEEE Conference on Intelligent Transportation Systems (ITSC), pp. 1609–1615. IEEE, Washington (2011)
21. Kogos, K.G., Filippova, K.S., Epishkina, A.V.: Fully homomorphic encryption schemes: the state of the art. In: 2017 IEEE Conference of Russian Young Researchers in Electrical and Electronic Engineering (EIConRus), pp. 463–466, February 2017. https://doi.org/10.1109/EIConRus.2017.7910591
22. Lamberti, F., Gatteschi, V., Demartini, C., Pelissier, M., Gomez, A., Santamaria, V.: Blockchains can work for car insurance: using smart contracts and sensors to provide on-demand coverage. IEEE Consum. Electron. Mag. **7**(4), 72–81 (2018)
23. Lepoint, T., Ciocarlie, G., Eldefrawy, K.: Blockcis–a blockchain-based cyber insurance system. In: 2018 IEEE International Conference on Cloud Engineering (IC2E), pp. 378–384. IEEE (2018)
24. Li, N., Jain, J.J., Busso, C.: Modeling of driver behavior in real world scenarios using multiple noninvasive sensors. IEEE Trans. Multimed. **15**(5), 1213–1225 (2013)
25. Monreale, A., Trasarti, R., Pedreschi, D., Renso, C., Bogorny, V.: C-safety: a framework for the anonymization of semantic trajectories. Trans. Data Priv. **4**(2), 73–101 (2011)
26. Nakamoto, S.: Bitcoin: A peer-to-peer electronic cash system. www.bitcoin.org (2008)
27. News, B.: Car and house insurance faces price probe (2018). https://www.bbc.com/news/business-46042087. Accessed 28 Mar 2019
28. Ogburn, M., Turner, C., Dahal, P.: Homomorphic encryption. Proc. Comput. Sci. **20**, 502–509 (2013)
29. Oosting, J.: Whitmer orders audit as michigan auto insurance fee rises to \$220 (2019). https://www.detroitnews.com/story/news/local/michigan/2019/03/27/michigan-auto-insurance-mandatory-fee-rising-record-high/39264081/. Accessed 28 Mar 2019
30. Raikwar, M., Mazumdar, S., Ruj, S., Gupta, S.S., Chattopadhyay, A., Lam, K.Y.: A blockchain framework for insurance processes. In: 2018 9th IFIP International Conference on New Technologies, Mobility and Security (NTMS), pp. 1–4. IEEE (2018)
31. Romanosky, S., Ablon, L., Kuehn, A., Jones, T.: Content analysis of cyber insurance policies: How do carriers write policies and price cyber risk? (2017)
32. Saravanan, M., Shubha, R., Marks, A.M., Iyer, V.: SMEAD: A secured mobile enabled assisting device for diabetics monitoring. In: 2017 IEEE International Conference on Advanced Networks and Telecommunications Systems (ANTS), pp. 1–6, December 2017. https://doi.org/10.1109/ANTS.2017.8384099

33. Shae, Z., Tsai, J.J.P.: On the design of a blockchain platform for clinical trial and precision medicine. In: 2017 IEEE 37th International Conference on Distributed Computing Systems (ICDCS). pp. 1972–1980, June 2017. https://doi.org/10.1109/ICDCS.2017.61
34. Solove, D.: Understanding privacy (2008)
35. Sweeney, L.: Achieving k-anonymity privacy protection using generalization and suppression. Int. J. Uncertainty Fuzziness Knowl.-Based Syst. **10**(05), 571–588 (2002)
36. Szabo, N.: Formalizing and securing relationships on public networks. FirstMonday **2**(9) (1997)
37. Tefft, B.: American Driving Survey: 2015–2016. AAA Foundation, Washington (2018)
38. Underwood, S.: Blockchain beyond bitcoin. Commun. ACM **59**(11), 15–17 (2016). https://doi.org/10.1145/2994581
39. Vahdati, M., HamlAbadi, K.G., Saghiri, A.M., Rashidi, H.: A self-organized framework for insurance based on internet of things and blockchain. In: 2018 IEEE 6th International Conference on Future Internet of Things and Cloud (FiCloud), pp. 169–175. IEEE (2018)
40. Wang, L., Shen, X., Li, J., Shao, J., Yang, Y.: Cryptographic primitives inblockchains. J. Netw. Comput. Appl. **127**, 43–58 (2019). https://doi.org/10.1016/j.jnca.2018.11.003. http://www.sciencedirect.com/science/article/pii/S108480451830362X
41. Warekar, R., Patil, S.: Efficient approach for anonymizing tree structured dataset using improved greedy search algorithm. Int. J. Sci. Res. (IJSR), Impact Factor (2014)
42. Westin, A.F., Ruebhausen, O.M.: Privacy and Freedom, vol. 1. Atheneum, New York (1967)
43. Wood, G.: Ethereum: A secure decentralised generalised transaction ledger. Ethereum Project Yellow Paper **151**, 1–32 (2014)
44. Wuille, P.: Bip32: Hierarchical deterministic wallets (2012). https://github.com/genjix/bips/blob/master/bip-0032.md
45. Yao, Y.: Evolution of insurance: a telematics-based personal auto insurance study. Honors Scholar Theses (2018)

WiP: Criminal Smart Contract for Private Key Theft in End to End Encrypted Applications

Priyanka Pal[✉], Sudharsana K J L, and Rohith Balaji S

Aditya Empress Towers,
Aziz Bagh Colony, Shaikpet, Hyderabad 500008, Telangana, India
priyankapal330@gmail.com

Abstract. Cryptocurrencies such as Bitcoin [1], Ethereum [2] are becoming very popular among people due to their properties such as pseudo-anonymity which can be used for both good and bad. In this paper, we show how smart contracts can be used to build criminal applications. Here we construct an application that allows contractors to get the stolen private key of a target user from perpetrators in an end to end encrypted message application.

Keywords: Smart contract · Criminal smart contract · Blockchain · Cryptography · End to end encryption

1 Introduction

On 3rd January 2009, the bitcoin [1] network came into existence with Satoshi Nakamoto mining the genesis block of bitcoin which had a reward of 50 bitcoins. Since then the publicity of bitcoin steeply increased which led to a bitcoin boom during which the value of bitcoin reached a peak. Bitcoin became very popular quickly because of its characteristics such as pseudo-anonymity, no central authority, etc. Soon Ethereum [2] came into existence which gave the freedom to write better smart contracts [3] easily that holds the business logic of the application. This helped in developing various decentralized applications using blockchain [4] technology. This paved the way for the existence of many criminal applications as well. Such decentralized criminal applications [5] make it difficult to keep a track of the crime. This opened the gateway to build such criminal applications using blockchain which makes it difficult to trace back. Also, such applications support commission-fairness where there is a fool-proof reward system. In this paper, we build one such application that can be used to trade the stolen private key of a targeted user in an end to end encrypted system between a contractor and perpetrator. We also discuss the various security issues that arise even in such a fool-proof workflow.

© Springer Nature Switzerland AG 2019
D. Garg et al. (Eds.): ICISS 2019, LNCS 11952, pp. 21–32, 2019.
https://doi.org/10.1007/978-3-030-36945-3_2

2 Background and Related Work

2.1 Blockchain

A blockchain [4] is a distributed ledger technology that consists of a linked list of records that are linked using cryptographic schemes. Each block has a collection of transactions or data records stored in the form of a Merkle tree. Each block stores a hash pointer pointing to the previous block which stores the address of the previous block along with the hash of its contents. Blockchain technology is immutable and relies on a peer to peer network of nodes that follow distributed consensus algorithms to generate blocks, validate them and store them on the blockchain.

2.2 Smart Contracts

Smart contracts [3] hold the business logic of the decentralized application. It can be built using Turing complete languages such as solidity and compiled using a framework such as Truffle. Smart contracts are generally visible to all the users in the blockchain network. Contracts can be made partially or fully self-executing, self-enforcing, or both. Smart contracts aim to provide security that is superior to traditional contract laws and to reduce other transaction costs associated with contracting.

Smart contracts are advantageous than traditional cryptocurrencies like Bitcoin because of the reasons listed below:

– Mutually distrustful parties can have fair exchange by abiding by rules embedded in the contracts without any need for third-party intermediaries.
– Minimal interactions happen between the parties which reduce unwanted monitoring and tracking.
– Input can be taken from external sources with the help of authenticated data feeds.

The usage of smart contracts in Ethereum [6,7] is growing at a fast rate with arising utilization in criminal applications. The decentralized platform with smart contracts is particularly conducive for criminal activities because of the reasons listed below:

– Parties can have fair exchange without any third party involvement, so any kind of law enforcing body stays uninvolved and hence the criminal transactions can happen unchecked.
– Minimal interactions between the parties make it harder to monitor or track criminal transactions.
– Usage of authenticated data feeds enhances criminal smart contracts.

2.3   Criminal Smart Contracts

Definition. Criminal smart contracts (CSCs) [5] can facilitate leakage of confidential information, theft of cryptographic keys, and real-world crimes (murder, arson, terrorism). We refer to smart contracts that facilitate crimes in distributed smart contract systems as criminal smart contracts (CSCs). An example of a CSC is a smart contract for private-key theft [5]. Such a CSC might pay a reward for confidential delivery of a target key sk, such as a certificate authority's private digital signature key.

The following properties should be held by criminal smart contracts to build a foolproof criminal application in the blockchain:

- *Fair exchange.* The contract should ensure that the perpetrator is paid only for a fair exchange of the requirement specified by the contractor.
- *Commission fairness.* The execution of a smart contract should ensure that both the commission of a crime and the payment of reward should be atomic. The following challenges may occur if the above-mentioned properties are ignored:
    - *Challenge 1A.* Contractor C posts a request for theft and delivery of the signing key sk_V of a victim certificate authority(CA). C offers a reward $reward to a perpetrator P for (confidentially) delivering the private key sk_V to C. In this scenario, the contract should ensure that the perpetrator has completed the task committed. There can be a challenge possible where perpetrator P fools contractor C by giving him a false private key. P should not be allowed to access the reward without submitting a valid key to the contract which should be given to the contractor.
    - *Challenge 1B.* The Certificate Authority can act as a perpetrator and reveal the valid secret key, gain all the $reward and immediately change its secret key. These challenges should also be handled by the contract to ensure a fair exchange. These challenges are discussed in [5].
- *Fool proof-verification methods.* The verification methods for commission fairness depend on the type of criminal applications to be built. This should be unbiased and no authority should have control over it. The practicality of building such criminal smart contracts is still a difficult task. In this paper, we have presented one such application which allows theft of private keys in the end to end encryption. There is much scope to explore multiple such criminal applications and the construction of their criminal smart contracts.

3   CSC for End to End Encryption Key Theft

3.1   End to End Encryption

Definition. End to end encryption [8] is a secure way of communication between two or more parties so that any third party despite having access to the network used for communication cannot have access to the data that is being communicated amongst the parties involved in the communication. When data is end to end encrypted between two clients, the data is encrypted on the sender's device in such a way that it can be decrypted only by the recipient device.

In today's age of widespread usage of numerous messaging and file sharing apps end to end encryption is being used widely for ensuring secure communication. Here we have worked with an end to end encryption system that is implemented by the LINE messaging application [9].

Algorithms Used. The end to end encryption scheme, chosen for the attack is defined using the following algorithms.

- *Key exchange algorithm.* ECDH over Curve25519
- *Message encryption algorithm.* AES-256 in CBC mode
- *Message hash function* SHA-256

Private Message Encryption. A message between two parties is encrypted by using the schemes listed below:

- *Key Generation and Registration.* Each client generates an ECDH key pair that gets saved securely in the storage area reserved for the application. The key pair is generated when the application is first launched in a client device. The public key of the key pair is then registered with the application server which replies with a unique key ID for the client that represents the current version of the user's public key. Every time the application is re-installed or if the user migrates to a new device a new key(ECDH pair along with a unique key ID to be used as the client's public key) is generated.
- *Client-to-Client Key Exchange.* In order to exchange encrypted messages, the two parties must have a shared secret. Each of the two clients in a conversation generates a shared secret by using its own private key and the other client's public key. The shared secret formed on both sides is the same. Shared secret is generated as illustrated below.

$$SharedSecret = ECDH_{curve25519}(key_{private}^{user1}, key_{public}^{user2}) \qquad (1)$$

$$SharedSecret = ECDH_{curve25519}(key_{public}^{user1}, key_{private}^{user2}) \qquad (2)$$

- *Message Encryption.* Each message is encrypted with a unique encryption key and IV. The encryption key and IV are derived from the shared secret and a randomly generated 8-byte salt is also generated as follows

$$Key_{enc} = SHA256(SharedSecret||salt||``Key") \qquad (3)$$

$$IV_{pre} = SHA256(SharedSecret||salt||``IV") \qquad (4)$$

$$IV_{encrypt} = IV_{pre}[0:15] \oplus IV_{pre}[16:31] \qquad (5)$$

AES in CBC mode is used to encrypt the message using the encryption key and IV generated above and a MAC is calculated for the message to confirm that it has been sent from the stated sender.

$$C = AESCBC(Key_{encrypt}, IV_{encrypt}, M) \qquad (6)$$

$$MAC_{pl} = SHA256(C) \tag{7}$$

$$MAC_{enc} = AESECB(Key_{enc}, MAC_{pl}[0:15] \oplus MAC_{pl}[16:31]) \tag{8}$$

The sender key ID, the recipient key ID, salt and MAC are sent along with the ciphertext. The sender key ID helps to retrieve the public key of the sender and the recipient ID helps to check whether the message can be decrypted with the recipient's private key and once it is verified the recipient can generate the shared secret and derive the symmetric encryption key and the IV with the help of the salt sent. The MAC of the received ciphertext is also calculated and compared with the MAC sent. If it matches, the recipient goes ahead with decrypting the message with the generated symmetric encryption key and IV.

3.2 E2EE Key Theft Model

We introduce a CSC which is created and deployed by a contractor C, who wants to decrypt the end to end encrypted messages exchanged between two clients. To accomplish this, according to the end to end encryption model demonstrated in the above section, stealing the private key of one of the victim clients is sufficient. C deploys the contract with the public key pk_v of one of the victim clients V whose private key sk_v is to be stolen. The reward money for the commission of the crime is transacted to the contract during deployment. So the CSC is implemented such that it rewards the perpetrator P who reveals the sk_v associated with pk_v to the contractor C.

After submission of the stolen private key in a claim message by a perpetrator P, the contractor will verify the claim message. The perpetrator will get the reward money if it is valid. If the claim message is invalid, the contractor invalidates the claim and checks for other submissions. If the contract reaches its termination time without anyone submitting a valid claim message, the contract returns the reward money to C.

Once the private key of the victim is stolen, to decrypt any arbitrary ciphertext exchanged between any targeted pair of clients, the contractor has to intercept the ciphertext and the salt associated with it. The contractor can use the stolen private key of the victim, the public key of the other client to generate the shared secret. The contractor has to use the salt and shared secret to generate the symmetric encryption key and IV. With the help of the IV and symmetric encryption key, the intercepted ciphertext can be decrypted. Both the scenarios have been shown in Fig. 1.

Improvements: Our improvement of the above existing scheme comes in with the implementation of how the perpetrator submits the claim message and how the contractor invalidates the claim if it is invalid without loss of fair-exchange and commission-fairness.

The list of claim messages submitted by perpetrators is stored in the contract and verified one by one. Each such submitted claim message is given a time

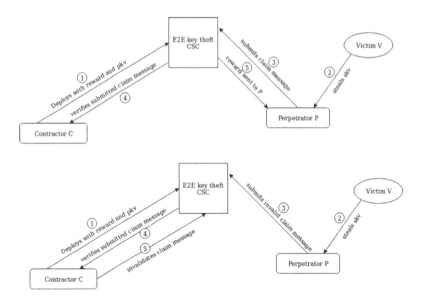

Fig. 1. Valid (top) and Invalid (bottom) key submission flow.

window within which the contractor either invalidates the claim by proving it to be invalid or chooses to do nothing, which makes the claim valid by default. The perpetrator can then claim the reward. Given below is the implementation of the steps mentioned above.

– The stolen secret key is submitted to the contract as a claim message after encrypting the key with the public key of the contractor. The contractor will be given some time within which he can choose to invalidate the claim.

$$claim\_message = enc(pk_c, sk_v) \tag{9}$$

– The contractor takes up the submitted claim message, decrypts it and verifies if it is a valid secret key. If the key is invalid, the contractor tries to invalidate the claim by sending the decrypted key back to the contract.

$$sk_v^* = dec(sk_c, claim\_message) \tag{10}$$

– The contract verifies whether the key is indeed invalid and if found so, invalidates the claim. If the key is found to be valid by the contract, it does nothing and so the deadline to invalidate the claim passes. The perpetrator can then claim the reward. The contract verifies the validity of the key by constructing the shared key used in the end-to-end encryption and verifying a known pair of (message, ciphertext) (Fig. 2).

  verify (claim_message == enc(pk_c, sk_v^*))
  shared_key = construct E2EE_shared_key from sk_v^*
  if (ciphertext == E2EE_enc(shared_key, message))

do nothing
else
invalidate the claim

Algorithm

- *CREATE.* On receiving *("create", \$reward, pk_v, intent_end, report_duration, token_window, contract_end, message, cipher_text, $pk_{recipient}$, salt)* from a contractor C,

    Transfer \$reward to contract.
    Set state = CREATED
    Set counter = 0

- *INTENT TO REVEAL.* On receiving *("intent", commit)* from a perpetrator P,

    Assert state = CREATED
    Assert time <intent_end
    (counter = counter + 1)
    Store the pair (commit, P)
    return counter

- *CLAIM.* On receiving *("claim", claim_message, token)* from a perpetrator P,

    Assert token belongs to P
    *Assert   intent_end + token_window * token<time<intent_end + token_window * (token + 1) − report_duration*
    $commit_P$ = Fetch commit of perpetrator P
    Assert $SHA256(claim\_message \parallel pk_p) == commit_P$
    Store (claim_message, pk_p, token)

- *INVALIDATE CLAIM.* On receiving *("invalidate_claim", sk_v^*, token)* from contractor C,

    $claim\_message_{token}$ = Fetch claim_message corresponding to token
    Assert $Enc(sk_v^*) = claim\_message_{token}$
    $shared\_secret^* = ECDH(sk_v^*, pk_{recipient})$
    $message\_key^* = SHA256(shared\_secret^* \parallel salt \parallel "key")$
    $IV_{pre}^* = SHA256(shared\_secret^* \parallel salt \parallel "IV")$
    $IV_{encrypt}^* = IV_{pre}^*[0:15] \ xor \ IV_{pre}^*[16:31]$
    $ciphertext^* = AESCBC(message\_key^*, IV_{encrypt}^*, message)$
    $if \ ciphertext^*! = ciphertext$
    $(Invalidate \ claim\_message_{token})$

- *RECEIVE REWARD.* Upon receiving ("receive_reward, token") from perpetrator P,

    Assert the token belongs to P
    $claim\_message_{token}$ = Fetch claim_message corresponding to token
    Check if report_duration time has elapsed since the $claim\_message_{token}$ submission time
    Assert the $claim\_message_{token}$ has not been invalidated by contractor
    Transfer \$reward to P
    Set STATE = CLAIMED

– *RETRACT REWARD.* On receiving ("retract_reward") from contractor C,
 Assert time >contract_end
 Assert state = CREATED
 Transfer $reward to C
 Set STATE = ABORTED

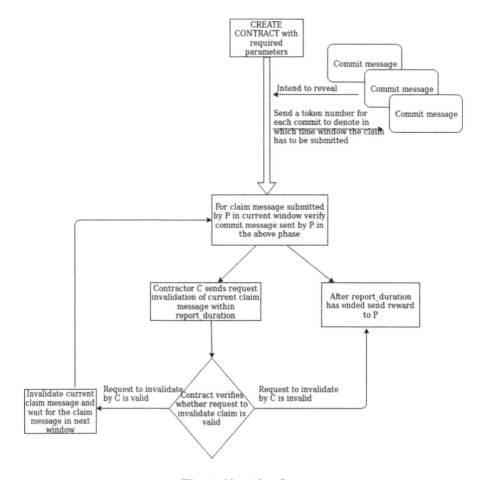

Fig. 2. Algorithm flow

3.3   Contract Protocol

The algorithm assumes the contractor has a message and its corresponding data intercepted when the message was sent to the recipient in an end to end encrypted form. One can get access to such data by snooping into the communication network. The data we need from the interception are ciphertext, salt, and pk_recipient. So, the contractor knows, the message, its ciphertext, and the salt used to generate the message key.

Contract Deployment. The contractor deploys the contract with the following parameters:

- $reward, the amount transferred to contract while deploying which will be paid to the perpetrator on submitting the valid key
- pk_v, public key of the victim
- *salt*, salt from the intercepted data
- *message*, plaintext message corresponding to the intercepted data
- *pk_recipient*, public key of the recipient to whom the message was sent
- *ciphertext*, ciphertext of the message
- report_duration: the duration within which the contractor has to report if the key is invalid
- *token_window*, the time interval for each perpetrator to reveal the key
- *intent_end*, end time for the perpetrators to commit his intent to reveal
- *contract_end*, end time of the contract

Intent Reveal Phase. As soon as the contract is deployed, the perpetrators will be given the option to submit a commit and get a token number. The contract will have a counter which will allow a unique token value for each of the commit submitted. The maximum number of commits that can be submitted is,

$$max\_commits = (contract\_end - intent\_end)/token\_window \qquad (11)$$

The commit is calculated as follows,

$$commit = SHA256(Enc(pk_c, sk_v)\|pk_p) \qquad (12)$$

where, pk_c -> public key of the contractor
sk_v -> secret key of the victim
pk_p -> public key of the perpetrator

There will not be any spam of commits as each commit requires the perpetrator to pay some amount of gas for their commits to be stored in the contract. The ith commit submission will be returned the token value of i starting from 1.

Key Reveal Phase. The token given in the previous step is used to allot time intervals at which the perpetrator can choose to reveal the encrypted secret key(encrypted with the public key of the contractor) of the victim as a claim message. The perpetrator having token i can reveal the claim_message between, $(intent\_end + token\_window * i)$ and $(intent\_end + token\_window * (i + 1) - report\_duration)$.

$$claim\_message = Enc(pk_c, sk_v^*) \qquad (13)$$

The stolen secret key encrypted with the public key of the contractor is submitted in the claim by perpetrator P. The contract then verifies if the hash of claim_message appended with the public key of perpetrator matches the commit. Check,

$$SHA256(claim\_message\|pk_p) == commit \qquad (14)$$

Invalidate Claim Phase. For each such claim, the contractor decrypts the key and checks if it is valid. If the key is not valid, the contractor sends a request to the contract to invalidate the claim. This request is sent with the decrypted secret key sent by the perpetrator and the perpetrator's address. The reporting of an invalid claim has to be done before the report_duration ends. The contract then verifies the data and invalidates the claim if it is invalid. Once a claim is invalidated, the next claim is checked. If there are no more claims left, then the reward money is refunded back to the contractor.

Transfer Reward Phase. Once a claim has passed report_duration since it is submitted and it has not been invalidated yet, the perpetrator can claim the reward and the state is set to CLAIMED.

If the contract_end time has passed and there has been no valid claim till then, the contractor gets back the reward money with which the contract had been deployed.

3.4   Security Analysis

Need for Sequencing Key Reveal Phase. The above approach has a limit on how many perpetrators can participate in the scheme. The removal of tokens and allowing the perpetrators to submit commits and claims may seem to solve the problem, but it introduces 2 other problems.

1. If all the perpetrators submit the claim_message within a short period, it will be difficult for the contractor to report back the invalid ones within the report_duration.
2. The contractor himself can pose to be a perpetrator who can commit with a random commit and then a claim_message with a random invalid key. He can choose not to report his claim_message as invalid and later claim the reward. The reward money will get refunded to the contractor while an actual perpetrator might have revealed the valid key, thus contradicting commission fairness.

where, v_p -> perpetrator with valid key
c_p -> contractor posing as a perpetrator

Intent Reveal phase

$$commit_{c_p} = SHA256(Enc(pk_c, \text{`invalid'})||pk_{cp})$$

$$commit_{v_p} = SHA256(Enc(pk_c, sk_v)||pk_{vp})$$

Key Reveal phase

$$claim\_message_{cp} = Enc(pk_c, \text{'}invalid\text{'})$$

$$claim\_message_{vp} = Enc(pk_c, sk_v)$$

If v_p submits claim_message after c_p submitted and before report_duration time from c_p's submission, then the contractor will learn the valid secret key from v_p's submission and will not report c_p's claim_message, allowing c_p to get the reward.

Rushing Attack. Theoretically, when a perpetrator gets hold of the private key sk_v of the victim, he can encrypt it with the public key of the contractor and send it to the contract but an attack called the rushing attack mentioned in [5] might take place where a corrupt C can decrypt and use the sk_v to construct a valid claim and make it reach the contract before the valid one.

To avoid the rushing attack, we proposed the following scheme. The perpetrator reveals the key in two phases. In the first phase, the perpetrator expresses an intent to reveal the key by submitting a commitment of the claim message. He then waits until the start of the next phase to reveal the claim message. The previous sections explain the commitment and claim message formats. The contractor will then verify the claim message, and the perpetrator will receive the reward if it is valid. If the claim message is invalid, the other submissions are checked. If the contract reaches its end without anyone claiming the reward, the reward is returned to the contractor's account.

3.5   Scope for Improvement

To verify that the stolen key submitted is a valid one, we have presented in our algorithm an interactive mechanism whereby the contractor reports an invalid key submission within a deadline and the contract verifies the reporting. Since the tools and features implementable in Smart Contracts are very limited, using these interactive mechanism solves a lot of implementation challenges and removes the need for the smart contract building tools to support every required feature for automation. This deadline-based interactive mechanism also opens up more opportunities to design CSCs which require the contractor's verification.

The obvious downside for the approach is that the contractor is required to be online to check every claim within the report_duration from the moment the claim arrived. The solution to this might be to have a script running at all times watching for any new claim and perform required checks and invalidate the claim if it is invalid. We can go for an alternative non-interactive zero-knowledge proof mechanism to serve the same purpose by using ZK-SNARKS [10].

4   Conclusion

We have worked on formulating a criminal smart contract that helps to achieve commission fairness in the scenario of an end to end encryption key theft. This can be extended to other such criminal activities. Even though it is fool-proof, there are security issues that arise in such scenarios as well such as thwarting attacks. This work along with other criminal applications supported by smart contract systems like Ethereum demonstrated in [5] stresses the urgent need to develop safeguards against such criminal usage of smart contracts that otherwise are used for numerous beneficial applications.

References

1. Nakamoto, S.: Bitcoin: a peer-to-peer electronic cash system (2009). http://www.bitcoin.org/bitcoin.pdf
2. Buterin, V.: Ethereum white paper: a next-generation smart contract and decentralized application platform (2013). https://github.com/ethereum/wiki/wiki/White-Paper
3. Nakamoto, W.S.: A next-generation smart contract decentralized application platform (2015)
4. Yuan, Y., Wang, F.: Blockchain and cryptocurrencies: model, techniques, and applications. IEEE Trans. Syst. Man Cybern.: Syst. **48**(9), 1421–1428 (2018)
5. Juels, A., Kosba, A.E., Shi, E.: The ring of Gyges: investigating the future of criminal smart contracts. IACR Cryptol. ePrint Arch. **2016**, 358 (2016)
6. Luu, L., Chu, D.-H., Olickel, H., Saxena, P., Hobor, A.: Making smart contracts smarter, pp. 254–269, October 2016
7. Delmolino, K., Arnett, M., Kosba, A., Miller, A., Shi, E.: Step by step towards creating a safe smart contract: lessons and insights from a cryptocurrency lab. In: Clark, J., Meiklejohn, S., Ryan, P.Y.A., Wallach, D., Brenner, M., Rohloff, K. (eds.) FC 2016. LNCS, vol. 9604, pp. 79–94. Springer, Heidelberg (2016). https://doi.org/10.1007/978-3-662-53357-4_6
8. Ermoshina, K., Musiani, F., Halpin, H.: End-to-end encrypted messaging protocols: an overview. In: Bagnoli, F., Satsiou, A., Stavrakakis, I., Nesi, P., Pacini, G., Welp, Y., Tiropanis, T., DiFranzo, D. (eds.) INSCI 2016. LNCS, vol. 9934, pp. 244–254. Springer, Cham (2016). https://doi.org/10.1007/978-3-319-45982-0_22
9. Line encryption overview, September 2016. https://scdn.line-apps.com/stf/linecorp/en/csr/line-encryption-whitepaper-ver1.0.pdf
10. Ben-Sasson, E., Chiesa, A., Tromer, E., Virza, M.: Succinct non-interactive zero-knowledge for a Von Neumann architecture. In: USENIX Security Symposium (2014)

Formal Techniques

Trustworthy Isolation of DMA Enabled Devices

Jonas Haglund[✉] and Roberto Guanciale[✉]

KTH Royal Institute of Technology, Stockholm, Sweden
{jhagl,robertog}@kth.se

Abstract. We present a mechanism to trustworthy isolate I/O devices with Direct Memory Access (DMA), which ensures that an isolated I/O device cannot access sensitive memory regions. As a demonstrating platform, we use the Network Interface Controller (NIC) of an embedded system. We develop a run-time monitor that forces NIC reconfigurations, defined by untrusted software, to satisfy a security rule. We formalized the NIC in the HOL4 interactive theorem prover and we verified the design of the isolation mechanism. The verification is based on an invariant that is proved to be preserved by all NIC operations and that ensures that all memory accesses address allowed memory regions only. We demonstrate our approach by extending an existing Virtual Machine Introspection (VMI) with the monitor. The resulting platform prevents code injection in a connected and untrusted Linux (The HOL4 proofs and the source code of the monitor are published at https://github.com/kth-step/NIC-formalization-monitor.).

Keywords: Formal verification · System security · Network Interface Controller

1 Introduction

Formally verified execution platforms (microkernels [10], hypervisors [11] and separation kernels [6]) constitute an infrastructure for implementing secure IoT devices. By guaranteeing memory isolation and controlling communication between software components, they prevent faults of non-critical software (e.g. HTTP interfaces, optimizations based on machine learning, and software providing complex functionality or with short life cycle) from affecting software that must fulfill strict security and safety requirements. This enables verification of critical software without considering untrusted software.

A problem with these platforms is that the verification does not consider devices with direct memory access (DMA). Current systems either disable them, use a special System MMU (which is usually not available in embedded systems) to isolate potentially misconfigured devices, or trust the (usually large) controlling software.

We address this issue by designing a secure IoT system based on component isolation and the principle of complete mediation: The software controlling the

© Springer Nature Switzerland AG 2019
D. Garg et al. (Eds.): ICISS 2019, LNCS 11952, pp. 35–55, 2019.
https://doi.org/10.1007/978-3-030-36945-3_3

I/O device is untrusted and monitored by a secure component, which verifies that the configurations defined by untrusted software cannot enable the device to access sensitive memory regions. This monitor preserves a security policy which can be described by an invariant. The rationale is that the monitor can be substantially simpler than the untrusted software and therefore it is easier to analyze and verify. In this context, security depends mainly on three properties: (1) The monitor is correctly isolated from the other, possibly corrupted, components of the system (e.g. the execution platform is formally verified or vulnerabilities are unlikely due to the small code base of the kernel); (2) The monitor is functionally correct and denies configurations that violate the invariant (e.g. the monitor is verified or its small code minimizes the number of critical bugs); (3) The security policy (i.e. the invariant) is strong enough to guarantee that the I/O device cannot violate memory isolation.

We contribute with the first formal verification of (3) for a real I/O device of significant complexity. As a demonstrating platform we use the development board/embedded system Beaglebone Black and its Network Interface Controller (NIC). We provide a formal model of the NIC and we define the security policy as an invariant of the state of the NIC. We then demonstrate that this policy is sound: The invariant is preserved by the NIC and it restricts memory accesses to predetermined memory regions. The analysis is implemented in the HOL4 interactive theorem prover, which guarantees soundness of our reasoning.

To demonstrate the applicability of this approach we implemented a secure connected system. Real systems often: need complex network stacks and application frameworks, have short time to market, require support of legacy features, and adopt of binary blobs. For these reasons many applications are dependent on commodity OSs. Our goal is to provide a software architecture that satisfies some desired security properties (e.g. absence of malware), even if the commodity software is completely compromised. Here, we extend the framework MProsper [5] with secure support for network connectivity to guarantee that a connected Linux system, which is in control of the NIC, is free from code injection.

2   DMA Controllers

We briefly summarize the main traits of DMA controllers (DMAC). These are hardware modules that offload the CPU by performing transfers between memory and I/O devices. From a security point of view, it is important to restrict the memory accesses performed by DMACs to certain memory regions, since unrestricted accesses can overwrite or disclose code and sensitive data. DMACs can be standalone hardware modules, or embedded in I/O devices such as NICs and USBs.

There are three common interfaces to configure DMACs (we reviewed 27 DMACs, including NICs, USBs, and standalone DMACs from twelve vendors: ARM, Intel, and Texas Instruments, among others). In the simplest DMACs (3 USBs), source, destination, and size of memory buffers to transfer are configured via dedicated registers of the controller. The seemingly most common configuration method (22 controllers of all kinds) is by means of linked lists of Buffer Descriptors (BD), an example of which is given in Fig. 1. Finally, some DMACs (2 standalone DMACs) are programmable: A program is stored in memory, and which is subsequently fetched and executed by the DMAC to perform the specified memory transfers.

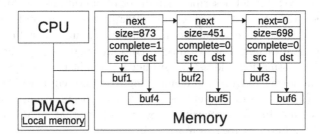

Fig. 1. An example DMAC that performs memory-to-memory transfers and is configured via linked list of BDs. The list is stored in memory, where BDs specify source (buf1 to buf3) and destination buffers (buf4 to buf6) by means of pointers and sizes. DMA transfers are activated by writing the address of the head of the list to a specific DMAC register. The DMAC then processes the list in order. First, the current BD is fetched to its local memory. Then a number of bytes are read from the source buffer and written to the destination buffer via local memory. This step is repeated until all bytes of the buffer have been transferred, at which point the complete bit is set to signal that the transfer is complete. The DMAC then processes the next BD, which is addressed by the next descriptor pointer. This procedure continues until the DMAC reaches the end of the list. In this example, the first BD has been processed and the DMAC is currently processing the second BD.

3   Security Threats, Challenges, and Scope

The main concern when DMACs are controlled by untrusted software is that the destination addresses of BDs can be set arbitrarily. Therefore a malicious software could use the DMAC to inject code and data into the execution platform or other components, or modify page tables and escalate its privileges. Similarly, by controlling the source addresses of BDs, an attacker can use a DMAC to leak arbitrary regions of memory. Finally, the untrusted software may configure a DMAC in ways that do not follow the specification, causing the system to perform unpredictable operations.

Easy protection against these threats is to completely isolate the DMAC from sensitive memory regions via a System MMU. This is a hardware component that restricts the memory accesses of I/O devices. Unfortunately, even capable embedded systems do not have a System MMU. Moreover, a System MMU may negative impacts on cost, performance, and power consumption, and introduce I/O jitter.

Software prevention against these threats requires a clear understanding of the DMAC. We address this by defining an unambiguous mathematical model of the DMAC under analysis: The NIC of BeagleBone Black. This task is challenging because the NIC specification is ambiguous, dispersive, self-contradictory and vague, and contains many details that are not security relevant.

An additional challenge is the identification of the security invariant. Each transition of the NIC model describe a small set of operations, leading to many state variables. Also, the NIC writes BDs after transmission and reception of frames. Many of these state variables, and all these writes must be considered when defining the invariant. For instance, if BDs are overlapping, when the NIC writes a BD the destination address of another BD might be modified. All these details make the formal verification challenging, but allowed us to identify bugs in the Linux NIC device driver, errors in the NIC specification, and define a monitor policy that includes security relevant details that may otherwise be overlooked. These findings are summarized in Sect. 9.

We remark that our goal is to define and verify the security policy of the NIC monitor, that is, validating the security of the system design described in Sect. 7. Verifying that the NIC hardware implements its specification and that the C implementation of the monitor is correct are not considered in this work.

4   Hardware Platform and Formal Model

Our analysis concerns the development board BeagleBone Black. We take into account only the Ethernet NIC and assume that the other DMACs of the SoC (e.g. USB) are disabled.

Our formal model of the SoC uses the device model framework by Schwarz et al. [15], which describes executions of computers consisting of one ARMv7 CPU, memory and a number of I/O devices. The state of the CPU-memory subsystem [8] is represented by a pair $s = (c, m)$, where c is a record representing the contents of the CPU registers, and m is a function from 32-bit words to 8-bit bytes representing the memory.

The state of the NIC is described by a pair $n = (reg, a)$. The first component describes the interface between the CPU and the NIC, consisting of the memory-mapped NIC registers: Ten 32-bit registers $reg.r$ and an 8-kB memory $reg.m$. The second component, $a = (it, tx, rx, td, rd)$, describes the internal state of the NIC, consisting of five records storing values of five automata. Each automaton describes the behavior of one of the five NIC functions: *initialization* (it), *transmission* (tx) and *reception* (rx) of frames, and *tear down* of *transmission* (td) and *reception* (rd).

The NIC specification [1] describes a programming guideline for device drivers, but it does not describe the behavior of the NIC when this guideline is not followed. A NIC transitions results in the undefined state $\perp$ if the transition models a NIC operation that is either: (1) not consistent with the device driver guideline, (2) not described by the specification (e.g. the behavior in the case of a DMA request that does not address RAM is unspecified), or (3) not supported by our formal NIC model.

The execution of the system is described by a transition relation $(s, n) \rightarrow (s', n')$, which is the smallest relation satisfying the following rules

$$\frac{s \xrightarrow{\tau_{cpu}} s'}{(s, n) \rightarrow (s', n)} \qquad \frac{s \xrightarrow{request(add)} s'' \qquad s'' \xrightarrow{process(add,n.reg[add])} s'}{(s, n) \rightarrow (s', n)}$$

$$\frac{s \xrightarrow{write(add,v)} s' \qquad n \xrightarrow{update(add,v)} n'}{(s, n) \rightarrow (s', n')}$$

$$\frac{n \xrightarrow{\tau_{atm}} n'}{(s, n) \rightarrow (s, n')} \qquad \frac{n \xrightarrow{write(add,v)} n'}{(c, m, n) \rightarrow (c, m[add := v], n')}$$

$$\frac{n' \xrightarrow{request(add)} n'' \qquad n'' \xrightarrow{process(add,m[add])} n'}{(c, m, n) \rightarrow (c, m, n')}$$

where $s \xrightarrow{l} s'$ and $n \xrightarrow{l} n'$ denote the transition relations of the CPU-memory subsystem and the NIC, respectively. Notice that these rules are general enough to handle other types of DMACs. To include fine-grained interleavings of the operations of the CPU and the NIC, each NIC transition describes one single observable hardware operation: One register read or write, or one single memory access of one byte.

The first two rules do not affect the NIC: The CPU can execute an instruction that (1) does not access a memory mapped NIC register ($s \xrightarrow{\tau_{cpu}} s'$), or (2) that reads the NIC register at address add ($s \xrightarrow{request(add)} s''$) and processes the result ($s'' \xrightarrow{process(add,n.reg[add])} s'$). The third rule describes executions of CPU instructions writing a value v to the NIC register at address add ($s \xrightarrow{write(add,v)} s'$). Register writes configure the NIC and may activate an automaton ($n \xrightarrow{update(add,v)} n'$).

The other three rules involve transitions of active automata. An internal transition of an automaton $atm \in \{it, tx, rx, td, rd\}$ ($n \xrightarrow{\tau_{atm}} n'$) does not affect the CPU. Memory write requests of writing a byte value v to a location with the address add ($n \xrightarrow{write(add,v)} n'$) are issued only by the transmission automaton tx. Memory read requests of reading the memory byte at an address add ($n' \xrightarrow{request(add)} n''$) are issued only by the reception automaton rx, and the byte value at the addressed memory location ($m[add]$) is immediately processed by the NIC ($n'' \xrightarrow{process(add,m[add])} n'$).

The remainder of this section describes the five automata.

Initialization. Figure 2 depicts the initialization automaton. Initially, the automaton is in the state *power-on* ($n.a.it.s = power-on$). Initialization is activated by writing 1 to the reset register, causing the automaton to transition to the state *reset*. Once the reset is performed, the automaton transitions to the

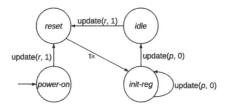

Fig. 2. Initialization automaton: r is the address of the reset register. p ranges over the addresses of those NIC registers that are cleared to complete the initialization of the NIC.

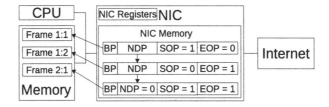

Fig. 3. A buffer descriptor queue consisting of three BDs located in the memory of the NIC. The queue starts with the topmost BD, which addresses the first buffer of the first frame (SOP = 1) and is linked to the middle BD. The middle BD addresses the last (and second) buffer of the first frame (EOP = 1) and is linked to the bottom BD. The bottom BD is last in the queue (NDP = 0) and addresses the only buffer of the second frame (SOP = EOP = 1).

state *init-reg*. The CPU completes the initialization by clearing some registers, causing the automaton to enter the state *idle*. The NIC can now be used to transmit and receive frames. If any register is written with a different value or when the initialization automaton is in a different state than described, then the NIC enters $\bot$ (i.e. $n' = \bot$).

Transmission and Reception. The NIC is configured via linked lists of BDs. One frame to transmit (receive) can be stored in several buffers scattered in memory, the concatenation of which forms the frame. The properties of a frame and the associated buffers are described by a 16-byte BD. Differently than the example of Fig. 1, the lists of BDs are located in the private NIC memory $n.reg.m$. There is one queue (list) for transmission and one for reception, which are traversed by the NIC during transmission and reception of frames. Each BD contains among others the following fields: Buffer Pointer (BP) identifies the start address of the associated buffer in memory; Buffer Length (BL) identifies the byte size of the buffer; Next Descriptor Pointer (NDP) identifies the start address of the next BD in the queue (or zero if the BD is last in the queue); Start/End Of Packet (SOP/EOP) indicates whether the BD addresses the first/last buffer of the associated frame; Ownership (OWN) specifies whether the NIC has completed the processing of the BD or not; End Of Queue (EOQ) indicates whether

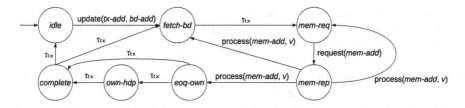

Fig. 4. Transmission automaton: *tx-add* is the address of the transmission head descriptor pointer register, which is written to trigger transmission of the frames addressed by the BDs in the queue whose head is at *bd-add*. The address *mem-add* is the memory location requested to read, and *v* is the byte value in memory at that location.

the NIC considered the BD to be last in the queue when the NIC processed that BD (i.e. NDP was equal to zero). Figure 3 shows an example of a BD queue.

The initial state of the transmission automaton (Fig. 4) is $n.a.tx.s = idle$. The CPU activates transmission by writing the transmission head descriptor pointer register with the address of the first BD in the queue addressing the frames to transmit. Such a NIC register write causes $n.a.tx.bd\text{-}add$ to be assigned the written address, recording the address of the currently processed BD, and the next state to be *fetch-bd*.

The transition from *fetch-bd* reads the current BD from $n.reg.m$ located at $n.a.tx.bd\text{-}add$, assigns fields of the record $n.a.tx$ to values identifying the memory location of the buffer addressed by the current BD, and sets the state to *mem-req*.

As long as there are bytes of the buffer left to read, the automaton transitions between *mem-req* and *mem-rep*, fetching and processing in each cycle one byte via DMA. When the last byte of the buffer addressed by the current BD has been processed, and if the currently transmitted frame consists of additional buffers (i.e. the EOP-flag is not set of the current BD) then the automaton moves from *mem-rep* to *fetch-bd* and sets $n.a.tx.bd\text{-}add$ to the address of next BD. Once all bytes of the currently transmitted frame have been processed (i.e. the EOP-flag is set of the current BD), the automaton moves to *eoq-own*.

Once in state *eoq-own*, if the current BD is not last in the queue (i.e. the NDP-field of the current BD is not 0) then the automaton clears the OWN-flag of the SOP-BD (the BD of the currently transmitted frame with the SOP-flag set; signaling to a device driver that the NIC memory area of the BDs of the transmitted frame can be reused), sets $n.a.tx.bd\text{-}add$ to the address of next the BD, and enters the state *complete*. If the current BD is last in the queue then the automaton sets the EOQ-flag of the current BD (used by a device driver to check whether a BD was appended just after the NIC processed a BD, which would result in the NIC not processing the appended BD, meaning that a device driver must restart transmission) and enters the state *own-hdp*.

The transition from *own-hdp* clears the OWN-flag of the SOP-BD and the head descriptor pointer register (the latter register clear signals to a device driver that transmission is complete).

The transition from *complete* writes the address of the processed BD to a register to inform a device driver of which is the last processed BD. Furthermore, if all BDs in the BD queue have now been processed, or initialization or transmission teardown was requested during the processing of the BDs of the last transmitted frame, then the next state is *idle*. Otherwise the next state is *fetch-bd* to begin the processing of the first BD of the next frame.

The structure of the reception automaton is similar to the structure of the transmission automaton but with four notable differences: (1) After the reception head descriptor pointer has been written with a BD address to enable reception, it is non-deterministically decided when a frame is received to activate the reception automaton. (2) The BDs in the reception queue address the buffers used to store received frames. Since reception do not get memory read replies there is only one state related to memory accesses. (3) The transmission automaton has two states (*eoq-own* and *own-hdp*) to describe BD writes (of the flags EOQ and OWN). Reception writes sixteen BD fields (e.g. the length of a frame and the result of a CRC check), leading to fourteen additional states. (4) Since content of received frames are unknown, values written to memory and some BD fields are selected non-deterministically.

Tear Down. Transmission and reception tear down are similar to each other, and are activated by writing 0 to the associated tear down register. First, the NIC finishes the processing of the currently transmitted (received) frame (the corresponding automaton enters the state *idle*). Then the tear down automaton performs four (six) transitions, each one describing one observable hardware operation (for the CPU). If the corresponding queue has not been completely processed ($n.a.tx.bd\text{-}add \neq 0$), then certain fields are written of the BD ($n.a.tx.bd\text{-}add$) that follows the last processed BD. The last two transitions clear the head descriptor pointer register and $n.a.tx.bd\text{-}add$, and writes a specific value to a register to signal to the CPU that the tear down is complete, respectively.

5   Formal Verification of Isolation

The main verification goal is to identify a NIC configuration that isolates the NIC from certain memory regions. This means that the NIC can only read and write certain memory regions, denoted by R and W, respectively. We identify such a configuration by an invariant $\mathcal{I}(n, R, W)$ that is preserved by internal NIC transitions ($l \neq update(add, v)$) and that restricts the set of accessed memory addresses:

Theorem 1. *If $\mathcal{I}(n, R, W) \wedge n \xrightarrow{l} n' \wedge l \neq update(add, v)$, then*

1. $\mathcal{I}(n', R, W)$,
2. $l = request(add) \implies add \in R$, and
3. $l = write(add, v) \implies add \in W$.

5.1 Definition of the Invariant

The invariant states that the NIC state is not undefined and that the transmission and reception queues are not overlapping, and restricts the values of the state components of each automaton (stored in $n.a.atm$, $atm \in \{it, tx, rx, td, rd\}$) and the contents of the BDs in the BD queues:

$$\mathcal{I}(n, R, W) \triangleq n \neq \perp \wedge \mathcal{I}_{qs}(n) \wedge \mathcal{I}_{it}(n, R, W) \wedge \mathcal{I}_{tx}(n, R, W) \wedge \mathcal{I}_{rx}(n, R, W)$$

Disjoint Queues. $\mathcal{I}_{qs}$ states that when the transmission and reception automata are active, their queues do not overlap (no byte in $n.reg.m$ is used by both a BD in the transmission queue and a BD in the reception queue):

$$\mathcal{I}_{qs}(n) \triangleq n.a.tx.s \neq idle \wedge n.a.rx.s \neq idle \implies DISJOINT(q_{tx}(n), q_{rx}(n))$$

The functions q_{tx} and q_{rx} return the list of the addresses of the BDs in transmission and reception queues respectively. A queue is considered empty when the corresponding automaton is idle.

Initialization. $\mathcal{I}_{it}$ states that during initialization the transmission and reception automata are idle:

$$\mathcal{I}_{it}(n, R, W) \triangleq n.a.it.s \neq idle \implies n.a.tx.s = idle \wedge n.a.rx.s = idle$$

This implies that when initialization finishes, the transmission and reception automata are idle. Therefore, after initialization $\mathcal{I}_{tx}$ and $\mathcal{I}_{rx}$ hold vacuously (see the definition of $\mathcal{I}_{tx}$ in the next paragraph).

Transmission. $\mathcal{I}_{tx}$ consists of two conjuncts:

$$\mathcal{I}_{tx}(n, R, W) \triangleq (n.a.tx.s \neq idle \implies \mathcal{I}_{tx\text{-}wd}(n) \wedge \mathcal{I}_{tx\text{-}mr}(n, R)) \wedge$$
$$(n.a.tx.s = idle \implies$$
$$n.a.tx.bd\text{-}add \neq 0 \implies DISJOINT([n.a.tx.bd\text{-}add], q_{rx}(n)))$$

The first conjunct ensures that the transmission automaton cannot cause the NIC to enter $\perp$ ($\mathcal{I}_{tx\text{-}wd}(n)$) and that only readable memory is read ($\mathcal{I}_{tx\text{-}mr}(n, R)$).

$\mathcal{I}_{tx\text{-}wd}$ states for example that the transmission queue is acyclic; no pair of BDs overlap; all BDs are appropriately configured (e.g. the OWN-flag is cleared); the queue is not empty while a BD is processed ($n.a.tx.s \neq idle \wedge n.a.tx.s \neq complete$); and the currently processed BD ($n.a.tx.bd\text{-}add$) is the head of the queue.

$\mathcal{I}_{tx\text{-}mr}$ states that the buffers addressed by the BDs in the queue are located in R. $\mathcal{I}_{tx\text{-}mr}$ also states that if the transmission automaton is in the DMA loop, then the state components used to compute the memory addresses do not cause overflow, and the addresses of the future memory read requests issued during the processing of the current BD are in R; that is, if $n.a.tx.s = mem\text{-}req \vee n.a.tx.s =$

mem-rep then $\forall 0 \leq i < n.a.tx.left$ $(n.a.tx.mem\text{-}add + i \in R)$, where $n.a.tx.left$ records the number of bytes left to read of the buffer addressed by the current BD, and $n.a.tx.mem\text{-}add$ records the address of the next memory read request (see Fig. 4).

The second conjunct ensures that the transmission tear down automaton does not modify the reception queue when writing the NIC memory $n.reg.m$. This prevents the tear down automaton from affecting the reception automaton to cause the NIC to enter $\bot$ or issue a memory write request outside W.

Reception. The invariant for reception is similar to the invariant for transmission. The main difference is the definition of $\mathcal{I}_{rx\text{-}wd}$, since reception BDs specify different properties than transmission BDs. Also, the invariant states that BDs in the reception queue address buffers located in W, and that $n.a.rx.bd\text{-}add$ is disjoint from the transmission queue.

5.2   Proof of Theorem 1

Consider Theorem 1.2. Transitions of the form $n \xrightarrow{request(add)} n'$ occur only when $n.a.tx.s = mem\text{-}req$, where $add = n.a.tx.mem\text{-}add$. $\mathcal{I}_{tx\text{-}mr}(n, R)$ implies $n.a.tx.s = mem\text{-}req \implies n.a.tx.mem\text{-}add \in R$. Hence, the requested address is readable: $add \in R$. The proof of Theorem 1.3 has the same structure but follows from $\mathcal{I}_{rx}(n, R, W)$.

Defining the invariant in terms of conjuncts specialized for each automaton gives a natural structure to the proof of Theorem 1.1. The proof is therefore described in terms of the three actions the NIC performs: initialization, transmission and reception, $act \in \{it, tx, rx\}$. The labels of the transitions describing one of the three actions are identified by $L(act)$, where $L(it) \triangleq \{\tau_{it}\}$, $L(tx) \triangleq \{\tau_{tx}, \tau_{td}\} \cup \bigcup_{add,v}\{request(add), process(add, v)\}$, and $L(rx) \triangleq \{\tau_{rx}, \tau_{rd}\} \cup \bigcup_{add,v}\{write(add, v)\}$.

The following two lemmas formalize properties of the NIC model: Transitions of an action do not modify state components of other actions; and an automaton can leave the idle state only when the CPU writes a NIC register.

Lemma 1. *For every act if $n \xrightarrow{l} n'$ and $l \notin L(act)$ then $n'.a.act = n.a.act$.*

Lemma 2. *For every atm if $n \xrightarrow{l} n'$, $n.a.atm.s = idle$, and $n'.a.atm.s \neq idle$ then $l = update(add, v)$.*

Lemma 3 states that all transitions of each action, $act \in \{it, tx, rx\}$, preserve the corresponding invariant:

Lemma 3. *For every act if $\mathcal{I}(n, R, W)$, $n \xrightarrow{l} n'$, and $l \in L(act)$ then $\mathcal{I}_{act}(n', R, W)$ and $n' \neq \bot$.*

Proof. We sketch the proof for $act = tx$, since reception is analogous and initialization is straightforward. The transition l belongs to the transmission or the transmission tear down automaton. There are four cases depending on whether $n.a.tx.s$ and $n'.a.tx.s$ are equal to *idle* or not.

The case $n.a.tx.s = idle \wedge n'.a.tx.s \neq idle$ cannot occur by Lemma 2.

If $n.a.tx.s \neq idle \wedge n'.a.tx.s \neq idle$ then the transition is performed by the transmission automaton. We first analyze modifications of the transmission queue. The transmission automaton can only modify the flags OWN and EOQ of the currently processed BD and advance the head of the transmission queue (but not atomically). $\mathcal{I}_{tx\text{-}wd}(n)$ implies that the current BD is the head of $q_{tx}(n)$ and that the BDs in $q_{tx}(n)$ do not overlap. Therefore, the two flag modifications do not alter the NDP-fields of the current BD nor the following BDs in $q_{tx}(n)$. For this reason the queue is only either *unmodified or shrinked*, thereby implying $\mathcal{I}_{tx\text{-}wd}(n')$. Moreover, the buffers addressed by the BDs in $q_{tx}(n')$ are still located in R, therefore $\mathcal{I}_{tx\text{-}mr}(n', R)$ holds. The modifications of OWN and EOQ of the current BD do not violate the invariant, since the queue is acyclic, implying that the current BD is not part of the queue when the head is advanced.

We now analyze modifications of the state components that are used for address calculations and the DMA read requests, which are restricted by $\mathcal{I}_{tx\text{-}mr}(n, R)$. If the transition is from *fetch-bd*, then the automaton fetches the current BD from the NIC memory, and assigns certain state components. $\mathcal{I}_{tx\text{-}mr}(n, R)$ ensures that the overflow restrictions are satisfied by the relevant state components in n' and that the buffer of the fetched BD is in readable memory. These properties are preserved by transitions from *mem-rep* and *mem-req*.

If $n.a.tx.s \neq idle \wedge n'.a.tx.s = idle$ then the transition is performed by the transmission automaton and $n.a.tx.s = complete$. Such a transition does not modify $n.a.tx.bd\text{-}add$, $n.a.reg.m$, nor $n.a.rx$. The BD at $n'.a.tx.bd\text{-}add$ does not overlap any BD in $q_{rx}(n')$ due to $\mathcal{I}_{qs}(n)$, $\mathcal{I}_{tx\text{-}wd}(n)$, and the fact that q_{rx} is unmodified since neither $n.a.reg.m$ nor $n.a.rx$ is modified.

The last case is $n.a.tx.s = idle \wedge n'.a.tx.s = idle$. These transitions are performed by the transmission tear down automaton, and only assign fields of the BD at $n.a.tx.bd\text{-}add$ (provided $n.a.tx.bd\text{-}add \neq 0$) and set $n.a.tx.bd\text{-}add$ to 0. The second conjunct of $\mathcal{I}_{tx}(n, R, W)$ implies that the BD at $n.a.tx.bd\text{-}add$ does not overlap $q_{rx}(n)$, therefore $q_{rx}(n) = q_{rx}(n')$ and $\mathcal{I}_{tx}(n', R, W)$ holds.   □

The following definitions, lemmas and corollary are used to prove that each action preserves the invariant of other actions and it does not make the queue overlapping. First, for each action act, we introduce a relation on NIC states, $n \succcurlyeq_{act} n'$, with the meaning that the invariant $\mathcal{I}_{act}$ is preserved from n to n'. For initialization, the relation $n \succcurlyeq_{it} n'$ requires that the state components of the initialization automaton are equal ($n.a.it = n'.a.it$) and that the transmission and reception automata remain in their idle states ($\wedge_{atm \in \{tx,rx\}}(n.a.atm.s = idle \implies n'.a.atm.s = idle)$). For $act \in \{tx, rx\}$, $n \succcurlyeq_{act} n'$ states that the:

- state components of the corresponding automaton are equal ($n.a.act = n'.a.act$).
- locations of the corresponding queues are equal ($q_{act}(n) = q_{act}(n')$).
- content of the corresponding queues are equal ($\forall add \in q_{act}(n).\ bd(n, add) = bd(n', add)$, where $\in$ denotes list membership and $bd(n, add)$ is a record with

its fields set to the values of the corresponding fields of the BD at address add in the state n).

– other queue is not expanded ($\forall add.\ add \in q_{act'}(n') \implies add \in q_{act'}(n)$, where $act' = tx$ if $act = rx$ and $act' = rx$ if $act = tx$).

The following Lemma states that $n \succ_{act} n'$ indeed preserves the corresponding invariant $\mathcal{I}_{act}$:

Lemma 4. *For every act if $\mathcal{I}_{act}(n, R, W)$ and $n \succ_{act} n'$ then $\mathcal{I}_{act}(n', R, W)$.*

To complete the proof we introduce a relation for every action act, $n \sqsupseteq_{act} n'$, which formalizes that the location of the corresponding queue is unmodified and that all bytes outside the queue are unmodified:

$$n \sqsupseteq_{act} n' \triangleq (\forall add \in q_{act}(n)(bd(n, add).ndp = bd(n', add).ndp)) \wedge$$
$$(\forall add \notin \mathcal{A}(q_{act}(n))(n.reg.m(add) = n'.reg.m(add)))$$

(where $\mathcal{A}(q_{act}(n))$ is the set of byte addresses of the BDs in $q_{act}(n)$, and the imaginary "initialization-queue" is defined to be empty: $q_{it}(n) \triangleq [\ ]$). The following Lemma states that each action preserves this relation, provided that the corresponding invariant holds in the pre-state:

Lemma 5. *For every act if $\mathcal{I}_{act}(n, R, W)$, $n \xrightarrow{l} n'$ and $l \in L(act)$ then $n \sqsupseteq_{act} n'$.*

Proof. The lemmas follows immediately for initialization since the initialization automaton does not modify $n.reg.m$.

For transmission and reception, the first conjunct of $n \sqsupseteq_{act} n'$ holds since the corresponding automaton does not modify the NDP-fields of the BDs in $q_{act}(n)$, and $q_{act}(n)$ contains no overlapping BDs (by $\mathcal{I}_{act}(n, R, W)$). The second conjunct holds since the automaton assigns only fields of BDs in $q_{act}(n)$ (by $\mathcal{I}_{act}(n, R, W)$). $\square$

The next Lemma states that each action either shrinks the corresponding queue or does not modify its location (the symbol @ denotes concatenation):

Lemma 6. *For every act if $\mathcal{I}_{act}(n, R, W)$, $n \xrightarrow{l} n'$, and $l \in L(act)$ then $\exists q\ (q_{act}(n) = q @ q_{act}(n'))$.*

Proof. $q_{act}(n)$ is non-overlapping (by $\mathcal{I}_{act}(n, R, W)$) and no automaton assigns an NDP-field of a BD. Therefore, no automaton can change the location of the BDs in its queue. If the state component identifying the head of q_{act} is not modified, the location of the queue is not modified; and if it is modified, then it is set to either zero (emptying the queue) or to a member of $q_{act}(n)$ (by $\mathcal{I}_{act}(n, R, W)$; shrinking the queue). $\square$

We finally show that each action preserves the invariant of the other actions:

Corollary 1. *For every act $\neq$ act' if $\mathcal{I}(n, R, W)$, $n \xrightarrow{l} n'$, and $l \in L(act)$ then $n \succeq_{act'} n'$.*

Proof. For $act' = it$, $act \in \{tx, rx\}$. Lemma 1 gives $n \succeq_{act'} n'$, and Lemma 2 gives $n.a.atm.s = idle \implies n'.a.atm.s = idle$ for $atm \in \{tx, rx\}$. Therefore, $n \succeq_{it} n'$ holds.

If $act = it$ then the transition is performed by the initialization automaton, which does not modify $n.a.tx$, $n.a.rx$ (by Lemma 1), nor $n.reg.m$. Therefore the q_{tx} and q_{rx} are unchanged.

If $act = tx$ and $act' = rx$, then Lemmas 1, 5, and 6 imply $n \succeq_{rx} n'$. The same reasoning applies for $act = rx$ and $act' = tx$. $\qquad\square$

Corollary 2. *For every act $\neq$ act' if $\mathcal{I}(n, R, W)$, $n \xrightarrow{l} n'$, and $l \in L(act)$ then $\mathcal{I}_{act'}(n', R, W)$.*

Proof. Follows from Corollary 1 and Lemma 4. $\qquad\square$

Corollary 3. *For every act if $\mathcal{I}(n, R, W)$, $n \xrightarrow{l} n'$, and $l \in L(act)$ then $\mathcal{I}_{qs}(n')$.*

Proof. Lemmas 5, 1 and $\mathcal{I}_{qs}(n)$ imply that an action cannot modify the queue of another action. This property, Lemma 6, and $\mathcal{I}_{qs}(n)$, imply that the queues remain disjoint. $\qquad\square$

6 HOL4 Implementation

The model and the proof have been implemented with the HOL4 interactive theorem prover [16]. Hereafter we briefly summarize some details of the implementation.

The HOL4 model uses an oracle to decide which automaton shall perform the next NIC transition and to identify properties of received frames (e.g. when a frame is received, its content, and presence of CRC errors). The oracle is also used to resolve some of the ambiguities in the NIC specification [1].

The NIC transition relation is defined in terms of several functions, one for each automaton state: $n \xrightarrow{l} n'$ is represented in HOL4 as $n' = \delta^{atm}_{n.a.atm.s}(n)$, where atm is the automaton causing transition l and $\delta^{atm}_{n.a.atm.s}$ is the transition function of atm from the state $n.a.atm.s$.

The implementation of the proof of Lemma 5 is based on the following strategy:

1. For each BD-field f we introduce a HOL4 function, $w_i(m, add, v)$, which updates the NIC memory m by writing the BD-field f of the BD at address add with the value v.
2. The HOL4 function $write$ performs several field writes sequentially:

$$write([], m) \triangleq m$$
$$write([(w_1, a_1, v_1), \ldots, (w_k, a_k, v_k)], m) \triangleq$$
$$write([(w_2, a_2, v_2), \ldots, (w_k, a_k, v_k)], w_1(m, a_1, v_1))$$

3. For each transition function δ_s^{atm}, we define a (possibly empty) list $W_s^{atm}(n) = [t_1(n), \ldots, t_k(n)]$, where $t_i(n)$ is a triple of the form (w, a, v) (denoting a field writer, address and value, respectively) and w, a and v depend on the state n. We prove that δ_s^{atm} and W_s^{atm} update $n.reg.m$ identically: $\delta_s^{atm}(n).reg.m = write(W_s^{atm}(n), n.reg.m)$. For tx and rx, we also prove that the written BDs are in the corresponding queue ($\{t_1.a, \ldots, t_k.a\} \subseteq q_{atm}(n)$), and for td and rd that the written BD is the BD following the last processed BD ($\{t_1.a, \ldots, t_k.a\} \subseteq \{n.a.tx.bd\text{-}add\}$ and $\{t_1.a, \ldots, t_k.a\} \subseteq \{n.a.rx.bd\text{-}add\}$ respectively).

4. We prove that each w_i writes only the BD at the given address and preserves the NDP-field:

$$(\forall add' \notin \mathcal{A}([add]) \ (m(add') = w_i(m, add, v)(add'))) \wedge$$
$$bd(m, add).ndp = bd(w_i(m, add, v), add).ndp$$

5. Finally, we prove Lemma 5 for every update $write(W_s^{atm}(n), n.reg.m)$, provided that all possible pairs of BDs at the addresses in $W_s^{atm}(n)$ are non-overlapping (that is, $t_i.a$ and $t_j.a$ are not overlapping for $\{t_i, t_j\} \subseteq W_s^{atm}(n)$). The non-overlapping is guaranteed by $\mathcal{I}(n, R, W)$.

HOL4 requires a termination proof for every function definition. For this reason the function q_{tx} returning the list of BDs in the transmission queue cannot be implemented by recursively traversing the NDP-fields of the BDs, since in general the (linked) list can be cyclic and therefore the queue can be infinite. This problem is solved as follows. We introduce a predicate $BD\_Q(q, add, m)$ that holds if the queue q is the list (which is finite by definition in HOL4) of BDs in NIC memory m starting at address add, linked via the NDP-fields, and containing a BD with a zero NDP-field (the last BD). This predicate is defined by structural induction on q and its termination proof is therefore trivial. We show that the queue starting from a given address in a given NIC memory m is unique:

$$\forall q \ q' \ add \ m \ .(BD\_Q(q, add, m) \wedge BD\_Q(q', add, m)) \implies q' = q$$

$\mathcal{I}_{tx\text{-}wd}$ includes a conjunct stating that there exists a list q satisfying $BD\_Q(q, n.a.tx.head\text{-}add, n.reg.m)$ ($n.a.tx.head\text{-}add$ denotes the address of the first BD in the transmission queue, which is defined to be empty if $n.a.tx.head\text{-}add = 0$). This enables to define $q_{tx}(n)$ using Hilbert's choice operator applied on the set $\{q \mid BD\_Q(q, n.a.tx.head\text{-}add, n.reg.m)\}$, returning the unique queue satisfying the predicate. The same approach is used for the reception queue.

The model of the NIC consists of 1500 lines of HOL4 code. Understanding the NIC specification, experimenting with hardware, and implementing the model required (roughly) three man-months of work. The NIC invariant consists of 650 lines of HOL4 code and the proof consists of approximately 55000 lines of HOL4 code (including comments). Identifying the invariant, formalizing it HOL4, defining a suitable proof strategy, and implementing the proof in HOL4 required (roughly) one man-year of work. Executing the proof scripts take approximately 45 min on a 2.93 GHz Xeon(R) CPU X3470 with 16 GB RAM.

7   Prevention of Code-Injection in IoT System

To demonstrate the applicability of our approach we developed a software platform to prevent code injection in an embedded connected Linux system running on BeagleBone Black.

Existing Platform. MProsper [5] is a formally verified platform that guarantees component isolation and absence of code injection. The latter is based on Virtual Machine Introspection (VMI) and code hashing: MProsper prevents execution of code (i.e. memory page) whose hash value is not in the database of trusted program hashes, referred to as the "golden image".

MProsper and Linux are guests of the Prosper hypervisor [12], which has been formally verified to isolate itself and its guests. Linux is paravirtualized, implying that both Linux and the applications are executed in user mode. Only the hypervisor is executed in privileged mode and which is invoked via hypercalls. In order to guarantee isolation, the hypervisor is in control of the MMU and virtualizes the memory subsystem via direct paging: Linux allocates the page tables inside its own memory area and can directly modify them while the tables are not in active use by the MMU; once the page tables are in active use by the MMU, the hypervisor guarantees that those page tables can only be modified via hypercalls.

Since the hypervisor supervises all modifications of the page tables, MProsper can intercept all modifications of the virtual memory layout. Whenever Linux requests to change a page table, MProsper identifies the physical pages that are requested to be made executable (if the request involves executable permissions), computes the hash values of those pages, and checks that the hash values are in the golden image. Additionally, MProsper forces Linux to obey the executable space protection policy: A memory page can be either executable or writable, but not both. These policies guarantee that the hash values of the code have been checked by MProsper before the code is executed and that executable code remains unmodified after validation.

Attacker Model. Concerning the Linux guest it is not realistic to restrict the attacker model, since it has been repeatedly demonstrated that software vulnerabilities have enabled complete Linux systems to be overtaken via privilege escalation. For this reason we assume that the attacker has complete control of the Linux guest. The attacker can force applications and the kernel to execute arbitrary code and access arbitrary data. It is assumed that the goal of the attacker is to run an arbitrary binary program.

Secure Network Connectivity via Monitoring. MProsper prevents code injection if the CPU is the only hardware component that can modify memory [5]. However, if Linux can control a DMA device then Linux can indirectly perform arbitrary memory accesses with catastrophic consequences: modify page

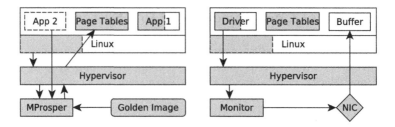

Fig. 5. The hypervisor prevents Linux from directly modifying the trusted components, page tables, and NIC registers (gray elements). Mprosper intercepts all changes to page tables, guaranteeing that executable code is read only (dashed gray elements) and that the hash values of the executable pages (e.g. code of App 2) are in the golden image. The NIC monitor intercepts all attempted NIC reconfigurations, guaranteeing that the invariant is preserved.

```
 1   bool nic_ram_handler(a: word, v: word)
 2     update_q_heads();
 3     for op in [tx, rx]:
 4       case q_overlap(a, op) of
 5       LAST_NDP:
 6         if (not queue_secure(v, op))
 7           return false;
 8       ILLEGAL: return false;
 9       NO: continue
10     m[a] := v;
11     return true;
```

Fig. 6. Pseudo-code of the NIC Monitor handling writes to internal NIC memory.

tables, enabling Linux to escape its memory confinement; inject code and data into the hypervisor or other guests (providing e.g. secure services); modify the golden image; or inject code into Linux executable memory.

We extend the system with secure Internet connectivity while preventing Linux from abusing the DMAC of the NIC. We deploy a new monitor within the hypervisor that validates all NIC reconfigurations (see Fig. 5). The hypervisor forces Linux to map the NIC registers with read-only access (NIC register reads have no side effects). When the Linux NIC driver attempts to configure the NIC, by writing a NIC register, an exception is raised. The hypervisor catches the exception and, in case of a NIC register write attempt, invokes the monitor. The monitor checks whether the write preserves the NIC invariant, and if so re-executes the write, and otherwise blocks it.

Figure 6 presents the pseudo-code of the monitor that checks writes (of the value v) to (the address a of) the NIC memory. The monitor uses the variables tx_q and rx_q to store the addresses of the heads of the transmission and reception queues, respectively. Initially (line 2), the monitor updates tx_q and rx_q by traversing the queues until a BD with a cleared OWN-flag is encountered (i.e. the monitor updates its view of which BDs are in use by the NIC). The monitor then checks the write with respect to both transmission and reception queues (line 3). If Linux is attempting to overwrite a BD of a queue then the queue is only allowed to be extended: The updated BD must be last in the queue and the address a must be the corresponding NDP field (line 5). In this case the appended queue (i.e. the one starting from address v) must be secure: All BDs are properly initialized, it is not circular and does not point to BDs of the existing nor have overlapping BDs, it does not overlap the other queue, and all addressed buffers belong to Linux memory. Moreover, reception buffers must not be executable. Any other update (line 8) of an existing queue is prohibited. Finally, if the queue extension is secure or no queue is modified then the monitor performs the write (line 10). The actual code of the monitor is slightly more complex, due to data structures recording which BDs are potentially in use by the NIC, in order to speed up the checks of whether a request attempts to modify a BD that can affect the operation of the NIC.

In addition to the NIC monitor, we extended the checks of MProsper to ensure that page tables and executable code are not allocated in buffers address by BDs in the reception queue, since those buffers are written when frames are received.

Secure Remote Upgrade. In addition to enabling Internet connectivity to Linux applications, the new system design also enables connectivity for the secure components, which can use Linux as an untrusted "virtual" gateway. We used this feature to implement secure remote upgrade of Linux applications. New binary code and corresponding hash values are signed using the administration private key and published by a remote host. Linux downloads the new binaries, hash values, and signatures and requests an update of the golden image via a hypercall. The hypervisor forwards the request to MProsper. The signature is checked by MProsper using the administration public key, and if it is valid, the golden image is updated with the new hash values. The use of digital signatures makes the upgrade trustworthy, even though Linux acts as a network intermediary, and furthermore, even if Linux is compromised. A similar approach is used to revoke hash values from the golden image.

Having the NIC driver in Linux in contrast to developing a NIC driver for the hypervisor has several advantages. It keeps the code of the hypervisor small, avoiding verification of code that manages initialization, power management, routing tables and statistics of the NIC. It makes the interface of the NIC independent of the guest OS, since the monitor code does not depend on the Linux networking stack. It also enables the same hypervisor and monitor to be used with different OSs, OS versions, and device driver versions. Finally, it demonstrates a general mechanism to secure DMACs that are configured via linked lists and can easily be adapted to support other DMACs.

Evaluation. Network performance was evaluated for BeagleBone Black (BBB), Linux 3.10, with netperf 2.7.0. BBB was connected with a 100 Mbit Eth-

ernet point-to-point link to a PC, with netperf 2.6.0. The benchmarks are:
TCP_STREAM and TCP_MAERTS transfer data with TCP from BBB to the
PC and vice versa; UDP_STREAM transfers data with UDP from BBB to
the PC; and TCP_RR and UDP_RR use TCP and UDP, respectively, to send
requests from BBB and replies from the PC. Each benchmark lasted for ten
seconds and was performed five times. Table 1 reports the average value for each
test.

Table 1. Netperf benchmarks. TCP_STREAM, TCP_MAERTS and UDP_STREAM
are measured in Mbit/second, and TCP_RR and UDP_RR are measured in transac-
tions/second.

Configuration	Benchmark				
	TCP_STREAM	TCP_MAERTS	UDP_STREAM	TCP_RR	UDP_RR
Native	94.1	93.9	96.2	3365.1	3403.4
Native+Monitor	94.1	93.9	96.2	3317.6	3402.2
Hyper	16.2	45.6	29.3	924.9	1009.0
Hyper+Monitor	15.3	41.0	27.6	891.3	982.6

We compare the network performance of the system (Hyper+Monitor) shown
in Fig. 5 with the MProsper system (Hyper) where Linux is free to directly
configure the NIC, and therefore being able to violate all security properties.
The performance of the new system are between 89.9% and 97.4% of the original
system. This performance loss is expected due to the additional context switches
caused by the Linux NIC driver attempting to write NIC registers.

To validate the monitor design we also experimented with a different system
setup. In this case we consider a trusted Linux kernel that is executed without
the hypervisor but with a potentially compromised NIC driver (Native). This
is typically the case when the driver is a binary blob. In order to prevent the
driver from abusing the NIC DMA the monitor is added to the Linux kernel
(Native+Monitor). The Linux NIC driver has been modified to not directly
write NIC registers but instead to invoke the monitor function when a NIC
register write is required. The monitor is similar to the one in the hypervisor,
and the C file containing the monitor code is located in the same directory as the
Linux NIC driver. The overhead introduced by this configuration is negligible, as
demonstrated by the first two lines of Table 1. The same approach can be used
to monitor an untrusted device driver that is executed in user mode on top of a
microkernel (e.g. seL4 and Minix).

In addition to being OS and device driver version independent, the monitor
minimizes the trusted computing base controlling the NIC. In fact, the monitor
consists of 900 lines of C code (excluding address conversion) while the Linux
device driver consists of 4650 lines of C.

8   Related Work

Several projects have done pervasive verification of low level execution platforms (e.g. [6,9–11,19]). These projects usually do not take I/O devices into account. If I/O devices are taken into account then there are four approaches to show security properties of these platforms: (1) block disallowed memory accesses by disabling DMA or using explicit hardware support, like IOMMU for x86 (e.g. Vasudevan et al. [18]); (2) verify a privileged device driver; (3) monitor the configurations established by an untrusted and unprivileged device driver; and (4) synthesize a driver that is correct by construction. In the last three cases formal models of the I/O devices (the NIC in our case) are necessary.

Alkassar et al. [2] and Duan [7] have verified device drivers for UART devices. Alkassar et al. [3] have verified a page fault handler of a microkernel that controls an ATAPI disk, proving that after the driver has terminated, a specific page in memory has been copied to a sector of the disk. In all these cases, data transfers to and from the device occur via the CPU and no DMA is involved, therefore these devices do not constitute a threat to memory isolation.

The system design presented in [20] is similar to the system design of Fig. 5a and consists of a hypervisor, a monitor, and untrusted guests. The hypervisor is based on XMHF [18] and configures the hardware to protect: the hypervisor from the monitor and from the guests; the monitor from the guests; and the guests from each other. The monitor (called wimpy kernel) checks device configurations built by guests to ensure isolation. Although memory integrity of the hypervisor has been verified, I/O devices are not considered in the verification since their memory accesses are checked by an IOMMU.

Device driver synthesis is a method for automatically generating device drivers that are correct by construction. Some of these methods (e.g. [13,14]) require a specification of the protocol of the communication between the OS and the device driver and between the device driver and the I/O device. Current results cannot synthesize device drivers for I/O devices with DMA. When only security properties are needed (and not functional correctness), communication protocols are not necessary for synthesis and a security invariant can be used to drive the synthesis of a run-time monitor (e.g. generation of a debugging monitor [17]).

9   Concluding Remarks

We modeled the NIC of an embedded system and demonstrated that the NIC can be securely isolated. Isolation is formally verified by means of an invariant, which is preserved by all NIC operations, and which implies that all memory requests address only readable and writable memory regions. The invariant provides a blueprint for securing the NIC: Either the device driver ensures preservation of the invariant, or a run-time monitor is used to prevent potentially compromised software to violate the invariant. Section 7 demonstrates that the second method is practical, by evaluating two different deployments of the monitor.

Hardware specifications are often incomplete (e.g. tests on hardware show undocumented updates of BD-fields), unclear, ambiguous, and self-contradictory (e.g. one section of the specification specifies SOP-BD and another specifies EOP-BD). To get a clear understanding of the NIC, in addition to reading the specification, we inspected the source code of the Linux NIC driver and tested on the hardware some unclear configurations. We also exercised the model by means of several lemmas, each one representing a large set of test cases for one usage scenario. Finally we developed a primitive model of the NIC and a device driver in NuSMV [4]. This allowed us to identify an error in the model related to the order of execution of some operations.

The verification identified some properties of secure NIC configurations that are not explicitly stated by the specification and that may be overlooked by developers. For example, a queue must not contain overlapping BDs, since that could cause the NIC to modify the BP-field of a BD when updating the OWN-field of an overlapping BD.

We also identified a bug in the Linux driver while testing the monitor. When the driver module is unloaded, the driver (1) tears down reception; (2) frees the buffers in memory used for reception; (3) inadvertently re-enables reception; and (4) shuts down the DMA of the NIC. If a frame is received between (3) and (4), then the NIC writes into a freed buffer. In case of interrupt or parallel execution, this buffer may have been (re-)allocated to another software component, potentially causing data corruption. Moreover, this write after free can leak frame data to other software components.

Our approach can be adapted to secure other DMACs that are configured via linked lists. In case the linked lists are stored in memory instead of being stored in the DMAC, then their elements must not overlap with writable buffers addressed by the BDs or be directly writable by untrusted software. Also, the linked lists cannot reside in non-readable memory, since the DMAC can then leak their configuration/content. In case the DMAC does not modify BDs, the constraint of non-overlapping BDs and queues is not needed. Our approach can also handle register based DMACs by considering the registers used to configure memory accesses as a fixed queue. On the other hand, a general treatment of programmable DMACs is challenging, since they require a formal model of their instruction set, which can be used to define arbitrary behavior.

Acknowledgements. Work partially supported by the TrustFull project financed by the Swedish Foundation for Strategic Research.

References

1. AM335x and AMIC110 Sitara^{TM} Processors, Technical Reference Manual, Texas Instruments Rev. P. https://www.ti.com/lit/ug/spruh73p/spruh73p.pdf
2. Alkassar, E., Hillebrand, M., Knapp, S., Rusev, R., Tverdyshev, S.: Formal device and programming model for a serial interface. In: Proceedings of VERIFY, pp. 4–20 (2007)

3. Alkassar, E., Hillebrand, M.A.: Formal functional verification of device drivers. In: Shankar, N., Woodcock, J. (eds.) VSTTE 2008. LNCS, vol. 5295, pp. 225–239. Springer, Heidelberg (2008). https://doi.org/10.1007/978-3-540-87873-5_19
4. Cavada, R., et al.: NuSMV 2.4 user manual. CMU and ITC-IRST (2005)
5. Chfouka, H., Nemati, H., Guanciale, R., Dam, M., Ekdahl, P.: Trustworthy prevention of code injection in Linux on embedded devices. In: Pernul, G., Ryan, P.Y.A., Weippl, E. (eds.) ESORICS 2015. LNCS, vol. 9326, pp. 90–107. Springer, Cham (2015). https://doi.org/10.1007/978-3-319-24174-6_5
6. MDam, M., Guanciale, R., Khakpour, N., Nemati, H., Schwarz, O.: Formal verification of information flow security for a simple ARM-based separation kernel. In: CCS, pp. 223–234. ACM (2013)
7. Duan, J.: Formal Verification of Device Drivers in Embedded Systems. The University of Utah, Salt Lake City (2013)
8. Fox, A., Myreen, M.O.: A trustworthy Monadic formalization of the ARMv7 instruction set architecture. In: Kaufmann, M., Paulson, L.C. (eds.) ITP 2010. LNCS, vol. 6172, pp. 243–258. Springer, Heidelberg (2010). https://doi.org/10.1007/978-3-642-14052-5_18
9. Gu, R., et al.: CertiKOS: an extensible architecture for building certified concurrent OS kernels. In OSDI, pp. 653–669. USENIX (2016)
10. Klein, G., et al.: seL4: formal verification of an OS kernel. In: Operating Systems Principles, pp. 207–220. ACM (2009)
11. Leinenbach, D., Santen, T.: Verifying the microsoft hyper-V hypervisor with VCC. In: Cavalcanti, A., Dams, D.R. (eds.) FM 2009. LNCS, vol. 5850, pp. 806–809. Springer, Heidelberg (2009). https://doi.org/10.1007/978-3-642-05089-3_51
12. Nemati, H., Guanciale, R., Dam, M.: Trustworthy virtualization of the ARMv7 memory subsystem. In: Italiano, G.F., Margaria-Steffen, T., Pokorný, J., Quisquater, J.-J., Wattenhofer, R. (eds.) SOFSEM 2015. LNCS, vol. 8939, pp. 578–589. Springer, Heidelberg (2015). https://doi.org/10.1007/978-3-662-46078-8_48
13. Ryzhyk, L., Chubb, P., Kuz, I., Le Sueur, E., Heiser, G.: Automatic device driver synthesis with termite. In: SIGOPS, pp. 73–86. ACM (2009)
14. Ryzhyk, L., et al.: User-guided device driver synthesis. In: OSDI, pp. 661–676. USENIX (2014)
15. Schwarz, O., Dam, M.: Formal verification of secure user mode device execution with DMA. In: Yahav, E. (ed.) HVC 2014. LNCS, vol. 8855, pp. 236–251. Springer, Cham (2014). https://doi.org/10.1007/978-3-319-13338-6_18
16. Slind, K., Norrish, M.: A brief overview of HOL4. In: Mohamed, O.A., Muñoz, C., Tahar, S. (eds.) TPHOLs 2008. LNCS, vol. 5170, pp. 28–32. Springer, Heidelberg (2008). https://doi.org/10.1007/978-3-540-71067-7_6
17. Sun, J., Yuan, W., Kallahalla, M., Islam, N.: HAIL: a language for easy and correct device access. In: Proceedings of the 5th ACM International Conference on Embedded Software, pp. 1–9. ACM (2005)
18. Vasudevan, A., Chaki, S., Jia, L., McCune, J., Newsome, J., Datta, A.: Design, implementation and verification of an extensible and modular hypervisor framework. In: SP, pp. 430–444. IEEE (2013)
19. Verbeek, F., et al.: Formal API specification of the PikeOS separation kernel. In: Havelund, K., Holzmann, G., Joshi, R. (eds.) NFM 2015. LNCS, vol. 9058, pp. 375–389. Springer, Cham (2015). https://doi.org/10.1007/978-3-319-17524-9_26
20. Zhou, Z., Yu, M., Gligor, V.D.: Dancing with giants: wimpy kernels for on-demand isolated I/O. In: 2014 IEEE Symposium on Security and Privacy, pp. 308–323. IEEE (2014)

Access Control

Toward Implementing Spatio-Temporal RBAC Extensions

Aditya Dubey[1], Uttara Ravi[2], Somya Sharma[1], and Barsha Mitra[2(✉)]

[1] Department of EEE, BITS Pilani, Hyderabad Campus, Hyderabad, India
{f20150181,f20160216}@hyderabad.bits-pilani.ac.in
[2] Department of CSIS, BITS Pilani, Hyderabad Campus, Hyderabad, India
{f20150032,barsha.mitra}@hyderabad.bits-pilani.ac.in

Abstract. Role-Based Access Control (RBAC) restricts unauthorized user accesses by ensuring that only the permissions necessary for executing the respective tasks by the users are available through the roles assigned to them. In order to effectively deploy and sustain RBAC in an organization, a set of roles needs to be designed. This can be done using an approach known as role mining. In many cases, it may be essential to limit the accessibility of the roles to certain locations and time periods. Such kind of location and time dependent availability of roles can be enforced by the spatio-temporal extensions of the RBAC model. The implementation of these extended models requires the creation of spatially and temporally constrained roles which cannot be directly done using the traditional role mining algorithms. In this paper, we propose an approach known as *spatio-temporal role mining* to generate the roles for setting up spatio-temporal RBAC. We describe a suitable representation for depicting the input to spatio-temporal role mining, formally define the *Spatio-Temporal Role Mining Problem (STRMP)* and propose an algorithm for solving it. Experimental results obtained from synthetic and real-world datasets provide the performance evaluation of our proposed approach.

Keywords: Access control · Spatio-temporal RBAC · Spatio-temporal role mining · Role minimization · Algorithm

1 Introduction

Role-Based Access Control (RBAC) [26] has been widely used as a suitable means of enforcing access control. As the name of the model implies, *roles* is possibly the single most crucial element of RBAC. Thus, in order to deploy RBAC in any organization, a set of roles is required. The process of creating roles for implementing RBAC is known as *role engineering* [6]. There are 3 approaches to performing role engineering - (i) *top-down*, (ii) *bottom-up* and (iii) *hybrid*. A top-down approach [23] works by analyzing and repeatedly dividing the business processes to determine the permissions needed to complete a particular task. On the other hand, a bottom-up technique accepts the information describing

© Springer Nature Switzerland AG 2019
D. Garg et al. (Eds.): ICISS 2019, LNCS 11952, pp. 59–78, 2019.
https://doi.org/10.1007/978-3-030-36945-3_4

the permissions assigned to each of the users, also known as user-permission assignments, as input and creates a set of roles. *Role mining* [8,14,28,29] is a bottom-up technique of role engineering. The third type of role engineering approach, hybrid [22] combines both top-down and bottom-up techniques.

The input to role mining is a set of user-permission assignments which can be represented in the form of a boolean matrix known as the *User-Permission Assignment* or *UPA* matrix. The rows and columns of UPA correspond to users and permissions respectively. The assignment or non-assignment of a permission p to a user u is depicted by putting a 1 or a 0 respectively in the cell present in row u and column p of the UPA. The output given by role mining consists of a set of roles, a user-role assignment (UA) relation and a role-permission assignment (PA) relation. The UA contains the information regarding the roles given to each user and the PA describes the composition of each role in terms of permissions. Like the UPA, the UA and PA also have suitable boolean matrix representations.

Though RBAC has proven to be quite an appropriate means of access control, it is not without some inherent shortcomings. While in many cases, it may be sufficient to simply have a set of roles without any additional constraints, system administrators, sometimes, may want to prohibit the unrestricted availability of roles for the users. As a result, a system administrator may restrict a role to be available or enabled only from a certain location or during a specific time interval or both. Consequently, the permissions contained in the role will also be subjected to the same location and time constraints. Such kinds of constraints cannot be accommodated by RBAC. Hence several extensions of RBAC have been proposed. Some of these extensions allow enabling of roles based on time constraints and are known as the temporal extensions of RBAC like Temporal Role-Based Access Control (TRBAC) [2] and Generalized Temporal Role-Based Access Control (GTRBAC) [11]. Other extended models allow roles to be enabled from specific locations and are categorized as the spatial extensions of RBAC like GEO-RBAC [7], Location-Aware Role-Based Access Control (LRBAC) [24], and Proximity-based Spatially Aware RBAC (Prox-RBAC) [12]. Combining both spatial and temporal models, researchers have also proposed a number of spatio-temporal extensions of RBAC like Location and Time-Based RBAC (LoT-RBAC) [4], generalized Temporal and Spatial RBAC (TSRBAC) [5], Spatio-Temporal Role-Based Access Control [25], Spatio-Temporal Role-Based Access Control (STRBAC) [13], etc.

To implement the above mentioned extended RBAC models, roles having the appropriate constraints are required. Such kind of roles cannot be directly output by the traditional role mining algorithms since these approaches are capable of handling only boolean input. For this reason, *temporal role mining* [17–20,27] has been proposed to create roles suitable for the deployment of the temporally extended RBAC models. However, to the best of our knowledge, few attempts have been made for designing approaches for implementing the spatio-temporal extensions.

In this paper, we present an approach to mine roles for the deployment of spatio-temporal RBAC models. We name this process as *Spatio-Temporal Role Mining*. Spatio-temporal role mining takes as input a set of user-permission assignments having location and time-based constraints associated with them. We propose a representation for storing this input and name it as the *Spatio-Temporal User-Permission Assignment (STUPA) Matrix*. The output of the proposed role mining variant is a set of *spatio-temporal roles*. We formally define the problem of mining a minimal set of such roles as the *Spatio-Temporal Role Mining Problem (STRMP)*. Moreover, we propose an algorithm for solving STRMP which makes use of existing traditional role mining algorithms. The benefit of using the existing role mining techniques is the seamless migration from RBAC to spatio-temporal RBAC without having to create a new and computationally complex algorithm to handle the space and time constraints. In case, spatio-temporal RBAC is implemented from scratch, then also the proposed technique can be easily applied. We have evaluated the performance of our approach both on synthetically generated datasets as well as real-world datasets augmented with appropriate spatio-temporal constraints.

The rest of the paper is organized as follows. Section 2 presents a brief survey of the current literature on role mining and Sect. 3 discusses some fundamental aspects of RBAC, role mining, extended RBAC models and role mining approaches related to them. In Sect. 4, we introduce the Spatio-Temporal User-Permission Assignment (STUPA) Matrix for storing the input of spatio-temporal role mining and formally define the Spatio-Temporal Role Mining Problem (STRMP). The algorithm for solving STRMP is discussed in Sect. 5 and explained using an example. Experimental results depicting the performance evaluation of the proposed approach is presented in Sect. 6. Finally, Sect. 7 concludes the paper along with some insights into future research efforts.

2   Related Work

The current literature contains several works related to role mining. Over the years, the research in this area has progressed along 2 directions which are complementary to one another. On one hand, a number of optimization problem variants have been proposed and on the other, various algorithms for solving these problem variants have been presented. Therefore, in this section, we shall first discuss some of the role mining problem formulations and then review the associated solution approaches.

Basic-RMP [28] is the role mining problem variant which minimizes the total number of roles. It also derives an exact solution where the input matches the output without any deviations. In other words, each user acquires exactly those permissions through his/her assigned roles as the ones specified in the input. This problem has been shown to be NP-complete. Instead of computing an exact solution, a limited amount of inexactness can be allowed in the output such that certain users are deprived of some privileges. By accommodating this error margin, researchers have proposed 2 problem variants - *δ-approx RMP* [28] and *Min-Noise RMP* [28]. The former one minimizes the total number of roles by allowing for a limited degree of difference between the input and the output and the latter minimizes the total amount of input-output deviation for a fixed number of roles. Another problem similar to Min-Noise RMP is *Usage RMP* [15] which takes a UPA and a PA as input and derives the UA by minimizing the deviations of the output from the input. In addition to these, several other problem variants are present such as *Edge-RMP* [14] that minimizes the sum of the sizes of the UA and PA, *Role Hierarchy Building Problem* [10] which reduces the number of hierarchical relations between senior and junior roles, *Weighted Structural Complexity Optimization (WSCO) Problem* [22] which minimizes a weighted sum of the sizes of different RBAC elements, etc.

Different types of approaches have been proposed for performing role mining. In [28] and [29], Vaidya et al. present algorithms that create roles by combining the similar permission assignments of multiple users for solving Basic-RMP and δ-approx RMP. Graph theoretic approaches have been proposed in [8] and [10] for generating solutions for Basic-RMP and Role Hierarchy Building Problem respectively. For solving Usage RMP and Edge-RMP, researchers have come up with matrix decomposition based techniques [14,15]. WSCO has been solved by making used for formal concepts analysis [28]. Recently, role mining algorithms capable of limiting the maximum number roles to be assigned to a user and the maximum number of roles of which a permission can become a member of, have been proposed by Blundo et al. [3]. Other recent role mining approaches include role generation using multi-domain information [1] and role creation from web usage patterns [9].

In the past few years, a number of works have focused on mining roles for the deployment of the temporally extended RBAC models. In [17], the authors have formally defined the *Temporal Role Mining Problem (TRMP)* as the problem of creating a minimal set of *temporal roles* (roles having temporal constraints), proved TRMP to be NP-complete and have proposed a heuristic to solve it. This work has been extended in [18], where an inexact version of TRMP, known as the *Generalized Temporal Role Mining Problem (GTRMP)* has been presented. Apart from the number of temporal roles, other minimization metrics have also been proposed such as the *Cumulative Overhead of Temporal Roles And Permissions (CO-TRAP)* [19] and *Weighted Structural Complexity (WSC)* [27]. The problem variant that minimizes CO-TRAP along with TRMP have been solved using many-valued concepts in [19] and the one minimizing WSC has been solved by a combination of subset enumeration and role hierarchy creation [27].

To the best of our knowledge, no attempts have been made to create roles for the deployment of the spatio-temporal extensions of RBAC. A very recent work [16] focuses on dataset generation that can associate spatial constraints with user-permission assignments and also proposes a representation for depicting such datasets. However, in [16], the authors have not presented any role mining algorithm. This paper proposes an approach which can aid system administrators to migrate to a spatio-temporal RBAC extension without much computational overhead.

3   Basic Preliminaries

In this section, we discuss some of the background concepts related to RBAC, traditional role mining, spatial-temporal RBAC and temporal role mining.

3.1   Role-Based Access Control (RBAC)

RBAC [26] consists of the following components:

- A set of users, a set of permissions and a set of roles.
- A many-to-many relation known as the user-role assignment relation or UA which describes the set of roles assigned to each user. The UA can be represented as a boolean matrix. The rows of the matrix correspond to users and the columns correspond to roles. If a role r is assigned to a user u then the cell (u, r) of the UA matrix is set as 1, otherwise it is set as 0.
- A many-to-many relation known as the role-permission assignment relation or PA. The information regarding the set of permissions present in each role is captured in the PA. Like the UA, the PA can also be depicted as a boolean matrix where the roles are represented as rows and the permissions are represented as columns. The cell (r, p) of the PA matrix is set as 1 if role r includes permission p, otherwise the cell contains a 0.

In the current context, we do not discuss about sessions, role hierarchy and constraints like cardinality and separation of duty (SoD) constraints as these RBAC components are not directly related to our work.

3.2   Role Mining

Role mining [8, 14] is the approach that takes a set of user-permission assignments as input and as output, creates a set of roles, a UA and a PA. The input to role mining can be conveniently represented as a boolean matrix, the rows and columns of which correspond to users and permissions respectively. This matrix is termed as the UPA matrix. If a user is assigned a particular permission, then that corresponding cell of the UPA is set as 1. The non-assignment of a permission is represented by setting the corresponding cell as 0. During role mining, several optimization criteria are considered such as the total number of roles [28], the cumulative sizes of the UA and the PA [14] or a weighted structural complexity [21]. Depending upon the role mining criterion, various role mining algorithms have been proposed.

3.3   Spatio-Temporal Extensions of RBAC

The spatio-temporal RBAC extensions [4, 13] have 2 types of constraints associated with the enabling of roles - location and time. In these models, a role is enabled from a specific location and during a specific set of time intervals. As a result, the permissions present in a role are available to the users only in the corresponding locations and during the associated time intervals. The role remains disabled in the rest of the locations and during rest of the time.

The spatio-temporal RBAC models use a notion of 3-dimensional space to represent location based constraints. A location can correspond to a geometric shaped area such as a line, a rectangle, a circle, a polygon, etc. or can resemble a non-geometric irregular figure. In either case, a set of points lying on the boundary of the area can be used to represent a location. The extended RBAC models distinguish between a *physical location* and a *logical location*. When a location is tangibly represented using a set of points (being parts of a co-ordinate system), it is referred to as a *physical location*. A physical location, though can be very precisely represented, does not directly resemble the notion of spaces as perceived by human cognition. A *logical location*, on the other hand, corresponds to areas or locations as recognized by individuals without having to think about boundary points. Examples of logical locations include parking lot, playground, library, etc. However, for computational purposes, it is easier to work with physical locations rather than logical ones.

In order to represent the enabling durations of a role, the extended RBAC models use a construct known as *periodic expression*. A periodic expression denotes an infinite set of time intervals. The intervals recur according to a specific frequency as dictated by the expression itself. For e.g., The periodic expression $all.Years + \{6,9\}.Months + \{1,3\}.Weeks + \{2,4\}.Days + \{10\}.Hours \triangleright 3.Hours$ represents the set of time intervals beginning at 10 am of every Monday and Wednesday (Sunday being the first day of week) of the first and third weeks of the months of June and September (January being the first month) of every year and ending at 1 pm. $Years$, $Months$, $Weeks$, $Days$ and $Hours$ are known as Calendars. Since a periodic expression does not bound the size of the time interval set, this is done by using date expressions (written in mm/dd/yyyy format). Repeating our previous example, if we write, $[01/01/2018, 12/31/2019], all.Years + \{6, 9\}.Months + \{1, 3\}.Weeks + \{2, 4\}.Days + \{10\}.Hours \triangleright 3.Hours$, the above mentioned time intervals will apply only for the years 2018 and 2019.

It can be noted here that we do not discuss about any additional features of the spatio-temporal models like role hierarchy, constraints, etc.

3.4   Temporal Role Mining

For successful deployment of temporal RBAC models, a set of temporal roles is required which are enabled for specific sets of time intervals. The process to create such temporal roles has been termed as temporal role mining [17]. It takes as input a set of user-permission assignments having associated temporal constraints. These assignments can be represented in the form of a matrix known as the temporal user-permission assignment (TUPA) matrix. The number of rows of TUPA is equal to the total number of users and the number of columns is equal to the number of permissions. Each user is assigned one or more permissions for a specific set of time intervals. Therefore, if user u is assigned permission p for a set of time intervals t, then the cell (u, p) of TUPA contains t, otherwise it contains ϕ. After processing such a TUPA, temporal role mining generates a set of temporal roles, a UA, a PA and a Role Enabling Base (REB). The REB describes the set of time intervals for which each role is enabled. A number of temporal role mining algorithms have been proposed till date such as the ones presented in [17–20, 27].

4   Mining Spatio-Temporal Roles

We name the roles having both spatial and temporal constraints as *Spatio-Temporal Roles* and the process of generating them as *Spatio-Temporal Role Mining*. These roles are crucial for the implementation of any spatio-temporal extension of RBAC. In this section, we describe a suitable representation for the user-permission assignments having spatial as well as temporal constraints and also formally define the problem of mining the spatio-temporal roles.

4.1   Spatio-Temporal User Permission Assignment Matrix

Spatio-temporal role mining is a bottom-up method for creating spatio-temporal roles. It takes as input a set of user-permission assignments having spatial as well as temporal constraints associated with them and generates a set of spatio-temporal roles. We propose that these spatio-temporal user permission assignments can be represented in the form of a matrix which we name as the *Spatio-Temporal User Permission Assignment (STUPA) Matrix*. The rows of the STUPA correspond to users and the columns correspond to permissions. Since each user-permission assignment has location and time constraints, each cell of STUPA either contains a set of locations and a set of time intervals or contains ϕ. The presence of ϕ in a cell, say (u_i, p_j) of STUPA denotes that user u_i has not been assigned permission p_j. If, however, u_i is assigned p_j, then cell (u_i, p_j) will contain a set of locations $\mathcal{L}_{ij}$ and a set of time intervals $\mathcal{T}_{ij}$ implying that p_j is available to u_i for each location of $\mathcal{L}_{ij}$ and for each time interval of $\mathcal{T}_{ij}$. $\mathcal{T}_{ij}$ is represented using one or more periodic expressions [2]. Each location of $\mathcal{L}_{ij}$ can be considered as an area which corresponds to either a geometric or a non-geometric shape and can be represented using a set of points. In this context, it should be mentioned that we are only considering physical locations that are described in the spatio-temporal RBAC models and do not consider the logical locations. Since locations can either belong to a 2-dimensional (2D) space or a 3-dimensional (3D) space, we account for both in our STUPA matrix. If the areas belong to a 2D space, then we can represent each of them as a set of points in 2D space. If on the other hand, they belong to a 3D space, then we consider that it implies that the areas are present inside a building having multiple floors. In such a case, each area is represented using a floor number and a set of points depicting the area boundary. Such a concept of depicting locations has been discussed in [16].

An example STUPA matrix having 4 users and 4 permissions is depicted in Table 1. Here, for the sake of brevity, instead of showing a set of time intervals

Table 1. Example STUPA matrix

	p_1	p_2	p_3	p_4
u_1	$\{area_1\}$, $\{10$ am–11 am$\}$	ϕ	ϕ	$\{area_2\}$, $\{9$ am–12 pm$\}$
u_2	ϕ	$\{area_1\}$, $\{10$ am–11 am$\}$	$\{area_1\}$, $\{10$ am–11 am$\}$	$\{area_2\}$, $\{9$ am–12 pm$\}$
u_3	$\{area_1\}$, $\{10$ am–11 am$\}$	$\{area_1\}$, $\{9$ am–12 pm$\}$	$\{area_1\}$, $\{9$ am–12 pm$\}$	$\{area_2\}$, $\{10$ am–1 pm$\}$
u_4	$\{area_1\}$, $\{10$ am–1 pm$\}$	$\{area_2\}$, $\{10$ am–1 pm$\}$	ϕ	ϕ

and a set of locations, we have shown only one interval and one location. Each time interval present in a non-empty cell of the STUPA corresponds to a bounded periodic expression. For eg., For 10 am–11 am, the corresponding bounded periodic expression is $\langle[1/1/2015, \infty], all.Days + \{10\}.Hours \triangleright 1.Hours\rangle$. Also, the areas are depicted by their names instead of actually describing the set of points. The description of each area can be stored in a separate data structure.

In the example STUPA, user u_1 is assigned permission p_1 for the time interval 10 am to 11 am on all days and for the location $area_1$. Since u_1 is not assigned p_2, the cell (u_1, p_2) contains ϕ. The remaining cells of the STUPA can be interpreted similarly. The 2 locations $area_1$ and $area_2$ present in the example STUPA are assumed to be disjoint. It may be noted here that the STUPA representation has some similarities with the Temporal UPA (TUPA) representation proposed in [17] with respect to the depiction of the temporal constraints. Also, the representation of the spatial constraints is similar to the Spatial UPA (SUPA) representation proposed in [16].

4.2   Spatio-Temporal Role Mining Problem (STRMP)

The STUPA matrix described above is given as input to the process of spatio-temporal role mining. The output that is derived from the process consists of a set of spatio-temporal roles, a user-role assignment (UA) matrix, a role-permission assignment (PA) matrix, a spatial role enabling base (SREB) and a temporal role enabling base (TREB). SREB lists the set of locations in which each role is enabled and TREB contains the set of time intervals for which each role is enabled. Here, we consider 2 types of role enabling bases (REBs) - spatial and temporal, since a set of locations as well as a set of time intervals is associated with each individual role. In this paper, we consider that the output of spatio-temporal role mining is produced in such a manner that each user gets exactly the same set of permissions for the sets of locations and time intervals as depicted in the input STUPA through his/her assigned roles. We refer to this scenario as the output being *consistent* with the input.

We define the problem of creating a minimum sized set of spatio-temporal roles from an input STUPA as the *Spatio-Temporal Role Mining Problem (STRMP)*. The formal problem definition is as follows.

Definition 1. *STRMP: For a set of users U, a set of permissions P and a spatio-temporal user-permission assignment matrix STUPA given as input, find a set of spatio-temporal roles STR, a user-role assignment matrix UA, a role-permission assignment matrix PA, a spatial role enabling base $SREB$ and a temporal role enabling base $TREB$, such that the number of spatio-temporal roles is minimized.*

STRMP can be proved to be an NP-complete problem by reducing Basic-RMP which is a known NP-complete problem to STRMP in polynomial time. This reduction can be done by assuming that the same location and the same time interval is associated with all the user-permission assignments of the STUPA. In the current context, we only consider the number of roles as the minimization criterion. However, other optimization metrics can also be considered.

5   Algorithm for Mining Spatio-Temporal Roles

In this section, we present the algorithm for creation of the spatio-temporal roles. The algorithm takes an STUPA matrix as input and produces a UA, a PA, an SREB and a TREB. It works in several phases. In the first phase, we separately create a set of spatial roles (roles having only location constraints) and a set of temporal roles. In the next phase, these 2 sets of roles are combined to obtain the set of spatio-temporal roles. For doing this, it needs to be ensured that after combining, we do not end up with any role through which one or more users can acquire any permission for any time duration or from any location which was not specified in the input STUPA. In other words, we make sure that the output exactly matches with the input. Finally, in the last phase, the spatio-temporal roles are merged to reduce the size of the final role set. In the subsequent subsections, we discuss each of the phases in detail.

5.1   Creation of Spatial and Temporal Roles

This phase accepts an STUPA matrix as input and segregates out the location and time information from it. This is done by creating separate UPA matrices for each distinct location and each unique set of time intervals present in the STUPA. We consider each non-null element of the STUPA matrix as a quadruple of the form $\langle u_i, p_j, \mathcal{L}_{ij}, \mathcal{T}_{ij} \rangle$ implying that user u_{ij} has permission p_{ij} in each location of the set $\mathcal{L}_{ij}$ and in each time interval of the set $\mathcal{T}_{ij}$. This quadruple can be considered to be a combination of 2 triples - $\langle u_i, p_j, \mathcal{L}_{ij} \rangle$ and $\langle u_i, p_j, \mathcal{T}_{ij} \rangle$. We refer to the former one as a *spatial triple* and the latter one as a *temporal triple*. By scanning all the spatial triples present in the STUPA, we identify all the distinct locations present. Similarly, all the distinct sets of time intervals existing in the STUPA are determined by scanning all the temporal triples. Let $S_{\mathcal{L}}$ and S_T respectively denote the set of the unique locations and the set of the distinct time interval sets present in the STUPA. For each location $l \in S_{\mathcal{L}}$, a separate UPA is created as per the following steps - (i) if cell (i, j) of STUPA contains ϕ or a location l'' such that $l \cap l'' = \phi$, then the corresponding cell of the UPA contains 0 and, (ii) if cell (i, j) of STUPA contains a location l' and $l \subseteq l'$, then cell (i, j) of UPA contains a 1. We denote this UPA as UPA_l. Each such UPA is referred to as *location-specific UPA*. Similarly, for each distinct time interval set $T \in S_T$, we create a UPA which is denoted as UPA_T and is named as *time-specific UPA*. This process of creating the time-specific UPAs is similar to the approach of generating the timestamped UPAs described in [20].

After creating the location-specific and time-specific UPAs, a traditional role mining algorithm that minimizes the size of the role set is applied to each of them to obtain a set of corresponding type of roles. Since the location and time information have been segregated out from the input and the individual UPAs contain information only for a particular location or time interval, any conventional role mining approach capable of handling only boolean input can be used. Mining each location-specific UPA will generate a set of roles having spatial constraints and the output will consist of a UA, a PA and an SREB. Hence, the spatially-aware roles obtained from each UPA_l will be enabled from location l. From each time-specific UPA, we shall obtain a set of temporal roles and thus a UA, a PA and a TREB will constitute the output. As a result, the temporal roles generated from a UPA_T will be enabled for a set of time intervals T.

Algorithm 1 (*Create_Spatial_Temporal_Roles*) depicts the steps for this phase. It takes a p x q STUPA as input and generates a set $R_{\mathcal{L}}$ of spatial roles and a set R_T of temporal roles. Initially, both sets are initialized as empty sets (Lines 1 and 2). Line 3 identifies all distinct locations present in the STUPA and stores in set $S_{\mathcal{L}}$. Now, for each unique location l present in $S_{\mathcal{L}}$, a p x q location-specific UPA_l containing all 0s is created (Line 5). In Lines 6–12, each cell of the STUPA is scanned and if a cell containing a location l' is found where l is a subset of or equal to l', then the corresponding cell content of UPA_l is changed to 1. Line 13 creates a set SR_l of spatial roles from UPA_l by applying a traditional role mining algorithm and these spatial roles are added to $R_{\mathcal{L}}$ in Line 14. Similarly, in Lines 16–28, all distinct time interval sets of the STUPA are identified, for each unique time interval set T, a time-specific UPA_T is created, a temporal role set TR_T is computed from UPA_T and added to R_T. $R_{\mathcal{L}}$ and R_T generated out of this phase is input to the next phase.

5.2   Generate Spatio-Temporal Roles

This phase takes as input the set of spatial roles and the set of temporal roles created in the first phase. These spatial and temporal roles are now combined to generate the spatio-temporal roles. Each spatial role r_l has 3 components - (i) the set U_l of users who are assigned this role, (ii) the set P_l of permissions contained in the role and (iii) the location l from which the role is enabled. Also,

Algorithm 1. Create_Spatial_Temporal_Roles

Require: INPUT: p x q STUPA
Require: OUTPUT: $R_\mathcal{L}$ (set of spatial roles), $R_\mathcal{T}$ (set of temporal roles)
Require: $S_\mathcal{L}$: Set of all distinct locations of STUPA
Require: $S_\mathcal{T}$: Set of all distinct time interval sets of STUPA
Require: SR_l: Set of spatial roles generated from UPA$_l$
Require: TR_T: Set of temporal roles generated from UPA$_T$
1: $R_\mathcal{L} \leftarrow \phi$
2: $R_\mathcal{T} \leftarrow \phi$
3: Identify all distinct locations and store in $S_\mathcal{L}$
4: **for** each $l \in S_\mathcal{L}$ **do**
5:     Create p x q UPA$_l$ containing 0s
6:     **for** $i \leftarrow 1$ to p **do**
7:         **for** $j \leftarrow 1$ to q **do**
8:             **if** cell (i, j) of STUPA contains l' such that $l \subseteq l'$ **then**
9:                 Put 1 in cell (i, j) of UPA$_l$
10:             **end if**
11:         **end for**
12:     **end for**
13:     Create SR_l from UPA$_l$ using a role mining algorithm
14:     $R_\mathcal{L} \leftarrow R_\mathcal{L} \cup SR_l$
15: **end for**
16: Identify all distinct time interval sets and store in $S_\mathcal{T}$
17: **for** each $T \in S_\mathcal{T}$ **do**
18:     Create p x q UPA$_T$ containing 0s
19:     **for** $i \leftarrow 1$ to p **do**
20:         **for** $j \leftarrow 1$ to q **do**
21:             **if** cell (i, j) of STUPA contains T' such that $T \subseteq T'$ **then**
22:                 Put 1 in cell (i, j) of UPA$_T$
23:             **end if**
24:         **end for**
25:     **end for**
26:     Create TR_T from UPA$_T$ using a role mining algorithm
27:     $R_\mathcal{T} \leftarrow R_\mathcal{T} \cup TR_T$
28: **end for**

each temporal role r_T has 3 components - (i) the set U_T of users who are assigned this role, (ii) the set P_T of permissions present in the role and, (iii) the set T of time intervals for which the role is enabled. Thus, we can use the following notations - $r_l = (U_l, P_l, l)$ and $r_T = (U_T, P_T, T)$. The notation for temporal role was introduced in [17]. Combining of the spatial and temporal roles will be done by considering all of the 6 components. r_l and r_T will be combined to create a spatio-temporal role r if both the pairs U_l and U_T and P_l and P_T have non-empty intersections. Thus, $r = (U_l \cap U_T, P_l \cap P_T, l, T)$. Thus, a spatio-temporal role r will have 4 components. If either of the intersections of the user sets or the permission sets of r_l and r_T empty, then no spatio-temporal role can be constructed by combining r_l and r_T. We take the intersections of U_l and U_T and

P_l and P_T because we need to ensure that no user acquires any permission from any extra location or any additional time interval set other than those present in the input STUPA.

Algorithm 2. Generate_Spatio-Temporal_Roles

Require: INPUT: $R_{\mathcal{L}}$ (set of spatial roles), R_T (set of temporal roles)
Require: OUTPUT: R (set of spatio-temporal roles)
1: $R \leftarrow \phi$
2: **for** each $r_l \in R_{\mathcal{L}}$ **do**
3:     **for** each $r_T \in R_T$ **do**
4:         **if** $U_l \cap U_T \neq \phi$ and $P_l \cap P_T \neq \phi$ **then**
5:             Create spatio-temporal role $r = (U_l \cap U_T, P_l \cap P_T, l, T)$
6:             $R \leftarrow R \cup \{r\}$
7:         **else**
8:             Do not combine r_l and r_T
9:         **end if**
10:     **end for**
11: **end for**

The steps for the creation of the spatio-temporal roles is described in Algorithm 2 (*Generate_Spatio-Temporal_Roles*). Line 1 initializes the set R of spatio-temporal roles as an empty set. In the *for* loops of Lines 2–11, each spatial role r_l and each temporal role r_T are pairwise considered and are combined to create a spatio-temporal role r if the requisite conditions are satisfied. Finally, r is added to the set R (Line 6).

5.3   Merge Spatio-Temporal Roles

In the third and the final phase of our algorithm, we merge the spatio-temporal roles generated out of the previous phase to further reduce their number since our objective is to minimize the size of the final role set. For this, we consider the roles in a pairwise manner and take into account all the 4 components of the roles. Let $r_x = (U_x, P_x, l_x, T_x)$ and $r_y = (U_y, P_y, l_y, T_y)$ be 2 spatio-temporal roles. r_x and r_y can be merged to create a new role r_z if any one of the following conditions are satisfied.

(i) If U_x and U_y, l_x and l_y and T_x and T_y are equal, then replace r_x and r_y with $r_z = (U_x, P_x \cup P_y, l_x, T_x)$.
(ii) If P_x and P_y, l_x and l_y and T_x and T_y are equal, then replace r_x and r_y with $r_z = (U_x \cup U_y, P_x, l_x, T_x)$.
(iii) If U_x and U_y, P_x and P_y, l_x and l_y are equal and $T_x \cap T_y \neq \phi$ or T_x and T_y are consecutive, then replace r_x and r_y with $r_z = (U_x, P_x, l_x, T_x \cup T_y)$.
(iv) If U_x and U_y, P_x and P_y, T_x and T_y are equal and $l_x \cap l_y \neq \phi$ or l_x and l_y share a common boundary, then replace r_x and r_y with $r_z = (U_x, P_x, l_x \cup l_y, T_x)$.

After merging, a UA, a PA, an SREB and a TREB are created and these along with the final spatio-temporal role set R constitute the output. Algorithm 3 shows the steps of the merging phase. The 2 *for* loops beginning at Lines 1 and 2 respectively consider every pair of roles present in R. The conditions (i), (ii), (iii) and (iv) are respectively checked in Lines 3, 5, 7 and 9 and accordingly, the merged role r_z is created. Finally, in Line 12, the 2 roles that are merged are removed from R and the merged one is added to the set in Line 13.

Algorithm 3. Merge_Spatio-Temporal_Roles

Require: INPUT: R (set of spatio-temporal roles)
Require: OUTPUT: updated R
1: **for** $x \leftarrow 1$ to $|R|$ **do**
2:     **for** $y \leftarrow 1$ to $|R|$ - 1 **do**
3:         **if** $U_x = U_y$, $l_x = l_y$ and $T_x = T_y$ **then**
4:             Create $r_z = (U_x, P_x \cup P_y, l_x, T_x)$
5:         **else if** $P_x = P_y$, $l_x = l_y$ and $T_x = T_y$ **then**
6:             Create $r_z = (U_x \cup U_y, P_x, l_x, T_x)$
7:         **else if** $U_x = U_y$, $P_x = P_y$, $l_x = l_y$ and $T_x \cap T_y \neq \phi$ or T_x and T_y are consecutive **then**
8:             Create $r_z = (U_x, P_x, l_x, T_x \cup T_y)$
9:         **else if** $U_x = U_y$, $P_x = P_y$, $T_x = T_y$ and $l_x \cap l_y \neq \phi$ or l_x and l_y share a common boundary **then**
10:        Create $r_z = (U_x, P_x, l_x \cup l_y, T_x)$
11:       **end if**
12:       $R \leftarrow R$ - $\{r_x, r_y\}$
13:       $R \leftarrow R \cup \{r_z\}$
14:     **end for**
15: **end for**

5.4 Illustrative Example

In this sub-section, we explain the working of our proposed algorithm using the STUPA presented in Table 1. It contains 2 distinct locations - $area_1$ and $area_2$ and 3 unique time intervals - 10 am–11 am, 9 am–12 pm and 10 am–1 pm. The Spatial UPA (SUPA) and Temporal UPA (TUPA) corresponding to the STUPA

Table 2. SUPA matrix for STUPA of Table 1

	p_1	p_2	p_3	p_4
u_1	$\{area_1\}$	ϕ	ϕ	$\{area_2\}$
u_2	ϕ	$\{area_1\}$	$\{area_1\}$	$\{area_2\}$
u_3	$\{area_1\}$	$\{area_1\}$	$\{area_1\}$	$\{area_2\}$
u_4	$\{area_1\}$	$\{area_2\}$	ϕ	ϕ

Table 3. TUPA matrix for STUPA of Table 1

	p_1	p_2	p_3	p_4
u_1	{10 am–11 am}	ϕ	ϕ	{9 am–12 pm}
u_2	ϕ	{10 am–11 am}	{10 am–11 am}	{9 am–12 pm}
u_3	{10 am–11 am}	{9 am–12 pm}	{9 am–12 pm}	{10 am–1 pm}
u_4	{10 am–1 pm}	{10 am–1 pm}	ϕ	ϕ

Table 4. UPA$_{area_1}$

	p_1	p_2	p_3	p_4
u_1	1	0	0	0
u_2	0	1	1	0
u_3	1	1	1	0
u_4	1	0	0	0

Table 5. UPA$_{area_2}$

	p_1	p_2	p_3	p_4
u_1	0	0	0	1
u_2	0	0	0	1
u_3	0	0	0	1
u_4	0	1	0	0

Table 6. UPA$_{10\ am-11\ am}$

	p_1	p_2	p_3	p_4
u_1	1	0	0	1
u_2	0	1	1	1
u_3	1	1	1	1
u_4	1	1	0	0

Table 7. UPA$_{9\ am-12\ pm}$

	p_1	p_2	p_3	p_4
u_1	0	0	0	1
u_2	0	0	0	1
u_3	0	1	1	0
u_4	0	0	0	0

Table 8. UPA$_{10\ am-1\ pm}$

	p_1	p_2	p_3	p_4
u_1	0	0	0	0
u_2	0	0	0	0
u_3	0	0	0	1
u_4	1	1	0	0

are shown in Tables 2 and 3 respectively. We show these 2 matrices for ease of understanding of the example.

The location-specific UPAs obtained from the SUPA of Table 2 are shown in Tables 4 and 5 and the time-specific UPAs created from the TUPA of Table 3 are depicted in Tables 6, 7 and 8.

Next, the minimum biclique cover based role mining algorithm [8] is applied to each of the UPAs to obtain the spatial and the temporal roles. The spatial roles created from UPA$_{area_1}$ are -

- $sr_1 = (\{u_2, u_3\}, \{p_2, p_3\}, \{area_1\})$
- $sr_2 = (\{u_1, u_3, u_4\}, \{p_1\}, \{area_1\})$

The spatial roles generated from UPA$_{area_2}$ are -

- $sr_3 = (\{u_4\}, \{p_2\}, \{area_2\})$
- $sr_4 = (\{u_1, u_2, u_3\}, \{p_4\}, \{area_2\})$

From UPA$_{10\ am-11\ am}$, the following temporal roles are obtained -

- $tr_1 = (\{u_1, u_3\}, \{p_1, p_4\}, \{10\ am - 11\ am\})$

- $tr_2 = (\{u_2, u_3\}, \{p_2, p_3, p_4\}, \{10\text{ am - 11 am}\})$
- $tr_3 = (\{u_4\}, \{p_1, p_2\}, \{10\text{ am - 11 am}\})$

2 temporal roles that are created from $UPA_{9\ am-12\ pm}$ are -

- $tr_4 = (\{u_3\}, \{p_2, p_3\}, \{9\text{ am - 12 pm}\})$
- $tr_5 = (\{u_1, u_2\}, \{p_4\}, \{9\text{ am - 12 pm}\})$

Finally, from $UPA_{10\ am-1\ pm}$, 2 temporal roles are obtained -

- $tr_6 = (\{u_4\}, \{p_1, p_2\}, \{10\text{ am - 1 pm}\})$
- $tr_7 = (\{u_3\}, \{p_4\}, \{10\text{ am - 1 pm}\})$

On combining these roles, the following spatio-temporal roles are obtained:

- $r_1 = (\{u_1, u_3\}, \{p_1\}, \{area_1\}, \{10\text{ am - 11 am}\})$
- $r_2 = (\{u_2, u_3\}, \{p_2, p_3\}, \{area_1\}, \{10\text{ am - 11 am}\})$
- $r_3 = (\{u_2, u_3\}, \{p_4\}, \{area_2\}, \{10\text{ am - 11 am}\})$
- $r_4 = (\{u_4\}, \{p_1\}, \{area_1\}, \{10\text{ am - 11 am, 10 am - 1 pm}\})$
- $r_5 = (\{u_4\}, \{p_2\}, \{area_2\}, \{10\text{ am - 11 am, 10 am - 1 pm}\})$
- $r_6 = (\{u_3\}, \{p_2, p_3\}, \{area_1\}, \{9\text{ am - 12 pm}\})$
- $r_7 = (\{u_1, u_2\}, \{p_4\}, \{area_2\}, \{9\text{ am - 12 pm}\})$
- $r_8 = (\{u_3\}, \{p_4\}, \{area_2\}, \{10\text{ am - 1 pm}\})$

The merging phase does not reduce the number of roles any further and thus, the final output consists of 8 spatio-temporal roles.

6 Experimental Results

In this section, we present the experimental results of our proposed approach. Since currently, there are no real-world datasets directly available which have associated spatio-temporal constraints, we have conducted the experiments in a 2-fold manner. On one hand, we have generated synthetic datasets and on the other, we have augmented the real-world datasets [8] reported in the existing literature by adding suitable spatio-temporal constraints. For both kinds of datasets, a single location and a single time interval is associated with each user-permission assignment. In Subsect. 6.1, we describe how the synthetic datasets have been created and present the results obtained from them. In Subsect. 6.2, we describe the process of augmenting the real-world datasets with spatio-temporal constraints as well as present the experimental results generated by using them as inputs.

6.1 Results from Synthetic Datasets

For creating the synthetic datasets, we have created several UA and PA matrices of different sizes by varying the number of users and permissions. We have also considered 3 locations (say l_1, l_2 and l_3) and 3 time intervals (say t_1, t_2 and t_3). The UA and the PA are randomly generated and the total number of 1s for both

UA and PA have been fixed at 2% of the total number of entries of the respective matrices. This has been done after analyzing the different characteristics of the real-world datasets [8]. The number of roles for the UA and PA has been considered to be 10% of the total number of users considered.

Out of the 3 locations, l_1 and l_2 are overlapping and l_3 is completely contained inside l_1. Currently, we have considered all 3 locations as axis-parallel rectangles belonging to a 2D space, each of which is represented using the following parameters - x and y co-ordinates of the bottom left vertex, length of side along the x-axis and length of side along the y-axis. The rectangles can also be represented using 4 pairs of x and y co-ordinates for the 4 vertices. Out of the 3 time intervals, t_1 and t_2 and, t_2 and t_3 are overlapping and t_1 is completely contained inside t_3. For each role, one location and one time interval have been randomly selected to create the SREB and the TREB respectively. Finally, the UA, PA, SREB and TREB are combined together to create the respective STUPA matrices. Since these datasets are randomly generated, for each combination of number of users and number of permissions, we have created 30 pairs of UA and PA matrices and for each pair, a different SREB and TREB are generated. Consequently, we have obtained 30 STUPA matrices for each parameter setting. The proposed algorithm has been implemented in Java and executed on a desktop computer having Intel Xeon processor, 64 GB RAM and Ubuntu 18 as the operating system. The minimum biclique cover based approach have been used as the traditional role mining algorithm which is applied to the individual location-specific and time-specific UPAs in the first phase of our algorithm. We report the median number of spatio-temporal roles (rounded off to the nearest higher integer) and the average execution time of the 30 STUPA matrices corresponding to each parameter setting. The parameter settings along with the results are presented in Table 9.

Table 9. Results for synthetic datasets

#Users	#Permissions	#Roles	#Spatio-Temporal Roles	Time (secs.)
200	200	20	24	0.18
400	400	40	114	0.51
600	600	60	434	1.74
800	800	80	1366	5.47
1000	1000	100	3176	16.47

In the above table, the first column denotes the number of users, the second one the number of permissions and the third one the number of regular (unconstrained) roles considered to construct the UA and PA matrices. The number of spatio-temporal roles output by our approach is shown in the fourth column and the last column presents the average execution time in seconds. As can be observed from the results, the number of spatio-temporal roles as well as the execution time increases as the size of the STUPA matrices increase. In fact, only for STUPAs of size 200×200, the number of spatio-temporal roles is close to the number of unconstrained roles. The reason for the increase in the number of spatio-temporal roles obtained is because of the fact that the role minimization algorithm is applied to the individual UPAs and not the STUPA as a whole. Using a role minimization approach on the entire STUPA can lead to lesser number of roles, but probably at the cost of higher computation and greater execution time. Moreover, it will require a new role mining algorithm capable of handling the spatio-temporal constraints present in the input. The benefit of our approach is that no new algorithm is required. The spatio-temporal roles are obtained by utilizing an existing traditional role creation method along with other steps. Thus, an organization using RBAC as an access control model can easily migrate to any one of its spatio-temporal extensions without having to integrate any sophisticated spatio-temporal role generation procedure. In addition to this, the execution time is also not too high.

6.2 Results from Real-World Datasets

The 9 real-world datasets reported in [8] have been extensively used to evaluate the performance of role mining algorithms. However, these datasets are boolean in nature (available as UPA matrices) and do not contain any associated spatial or temporal constraints. Therefore, we have augmented the datasets using spatio-temporal constraints to generate the corresponding STUPA matrices. For this, we have used an approach similar to the one described in the previous sub-section. First, for each dataset, we have obtained the UA and PA matrices by applying the role mining algorithm based on minimum biclique cover. After that, for every UA and PA pair, an SREB and a TREB is randomly generated. This is done by selecting 1 location and 1 time interval respectively out of 4 equi-probable locations and 4 equi-probable time intervals for each unconstrained role of each dataset. The 4 locations are related among themselves via containment, overlap and disjoint relationships. The same relationships apply for the time intervals as well. Since the SREB and TREB are randomly generated, 30 such SREBs and TREBs are created for every real-world dataset. We report the median number of roles (rounded off to the nearest highest integer) and the average execution time over the 30 executions for the individual datasets. Table 10 shows the number of users (#Users), number of permissions (#Perms), number of user-permission assignments (#User-Perm Assignments), number of unconstrained roles (#Roles) obtained from each dataset as well as the number of spatio-temporal roles (#Spatio-Temporal Roles) generated by our role mining method and its execution time in seconds (last column).

In case of the datasets having smaller sizes like *emea*, *healthcare*, *domino* and *firewall2*, the number of spatio-temporal roles output by our algorithm is close to the number of unconstrained roles. However, still there is an increase in the number of roles given by our method. For the larger datasets like *apj*, *firewall1*, *americas small*, *americas large* and *customer*, the increase in the number of spatio-temporal roles over that of the unconstrained roles is quite significant. The reason behind the increase in the size of the final role set is similar to

Table 10. Results for real-world datasets

Dataset	#Users	#Perms	#User-Perm Assignments	#Roles	#Spatio-Temporal Roles	Time (secs.)
apj	2,044	1,164	6,841	456	694	36.96
emea	35	3,046	7,220	34	34	0.39
healthcare	46	46	1,486	15	31	0.08
domino	79	231	730	20	29	0.16
firewall2	325	590	36,428	10	18	0.39
firewall1	365	709	31,951	69	168	0.80
americas small	3,477	1,587	1,05,205	211	707	90.99
americas large	3,485	10,127	1,85,294	421	623	2549.33
customer	10,021	277	45,427	276	426	103.44

that discussed in the previous sub-section. Moreover, the execution time also increases with the increase in the size of the datasets. The highest time required for a single execution of our algorithm is recorded for the *americas large* dataset and is around 45 min. This shows that the proposed approach computes the output in a reasonable amount of time. In summary, it can be said that the trend observed in the number of roles generated and the overall execution time for the proposed spatio-temporal role mining algorithm is similar for both synthetic and real-world datasets.

It may be noted here that our proposed approach can also be used for creating roles having only spatial constraints. This can be done by eliminating the steps of creating the time-specific UPAs in the first phase. This flexibility is possible because of the segregation of the spatial and temporal information present in the input. Moreover, our approach can also be extended and used for the RBAC models where additional constraints are considered other than the location and time-based ones.

7   Conclusion and Future Work

Implementing any spatio-temporal extension of RBAC in an organization enables the system administrator to associate space and time constraints with the enabling of roles which in turn, allows for a finer level of granularity in access control. In order to deploy such an extended RBAC model, a set of roles capable for enforcing the spatio-temporal constraints is required. Spatio-temporal role mining is crucial in this regard. In this paper, we have proposed a suitable way of representing user-permission assignments having spatial and temporal information which serve as input to spatio-temporal role mining, have formally defined the Spatio-Temporal Role Mining Problem (STRMP) and have presented an approach for creating spatio-temporal roles. Our method separates out the location and time information associated with the input to create several location-specific and time-specific UPAs, mines each of the UPAs using a traditional role mining algorithm, combines the roles obtained from the individual UPAs to generate the final spatio-temporal roles.

STRMP aims to minimize the total number of roles. In future, other optimization metrics can be considered like the sizes of the user-role assignment and role-permission assignment relations as well as the sizes of the spatial and the temporal role enabling bases. This can result in the creation of more semantically meaningful role. Also, other variants of the spatio-temporal role mining problem can be taken up where a certain amount of deviation of the output from the input may be allowed. The deviation will be in terms of the privileges acquired by the users and the associated locations and time intervals through one or more assigned spatio-temporal roles.

Acknowledgement. This work is funded by the Research Initiation Grant sanctioned by BITS Pilani, Hyderabad Campus having the grant number BITS/GAU/RIG/2017/93 and project ID 717 as on 27/11/2017.

References

1. Bai, W., Pan, Z., Guo, S., Chen, Z.: RMMDI: a novel framework for role mining based on the multi-domain information. Secur. Commun. Netw. J. **2019**, 15 (2019)
2. Bertino, E., Bonatti, P.A., Ferrari, E.: TRBAC: a temporal role-based access control model. ACM Trans. Inf. Syst. Secur. **4**(3), 191–233 (2001)
3. Blundo, C., Cimato, S., Siniscalchi, L.: PostProcessing in constrained role mining. In: Yin, H., Camacho, D., Novais, P., Tallón-Ballesteros, A.J. (eds.) IDEAL 2018. LNCS, vol. 11314, pp. 204–214. Springer, Cham (2018). https://doi.org/10.1007/978-3-030-03493-1_22
4. Chandran, S.M., Joshi, J.B.D.: *LoT-RBAC*: a location and time-based RBAC model. In: Ngu, A.H.H., Kitsuregawa, M., Neuhold, E.J., Chung, J.-Y., Sheng, Q.Z. (eds.) WISE 2005. LNCS, vol. 3806, pp. 361–375. Springer, Heidelberg (2005). https://doi.org/10.1007/11581062_27
5. Chen, H., Wang, S., Wen, J., Huang, Y., Chen, C.: A generalized temporal and spatial role-based access control model. J. Netw. **5**(8), 912–920 (2010)
6. Coyne, E.J.: Role engineering. In: Proceedings of 1st ACM Workshop on Role-Based Access Control, pp. 15–16, November 1995
7. Damiani, M.L., Bertino, E., Catania, B., Perlasca, P.: GEO-RBAC: a spatially aware RBAC. ACM Trans. Inf. Syst. Secur. **10**(1), 2 (2007)
8. Ene, A., Horne, W., Milosavljevic, N., Rao, P., Schreiber, R., Tarjan, R.E.: Fast exact and heuristic methods for role minimization problems. In: Proceedings of 13th ACM Symposium on Access Control Models and Technologies, pp. 1–10, June 2008
9. Gal-Oz, N., Gonen, Y., Gudes, E.: Mining meaningful and rare roles from web application usage patterns. Comput. Secur. **82**, 296–313 (2019)
10. Guo, Q., Vaidya, J., Atluri, V.: The role hierarchy mining problem: discovery of optimal role hierarchies. In: Proceedings of 24th Annual Computer Security Applications Conference, pp. 237–246, December 2008
11. Joshi, J.B.D., Bertino, E., Latif, U., Ghafoor, A.: A generalized temporal role-based access control model. IEEE Trans. Knowl. Data Eng. **17**(1), 4–23 (2005)
12. Kirkpatrick, M.S., Damiani, M.L., Bertino, E.: Prox-RBAC: a proximity-based spatially aware RBAC. In: Proceedings of 19th ACM SIGSPATIAL International Conference on Advances in Geographic Information Systems, pp. 339–348, November 2011

13. Kumar, M., Newman, R.E.: STRBAC - an approach towards spatio-temporal role-based access control. In: Proceedings of the 3rd IASTED International Conference on Communication, Network, and Information Security, pp. 150–155, October 2006

14. Lu, H., Vaidya, J., Atluri, V.: Optimal boolean matrix decomposition: application to role engineering. In: Proceedings of 24th IEEE International Conference on Data Engineering, pp. 297–306, April 2008

15. Lu, H., Vaidya, J., Atluri, V.: An optimization framework for role mining. J. Comput. Secur. **22**(1), 1–31 (2014)

16. Mitra, B., Harika, B.: Enhancing user access information with spatial data. J. Inf. Optim. Sci. **40**(2), 203–217 (2019)

17. Mitra, B., Sural, S., Atluri, V., Vaidya, J.: Toward mining of temporal roles. In: Wang, L., Shafiq, B. (eds.) DBSec 2013. LNCS, vol. 7964, pp. 65–80. Springer, Heidelberg (2013). https://doi.org/10.1007/978-3-642-39256-6_5

18. Mitra, B., Sural, S., Atluri, V., Vaidya, J.: The generalized temporal role mining problem. J. Comput. Secur. **23**(1), 31–58 (2015)

19. Mitra, B., Sural, S., Vaidya, J., Atluri, V.: Mining temporal roles using many-valued concepts. Comput. Secur. **60**, 79–94 (2016)

20. Mitra, B., Sural, S., Vaidya, J., Atluri, V.: Migrating from RBAC to temporal RBAC. IET Inf. Secur. **11**(5), 294–300 (2017)

21. Molloy, I., et al.: Mining roles with semantic meanings. In: Proceedings of 13th ACM Symposium on Access Control Models and Technologies, pp. 21–30, June 2008

22. Molloy, I., et al.: Mining roles with multiple objectives. ACM Trans. Inf. Syst. Secur. **13**(4), 36:1–36:35 (2010)

23. Neumann, G., Strembeck, M.: A scenario-driven role engineering process for functional RBAC roles. In: Proceedings of 7th ACM Symposium on Access Control Models and Technologies, pp. 33–42, June 2002

24. Ray, I., Kumar, M., Yu, L.: LRBAC: a location-aware role-based access control model. In: Bagchi, A., Atluri, V. (eds.) ICISS 2006. LNCS, vol. 4332, pp. 147–161. Springer, Heidelberg (2006). https://doi.org/10.1007/11961635_10

25. Ray, I., Toahchoodee, M.: A spatio-temporal role-based access control model. In: Barker, S., Ahn, G.-J. (eds.) DBSec 2007. LNCS, vol. 4602, pp. 211–226. Springer, Heidelberg (2007). https://doi.org/10.1007/978-3-540-73538-0_16

26. Sandhu, R.S., Coyne, E.J., Feinstein, H.L., Youman, C.E.: Role-based access control models. IEEE Comput. **29**(2), 38–47 (1996)

27. Stoller, S., Bui, T.: Mining hierarchical temporal roles with multiple metrics. J. Comput. Secur. **26**(1), 121–142 (2017)

28. Vaidya, J., Atluri, V., Guo, Q.: The role mining problem: a formal perspective. ACM Trans. Inf. Syst. Secur. **13**(3), 27:1–27:31 (2010)

29. Vaidya, J., Atluri, V., Warner, J.: Role miner: mining roles using subset enumeration. In: Proceedings of 13th ACM Conference on Computer and Communications Security, pp. 144–153, October 2006

VisMAP: Visual Mining of Attribute-Based Access Control Policies

Saptarshi Das[1], Shamik Sural[1(✉)], Jaideep Vaidya[2], Vijayalakshmi Atluri[2], and Gerhard Rigoll[3]

[1] Indian Institute of Technology Kharagpur, Kharagpur, India
saptarshidas13@iitkgp.ac.in, shamik@cse.iitkgp.ac.in
[2] Rutgers University, New Brunswick, USA
jsvaidya@business.rutgers.edu, atluri@rutgers.edu
[3] Technical University of Munich, Munich, Germany
rigoll@mmk.ei.tum.de

Abstract. Policy mining has been identified as one of the most challenging tasks towards deployment of Attribute-Based Access Control (ABAC) in any organization. This work introduces a novel approach for visual mining of ABAC policies. The fundamental objective is to graphically portray the existing accesses to facilitate visual elucidation and mining of meaningful authorization rules. We represent the existing accesses in the form of a binary matrix and formulate the problem of finding the best representation of the binary matrix as a minimization problem. The authorization rules are then extracted from the visual representation of the access control matrix in such a way that the number of rules required to satisfy all the existing accesses is minimum. The problem is shown to be NP-Complete and hence, heuristic solution is proposed. We experimentally evaluate our proposed approach on a number of synthetically generated data sets to study its robustness and scalability in a variety of situations.

Keywords: Attribute-Based Access Control · Policy mining · Visual policy representation

1 Introduction

Access control models mediate controlled access to organizational resources. Traditional access control models include Mandatory Access Control [25], Discretionary Access Control [27] and Role-Based Access Control (RBAC) [26]. Of these, RBAC has emerged as the *de facto* standard in a majority of organizations. Roles are the primary elements of RBAC. Each role is assigned a set of permissions and each user is assigned to a set of roles. While RBAC suffices in mediating efficient access control in situations where all the users of an organization are known beforehand, it is not sufficiently flexible for handling scenarios which mandate sharing of resources among organizations and the total number of users cannot be precisely quantified. Attribute-Based Access Control (ABAC)

© Springer Nature Switzerland AG 2019
D. Garg et al. (Eds.): ICISS 2019, LNCS 11952, pp. 79–98, 2019.
https://doi.org/10.1007/978-3-030-36945-3_5

[15] has recently been proposed to address such shortcomings of RBAC. Basically, attributes are properties of users, resources and environment conditions. They capture information in the form of an attribute-value and entity is characterized by a set of attribute-value pairs. A request for accessing any resource in ABAC is permitted or denied by evaluating the sets of attribute-value pairs of the requesting user, requested resource and the environment condition in which the request is made against a set of authorization rules, called the ABAC policy. Each rule is also defined by a set of attribute-value pairs. Therefore, the process of devising an ABAC policy, known as *policy engineering*, is necessary for the deployment of ABAC in any organization [28].

As manually defining an ABAC policy is both time consuming and cost intensive [20], several algorithmic techniques [8, 22–24] have been proposed for efficient policy engineering. Generally, policy engineering techniques that construct an ABAC policy from the existing access permissions in the organization are referred as *policy mining*. The existing algorithms [12,32] have shown to be efficient in mining legitimate authorization rules. However, in certain scenarios, the automatically constructed rules may not reflect actual organizational processes. Moreover, inadvertent presence of any unauthorized access adversely affects the constructed policy. There is no easy way of identifying such unauthorized accesses. Further, despite forming the rules, it is difficult to visually interpret the accesses allowed by each rule. In this work, we propose a method that constructs rules from a given visual pattern of existing accesses. Additionally, we propose another method called CovAc that enables visualization of the existing accesses of an organization by arranging them into comprehensible patterns.

The motivation behind our proposed approach is that visually representing the existing accesses can improve the understandability of the organizational processes. Further, correlations among rules are shown as overlapping patterns. We depict the similarity between the authorization rules as overlapping clusters, thereby helping in the identification of redundant rules, i.e., the rules whose accesses can be granted by other rules in the policy. Besides improving the visual interpretability of the rules, our proposed techniques also helps in identifying possible unauthorized accesses.

The rest of the paper is organized as follows. Section 2 discusses the preliminaries of an ABAC system. Section 3 formally defines CovAc and analyses its complexity. In Sect. 4, we provide a heuristic solution called VisMAP that facilitates visual mining of ABAC policies. Section 5 presents experimental evaluation of VisMAP on various data sets. Section 6 discusses related work. Finally, Sect. 7 concludes the paper and provides directions of future research.

2   Preliminaries

In this section, we describe the basic components of ABAC along with the assumptions we consider in this work. A set of formal notations is given below which will be used for precise formulation of the problem being addressed and its solution.

- U: Set of users. Each element of U is represented as u_i, for $1 \leq i \leq |U|$.
- R: Set of organizational resources. Each element of R is represented as r_i, for $1 \leq i \leq |R|$.
- E: Set of possible environmental conditions in which access to a resource can be requested. Each element of E is represented as e_i, for $1 \leq i \leq |E|$.
- U_a: Set of user attributes. Each element of U_a is represented as ua_i, for $1 \leq i \leq |U_a|$. Sets R_a and E_a are similarly defined for resource attributes and environment attributes, respectively.
- OP: Set of operations. Each element of OP is represented as op_i, for $1 \leq i \leq |OP|$.
- AR: Set of authorization rules comprising an ABAC policy. Each element of AR is an authorization rule represented as ar_i, for $1 \leq i \leq |AR|$.
- UV: A set containing assignment of values to all the user attributes, also referred to as user attribute-value pairs, for all the users. Likewise, RV and EV denote the sets of attribute-value pairs for all objects and environments, respectively.

Each rule $ar \in AR$ is a 4-tuple of the form $<UC, RC, EC, op>$, where UC, RC and EC represent a set of user attribute-value pairs, a set of resource attribute-value pairs and a set of environment attribute-value pairs, respectively. An access is represented by a 4-tuple. For example, an access $<u, r, e, op>$ means that a user u can perform an operation op on a resource r under an environment condition e. For the sake of brevity, in this work, we have not considered the environment attributes. We also limit the number of operations in the system to 1, i.e., either a user is allowed to access a resource or not.

3   Visual Representation and Covering of Accesses

ABAC policy mining algorithms consider the existing accesses in an organization in order to construct a set of authorization rules. Intuitively, these existing accesses can be represented as a binary matrix A, where each row and each column corresponds to a user and a resource, respectively. An element $a_{ij} \in A$ is assigned 1 if user u_i is permitted to access resource r_j, and 0 otherwise. To make the binary access control matrix (ACM) visually appealing and more understandable, each cell of the matrix having 1 is colored *black* and the others are colored *white*. Consider a hypothetical organization having 10 users and 10 resources. The attributes and the associated values for the users and resources of the organization are shown in Tables 1 and 2, respectively.

An illustrative ACM for the organization is shown in Fig. 1a. Although the existing accesses are identifiable in this figure, the representation is rather confusing. In other words, it is arduous to analyze and identify the rules from such a representation. Therefore, an alternative representation is essential to facilitate the construction of rules. From Fig. 1b, it is evident that an intuitive re-arrangement of the users and resources of the access matrix enhances its visual interpretability. It is relatively easier to detect patterns in Fig. 1b where the users and resources have been re-arranged. These patterns of black or 1s are

Table 1. Attributes and their values for all users

User	Designation	U_Department
u_0	Clerk	Finance
u_1	Auditor	Finance
u_2	Technical staff	Security
u_3	Technical staff	Research
u_4	Manager	Finance
u_5	Auditor	Finance
u_6	Manager	Research
u_7	Technical staff	Finance
u_8	Technical staff	Finance
u_9	Clerk	Finance

Table 2. Attributes and their values for all users

Resource	Type	R_Department
r_0	Log book	Finance
r_1	Log book	Finance
r_2	Technical report	Finance
r_3	Technical tender	Security
r_4	Master key	Security
r_5	Technical report	Finance
r_6	Bill	Security
r_7	Technical report	Finance
r_8	Master key	Research
r_9	Log book	Research

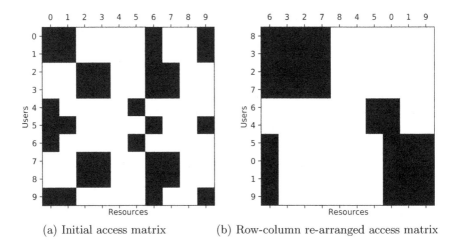

(a) Initial access matrix   (b) Row-column re-arranged access matrix

Fig. 1. Access matrix for the organization

rectangular in shape and known as *tiles*. For instance, compared to Fig. 1a, from Fig. 1b, it is easier to discern that users u_8, u_3, u_2 and u_7 are permitted to access the same set of resources, i.e., r_6, r_3, r_2 and r_7, in Fig. 1b. ABAC authorization rules that can easily be constructed from the four visible tiles. Therefore, such representation also reduces the number of rules in an ABAC policy. Moreover, singleton tiles that may depict inadvertently granted accesses, can easily be identified. Basically, the idea is to cover an ACM with the least possible number of tiles. Since the accesses in the ACM are immutable, the only way to suitably represent the ACM is by re-arrangement of the sequence of rows and columns. Essentially, we aim to provide an intuitive re-arrangement of rows and columns of an ACM which ensures the coverage of all the accesses less number of tiles. Additionally, rules are constructed corresponding to each of the identified tiles.

3.1   Problem Definition

We now formally define the problem of covering the accesses in an ACM with the minimum number of tiles. We refer to this problem as Covering Accesses Problem (CovAc). The formal definition of CovAc is given below.

Definition 1. *Covering Accesses Problem (CovAc)*
Given a binary ACM A where rows and columns correspond to a user $u_i \in U$ and a resource $r_j \in R$, respectively, cover all the accesses in A such that the number of tiles required to cover all the 1s in A is minimum.

3.2   Complexity Analysis for CovAc

Now, we prove that CovAc is NP-Complete. To prove the NP-Completeness of CovAc, first, we formulate a decision version of CovAc.

Definition 2. *Decision version of CovAc (D-CovAc)*
Given a binary ACM A where rows and columns correspond to a user $u_i \in U$ and a resource $r_j \in R$, respectively, is it possible to cover all the accesses in A such that the number of tiles required to cover all the 1s in A less than or equal to k.

We use the Minimum Set Cover problem (MSC) problem, which is a known NP-Complete problem to show that CovAc is NP-Complete. The formal definition of MSC is given below.

Definition 3. *Minimum Set Cover Problem*
Given a universal set U and a collection S of subsets of U, find a minimum number of subsets $s_1, s_2, \ldots, s_m$, where each $s_i \in ST$ and $s_1 \cup s_2 \cup \ldots \cup s_m = U$.

We now define a decision version of MSC.

Definition 4. *Decision version of MSC (D-MSC)*
Given a universal set U and a collection S of subsets of U, find a minimum number of subsets $s_1, s_2, \ldots, s_m$ which covers all the elements in U and $m \leq t$?

Theorem 1. *D-CovAc is NP-Complete.*

Proof. First, we show that CovAc is in NP. Let A be an ACM, T be the set of all the tiles of 1s and k be an integer. Therefore, $\langle A, T, k \rangle$ is an instance of CovAc. Given a subset $T^{'} \in T$, it can be verified in polynomial time whether $T^{'}$ is a valid solution of $\langle A, T, k \rangle$ by verifying that all the tiles in $T^{'}$ cover all the accesses of A in $O(\sum_{i=0}^{|T^{'}|}|T_i^{'}|)$ time. The checking whether $|T|^{'} \leq k$ takes $O(1)$ time.

Now, we show that D-MSC $\leq_p$ D-CovAc. Let $\langle U, S, t \rangle$ be an instance of D-MSC. Then, an instance of D-CovAc, $\langle A, T, k \rangle$ can be obtained in polynomial time using a function f such that $f(u_i) = (\lfloor \frac{u_i}{c} \rfloor, u_i \% c)$ where, $u_i \in U$, $(\lfloor \frac{u_i}{c} \rfloor, u_i \% c) \in A$ and c is a constant. Essentially, the function f convert a given element into an access (2-tuple). Here, A is an ACM with c columns and $\lceil \frac{max(U)}{c} \rceil$ rows. A collection T of sets of tiles of 1s can be obtained from S using the function f. Finally, we set $k = t$ where, k is an integer. Now, let Z_m and Z_r be the solutions to the instances of D-MSC and D-CovAc, respectively. Next, we show that a solution Z_m to the instance of D-MSC is a valid solution if and only if the solution Z_r to the instance of D-CovAc is valid.

We now construct a solution to the instance of D-MSC from the solution to the instance of D-CovAc, i.e., Z_r. Since, each access $(x, y) \in Z_r$ can be mapped to an element $u_i \in Z_m$ using the function f^{-1} where, $f^{-1}(x, y) = (x \times c) + y$. Therefore, if the number of tiles of 1s in Z_r is less than or equal to t, the number of sets in Z_m is definitely less than or equal to t. Moreover, if Z_r contains all the tiles in A, that implies that Z_m contains all the elements in U.

Thus, the solution to the instance of D-MSC constructed from the solution to the instance of D-CovAc is a valid solution. Likewise, the converse can also be proved. Therefore, D-CovAc is NP-Hard. Since D-CovAc is in NP and NP-Hard, it is NP-Complete.

4   Heuristic Solution for Visual Mapping of ABAC Policies (VisMAP)

Since CovAc is NP-Complete, it is unlikely that a polynomial time algorithm can be designed for covering all the accesses of an ACM with the minimum number of tiles. So we propose a heuristic approach for solving CoVAC. As discussed in Sect. 3, first we find an appropriate sequence of rows and columns of a given ACM which places the users with similar access patterns together. The procedure for rearranging the sequence of rows and columns is referred as VisMAP Rearranger (VisMAP_R). Finally, the tiles are identified from the ACM and rules are constructed from the identified tile. The procedure is given in Algorithm 3. The steps are elaborately explained in the sub-sections to follow. Visual mapping of ABAC policies is achieved using VisMAP_R and CovAc. The overall solution is termed VisMAP.

4.1   Rearrange the Rows and Columns (VisMAP_R)

The algorithm for VisMAP_R is given in Algorithm 1. First, VisMAP_R (Lines 1–4) constructs the distance matrices for the rows and columns of the access matrix A. Since the access matrix is binary in nature, each row (or column) is a binary vector of the same length. Therefore, the difference or distance between a pair of rows can be quantified using Hamming distance [14] as defined below.

Algorithm 1. *VisMAP_R*

Input: An access matrix A
Output: An modified access matrix A
1 $A_r \leftarrow$ sequential list of rows of A
2 $D_r \leftarrow$ Hamming distance matrix for rows of A
3 $A_c \leftarrow$ sequential list of columns of A
4 $D_c \leftarrow$ Hamming distance matrix for columns of A
5 $R_r \leftarrow$ *generate-route*(D_r)
6 $A \leftarrow$ arrange the rows of A w.r.t. R_r
7 $R_c \leftarrow$ *generate-route*(D_c)
8 $A \leftarrow$ arrange the columns of A w.r.t. R_c
9 *return* A

Definition 5. *Hamming Distance*
Given two equal-length binary strings $x, y \in \{0 + 1\}^+$, the Hamming distance between x and y, $D(x, y)$ is defined as the number of positions where x and y differ.

For example, if $x = 100110$ and $y = 110011$, $D(x, y) = 3$. Intuitively, the distance between any two rows of the ACM increases with the number of positions in which they differ.

Jaccard similarity can also be used to measure the distance between a pair of rows. Jaccard similarity is also capable of handling sets that are not binary in nature and of different sizes. As the sets of authorizations (including granted and denied accesses) are of binary nature, as well as of the same cardinality, we use Hamming distance to calculate the difference. After the computation of Hamming distances between each pair of row (and column) Algorithm VisMAP_R (Lines 5–8) finds an appropriate sequence of rows (and columns) such that the sum of distances between the consecutive rows (and columns) is minimum. In other words, it is required to arrange the rows (and columns) of the access matrix in an order which places the similar rows (and columns) together. As discussed above, row/column similarity is measured in terms of Hamming distance. We consider each row of the access matrix as a city. The distance matrix for the rows is obtained from the previous phase. Now, we need to find a sequence where the distance between the adjacent rows (cities) is minimum. First, we perform a complexity analysis of VisMAP_R.

Complexity Analysis of VisMAP_R
VisMAP_R has two steps, finding an appropriate re-arrangement of the rows and then, finding an appropriate re-arrangement of the columns. For notational simplification, we refer to finding a suitable re-arrangement of rows as VisMAP_R. To devise the proof, we first give a formal definition of VisMAP_R. Re-arrangement of columns is obtained similarly.

Definition 6. *VisMAP_R*
Given an ACM A and a list D of Hamming distances between pairs of rows, find

a re-arrangement of rows $u_1, u_2, \ldots, u_{n-1}$ *of A such that the sum of distances between the adjacent rows in the re-arrangement is minimum, i.e.,*

$$minimize \left(\sum_{i=0}^{n-2} D(u_i, u_{i+1}) \right)$$

where, $D(u_i, u_{i+1})$ *is the distance between rows* u_i *and* u_{i+1}.

Next, we formulate a decision version of VisMAP_R.

Definition 7. *Decision version of VisMAP_R (D-VisMAP_R)*
Given an access matrix A and a list D of Hamming distances between each pair of rows, is there a re-arrangement of rows $u_1, u_2, \ldots, u_{n-1}$ *of A such that the sum of distances between the adjacent rows in the re-arrangement is less than or equal to k, i.e.,*

$$\sum_{i=0}^{n-2} D(u_i, u_{i+1}) \leq k$$

We use a known NP-Complete problem, namely, Hamming Traveling Salesman Problem (HTSP) [10] to show that VisMAP_R is NP-Complete. HTSP consists of a salesman, a set of cities represented using bit strings and the list of Hamming distances between each pair of cities. The salesman needs to visit each city starting from a specific city, known as the hometown, and returning to the same city. The objective of the salesman is to minimize the total Hamming distance traveled for the complete trip. The formal definition of HTSP is given below.

Definition 8. *Hamming Traveling Salesman Problem (HTSP)*
Given a set of n cities $C = \{c_1, c_2, \ldots, c_n\}$ *represented by bit strings, and distances between each* $c_i, c_j \in C \times C$, *determine a route* R_c *that starts from an initial city* c_s, *visits each* $c_i \in C$ *exactly once and returns to the starting city* c_s *in such a way that the Hamming distance covered by* R_c *is minimum.*

We now define a decision version of HTSP.

Definition 9. *Decision Version of HTSP (D-HTSP)*
Given a set of n cities $C = \{c_1, c_2, \ldots, c_n\}$ *represented by bit strings, the Hamming distances between each* $c_i, c_j \in C \times C$ *and an integer t, does there exist a route* R_c *that starts from city* c_s, *visits all the cities exactly once and returns to the starting city* c_s *in such a way that the Hamming distance covered by* R_c *is less than or equal to t.*

Theorem 2. *D-VisMAP_R is NP-Complete.*

Proof. First, we show that D-VisMAP_R is in NP. Let A be an ACM, D_r be a list containing the distances between each pair of rows in A and k be an integer. Therefore, $\langle A, D_r, k \rangle$ is an instance of D-VisMAP_R. Given a sequence of rows SR, it can be verified in polynomial time whether SR is a valid solution of $\langle A, D_r, k \rangle$. Initially, the first and the last element of SR are checked for similarity in $O(1)$ time. Next, it is verified whether SR contains all the rows in A in $O(|SR|)$ time. Finally, the sum of distances between adjacent rows in SR is obtained from D_r in $O(|SR|)$ time.

Now, we show that D-HTSP $\leq_P$ D-VisMAP_R. Let $\langle C, D_c, t \rangle$ be an instance of D-HTSP where C is a list of cities where each $c_i \in C$ is represented by a bit string, D_c contains the Hamming distances between each pair of cities in C and t is an integer. Then, an instance of D-VisMAP_R, $\langle A, D_r, k \rangle$ can be obtained in polynomial time by setting $A = C$, $D_r = D_c$ and $t = k$. Here, A is a matrix having the same number of rows as the number of cities in C, D_r is the list of Hamming distances between each pair of rows of A, and k is an integer. Now, let R_c and R_r be solutions to the instances D-HTSP and D-VisMAP_R, respectively. For completing the proof, we show that a solution R_c to the instance of D-HTSP is a valid solution if and only if the solution R_r to the instance of D-VisMAP_R is a valid solution.

We now construct a solution to the instance of the D-HTSP from the solution to the instance of D-VisMAP_R, i.e., R_c. Since each city in C corresponds to a row of A, the distances between a pair of cities of C in D_c are mapped to the distance between the corresponding rows of A in D_r. Therefore, if the sum of distances for the sequence R_c is less than or equal to t, the sum of distances between the sequence of rows of A is definitely less than or equal to t. Thus, the solution to the instance of D-VisMAP_R constructed from the instance of D-HTSP is a valid solution. Likewise, the converse can also be proved. Thus, D-VisMAP_R is NP-Hard. Since D-VisMAP_R is in NP and is NP-Hard, it is NP-Complete.

Therefore, solving VisMAP_R is similar to solving HTSP. Essentially, the starting city for HTSP is fixed. In the majority of instances of access matrices, if the starting row is made immutable, the resulting sequence may not be the best one. To avoid such situations, an extra pseudo-row (city) is added to the distance matrix having distance 0 to all the rows (cities). This pseudo-row is considered as the starting row. After obtaining the desired sequence of rows (cities), the pseudo-row and the last row (which essentially is the starting row) are removed. Since HTSP is a known NP-Complete problem, in this work, we use the 2-opt heuristic [6] for solving HTSP. Chandra et al. [1] show that the 2-opt heuristic approach has an approximation ratio with an upper bound of $4\sqrt{m}$ where m is the number of cities. The algorithm for the 2-opt heuristic is given in Algorithm 2.

The 2-opt heuristic approach relies on local searches to solve HTSP. The basic methodology of the 2-opt heuristic is shown in Fig. 2. Primarily, the 2-opt heuristic removes a crossed-over path by re-ordering the nodes. For each distinct pair of cities, if the distance of a cross-over route between them is greater than

---

Algorithm 2. *generate-route*

Input: A distance matrix D
Output: A route of cities R_c
1 $R_c \leftarrow$ a random initial route
2 **for** *each pair of distinct cities (x,y), (u,v)* **do**
3 $\quad$ **if** $D(x,u) + D(y,v) < D(x,y) + D(u,v)$ **then**
4 $\quad\quad$ $R_c \leftarrow \{R_c - \{(x,y),(u,v)\}\} \cup \{(x,u),(y,v)\}$

5 $R_c \leftarrow R_c -$ last city of R_c
6 ***return*** R_c

---

the distance of the route obtained by re-ordering the cities, the re-ordered route is taken to obtain a feasible Hamiltonian cycle [11] (Lines 2–4). For instance, considering each row of the access matrix given in Fig. 1a as a city, the pair of edges (u_0, u_3) and (u_1, u_2) is a cross-over. Now, assume that the cross-over is part of the path having the minimum distance. The total distance of the two edges in the cross-over is the sum of Hamming distances between the corresponding rows. As shown in Fig. 2a, the distance between u_0 and u_3 is 6. Likewise, the distance between u_1 and u_2 is also 6. Therefore, the total distance in the cross-over is 12. The cross-over is removed by considering the edges (u_0, u_1) and (u_2, u_3) where the sum of distances is 0. Since the distance of edges (u_0, u_1) and (u_2, u_3) is less than that of the distance of the edges (u_0, u_3) and (u_1, u_2), the former is included in the route while the latter is removed. The modified route is shown in Fig. 2b. This approach only finds locally optimal routes involving two edges at a time. However, this does not guarantee an optimal solution for HTSP but finds an optimal route in a short span of time. For this work, the complete cycle is not required, therefore, we remove the last city from the obtained Hamiltonian cycle (Line 5) to obtain an optimal sequence.

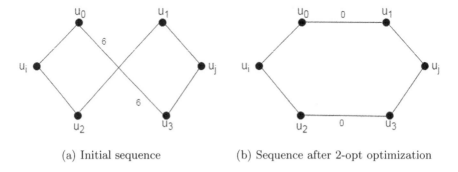

(a) Initial sequence   (b) Sequence after 2-opt optimization

Fig. 2. Finding local optima using 2-opt heuristic

Finally, the rows of the access matrix are arranged with respect to the sequence obtained using Algorithm 2. The ACM after arranging the rows is shown in Fig. 3. Likewise, the same procedure is repeated for the columns to arrange them in the desired order. The final ACM after the row and column re-arrangements is given in Fig. 1b.

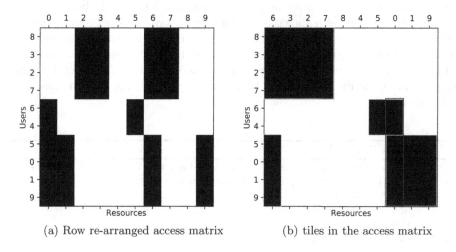

(a) Row re-arranged access matrix   (b) tiles in the access matrix

Fig. 3. Access matrix for the organization

As discussed in Subsect. 3.2, VisMAP is NP-Complete. Therefore, we propose a heuristic solution for VisMAP. The overall algorithm for VisMAP is given in Algorithm 3. Now, we elaborate a heuristic solution for VisMAP.

4.2   Find Tiles and Construct Rules from the ACM

Initially, Algorithm 3 (Lines 1–8) identifies all the tiles in the modified ACM obtained from the previous step. Finally, it finds the minimum number of tiles required for covering all the access. For finding the tiles, continuous rows with 1s which share continuous columns are identified. The algorithm for detecting the tiles is straight-forward and hence, omitted. Each tile is obtained as a collection of two sets, containing the set of rows and the set of columns. For example, five tiles obtained from the access matrix are highlighted in Fig. 3b. The tiles are as follows.

$$t_0 = \langle \{u_8, u_3, u_2, u_7\}, \{r_6, r_3, r_2, r_7\} \rangle \qquad t_1 = \langle \{u_6, u_4\}, \{r_5, r_0\} \rangle$$

$$t_2 = \langle \{u_5, u_0, u_1, u_9\}, \{r_6\} \rangle \qquad t_3 = \langle \{u_6, u_4, u_5, u_0, u_1, u_9\}, \{r_0\} \rangle$$

$$t_4 = \langle \{u_5, u_0, u_1, u_9\}, \{r_0, r_1, r_9\} \rangle$$

In Fig. 3b, the tiles t_1, t_3 and t_4 are overlapping. Next, VisMAP finds the minimum number of tiles required to cover all the accesses. The problem is similar to the Minimum Set Cover (MSC) problem discussed in Sub-section comprex.

Here, each tile is considered a subset and all the accesses taken together constitute the universe. It is known that MSC is an NP-Complete problem [29]. We therefore use a heuristic approach to find the minimum number of tiles. We use the same heuristic [3] used for solving MSC, i.e., in each iteration, the tile which covers the most number of uncovered 1s is selected. The greedy heuristic used for solving MSC has been shown by Chvatal [3] to have an exact approximation ratio of $\ln n - \ln \ln n + \Theta(1)$ where n is the number of elements in the universe set. The approach is given in Algorithm 3 (Lines 4–7). The procedure is repeated while there are still uncovered accesses in the access matrix. As shown by highlighted borders in Fig. 3b, the four tiles, namely, t_0, t_1, t_2 and t_4 are required to cover all the accesses.

Algorithm 3. $CovAc$

Input: An access matrix A, set of attribute-value pairs of all users UV, set of
        all attribute-values pairs of all resources RV
Output: A policy P
1   $T \leftarrow$ find all the tiles in A
2   $U \leftarrow t_0 \cup t_1 \cup ... \cup t_{|T|-1}$
3   $T_m \leftarrow \Phi$
4   **while** $U \neq \Phi$ **do**
5      $N_j \leftarrow |t_j| \cap U$
6      $j \leftarrow argmax_{i \in \{0,1,...,|T-1|\}} N_j$
7      $T_m \leftarrow T_m \cup \{j\}$
8      $U \leftarrow U \setminus t_j$
9   $P \leftarrow extract\text{-}rules(T_m, UV, RV)$
10 **return** P

Finally, Algorithm 3 (Line 9) constructs the rules of the ABAC policy. Essentially, there is a rule in the policy corresponding to each tile obtained by solving VisMAP_M. For each tile, a rule is constructed by selecting the common attribute-value pairs from the users and resources corresponding to the rows and columns of the tile, respectively. For instance, tile t_1 has users u_6 and u_4, the attribute-value pair common to u_6 and u_4 is (Designation: manager). For resources r_5 and r_0 in t_1, the common attribute-value pair is (R_Department: finance). The selected attribute-value pairs are used to construct the rules.

The formed rule 1 corresponding to tile b_1 along with the other rules is given below. The authorization rules ar_0, ar_1, ar_2 and ar_4 correspond to tiles t_0, t_1, t_2 and t_4, respectively.

    ar_0: $\langle$(Designation: technical staff), (R_Department: finance)$\rangle$
    ar_1: $\langle$(Designation: manager), (R_Department: finance)$\rangle$
    ar_2: $\langle$(U_Department: finance), (Type: bill), (R_Department: security)$\rangle$
    ar_4: $\langle$(U_Department: finance), (Type: log book)$\rangle$

Thus, VisMAP enables organizations to construct an ABAC policy as well as visualize the policy for better understanding of the organizational processes.

It may be noted that, in the entire discussion above, for ease of understanding of the basic approach, we consider only a single operation in the system. Handling of more than one operation can be done by defining a separate ACM for every operation and applying VisMAP for each such ACM independently. After the independent rules are obtained, they can be merged if the same combination of user and resource attribute values is given access to more than one operation, thereby reducing the overall number of rules in the ABAC policy.

5   Experimental Results

ABAC is gradually being deployed in many organizations. However, no benchmark access data is yet available by any organization. VisMAP can be used on a given ACM to enhance the visual interpretability, as well as to obtain a minimal set of ABAC authorization rules. First, we evaluate the performance of the proposed solution, i.e., VisMAP on the data sets given in [31]. While these data sets have been widely used for comparative study of various ABAC policy mining algorithms, for further analysis with more variations, we also evaluated the performance of VisMAP on a number of synthetically generated data sets. These data sets comprise sets of users, resources and access matrices along with the attribute-value pair assignments for all the entities. Both the proposed approaches were implemented in Python 3.7.1 and run on an 1.60 GHz Intel i5 CPU having 8 GB of RAM.

Essentially, VisMAP produces a visually interpretable representation of a given binary access matrix. Additionally, VisMAP attempts to find the minimum number of tiles required to cover all the 1s in a binary matrix. Therefore, the performance VisMAP depends on the size of the input binary matrix. We present the obtained results using number of users $|U|$, number of resources $|R|$, size of the constructed policy $|P|$ and the execution time T measured in seconds. The size of $|P|$ and T are obtained by taking an average of 10 executions of VisMAP on different synthetic data sets having similar parameters. The represented values of $|P|$ and T are rounded off to the nearest integer and up to two decimal places, respectively. For the data sets in [31], $|U_a|$, $|R_a|$, OP and $|P_{[31]}|$ denote the number of user attributes, number of resource attributes, number of operations and the number of rules in the policy, respectively.

Table 3. Policy size and execution time for the data sets in [31]

Data set	$|U|$	$|U_a|$	$|R|$	$|R_a|$	$|OP|$	$|P_{[31]}|$	$|P|$	$T(in\ s.)$
Healthcare	21	6	16	7	8	11	7	0.02
University	20	6	34	5	10	10	10	0.02
Project management	16	7	40	6	11	19	12	0.03

Table 3 shows the experimental evaluation of VisMAP on the data sets in [31] which involve multiple operations. However, The aforementioned data sets contain complex rules involving various constraints between attribute values. For such complex rules, we have broken them into simpler rules of the form defined in Sect. 2. For multi-valued attributes, we consider each set of such values as a distinct atomic value. The values in Table 3 represent the modified data sets. For each distinct operation, a separate ACM is constructed and VisMAP is applied on each such ACM. It is seen that the execution of VisMAP constructs a policy with lesser number of rules for the *Healthcare* and the *Project management* data sets. The number of rules remains the same for the *University* data set. Therefore, it is evident that the proposed approaches used sequentially are capable of forming a compact policy along with providing a visual representation.

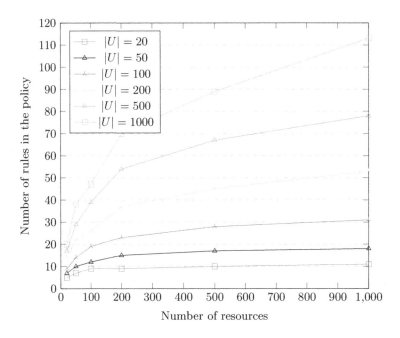

Fig. 4. Variation in the number of rules generated by using VisMAP with the number of users and resources

For synthetically generated data sets, first, we evaluate the performance of VisMAP for different number of users and resources. Figure 4 shows the variation in the average number of rules in the constructed policy for different number of resources. The average number of constructed rules increases with the number of resources. For taking results, we have varied the number of users and resources from 20 to 1000. From Fig. 4, it is seen that for a small number of resources, e.g., for 50 resources, the average number of rules generated varies from 7 to 29, which a variation of 22 rules. In contrast, when the number of resources is

1000, the average number of generated rules varies from 11 to 113 which is a variation of 102 rules. Although the number of rules increases with the number of resources, the increase is more prominent when the number of resources is large. This is attributed to the fact that the tiles identified by VisMAP are basically access patterns. Higher variation of access pattern is expected when the number of resources is more. This results in a relatively larger variation in the number of generated rules when the number of resources is large.

Next, we discuss the variation in the number of users. It is seen that, for a small number of users, e.g., 20 users, the number of constructed rules vary by 6, i.e., from 5 to 11, when the number of resources is varied from 20 to 1000. Conversely, the number of generated rules increases by 93, i.e., from 20 to 113, when the number of users is 1000 and the number of resources is varied from 20 to 1000. Therefore, relatively greater variation in the number of generated rules is observed when the number of users is large. This nature of variation is due to an increase in distinct access patterns with the number of users.

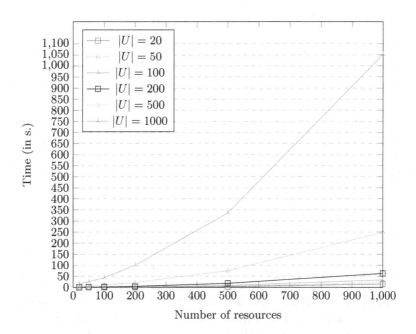

Fig. 5. Variation in execution time of VisMAP for different number of users and resources

In Fig. 5, we show the variation in execution time of our proposed approach for different number of users and resources. We use two iterations of HTSP for arranging the rows and columns of the access matrix. Finally, we use an iteration of MSC for obtaining the minimum number of tiles. Since we deploy heuristic solutions to two NP-Complete problems in our implementation, it is crucial to ensure that the time taken to solve VisMAP is within an acceptable range. It is observed that the execution time of VisMAP increases with the number of users and resources. This is attributed to the fact that increase in the number of users and resources implies a larger dimension of access matrices that require more time to rearrange using the 2-opt heuristic. Moreover, larger access matrices have a large number of tiles which increases the time required to find a minimum set of tiles to cover all the accesses using VisMAP. In Fig. 5, it is seen that, for less than 500 users, the total execution time of VisMAP is under 250 s. However, for more than 500 users, the execution time increases exponentially. Specifically, for 1000 users and resources, VisMAP took more than 1000 s to terminate. In such cases, an alternative way is to split the ACM into sub-matrices and solve each one using VisMAP. This provides a trade-off between the policy size and the execution time. Next, we show the results obtained by splitting an access matrix into multiple sub-matrices.

Table 4. Variation in policy size and execution time with number of sub-matrices

$|R| = 100$							$|R| = 200$					
Splits	1		2		4		1		2		4	
$|U|$	$|P|$	T(in s.)	$|P|$	T(in s.)	$|P|$	T(in s.)	$|P|$	T(in s.)	$|P|$	T(in s.)	$|P|$	T(in s.)
100	19	0.59	38	0.72	62	0.35	23	1.63	48	1.57	78	0.95
200	26	1.77	55	1.11	84	1.03	37	4.25	77	3.33	114	2.14
500	34	10.18	76	5.38	108	5.90	54	21.54	96	12.36	146	10.78
1000	47	43.28	96	20.46	197	10.92	70	100.4	145	43.01	197	39.77
$|R| = 500$							$|R| = 1000$					
100	28	8.27	50	9.78	89	4.72	31	33.84	60	47.46	109	10.09
200	45	17.64	91	16.41	156	9.39	53	62.47	100	70.63	180	33.43
500	67	75.23	141	49.92	224	33.57	78	248.87	175	174.30	282	100.21
1000	89	334.98	207	163.96	304	115.50	113	1052.78	218	695.67	335	452.52

Now, we consider access matrices corresponding to 100, 200, 500 and 1000 users and resources. For each matrix, we compare the number of rules generated and execution time in these three scenarios: (i) the complete access matrix is used as input (ii) the matrix is split into 2 sub-matrices which are used as inputs (iii) the matrix is split into 4 sub-matrices which are used as inputs. The obtained results are shown in Table 4. For a small number (say 100) of users and resources, the execution time increases with the number of sub-matrices the original matrix is divided into. However, when the number of users and resources is varied between 200 and 1000, the execution time decreases with the number of sub-matrices the original matrix is split into. For large data sets, involving 1000 users and resources, the execution time reduces to less than 50% when the original matrix is split into 4 sub-matrices. However, splitting the access matrix increases the number of rules generated. Splitting provides a trade-off between execution time and policy size. Therefore, the benefit of splitting is expressed only when the size of the access matrix is considerably large.

6 Related Work

Krautsevich et al. [18] show that the problem of policy mining in ABAC is similar to the problem of role mining in RBAC. Coyne [5] introduced the role engineering problem of RBAC. However, it was substantially different from role mining. The author defined the problem as a top-down approach. Kuhlmann et al. [19] introduced the term role mining for leveraging data mining algorithms to extract meaningful roles from access data. Mitra et al. [21] present a comprehensive survey on various techniques used for role mining in RBAC.

Xu and Stoller [31] first introduced the policy mining problem for ABAC. They use a set of candidate rules and an access control list (ACL) to derive an ABAC policy. Their algorithm iterates over the given ACL for selecting accesses to form a set of candidate rules. Next, a generalization of the candidate rules is obtained to include further accesses in the ACL. Once all the accesses in the ACL are satisfied by the candidate rules, the algorithm merges them and removes those rules whose accesses are covered by other rules. In contrast, from the policy mining perspective, the motivation behind VisMAP is to improve the visual elucidation of a given ACM. Additionally, VisMAP facilitates the identification of a minimal number of tiles to cover all the existing accesses. Such minimization of the number of tiles reduces the number of rules.

Das et al. [9] present a solution to the problem of policy mining in ABAC that uses Gini impurity to form an ABAC policy. They also include the environment attributes while mining the policy. Apart from role mining, policy mining in ABAC is similar to other problems too. Talukdar et al. [30] show that the problem of policy mining in ABAC is similar to that of identifying functional dependencies in database tables. In this context, they propose an ABAC policy mining algorithm which exhaustively enumerates all possible subject-object pairs. Iyer et al. [16] present a policy mining technique that constructs positive as well as negative ABAC authorization rules. Das et al. present an elaborate survey on various policy engineering techniques in RBAC and ABAC [7].

Various techniques have been proposed for visualization of data organized in the form of matrices [2]. However, they are not explicitly suited for binary matrices. As for visual representation of mined data, a few visualizers have been proposed in the current literature, and most of them are not explicitly designed for binary data [17]. Geerts et al. [13] present a method for tiled representation of data in databases. The authors also devise an algorithm to cover a database with a minimum number of tiles. Colantonio et al. [4] present a work involving visual mining of roles in RBAC. The authors introduce a quality metric for graphical representation of user-permission data in RBAC when a set of pre-defined roles are given. Further, they introduce an algorithm for visual elicitation of meaningful roles when a set of pre-defined roles is unavailable. In contrast, VisMAP enhances the visual interpretabilty of a given ACM in the absence of a pre-defined set of rules. Besides, VisMAP minimizes the number of rules in the constructed ABAC policy by eliminating redundant rules. To the best of our knowledge, the work proposed in this paper is the first-ever approach in ABAC paradigm that visually represents access data and extracts an optimal number of authorization rules from it.

7 Conclusion and Future Work

In this work, we have formally defined VisMAP_R that suitably represents the existing accesses in an organization. We have also proposed CovAC which forms an ABAC policy from a given ACM. We have shown both VisMAP_R and CovAc to be NP-Complete problems. We also provided a heuristic-based solution called VisMAP. Experimental evaluation of the proposed solution VisMAP on various data sets establishes the robustness of our proposed approach. The future direction of research in this area involves designing new heuristics which reach a solution in lesser time. Moreover, algorithms can be developed to merge the rules obtained from the sub-matrices in order to reduce the overall number of rules in a generated policy. Although the complete ABAC model description (Sect. 2) includes environmental conditions as well, our algorithm has not taken them into consideration. If these are to be considered, instead of black and white, different colors will have to be used corresponding to different environmental conditions in the ACM for visual elucidation. Suitably extending our algorithm for extracting rules from such multi-colored ACMs will be an important contribution, which is both interesting as well as challenging. Additionally, we plan to extend the proposed approach by considering multiple operations and design a graphical tool using which administrators can make manual decisions.

References

1. Chandra, B., Karloff, H., Tovey, C.: New results on the old k-opt algorithm for the traveling salesman problem. SIAM J. Comput. **28**(6), 1998–2029 (1999)
2. Chen, C.: Top 10 unsolved information visualization problems. IEEE Comput. Graph. Appl. **25**(4), 12–16 (2005)
3. Chvatal, V.: A greedy heuristic for the set-covering problem. Math. Oper. Res. **4**(3), 233–235 (1979)
4. Colantonio, A., Pietro, R.D., Ocello, A., Verde, N.V.: Visual role mining: a picture is worth a thousand roles. IEEE Trans. Knowl. Data Eng. **24**(6), 1120–1133 (2012)
5. Coyne, E.J.: Role engineering. In: ACM Workshop on Role-Based Access Control, vol. 29, no. 2, pp. 38–47 (1996)
6. Croes, G.A.: A method for solving traveling-salesman problems. Oper. Res. **6**(6), 791–812 (1958)
7. Das, S., Mitra, B., Atluri, V., Vaidya, J., Sural, S.: Policy engineering in RBAC and ABAC. In: Samarati, P., Ray, I., Ray, I. (eds.) From Database to Cyber Security. LNCS, vol. 11170, pp. 24–54. Springer, Cham (2018). https://doi.org/10.1007/978-3-030-04834-1_2
8. Das, S., Sural, S., Vaidya, J., Atluri, V.: HyPE: a hybrid approach toward policy engineering in attribute-based access control. IEEE Lett. Comput. Soc. **1**, 25–29 (2018)

9. Das, S., Sural, S., Vaidya, J., Atluri, V.: Using Gini impurity to mine attribute-based access control policies with environment attributes. In: ACM Symposium on Access Control Models and Technologies, pp. 213–215 (2018)
10. Ernvall, J., Katajainen, J., Penttonen, M.: NP-completeness of the Hamming salesman problem. BIT Numer. Math. **25**(1), 289–292 (1985)
11. Garrod, C.: Hamiltonian path-integral methods. Rev. Mod. Phys. **38**(3), 483–494 (1966)
12. Gautam, M., Jha, S., Sural, S., Vaidya, J., Atluri, V.: Poster: constrained policy mining in attribute based access control. In: ACM Symposium on Access Control Models and Technologies, pp. 121–123 (2017)
13. Geerts, F., Goethals, B., Mielikäinen, T.: Tiling databases. In: Suzuki, E., Arikawa, S. (eds.) DS 2004. LNCS, vol. 3245, pp. 278–289. Springer, Heidelberg (2004). https://doi.org/10.1007/978-3-540-30214-8_22
14. Hamming, R.: Error detecting and error correcting codes. Bell Syst. Tech. J. **26**(2), 14–160 (1950)
15. Hu, V.C., et al.: Guide to Attribute-Based Access Control (ABAC) definition and considerations. Technical report, NIST Special Publication (2014)
16. Iyer, P., Masoumzadeh, A.: Mining positive and negative attribute-based access control policy rules. In: ACM Symposium on Access Control Models and Technologies, pp. 161–172 (2018)
17. Jin, R., Xiang, Y., Fuhry, D., Dragan, F.F.: Overlapping matrix pattern visualization: a hypergraph approach. In: IEEE International Conference on Data Mining, pp. 313–322 (2008)
18. Krautsevich, L., Lazouski, A., Martinelli, F., Yautsiukhin, A.: Towards policy engineering for attribute-based access control. In: Bloem, R., Lipp, P. (eds.) INTRUST 2013. LNCS, vol. 8292, pp. 85–102. Springer, Cham (2013). https://doi.org/10.1007/978-3-319-03491-1_6
19. Kuhlmann, M., Shohat, D., Schimpf, G.: Role mining-revealing business roles for security administration using data mining technology. In: ACM Symposium on Access Control Models and Technologies, pp. 179–186 (2003)
20. Lim, Y.T.: Evolving security policies. Ph.D. dissertation, University of York (2010)
21. Mitra, B., Sural, S., Vaidya, J., Atluri, V.: A survey of role mining. ACM Comput. Surv. **48**(4), 1–37 (2016)
22. Mocanu, D.C., Turkmen, F., Liotta, A.: Towards ABAC policy mining from logs with deep learning. In: Intelligent Systems, pp. 124–128 (2015)
23. Narouei, M., Khanpour, H., Takabi, H., Parde, N., Nielsen, R.: Towards a top-down policy engineering framework for attribute-based access control. In: ACM Symposium on Access Control Models and Technologies, pp. 103–114 (2017)
24. Narouei, M., Takabi, H., Nielsen, R.: Automatic extraction of access control policies from natural language documents. IEEE Trans. Dependable Secure Comput. (2018)
25. Sandhu, R.S.: Lattice-based access control models. IEEE Comput. **26**(11), 9–19 (1993)
26. Sandhu, R.S., Coyne, E.J., Feinstein, H.L., Youman, C.E.: Role-based access control models. IEEE Comput. **29**(2), 38–47 (1996)
27. Sandhu, R.S., Samarati, P.: Access control: principle and practice. IEEE Commun. Mag. **32**(9), 40–48 (1994)
28. Servos, D., Osborn, S.L.: Current research and open problems in attribute-based access control. ACM Comput. Surv. **49**(4), 65:1–65:45 (2017)
29. Slavík, P.: A tight analysis of the greedy algorithm for set cover. J. Algorithms **25**(2), 237–254 (1997)

30. Talukdar, T., Batra, G., Vaidya, J., Atluri, V., Sural, S.: Efficient bottom-up mining of attribute based access control policies. In: IEEE International Conference on Collaboration and Internet Computing, pp. 339–348 (2017)
31. Xu, Z., Stoller, S.: Mining attribute-based access control policies. IEEE Trans. Dependable Secure Comput. **12**(5), 533–545 (2015)
32. Xu, Z., Stoller, S.D.: Mining attribute-based access control policies from logs. In: Atluri, V., Pernul, G. (eds.) DBSec 2014. LNCS, vol. 8566, pp. 276–291. Springer, Heidelberg (2014). https://doi.org/10.1007/978-3-662-43936-4_18

Policy Reconciliation and Migration in Attribute Based Access Control

Gunjan Batra[1]([✉]), Vijayalakshmi Atluri[1], Jaideep Vaidya[1], and Shamik Sural[2]

[1] MSIS Department, Rutgers Business School, Newark, USA
{gunjan.batra,atluri,jsvaidya}@rutgers.edu
[2] Department of Computer Science and Engineering, IIT Kharagpur,
Kharagpur, India
shamik@cse.iitkgp.ernet.in

Abstract. Today, organizations do not work in silos, but rather collaborate, work jointly and share data resources for various business benefits such as storage, management, analytics, etc. In this scenario, organizations want to ensure that their own security requirements are always met, even though they may be sharing/moving their resources to another organization. Hence, there is a need to evaluate the extent to which their policies are similar (or equivalent) i.e., to what extent do they both agree on a common set of security requirements (policy)? When the policies are not identical, there is also a need to evaluate the differences and see how these differences can be reconciled so that the organizations can be brought to agreement in terms of their security requirements.

To address this issue, in this paper, we first propose the notion of policy equivalence and develop methods to evaluate the policy similarity. We also propose two different approaches for accomplishing policy reconciliation where one is based on ABAC mining and the other is based on finding maximal common subsets. Both of the approaches guarantee that the organization's policies are never violated as they are both conservative in nature. Further, it is also possible that the organizations in the collaboration decide to pick one organization and each of them migrates to the policy. We propose a migration approach for organizations in this setting which will incur least migration cost for all the organizations. We compare both the reconciliation approaches and policy migration with respect to their reconciliation results as well as performance.

Keywords: ABAC · Policy equivalence · Policy similarity · Policy reconciliation · Policy migration

1 Introduction

Organizations of all types and sizes are collecting large amounts of data and processing it to improve customers' experiences and their business decisions and processes. This leads to business needs that cannot be fulfilled by themselves alone or by working in silos. Due to this, organizations outsource their needs such as infrastructure, software, analytics, storage, computation needs, etc., and

© Springer Nature Switzerland AG 2019
D. Garg et al. (Eds.): ICISS 2019, LNCS 11952, pp. 99–120, 2019.
https://doi.org/10.1007/978-3-030-36945-3_6

work together in collaborative environments. In this scenario, organizations want to ensure that all their resources are protected under the same set of security requirements, even though they are sharing/moving their resources to another organization. Hence, there is a need to evaluate if their security policies are similar (or equivalent) i.e., whether they both agree on a common set of security requirements (policies). And, to what extent these policies are similar? In case, their policies are different, there is a need to reconcile these differences so that these organizations can be brought to an agreement in terms of their security requirements. Further, Attribute Based Access Control (ABAC) is the most amenable form of enforcing security by organizations in collaborative environments because of its fine-grained nature as well as its identity less enforcement. Under ABAC, security policies are specified based on user attributes and object attributes rather than user and object identities. As such, we develop solutions for determining policy equivalence and reconciliation with minimum transition cost for all. Further, we also propose a solution in case the organizations in the collaboration decide to migrate to any one organization's policy.

Towards this end, we first propose a definition for *policy equivalence* based on the authorizations covered by a policy (or ABAC rules). To evaluate the policies of the organizations in terms of how similar (or dissimilar) they are, we propose a *policy similarity metric* based on the maximum common possible subset of accesses covered by their rules. In case of dissimilar policies among organizations, there is a need to overcome these differences through reconciliation in such a way that security requirements of no organization are compromised. We propose two reconciliation approaches - subset based and mining based. In the former approach, we compute the reconciled policy by identifying the maximal subset of initial policies that ensures no additional accesses are added when adopted by any organization. In the mining-based approach, we combine the attribute conditions of all the users and objects that result in authorizations and mine the policies from this set. Further in policy migration approach we propose, how a set of policies decide which policy to migrate to based on least possible migration cost and then how to migrate in an efficient way by modifying least possible rules. We perform an experimental comparison of the two approaches with respect to the resulting reconciliation policy in terms of changed authorizations, as well as performance. While the subset-based algorithm provides less changes in terms of rules, the mining-based algorithm results in less changes in the number of authorizations, thus providing a different tradeoff in terms of rules/authorizations.

The rest of this paper is organized as follows. Section 2 provides a brief overview of ABAC in the context of multiple organizations that wish to collaborate, and describes how to find the set of authorizations covered by a given ABAC policy. Section 3 defines equivalence between two ABAC policies and policy similarity metric, and proposes a method to determine policy similarity. Sections 4 and 5 present our two policy reconciliation approaches and Sect. 6 presents the policy migration algorithm. Section 7 presents an experimental analysis of these approaches. Section 8 reviews the related work. Finally, conclusions and future work are in Sect. 9.

2   Preliminaries

In this section, we briefly review the attribute-based access control (ABAC) model [10]. In ABAC, the authorization to perform an operation (e.g., read/write) is granted based on the attributes of the requesting user, requested object, and the environment in which a request is made. We assume there exist a set of organizations ORG, upon which we intend to perform policy reconciliation. We use G_k to denote an individual organization where $1 \leq k \leq |ORG|$. The basic components of ABAC adapted from [4,18] are as follows:

Users and Objects: We use U_k to denote the set of users of organization G_k and u_{ki} to denote a single user where $u_{ki} \in U_k$, O_k to denote the set of objects of an organization G_k and o_{ki} to denote a single object where $o_{ki} \in O_k$.

Environment: The set of environment conditions in organization G_k are denoted as E_k, and the set of environment conditions of all organizations are denoted as $E = \bigcup_{k=1}^{|ORG|} E_k$. We use e_i to denote an environment condition such that $e_i \in E$.

OPS: This represents a set of all possible operations/permissions on objects allowed in ORG. We use op_i to denote an operation where $op_i \in OPS$. In this paper, for the sake of simplicity, we have considered only one operation.

UA: This represents the set of user attribute names. Each attribute name $ua_i \in UA$ is associated with a set of possible values it can acquire.

OA: This represents a set of object attribute names. Each $oa_i \in OA$ is associated with a set of possible values it can acquire.
For the sake of simplicity, in this paper, we ignore environmental attributes.

UC: This represents the user attribute conditions. The set of user attribute conditions in organization G_k are denoted as UC_k. The set of all user attribute conditions of all organizations in ORG is $\bigcup_{k=1}^{|ORG|} UC_k$. We use uc_i to denote a user attribute condition where $uc_i \in UC$. Each uc_i is represented as equalities of the form $n = c$, where n is a user attribute name and c is either a constant or any. We denote the user attribute condition set of a user u_{ki}, by $u_{ki}.UC$.

OC: This represents the set of object attribute conditions. The set of object attribute conditions in organization G_k are denoted as OC_k. The set of all object attribute conditions of all organizations in ORG is $\bigcup_{k=1}^{|ORG|} OC_k$. We use oc_i to denote a object attribute condition where $oc_i \in OC$. Each oc_i is represented as equalities of the form $n = c$, where n is an object attribute name and c is either a constant or any. For an attribute name n, if the value of c is any, then the attribute n is not relevant for making the corresponding access decision. Therefore, as above, the condition $n = any$ does not have to be explicitly chosen. It is set only if at least one other condition for n is present. We denote the object attribute condition set of an object o_{ki}, by $o_{ki}.OC$.

ABAC policies ϕ: This represents the set of all ABAC policies for the organizations in ORG. We use Π_k to represent the set of ABAC policies of

Table 1. UAR, OAR, and Π for organization G_1

(a) UAR_1 (b) OAR_1 (c) Π_1

U_1	uc_1	uc_2	uc_3	uc_4	uc_6
u_{11}	1	0	1	0	0
u_{12}	1	0	1	0	0
u_{13}	0	1	0	0	0
u_{14}	0	0	0	1	1
u_{15}	0	0	0	1	1

O_1	oc_1	oc_2
o_{11}	1	0
o_{12}	0	1

Rule	Attributes
π_{11}	uc_3, oc_1, r
π_{12}	uc_2, oc_1, r
π_{13}	uc_4, oc_2, r

Table 2. UAR, OAR, and Π for organization G_2

(a) UAR_2 (b) OAR_2 (c) Π_2

U_2	uc_1	uc_2	uc_3	uc_4	uc_5
u_{21}	0	0	0	0	1
u_{22}	0	1	0	0	0
u_{23}	0	1	0	0	0
u_{24}	1	0	1	0	0
u_{25}	0	0	0	1	1

O_2	oc_1	oc_2
o_{21}	1	0
o_{22}	0	1

Rule	Attributes
π_{21}	uc_2, oc_1, r
π_{22}	uc_1, oc_1, r
π_{23}	uc_5, oc_2, r

organization $G_k \in ORG$. We use π_{ki} to denote a policy (or rule) of organization G_k, where $\pi_{ki} \in \Pi_k$, which is a quadruple of the form $\langle uc, oc, ec, op \rangle$. We use $\pi_{ki}.UC$, $\pi_{ki}.OC$, $\pi_{ki}.OPS$ to express the user attribute condition set and object attribute condition set and operations set of a rule π_{ki}, respectively. If a user makes a request to access an object, the policy base is searched for any rule through which the user can gain access. If such a rule exists, then access is granted, otherwise it is denied.

In UC and OC, we have represented the attribute conditions as equalities, however, our approach is flexible to include the complex attribute condition constructs (inequalities, negation, subset, etc.) by converting them to their corresponding list of attributes conditions. In the following, we define the mapping between users and user attribute conditions as well as objects and object attribute conditions.

UAR: User attribute relation $UAR \subseteq U \times UC$ is a many-to-many mapping of users and user attribute conditions. We use a $m \times n$ binary matrix to represent UAR, where $UAR[i, j] = 1$, if user u_i satisfies an attribute condition uc_j. Specifically, we denote UAR_k to represent the User Attribute Relation for Organization G_k. $UAR_k \subseteq U_k \times UC_k$ is a many-to-many mapping of users and the user attribute conditions in G_k. We use a $m \times n$ binary matrix to represent UAR_k, where $UAR_k[i, j] = 1$, if user u_{ki} satisfies an attribute condition uc_j.

OAR: The Object attribute relation, $OAR \subseteq O \times OC$ is a many-to-many mapping of objects and the set of all attributes conditions, where we again use a $m \times n$ binary matrix to represent $\mathcal{OAR}$. $OAR[i, j] = 1$ if an object o_i satisfies an object attribute condition oc_j. We denote OAR_k to represent the Object Attribute Relation for Organization G_k. $OAR_k \subseteq O_k \times OC_k$ is a many-to-many mapping of objects and the object attribute conditions in G_k. We use a $m \times n$ binary matrix to represent OAR_k, where $OAR_k[\mathrm{i}, \mathrm{j}] = 1$, if object o_{ki} satisfies an attribute condition oc_j.

Table 3. UAR, OAR, and Π for organization G_3

(a) UAR_3

U_2	uc_1	uc_2	uc_3	uc_4	uc_6
u_{31}	0	0	0	0	1
u_{32}	0	0	0	1	1
u_{33}	1	0	1	1	0
u_{34}	0	1	1	0	0
u_{35}	0	1	0	0	0

(b) OAR_3

O_1	oc_1	oc_2
o_{31}	1	0
o_{32}	0	1

(c) Π_3

$Rule$	$Attributes$
π_{31}	uc_1, oc_1, r
π_{32}	uc_2, oc_1, r
π_{33}	uc_6, oc_2, r

Authcovered(Π, G): We now define a function called "Authcovered" that returns a set of authorizations covered by Policy Π on an organization G. This function essentially first considers the set of Users U and Objects O of G, and computes UAR and OAR from the given UC and OC, and then computes all the authorization covered by this policy on those users and objects using the Algorithm 1. For example, if we wish to compute authorization covered by applying policy Π_l on organization G_k, then we essentially compute Authcovered(Π_l, G_k) by first finding UAR_k and OAR_k. We use A_k^l to denote these set of covered authorizations. Further, if we simply apply a specific rule π_{li}, where $\pi_{li} \in \Pi_l$ on G_k, we simply compute Authcovered(π_{li}, G_k) and use A_k^{li} to denote the authorizations returned by it.

Each authorization a in A_k^l is denoted by $\langle u_{ki}, o_{kj}, op_g \rangle$, which states that the user u_{ki} is allowed to perform an operation op_g on the object o_{kj}. For example, given an ABAC policy Π_1, and organization G_1 comprising of users and object U_1 and O_1, respectively, we say that authorization set A_1^1 is covered by Π_1 if for every user u_{1i} and object o_{1j} combination where u_{1i} is allowed to perform operation op_g on o_{1j}, there exists an authorization $a = \langle u_{1i}, o_{1j}, op_g \rangle \in A_1^1$. We use $a.u$, $a.o$ and $a.op$ to denote the user, object and operation of a, respectively. For example, in the above authorization a, $a.u = u_{1i}$. The set of authorizations covered by rule π_{lm} is denoted by a_{lm}. And the set of users and objects associated with a_{lm} are denoted by $a_{lm}.U$ and $a_{lm}.O$, respectively.

2.1 Generating Authorizations A_k^l

The steps to find authorization set for a policy are described in Algorithm 1. We have described the algorithm for one policy Π_l. The procedure can be repeated for all the policies. First, for each policy rule π_{lm} in Π_l, in Lines 3–7, we find all the users in the organization user set U_k, that can get access based on the user attribute conditions of the policy rule ($\pi_{lm}.UC$) and the user's attributes ($u_{ki}.UC$). We store these users in $a_{lm}.U$. Similarly, in Lines 8–12, for each rule, we go over all the objects o_{kj} in O_k and find the objects that satisfy the object attribute conditions of the policy rules ($\pi_{lm}.OC$) based on their object attributes ($o_{kj}.OC$). We save these in $a_{lm}.O$. Next, in Line 13, for each policy rule, we take all combinations of the users (in $a_{lm}.U$) and objects (in $a_{lm}.O$) in a_{lm}. From lines 14 to 16, we add the operation of the rule op_g to each user object combination in a_{lm} to get the authorizations given by each rule A_k^{lm} and finally authorizations A_k^l (Tables 4, 5 and 6).

Algorithm 1. Authcovered(Π_l, G_k):Generating A_k^l for policy Π_l over users and objects of organization G_k

---

Require: $U_k, O_k, UAR_k, OAR_k, \Pi_l$
1: Initialize:A_k^l , $a_{lm}.U$, $a_{lm}.O = \emptyset$
2: **for** ($\pi_{lm} \in \Pi_l$) **do**
3:     **for** ($u_{ki} \in UAR_k$) **do**
4:         **if** ($u_{ki}.UC \supseteq \pi_{lm}.UC$) **then**
5:             $a_{lm}.U \leftarrow a_{lm}.U + u_{ki}$
6:         **end if**
7:     **end for**
8:     **for** ($o_{kj} \in OAR_k$) **do**
9:         **if** ($o_{kj}.OC \supseteq \pi_{lm}.OC$) **then**
10:            $a_{lm}.O \leftarrow a_{lm}.O + o_{kj}$
11:        **end if**
12:    **end for**
13:    $a_{lm} \leftarrow \bigcup (u_{ki}\text{-}o_{kj}), \forall\, u_{ki} \in a_{lm}.U$ and $\forall\, o_{kj} \in a_{lm}.O$
14:    **for** a_q in a_{lm} **do**
15:        $A_k^l \leftarrow a_q + \pi_{lm}.op_g$
16:    **end for**
17: **end for**
18: return A_k^l

Table 4. Authorizations of G_1 when Π_1, Π_2 and Π_3 are applied

(a) A_1^1 (b) A_1^2 (c) A_1^3

Rule	a
π_{11}	$\langle u_{11}, o_{11}, r \rangle$
π_{11}	$\langle u_{12}, o_{11}, r \rangle$
π_{12}	$\langle u_{13}, o_{11}, r \rangle$
π_{13}	$\langle u_{14}, o_{12}, r \rangle$
π_{13}	$\langle u_{15}, o_{12}, r \rangle$

Rule	a
π_{21}	$\langle u_{13}, o_{11}, r \rangle$
π_{22}	$\langle u_{11}, o_{11}, r \rangle$
π_{22}	$\langle u_{12}, o_{11}, r \rangle$

Rule	a
π_{31}	$\langle u_{11}, o_{11}, r \rangle$
π_{31}	$\langle u_{12}, o_{11}, r \rangle$
π_{32}	$\langle u_{13}, o_{11}, r \rangle$
π_{33}	$\langle u_{14}, o_{12}, r \rangle$
π_{33}	$\langle u_{15}, o_{12}, r \rangle$

Table 5. Authorizations of G_2 when Π_1, Π_2 and Π_3 are applied

(a) A_2^1 (b) A_2^2 (c) A_2^3

Rule	a
π_{11}	$\langle u_{24}, o_{21}, r \rangle$
π_{12}	$\langle u_{22}, o_{21}, r \rangle$
π_{12}	$\langle u_{23}, o_{21}, r \rangle$
π_{13}	$\langle u_{25}, o_{22}, r \rangle$

Rule	a
π_{21}	$\langle u_{22}, o_{21}, r \rangle$
π_{21}	$\langle u_{23}, o_{21}, r \rangle$
π_{22}	$\langle u_{24}, o_{21}, r \rangle$
π_{23}	$\langle u_{21}, o_{22}, r \rangle$
π_{23}	$\langle u_{25}, o_{22}, r \rangle$

Rule	a
π_{31}	$\langle u_{24}, o_{21}, r \rangle$
π_{32}	$\langle u_{22}, o_{21}, r \rangle$
π_{32}	$\langle u_{23}, o_{21}, r \rangle$

UOP_{op}: User Object Permission Matrix UOP_{op}, is a $M \times N$ matrix, where $M = |U| \times |O|$ comprising of a row for each user-object pair, and $N = |UC| + |OC|$ + 1, comprising of a column for each object attribute condition, a column for each user attribute condition, and a column for the permission op. Specifically, we denote UOP_{op}^k as the UOP of permission op for organization k. Given a set of authorizations A_k^k, we construct UOP_{op}^k for a permission type op_n as follows: the columns of this matrix are all possible user attribute conditions and object attribute conditions of users and objects in A_k^k, respectively, and a column for op_n. There is a row in UOP_{op}^k for each user object pair of organization k. For each row, if the user attribute condition (object attribute condition) is true for a user (object), the corresponding cells to $u_{kl}.UC(o_{kl}.OC)$ is filled with 1, otherwise with 0. If there exists an $a = \{u_{kl}, o_{km}, op_n\}$, we insert a 1 in the op_n column of that $u_{kl} - o_{km}$. For the remaining rows, the op_n column is 0.

3   Policy Equivalence and Policy Similarity

The goal of policy equivalence to identify the policy rules in a set of organizations that lead to same access decisions (or authorizations). In this section, we formally define the notion of *Policy Equivalence* and the *Policy Similarity Metric*, and present an approach to calculate it, with a detailed example illustrating it.

Table 6. Authorizations of G_3 when Π_1, Π_2 and Π_3 are applied

(a) A_3^1

Rule	a
π_{11}	$\langle u_{33}, o_{31}, r \rangle$
π_{11}	$\langle u_{34}, o_{31}, r \rangle$
π_{12}	$\langle u_{34}, o_{31}, r \rangle$
π_{12}	$\langle u_{35}, o_{31}, r \rangle$
π_{13}	$\langle u_{32}, o_{32}, r \rangle$
π_{13}	$\langle u_{33}, o_{32}, r \rangle$

(b) A_3^2

Rule	a
π_{21}	$\langle u_{34}, o_{31}, r \rangle$
π_{21}	$\langle u_{35}, o_{31}, r \rangle$
π_{22}	$\langle u_{33}, o_{31}, r \rangle$

(c) A_3^3

Rule	a
π_{31}	$\langle u_{33}, o_{31}, r \rangle$
π_{32}	$\langle u_{34}, o_{31}, r \rangle$
π_{32}	$\langle u_{35}, o_{31}, r \rangle$
π_{33}	$\langle u_{31}, o_{32}, r \rangle$
π_{33}	$\langle u_{32}, o_{32}, r \rangle$

Table 7. ABAC Policy Π_a when applied to organization G_1 and G_2

(a) Π_a

Rule	Attributes
π_{a1}	uc_3, oc_1, r
π_{a2}	uc_2, oc_1, r

(b) A_1^a

Rule	a
π_{a1}	$\langle u_{11}, o_{11}, r \rangle$
π_{a1}	$\langle u_{12}, o_{11}, r \rangle$
π_{a2}	$\langle u_{13}, o_{11}, r \rangle$

(c) A_2^a

Rule	a
π_{a1}	$\langle u_{24}, o_{21}, r \rangle$
π_{a2}	$\langle u_{22}, o_{21}, r \rangle$
π_{a2}	$\langle u_{23}, o_{21}, r \rangle$

Table 8. ABAC Policy Π_b when applied to organization G_1 and G_2

(a) Π_b

Rule	Attributes
π_{b1}	uc_2, oc_1, r
π_{b2}	uc_1, oc_1, r

(b) A_1^b

Rule	a
π_{b1}	$\langle u_{13}, o_{11}, r \rangle$
π_{b2}	$\langle u_{11}, o_{11}, r \rangle$
π_{b2}	$\langle u_{12}, o_{11}, r \rangle$

(c) A_2^b

Rule	a
π_{b1}	$\langle u_{22}, o_{21}, r \rangle$
π_{b1}	$\langle u_{23}, o_{21}, r \rangle$
π_{b2}	$\langle u_{24}, o_{21}, r \rangle$

3.1   Policy Equivalence

First, we define Policy Equivalence for two policies of two different organizations based on the authorizations they cover on each other's users and objects.

Definition 1 (Policy Equivalence). Given two organizations G_i and G_j, and their corresponding ABAC policies Π_i and Π_j, we say $\Pi_i \equiv \Pi_j$, iff, $A_i^i = A_i^j$ and $A_j^j = A_j^i$.

Essentially, the above definition states that, two policies are equivalent if both policies give the same set of authorizations for each organization (even if the actual authorizations across both organizations are different). When only a single organization exists and would like to check if a different policy is equivalent to its policy, we can define policy equivalence as follows:

Definition 2 (Policy Equivalence with respect to G_i). Given an organization G_i and its corresponding ABAC policy Π_i and another policy Π_j we say $\Pi_i \equiv^i \Pi_j$, iff, $A_i^i = A_i^j$.

Example 1. Consider two ABAC Policies Π_a and Π_b as shown in Tables 7a and 8a, respectively. When Π_a and Π_b are applied on G_1, we use UAR_1 (Table 1a) and OAR_1 (Table 1b) and obtain A_1^a and A_1^b as shown in Tables 7b and 8b, respectively. Also, when Π_a and Π_b are applied on G_2, we use UAR_2 (Table 2a) and OAR_2 (Table 2b), we get A_2^a and A_2^b, shown in Tables 7c and 8c, respectively. Since $A_1^a = A_1^b$ and $A_2^a = A_2^b$, we have $\Pi_a \equiv \Pi_b$.

Since policies are a set of rules, similar to policy equivalence, it is also possible to describe equivalence in terms of ABAC rules and find *Equivalent ABAC Rules*, i.e., the subset of rules in two policies that cover the same set of authorizations.

3.2   Policy Similarity

In many cases, apart from equivalence, an organization may wish to know how similar another policy (Π_j) is with respect to its policy (Π_i). This can be done by measuring the degree of overlap between the authorizations obtained when each policy is adopted by the organization. Note however, that we measure the overlap in terms of the subset of rules of the policies that give the same set of authorizations (i.e., we measure the number of authorizations that are derived from equivalent ABAC rules across both policies). The reason for this is that we assume that a specific policy cannot simply be completely replaced with another policy, even if it is equivalent in terms of authorizations, but rather that once authorizations are excluded, the rules containing these authorizations are themselves revoked and need to be removed.

Definition 3. (Policy Similarity Metric). We define the Policy Similarity Metric between two policies Π_i and Π_j with respect to G_i as $|A_i^{S_i}|/|A_i^i \cup A_i^j|$ where $S_i \subseteq \Pi_i$ and $S_j \subseteq \Pi_j$ such that $S_i \equiv^i S_j$, and there does not exist another $S_k \subseteq \Pi_j$ where $A_i^{S_j} \subset A_i^{S_k}$ and $S_i \equiv^i S_k$.

Note that in the above definition we divide by the number of authorizations across both policies, assuming that both have the same importance. However, when one policy is more significant (i.e., it is the currently adopted policy of the organization), then the denominator can be changed to only the number of authorizations given by this policy (instead of the union across both policies). Furthermore, when we are interested in measuring similarity of several different policies with this specific policy, then since the denominator is the same across

Algorithm 2. Evaluate Policy Similarity from G_1's perspective:

Require: $UAR_1, OAR_1, \Pi_1, \Pi_2$
1: $\Pi_x \leftarrow \Pi_1, \Pi_y \leftarrow \Pi_2$
2: $UAR_x \leftarrow UAR_1, OAR_x \leftarrow OAR_1$
3: Compute A_x^x, A_x^y
4: **repeat**
5:     $ExtraA\_x \leftarrow A_x^x \setminus A_x^y$
6:     $ExtraA\_y \leftarrow A_x^y \setminus A_x^x$
7:     **for** $(a_i \in ExtraA\_x)$ **do**
8:         **if** $(a_i \in A_x^{xj})$ **then**
9:             $\Pi_x \leftarrow \Pi_x \setminus \pi_{xj}$
10:         **end if**
11:     **end for**
12:     **for** $(a_l \in ExtraA\_y)$ **do**
13:         **if** $(a_l \in A_x^{yj})$ **then**
14:             $\Pi_y \leftarrow \Pi_y \setminus \pi_{yj}$
15:         **end if**
16:     **end for**
17: **until** $(ExtraA\_x == \{\})$ $\wedge$ $(ExtraA\_y == \{\})$
18: return$(\Pi_x, \Pi_y, |A_x^x|, |A_x^y|)$

all the similarities, we can ignore it, and only compare by checking the numerator (the number of common authorizations) across the policies. We follow this procedure below.

To determine the policy similarity metric from G_i's perspective between its own policy and Π_i and another policy Π_j, we need to find S_i and S_j such that when S_i and S_j are applied to G_i they lead to a maximum possible set of authorizations that are essentially the same. On the other hand, if we were to find out policy similarity from G_j's perspective we need to determine S_i and S_j such that when S_i and S_j are applied on G_j they lead to a maximum possible set of authorizations that are same. The rules discovered S_i and S_j are **Equivalent Rules** and the authorizations covered by the rules S_i and S_j are the same. The **Policy Similarity Metric** is nothing but $|A_i^{S_i}| = |A_i^{S_j}|$. The key idea to compute $|A_i^{S_i}| = |A_i^{S_j}|$ is to remove rules iteratively from each policy that cover extra authorizations that are not covered by the other policy. When there are no such rules remaining in either policy, then the remaining set of rules are indeed equivalent. The detailed steps are given in Algorithm 2.

Example 2. Consider the 3 Organizations G_1, G_2, and G_3 having with User Attribute Relations UAR_1, UAR_2, UAR_3, Object Attribute Relations OAR_1, OAR_2, OAR_3 and ABAC policies Π_1, Π_2, and Π_3 respectively (all as depicted in Tables 1, 2 and 3). Organization G_1 has bids to be acquired by G_2 and G_3; G_1 is looking to find policies of which firm has more synergy with its own policy, so that it's Users and Objects can be easily integrated into the acquiring organization. Therefore, organization G_1 would like to find the policy Π_e among Π_2 and Π_3, which has a larger Policy Similarity with itself. Hence, we compute the Policy Similarity metric between G_1 and G_2, and between G_1 and G_3.

Now we begin with the evaluation of policy similarity metric. Policies Π_1, Π_2, and Π_3, lead to authorization sets A_1^1, A_1^2 and A_1^3 when applied on UAR_1, OAR_1.

Policy Similarity Metric Between G_1 and G_2:
$\Pi_1 = \{\pi_{11}, \pi_{12}, \pi_{13}\}$, $\Pi_2 = \{\pi_{21}, \pi_{22}, \pi_{23}\}$, $\Pi_x = \Pi_1$, $\Pi_y = \Pi_2$, $UAR_x = UAR_1$, $OAR_x = OAR_1$

Iteration 1:
$\text{ExtraA}\_x = A_x^x \backslash A_x^y$
$\qquad = \{\langle u_{14}, o_{12}, r\rangle, \langle u_{15}, o_{12}, r\rangle\}$
$\text{ExtraA}\_y = A_x^y \backslash A_x^x = \{\}$
$\Rightarrow$ Delete rule π_{13} from Π_x
$\Pi_x = \{\pi_{11}, \pi_{12}\}$, $\Pi_y = \{\pi_{21}, \pi_{22}, \pi_{23}\}$

Iteration 2:
$\text{ExtraA}\_x = A_x^x \backslash A_x^y = \{\}$
$\text{ExtraA}\_y = A_x^y \backslash A_x^x = \{\}$
$\Pi_x = \{\pi_{11}, \pi_{12}\}$, $\Pi_y = \{\pi_{21}, \pi_{22}, \pi_{23}\}$
$\Pi_x \equiv \Pi_y$

Policy Similarity Metric $= 3$; Authorizations: $\langle u_{11}, o_{11}, r\rangle, \langle u_{12}, o_{11}, r\rangle, \langle u_{13}, o_{11}, r\rangle$

Policy Similarity Metric Between G_1 and G_3:
$\Pi_1 = \{\pi_{11}, \pi_{12}, \pi_{13}\}$, $\Pi_3 = \{\pi_{31}, \pi_{32}, \pi_{33}\}$, $\Pi_x = \Pi_1$, $\Pi_y = \Pi_3$, $UAR_x = UAR_1$, $OAR_x = OAR_1$

Iteration 1:
$\text{ExtraA}\_x = A_x^x \backslash A_x^y = \{\}$
$\text{ExtraA}\_y = A_x^y \backslash A_x^x = \{\}$

$\Pi_x = \{\pi_{11}, \pi_{12}, \pi_{13}\}$, $\Pi_y = \{\pi_{31}, \pi_{32}, \pi_{33}\}$
$\Pi_x \equiv \Pi_y$

Policy Similarity Metric $= 5$; Authorizations: $\langle u_{11}, o_{11}, r\rangle, \langle u_{12}, o_{11}, r\rangle, \langle u_{13}, o_{11}, r\rangle, \langle u_{14}, o_{12}, r\rangle, \langle u_{15}, o_{12}, r\rangle$

Hence organization **G_3 will choose G_3** as Π_1 is more similar to Π_3.

4   Subset-Based Policy Reconciliation

When organizations want to collaborate, they desire to move to a conservative policy that does not lead to any additional accesses for any organization. In this section, we formally define the notion of *Reconciled Policies* for a set of n organizations, and show how to compute it, along with an example illustrating the process.

Definition 4. Given a set of organizations $\{G_1, \ldots, G_n\}$ and their corresponding ABAC policies $\Pi_1, \ldots \ldots \Pi_n$, respectively; we define the reconciled policy of each G_i as S_i where $S_i \subseteq \Pi_i$ and $\forall_{j \in \{1, \ldots, n\}} A_i^{S_i} \supseteq A_i^{S_j}$, and there does not exist another $S_k \subseteq \Pi_i$, where $A_i^{S_i} \subset A_i^{S_k}$ and $A_i^{S_k} \supseteq A_i^{S_j}$.

This essentially means that the reconciled policy for every organization is such that it does not give any additional authorizations for any of the other organizations, i.e., it does not violate the existing security policy of any organization. Similar to how an equivalent rule set was computed earlier, to create the reconciled policy, for every policy, we simply iteratively remove the rules that lead to additional authorizations in any other policy until there are no more changes. Note that it is acceptable if the authorizations produced by the reconciled policy are less than the original authorizations of the organization since we are adopting a conservative approach. The detailed steps are given in Algorithm 3.

Algorithm 3. Computing Reconciled Policies using subset-based approach

---
Require: $\Pi_1,...\Pi_n$
Require: $UAR_1,..,UAR_n$
Require: $OAR_1,..,OAR_n$
1: $\{S_1,...,S_n\} \leftarrow \{\Pi_1,...\Pi_n\}$
2: **repeat**
3:    **for** $i \in \{1,...,n\}, j \in \{1,...,n\}, j \neq i$ **do**
4:       $G_x \leftarrow G_i$
5:       $G_y \leftarrow G_j$
6:       Compute: A_x^x, A_x^y
7:       $ExtraA_y^x \leftarrow A_y^x \setminus A_y^y$
8:    **end for**
9:    **for** $(a_l \in ExtraA_j^i)\ \forall i \in \{1,..n\}, j \in \{1,..n\}$ **do**
10:       **if** $(a_l \in A_j^{ik})$ **then**
11:          $S_i \leftarrow S_i \setminus \pi_{ik}$
12:       **end if**
13:    **end for**
14: **until** $(ExtraA_j^i == \{\})\ \forall i \in \{1,..n\}, \forall j \in \{1,..n\}$
15: **return** $\{S_i,...S_n\}$

Example 3. Again consider the 3 Organizations G_1, G_2, and G_3 having with User Attribute Relations UAR_1, UAR_2, UAR_3, Object Attribute Relations OAR_1, OAR_2, OAR_3 and ABAC policies Π_1, Π_2, and Π_3 respectively (all as depicted in Tables 1, 2 and 3).

Organizations G_1, G_2 and G_3 intend to reconcile their policies conservatively in such a way that maximum possible accesses in the three policies are covered and no extra accesses are given based on another policy i.e., they would like to find $(\{S_1 \subseteq \Pi_1, S_2 \subseteq \Pi_2, S_3 \subseteq \Pi_3\})$ as per Definition 4, as follows:

Iteration 1:
i=S_1 and j=S_2:
$\Pi_x=S_1, UAR_x=UAR_1, OAR_x=OAR_1$
$\Pi_y=S_2, UAR_y=UAR_2, OAR_y=OAR_2$
$ExtraA_y^x=A_y^x\setminus A_y^y, ExtraA_2^1=A_2^1\setminus A_2^2=\{\}$

i=S_1 and j=S_3:
$\Pi_x=S_1, UAR_x=UAR_1, OAR_x=OAR_1$
$\Pi_y=S_3, UAR_y=UAR_3, OAR_y=OAR_3$
$ExtraA_3^1=A_3^1 \setminus A_3^3=\{\langle u_{33}, o_{32}, r\rangle\}$

i=S_2 and j=S_1:
$\Pi_x=S_2, UAR_x=UAR_2, OAR_x=OAR_2$
$\Pi_y=S_1, UAR_y=UAR_1, OAR_y=OAR_1$
$ExtraA_1^2=A_1^2 \setminus A_1^1=\{\}$

i=S_2 and j=S_3:
$\Pi_x=S_2, UAR_x=UAR_2, OAR_x=OAR_2$
$\Pi_y=S_3, UAR_y=UAR_3, OAR_y=OAR_3$
$ExtraA_3^2=A_3^2 \setminus A_3^3=\{\}$

i=S_3 and j=S_1:
$\Pi_x=S_3, UAR_x=UAR_3, OAR_x=OAR_3$
$\Pi_y=S_1, UAR_y=UAR_1, OAR_y=OAR_1$
$ExtraA_1^3=A_1^3 \setminus A_1^1=\{\}$

i=S_3 and j=S_2:
$\Pi_x=S_3, UAR_x=UAR_3, OAR_x=OAR_3$
$\Pi_y=S_2, UAR_y=UAR_2, OAR_y=OAR_2$
$ExtraA_2^3=A_2^3 \setminus A_2^2=\{\}$

$S_1=S_1-\pi_{13} = \{\pi_{11},\pi_{12}\};$
$S_2=S_2-\{\} = \{\pi_{21},\pi_{22},\pi_{23}\};$
$S_3=S_3-\{\} = \{\pi_{31},\pi_{32},\pi_{33}\}$

Iteration 2:
i=S_1 and j=S_2: $ExtraA_2^1=A_2^1\setminus A_2^2=\{\}$
i=S_1 and j=S_3: $ExtraA_3^1=A_3^1\setminus A_3^3=\{\}$
i=S_2 and j=S_1: $ExtraA_1^2=A_1^2\setminus A_1^1=\{\}$
i=S_2 and j=S_3: $ExtraA_3^2=A_3^2\setminus A_3^3=\{\}$
i=S_3 and j=S_1:
$ExtraA_1^3=A_1^3\setminus A_1^1=\{\langle u_{14}, o_{12}, r\rangle, \langle u_{15}, o_{12}, r\rangle\}$
i=S_3 and j=S_2: $ExtraA_2^3=A_2^3\setminus A_2^2=\{\}$

$S_1 = S_1 - \{\} = \{\pi_{11}, \pi_{12}\};$

$S_2 = S_2 - \{\} = \{\pi_{21}, \pi_{22}, \pi_{23}\};$

$S_3 = S_3 - \{\pi_{33}\} = \{\pi_{31}, \pi_{32}\}$

Iteration 3:

i$=S_1$ **and j**$=S_2$: $ExtraA_2^1 = A_2^1 \backslash A_2^2 = \{\}$

i$=S_1$ **and j**$=S_3$: $ExtraA_3^1 = A_3^1 \backslash A_3^3 = \{\}$

i$=S_2$ **and j**$=S_1$: $ExtraA_1^2 = A_1^2 \backslash A_1^1 = \{\}$

i$=S_2$ **and j**$=S_3$: $ExtraA_3^2 = A_3^2 \backslash A_3^3 = \{\}$

i$=S_3$ **and j**$=S_1$: $ExtraA_1^3 = A_1^3 \backslash A_1^1 = \{\}$

i$=S_3$ **and j**$=S_2$: $ExtraA_2^3 = A_2^3 \backslash A_2^2 = \{\}$

$S_1 = \{\pi_{11}, \pi_{12}\};\ S_2 = \{\pi_{21}, \pi_{22}, \pi_{23}\};$

$S_3 = \{\pi_{31}, \pi_{32}\}$

5 Mining-Based Policy Reconciliation

A very intuitive method of performing reconciliation is to combine the cross product of the UC and OC across each organization, and to perform ABAC Mining on the combined set. Note that when we consider authorizations across organizations, it is possible that a specific policy rule (combination of user and object attributes) might lead to a valid authorization in one organization, while it is invalid in another organization. Since our approach is conservative, we disallow such conflicting authorizations. We now formalize the concept of conflicting authorizations which will not be granted access in any organization:

Conflicting Authorizations (CA_i^j): Consider organizations G_i and G_j. An authorization a_x in G_i is called conflicting if the set of user conditions and object conditions associated with a_x are possessed by some user u and object o in G_j and u is not permitted to carry out the same operation on o in G_j.

Definition 5. Given a set of n Organizations $\{G_1, \ldots, G_n\}$, each with ABAC policy $\{\Pi_1, \ldots, \Pi_n\}$, the Reconciled Policy, Π_R for all the organizations is the minimum possible set of policy rules which cover the authorization set $(A_i^i - (CA_i^j))\ \forall\ i, j \in \{1, \ldots, n\}$.

This essentially means that we mine those policy rules that cover only all authorizations except the subdued authorizations. Whenever, conflicting authorizations are discovered in an organization, we adopt a conservative approach and remove them while mining rules for the reconciled policy Π_r.

Steps to Evaluate Reconciled Policy

Firstly, we create a UOP_{op}^i matrix for every organization. For simplicity we have considered only one operation. Next, from each UOP_{op}^i we remove the rows of conflicting authorizations. After this, we concatenate all the UOP_{op}^i create a combined $\mathcal{UOP}$. Then we use an ABAC Mining algorithm [18] (ABAC-SRM) to mine the reconciled policy Π_R. Finally, the participating organizations will replace their existing policies and implement the new policy generated by ABAC Mining algorithm.

The ABAC Mining algorithm ABAC-SRM requires the UOP, *permission1 Rules* and *permission0Rules*. *permission1Rules* are the rows in the UOP where the permission op is 1 and *permission0Rules* are the rows in UOP where permission op is 0. The algorithm is based on the concept of functional dependencies in a database. The idea of the algorithm is to find the set of user-object attribute conditions that covers all the *permission1Rules* and doesn't cover any *permission0Rules*. Given an authorization set, the algorithm mines the minimum set of ABAC policy rules by first discovering a candidate set of ABAC rules and then finding the most general rules from this candidate set of rules, thus finding the minimum set of ABAC rules covering a set of authorizations. In this paper, we refer to the algorithm as function abacMining(*permission1Rules*, *permission0Rules*) and pass the set of attribute condition set as arguments.

Example 4. Consider once again the 3 organizations G_1, G_2 and G_3 in Sect. 2. We separate the rows with $op = 1$ and $op = 0$ in the combined $\mathcal{UOP}_r$, and perform ABAC Mining. We obtain the reconciled policy rules as follows:

$$\pi_{r1} = uc_1, oc_1, r, \quad \pi_{r2} = uc_2, oc_1, r, \quad \pi_{r3} = uc_6, oc_2, r$$

6 Policy Migration for Reconciliation

When organizations want to collaborate, an alternative approach to reconciliation is that these organizations choose to migrate to the policy of one organization such that the cost of migration is minimum.

Calculating the Optimal Policy: We find out the Optimal policy to which all organizations should migrate to by first calculating Migration Cost (MC) as follows and then choose the one with the minimum MC. For each organization for $k = \{1, \ldots n\}$:

$MC(\Pi_k) = |A_1^1 - A_1^k| + |A_1^k - A_1^1| + |A_2^2 - A_2^k| + |A_2^k - A_2^2| + \ldots + |A_n^n - A_n^k| + |A_n^k - A_n^n|$. We pick the policy with lowest $MC(\Pi_k)$ as the Optimal Policy.

To migrate to the Optimal policy, we need to modify the ABAC policies of participating organizations. There are two ways to do this:

1. Directly applying the Optimal Policy: Replace the policy rules of an existing policy Π_k, entirely with the set of rules of the Optimal policy Π_x.
2. Policy Modification using Algorithm 4: Modifying policy by changing the existing rules by the following methods: Adding attributes to ABAC rules; Adding ABAC Rules; and Deleting ABAC Rules.

In the method of Policy Modification approach we try to achieve this by incurring least possible changes to the original policy. By least possible changes to an ABAC policy we mean to say that, in the process of migration, the number of Rule Changes(RC) in an ABAC Policy should be minimum.

Rule Changes(RC) = |Rules Added| + |Rules Deleted|

Now, let us discuss the process of Policy Migration in detail. In an ABAC Policy System ϕ, with n organizations, each having its own ABAC policy, and User-Object set. For each organization G_i, and ABAC policy Π_i we use it's policy rules to create the set of Authorizations on the User-Object sets of rest of the organizations (for $k = 1$ to n) using Algorithm 1, $A_1^i, A_2^i, A_3^i, \ldots, A_n^i$. Then we calculate the migration costs for each policy and choose the Optimal policy (Π_x) (one which has the lowest Migration Cost). Once we find the Optimal policy, we perform the policy modification algorithm to find how to transform each policy Π_i such that it covers authorizations A_i^x as $(\Pi_x$ when applied on U_i and $O_i)$.

Algorithm 4. Generating the modified policy $\Pi_i'(A_i^x)$ for policy $\Pi_i(A_i^i)$

Require: : $UAR_i, OAR_i, \Pi_i, \Pi_x$
1: **Initialize** $\Pi_i' = \Pi_i$
2: $DelA_i^e \leftarrow A_i^i \setminus A_i^x$, $AddA_i^e \leftarrow A_i^x \setminus A_i^i$
3: $Edit\pi_i \leftarrow$ Rule set to which authorizations in $DelA_i^e$ belong
4: **for** π_{ij} in $Edit\pi_i$ **do**
5:     keepa=[ ], removea=[ ], Allow=[ ], Deny=[ ]
6:     keepa $\leftarrow (A_i^{\pi_{ij}} \setminus DelA_i^e)$, removea $\leftarrow (A_i^{\pi_{ij}} \setminus keepA)$
7:     **if** keepa $== \phi$ **then**
8:         $\Pi_i' \leftarrow \Pi_i' \setminus \pi_{ij}$
9:     **else**
10:         Allow $\leftarrow$ [Allow + $((a_p.UC \cup a_p.OC) \setminus (\pi_{ij}.UC \cup \pi_{ij}.OC))$ **for** a_p in keepa]
11:         Deny $\leftarrow$ [Deny + $((a_q.UC \cup a_q.OC) \setminus (\pi_{ij}.UC \cup \pi_{ij}.OC))$ **for** a_q in removea]
12:         $semirules \leftarrow$ abacMining(Allow,Deny)
13:         $rules \leftarrow [rules.UC + rules.OC + \pi_{ij}.UC + \pi_{ij}.OC]$ **for** $rules$ in semirules
14:         $\Pi_i' \leftarrow \Pi_i' - \pi_{ij} + rules$
15:     **end if**
16: **end for**
17: Denytotal $\leftarrow DelA_i^e + (Ai - A_i^i - AddA_i^e)$ or Denytotal $\leftarrow Ai \setminus A_i^x$
18: perm1 $\leftarrow$ [q.UC+q.OC **for** q in $AddA_i^e$]
19: perm0 $\leftarrow$ [q.UC+q.OC **for** q in Denytotal]
20: $\Pi_i' \leftarrow \Pi_i' +$ abacMining(perm1,perm0)
21: **return** Π_i'

The idea of the policy modification algorithm (Algorithm 4) for organization i, is to modify each policy, Π_i, in such a way that only the authorizations allowed by the Optimal policy Π_x on Org i (A_i^x) are allowed, whereas, all other authorizations covered by Policy Π_i besides A_i^x are denied. The authorizations covered by policy Π_i, besides the A_i^x are called $DelA_i^e$. These authorizations need to be blocked. Also, we need to add authorizations that are present in A_i^x and are not covered by policy Π_i. These authorizations are called $AddA_i^e$. To begin with, in Line 1, we assign the Policy Π_i to modified policy Π_i'. Next, in Line 2, we find these set of authorizations, $DelA_i^e$ and $AddA_i^e$.

First, we modify policy Π_i so as to block the authorizations in $DelA_i^e$ in Lines 1–16. After that, we modify the policy to add the authorizations in Lines 17–20. In Line 3, we find the set of rules $(Edit\pi_i)$ in policy Π_i to which the authorizations in $DelA_i^e$ belong to. These are the set of rules on which we need to work on (modify rule/delete rule) in order to block authorization set $DelA_i^e$.

From Lines 4–16, we edit each rule one by one in $Edit\pi_i$. For every rule, we create two empty sets: (1) keepa, (2) removea; and two empty lists: (a) Allow, (b) Deny. 'keepa' is the set of authorizations that should be allowed by the rule. We find 'keepa' in Line 6 by subtracting set $DelA_i^e$ from $A_i^{\pi_{ij}}$ (the authorizations covered by rule π_{ij}). We also find 'removea' in Line 6 by subtracting 'keepa' from

$A_i^{\pi_{ij}}$. In Line 7, we check if (keepa $== \Phi$). If it's true, it means that there are no authorizations to be covered by the rule π_{ij} and so we delete rule π_{ij} from the policy Π_i' in Line 8.

In case, keepa is not NULL, in Lines 10–14, we modify the rule to allow the authorizations 'keepa' and block the authorizations 'removea'. We remove the attribute conditions of rule π_{ij} from the attribute condition set for each of the authorizations in 'keepa' and create the 'Allow' list in Line 10. Similarly, we create the 'Deny' list by removing the attribute conditions of rule π_{ij} from the attribute condition set for each of the authorizations in 'removea' and creating a list. In Line 12, we mine ABAC rules using the lists Allow and Deny in function abacMining. Allow and Deny signify the permission1rules and permission0rules in the abacMining algorithm by Talukdar et al. [18]. After we get the mined ABAC rules, we add back the attribute conditions of rule π_{ij} to the mined ABAC rules in Line 13. In Line 14, we remove the rule π_{ij} from the policy Π_i' and add the new rules instead. In Line 17–20, we describe how to add the authorizations $AddA_i^e$ to the policy. First, in Line 17, we find the total authorizations that should be denied (Denytotal). Denytotal is A_i^x subtracted from Ai (all possible authorizations) (Denytotal $\leftarrow$ Ai $\setminus A_i^x$).

Example 5. Consider once again the 3 organizations G_1, G_2 and G_3 in Sect. 2. We now calculate the Migration Cost (MC) for the three policies in each of the organizations.

$\mathrm{MC}(\Pi_1) = |A_2^1 - A_2^2| + |A_2^2 - A_2^1| + |A_3^1 - A_3^3| + |A_3^3 - A_3^1| = 0 + 1 + 1 + 1 = 3$

$\mathrm{MC}(\Pi_2) = |A_1^1 - A_1^2| + |A_1^2 - A_1^1| + |A_3^3 - A_3^2| + |A_3^2 - A_3^3| = 2 + 0 + 2 + 0 = 4$

$\mathrm{MC}(\Pi_3) = |A_1^1 - A_1^3| + |A_1^3 - A_1^1| + |A_2^2 - A_2^3| + |A_2^3 - A_2^2| = 0 + 0 + 2 + 0 = 2$

Since lowest Migration Cost of of Policy Π_3, we decide to migrate to Π_3.

For Policy Π_1:	**For Policy Π_2 :**
$DelA = A_1^1 \setminus A_1^3 = $ NULL	$DelA = A_2^2 \setminus A_2^3 = \{(u_{21}, o_{22}, r), (u_{25}, o_{22}, r)\}$
$AddA = A_1^1 \setminus A_1^3 = $ NULL	$AddA = A_2^3 \setminus A_2^2 = $ NULL
Do nothing as $A_1^3 = A_1^1$	Edit$\pi_i = \{\pi_{23}\}$
	For π_{23}, keepa = NULL
	$\Pi_2' = \Pi_2 \setminus \pi_{23}$

7 Experimental Evaluation

We now evaluate the effectiveness of the three approaches. Since it is difficult to find suitable real data sets, we have created synthetic data sets with specific parameter values. In the following experiments we only create data with a single permission, though the time required would scale linearly with the number of permissions. We consider a set of three organizations, $\{G_1, G_2, G_3\}$ each with a policy Π_1, Π_2 and Π_3. The key parameters in each organization are the set of users (U_1, U_2, U_3), set of objects (O_1, O_2, O_3), user and object attribute conditions (UC_1, UC_2, UC_3), object attribute conditions (OC_1, OC_2, OC_3), and the set of rules (Π_1, Π_2, Π_3). Each policy and the corresponding user object set were created such that a pre-defined percentage of rules in each policy were equivalent to one-another, called 'Overlap Percentage - Rules' (*ovpr*). The percentage of authorizations covered by these rules over total possible authorizations is called 'Overlap Percentage - Accesses' (*ovpa*) amongst the organizations. We have used the following default value of these parameters for experiments, unless the value of a specific parameter is varied for study.

$\|\Pi_1\|\backslash\|\Pi_2\|\backslash\|\Pi_3\|=40\backslash40\backslash40,$	$\|UC_1\|\backslash\|OC_1\|=400\backslash400,$	$ovpr$ in $\Pi_1 = 20,$
$\|U_1\|\backslash\|O_1\|=100\backslash100,$	$\|UC_2\|\backslash\|OC_2\|=400\backslash400,$	$ovpr$ in $\Pi_2 = 50,$
$\|U_2\|\backslash\|O_2\|=100\backslash100,$	$\|UC_3\|\backslash\|OC_3\|=400\backslash400,$	$ovpr$ in $\Pi_3 = 70$
$\|U_3\|\backslash\|O_3\|=100\backslash100,$	$ovpa=10$	

We use the following metrics to evaluate the performance of the approaches proposed above:

1. T: Runtime required for the algorithm.
2. RC_T: Count of rule changes during the transition when using the algorithm.
   $RC_T = (|\text{Rules Deleted}| + |\text{Rules Added}|)$ combined across all three policies.
3. RC_A: Count of rule changes in the policy administratively.
   $RC_A = (|\text{Final Rules}| - |\text{Initial Rules}|)$ combined across all three policies.
4. AC: Count of Authorization Changes in the algorithm.
   $AC = |\text{New Authorizations added}| + |\text{Authorizations lost}|)$ combined across all three policies.

We performed the experiments to evaluate the metrics keeping the following two goals in mind. Also, for each set, we varied the parameters mentioned below.

1. Comparing reconciliation approaches (Sects. 4 and 5)
   - varying # rules in each of the policies
   - varying # users-objects in each of the organizations
2. Comparing reconciliation approaches with Policy Migration (Sects. 4, 5 and 6)
   - varying Overlap among the policies

Further, we repeated each experiment 5 times (each time generating a new random set of policies) and reported the results by averaging over the five runs. The experiments are performed on an Intel Core i7 3.20 GHz machine with 32.00 GB memory running 64-bit Windows 10. As discussed before, for Mining-based reconciliation, we use the ABAC Mining algorithm (ABAC-SRM) proposed by Talukdar et al. [18].

Comparing Reconciliation Approaches

Our observations are similar when we observe the metrics discussed above for both Varying the # of Rules in each of the policies and Varying the # of Users/Objects in each of the organizations. Figures 1 and 2 show the results obtained for different metrics while varying count of Rules and User-Objects respectively while keeping the remaining parameters constant at their default value. It is intuitive that as # of rules in a policy or # of user-object of an

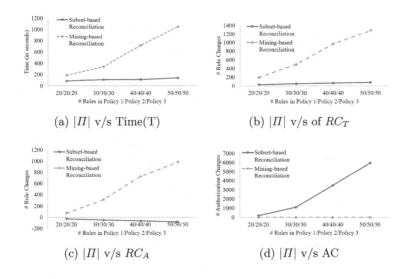

Fig. 1. Increasing # of Rules(Π) in G_1, G_2, G_3

organization increase, the count of authorizations covered by each of the policy sets also increases. Now let us see the effect on individual metrics when we vary the parameters.

Time: For Mining-based reconciliation, time increases with increase in number of rules as more rules lead to more authorizations to mine. For subset based reconciliation also, time increases as the number of rules are increasing as the algorithm will have to check more rules for reconciling. Comparing the two, since Mining-based reconciliation, goes over every authorization and its attribute conditions to evaluate the rules, it's time is much more and increases more rapidly, than Subset-based Reconciliation which only identifies the rules covering extra authorizations and removes them from the policy set policy (Figs. 1a and 2a).

Rule Changes in Transition: The rule changes during transition are more for Mining-based reconciliation as mining has to replace an entire rule set with a new one for all the policies where as Subset-based reconciliation only deletes rules (Figs. 1b and 2b).

Rule Changes Administrative: Mining-based reconciliation has a higher RC_A, which means more administrative cost as the new rule set covers authorizations of all the three organizations (policies). For subset based reconciliation, RC_T is always negative, as the rules are removed from the policy to achieve the reconciled policies, leading to a lower administrative cost (Figs. 1c and 2c).

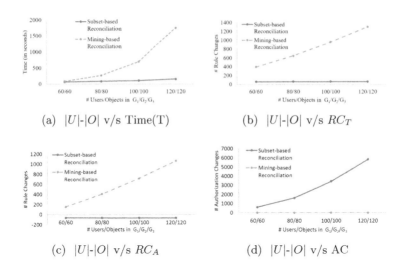

Fig. 2. Increasing # users and objects ($|U|$-$|O|$) in G_1, G_2, G_3

Authorization Changes: *AC* for mining is 0 as we have considered non-conflicting policies for our experiments. For reconciliation, *AC* increase with increasing users-objects/rules, as total authorizations generated by each policy are increasing, but the overlapping authorizations are constant (Figs. 1c and 2c).

Comparing Reconciliation Approaches and Policy Migration

Figure 3 show the results obtained for different metrics when the percent overlap in the authorizations of the three organizations is varied while keeping the remaining parameters constant at their default value. As the % of overlap increase, more percentage of the authorizations are covered by equivalent rules in the three organizations.

Time: For Mining-based reconciliation, time decreases with increase in *ovpa*; equivalent rule sets are covering the authorizations are increasing, thus making mining of rules faster. For Subset-based reconciliation, time increases slowly with the *ovpa* as the algorithm will have to check more extra authorizations while making the decision to eliminate/keep a rule, until it reaches its peak at highest overlap percentage and drops suddenly due to very less extra authorizations. And for migration, the time increases initially but then goes on decreasing with the increase in overlap due to less changes required in authorizations among policies. Policy Migration takes less time than both types of reconciliation approaches at any degree of overlap (Fig. 3a).

Rule Changes in Transition: Rule changes during transition go on decreasing for all the three approaches with increasing overlap. For Mining-based reconciliation the RC_T is maximum among the three, a new ruleset (covering all three policies) replaces the previous one for all the policies, whereas, Subset-based reconciliation only deletes rules and migration works on selected rules or sometimes

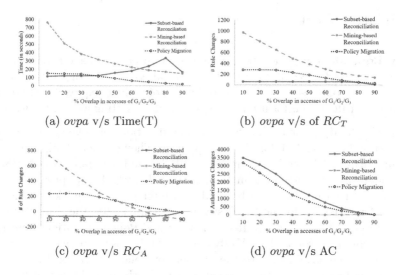

Fig. 3. Increasing % of overlap authorizations (*ovpa*) in G_1, G_2, G_3

adds few rules. To be fair, while counting rule changes in migration we included the rules that we modified by adding or deleting attributes (Fig. 3b).

Rule Changes Administrative: At low overlap, Mining-based reconciliation has the highest administrative cost followed by Migration and Subset-based reconciliation. However, as ovpa increases, the RC_A for both decreases. With increasing overlap RC_A for Subset-based reconciliation increases.

Authorization Changes: The number of authorization changes for mining is 0 as we have considered non-conflicting policies for our experiments. For both reconciliation and migration, the authorization changes increases with increasing overlap (Fig. 3d). All our results are intuitive in nature. Note that all of the above results are statistically significant. We formulated the null hypothesis and the alternative hypothesis in each case, and carried out a paired t-test to determine if the null hypothesis can be rejected. Overall, comparing reconciliation approaches, Mining based reconciliation is more accurate and optimal, as it covers all the authorizations of the three organizations. However, it generates a much larger number of rule sets, leading to more transition and administrative cost for the organizations. The subset-based reconciliation approach, covers less authorizations but has less rule changes in transition and low administration cost once the change is in effect. Migration and Subset based reconciliation perform better than Mining-based reconciliation in terms of time, transition cost and administrative cost, however, Mining-based reconciliation is able to cover all the authorizations for all the organizations. We see that migration performs fairly better considering all the metrics.

8   Related Work

Policy Equivalence: Concepts of Equivalence in policies have been discussed previously by Bertino et al. [5] and Bonatti et al. [6]. Comparing sets of authorizations in two policies, is analogous to the idea of multiset equivalence. We have modified their definition for a multiple organization setting as per our work.

Policy Similarity: One of the widely accepted notions of policy similarity was presented by Lin et al. [13] for XACML policies. They consider both categorical and numerical attributes in evaluating similarity and also integrate dictionary lookup and ontology matching in their extended work [13]. It provides a policy similarity measure that can be used as a filter phase to quickly reduce the number of policies for further analysis. We attempt to use the Policy Similarity measure as a basis of Policy Reconciliation and Policy Migration eventually. Another approach proposed by Vaidya et al. [20] is based on change detection tool XyDiff. They also deal with the problem of Policy Migration by using the results to further develop a policy composition algorithm and migrate to one of the policies at lowest transition cost. We take inspiration from them in defining policy similarity in terms of common access decisions. A similar notion of similarity is that of semantic similarity, used by Xu et al. [21], specifically for ABAC policies. However, we consider only those accesses covered by equivalent rules in two policies while evaluating similarity. Other work is in the area of policy analysis, which is about approaches for checking policy refinement and change analysis and can be used to verify that the policies are equivalent (which is complimentary to our work). Specifically, Fisler et al. [8] presented Margrave represents policies using MTBDDs and presents a policy verification and policy version change analysis algorithm. Backes et al. [2] proposes a policy refinement technique to compare policies and check if one policy is a subset of the other. Turkmen et al. [19] consider SMT as reasoning method to create a policy analysis framework to verify policy properties such as refinement, subsumption, change-impact. Many policy analysis approaches are based on the concept of model checking, e.g., [9].

Policy Reconciliation: Many approaches have been proposed to develop languages that can express multiple access control policies in single unified system (e.g., Jajodia et al. [11]). Barker et al. [3] describe a general access control model that could also be used for ABAC. Besides, several research efforts were made in the area of composing policies Bonatti et al. [6], Bruns et al. [7], McDaniel et al. [16]. In these the different access control policies can be integrated while retaining their own independence. Mazzoleni et al. [15] propose an XACML extension as a policy integration algorithm, which also includes an approach to evaluate policy similarity based on identifying most restrictive policy based on each common attribute in policies. Koch et al. [12] describe a graph-based approach for policy comparison, policy evolution, policy integration and policy transition. Other relevant work for policy reconciliation is that of policy ratification by Agarwal et al. [1] and policy conflict by Lupu et al. [14]. There are also works for secure interoperation in multi-organization environment (e.g. by Shafiq et al. [17], Lupu et al. [14]. These do not consider definition of policy similarity and are not directly related to our work.

9   Conclusions and Future Work

In this paper, we assumed the security policies of organizations in a collaborative setting are enforced using ABAC. We have proposed the notion of policy equivalence based on some past work and policy similarity metric and developed algorithms to evaluate policy similarity. We have also proposed two different approaches for accomplishing policy reconciliation where one is based on ABAC mining and the other is based on finding maximal common subsets. We have also proposed a Policy migration approach for the organizations in such a setting. We have performed extensive experiments to compare the performance of the proposed approaches with respect to a variety of metrics. Mining-based reconciliation is a straightforward way to reconcile policies and results in less changes in the policy in terms of authorizations, but may require more changes in the rules. Migration performs average for all the parameters. In the future, we plan to evaluate the performance of the approaches when the organizations in the collaborative setting are increased and by introducing conflicting authorizations.

Acknowledgments. Research reported in this publication was supported by the National Science Foundation under awards CNS-1624503 and CNS-1747728. The content is solely the responsibility of the authors and does not necessarily represent the official views of the agencies funding the research. We would like to thank Dr. Yiannis Koutis for his valuable suggestions.

References

1. Agrawal, D., Giles, J., Lee, K.W., Lobo, J.: Policy ratification. In: IEEE International Workshop on Policies for Distributed Systems and Networks, pp. 223–232 (2005)
2. Backes, M., Karjoth, G., Bagga, W., Schunter, M.: Efficient comparison of enterprise privacy policies. In: ACM Symposium on Applied Computing, pp. 375–382 (2004)
3. Barker, S.: The next 700 access control models or a unifying meta-model? In: ACM SACMAT, pp. 187–196 (2009)
4. Batra, G., Atluri, V., Vaidya, J., Sural, S.: Enabling the deployment of ABAC policies in RBAC systems. In: Kerschbaum, F., Paraboschi, S. (eds.) DBSec 2018. LNCS, vol. 10980, pp. 51–68. Springer, Cham (2018). https://doi.org/10.1007/978-3-319-95729-6_4
5. Bertino, E., Catania, B., Ferrari, E., Perlasca, P.: A logical framework for reasoning about access control models. ACM TISSEC **6**(1), 71–127 (2003)
6. Bonatti, P., De Capitani di Vimercati, S., Samarati, P.: An algebra for composing access control policies. ACM TISSEC **5**(1), 1–35 (2002)

7. Bruns, G., Dantas, D.S., Huth, M.: A simple and expressive semantic framework for policy composition in access control. In: Proceedings of the 2007 ACM Workshop on Formal Methods in Security Engineering, pp. 12–21. ACM (2007)

8. Fisler, K., Krishnamurthi, S., Meyerovich, L.A., Tschantz, M.C.: Verification and change-impact analysis of access-control policies. In: International Conference on Software Engineering, pp. 196–205 (2005)

9. Guelev, D.P., Ryan, M., Schobbens, P.Y.: Model-checking access control policies. In: Zhang, K., Zheng, Y. (eds.) ISC 2004. LNCS, vol. 3225, pp. 219–230. Springer, Heidelberg (2004). https://doi.org/10.1007/978-3-540-30144-8_19

10. Hu, V.: Attribute based access control (ABAC) definition and considerations. Technical report, National Institute of Standards and Technology (2014)

11. Jajodia, S., Samarati, P., Subrahmanian, V., Bertino, E.: A unified framework for enforcing multiple access control policies. ACM SIGMOD Rec. **26**, 474–485 (1997)

12. Koch, M., Mancini, L.V., Parisi-Presicce, F.: On the specification and evolution of access control policies. In: ACM SACMAT, pp. 121–130 (2001)

13. Lin, D., Rao, P., Ferrini, R., Bertino, E., Lobo, J.: A similarity measure for comparing XACML policies. IEEE TKDE **25**(9), 1946–1959 (2013)

14. Lupu, E.C., Sloman, M.: Conflicts in policy-based distributed systems management. IEEE Trans. Softw. Eng. **25**(6), 852–869 (1999)

15. Mazzoleni, P., Bertino, E., Crispo, B., Sivasubramanian, S.: XACML policy integration algorithms: not to be confused with XACML policy combination algorithms! In: Proceedings of the Eleventh ACM Symposium on Access Control Models and Technologies, pp. 219–227. ACM (2006)

16. McDaniel, P., Prakash, A.: Methods and limitations of security policy reconciliation. ACM TISSEC **9**(3), 259–291 (2006)

17. Shafiq, B., Joshi, J.B., Bertino, E., Ghafoor, A.: Secure interoperation in a multidomain environment employing RBAC policies. IEEE TKDE **17**(11), 1557–1577 (2005)

18. Talukdar, T., Batra, G., Vaidya, J., Atluri, V., Sural, S.: Efficient bottom-up mining of attribute based access control policies. In: IEEE International Conference on Collaboration and Internet Computing, pp. 339–348 (2017)

19. Turkmen, F., den Hartog, J., Ranise, S., Zannone, N.: Analysis of XACML policies with SMT. In: Focardi, R., Myers, A. (eds.) POST 2015. LNCS, vol. 9036, pp. 115–134. Springer, Heidelberg (2015). https://doi.org/10.1007/978-3-662-46666-7_7

20. Vaidya, J., Shafiq, B., Atluri, V., Lorenzi, D.: A framework for policy similarity evaluation and migration based on change detection. Network and System Security. LNCS, vol. 9408, pp. 191–205. Springer, Cham (2015). https://doi.org/10.1007/978-3-319-25645-0_13

21. Xu, Z., Stoller, S.D.: Mining attribute-based access control policies. IEEE TDSC **12**(5), 533–545 (2015)

Machine Learning

WiP: Generative Adversarial Network for Oversampling Data in Credit Card Fraud Detection

Akhilesh Kumar Gangwar[1,2] and Vadlamani Ravi[1(✉)]

[1] Center of Excellence in Analytics, Institute for Development
and Research in Banking Technology, Castle Hills Road #1,
Masab Tank, Hyderabad 500057, India
gangwar.akhilesh1993@gmail.com, rav_padma@yahoo.com
[2] School of Computer and Information Sciences, University of Hyderabad,
Hyderabad 500046, India

Abstract. In this digital world, numerous credit card-based transactions take place all over the world. Concomitantly, gaps in process flows and technology result in many fraudulent transactions. Owing to the spurt in the number of reported fraudulent transactions, customers and credit card service providers incur significant financial and reputation losses respectively. Therefore, building a powerful fraud detection system is paramount. It is noteworthy that fraud detection datasets, by nature, are highly unbalanced. Consequently, almost all of the supervised classifiers, when built on the unbalanced datasets, yield high false negative rates. But, the extant oversampling methods while reducing the false negatives, increase the false positives. In this paper, we propose a novel data oversampling method using Generative Adversarial Network (GAN). We use GAN and its variant to generate synthetic data of fraudulent transactions. To evaluate the effectiveness of the proposed method, we employ machine learning classifiers on the data balanced by GAN. Our proposed GAN-based oversampling method simultaneously achieved high precision, F1-score and dramatic reduction in the count of false positives compared to the state-of-the-art synthetic data generation based oversampling methods such as Synthetic Minority Oversampling Technique (SMOTE), Adaptive Synthetic Sampling (ADASYN) and random oversampling. Moreover, an ablation study involving the oversampling based on the ensemble of SMOTE and GAN/WGAN generated datasets indicated that it is outperformed by the proposed methods in terms of F1 score and false positive count.

Keywords: Fraud detection · Supervised classification · Deep learning · Generative Adversarial Network · Oversampling · SMOTE

1 Introduction

With the spectacular digitalization witnessed in the last decade, online payment methods become one of the significant offerings in the financial services industry. Online shopping, ticket booking, bill payments using credit card become the norm nowadays.

© Springer Nature Switzerland AG 2019
D. Garg et al. (Eds.): ICISS 2019, LNCS 11952, pp. 123–134, 2019.
https://doi.org/10.1007/978-3-030-36945-3_7

Fraudulent transactions involving credit cards for online payments are increasing owing to the shortcomings in the processes, technology and social engineering. Detecting these online card-based frauds and preventing them is a thriving research area. Implementing a powerful and versatile fraud detection system is paramount for any organization as they incur heavy monetary and reputational loss. State-of-the-art fraud detection systems take recourse to machine learning techniques which attempt to learn the profiles of fraudulent transactions from a dataset that contains normal as well as fraudulent transactions.

We now present the challenges in data-driven fraud detection. Data-driven fraud detection collapses into the classification task of supervised machine learning. Due to a disproportionately small number of fraudulent transactions vis-à-vis the normal ones, traditional classifiers incorrectly predict the fraudulent transaction as normal ones. For instance, fraudulent transactions account for 0.1% to 5% of the total data leading to the problem of data imbalance. Almost all machine learning based binary classifiers perform badly on the unbalanced data. However, fuzzy rule based classifiers, one-class classification using SVM, 3-layered or 5-layered auto encoders can work well in case of unbalanced data without having to balancing the data. Generating synthetic data of fraudulent transactions having the same distribution as that of the original data is a big challenge. There are many ways to oversample minority class data in data mining literature. But the problem with these methods is that they replicate the data, without bothering to learn the distribution of minority class. Consequently, false positive rates becomes very large. Cost of manually verifying false positives is much high compared to the cost incurred due to fraud.

We now briefly survey the related work. Sisodia et al. [1] evaluated the performance of class balancing techniques for credit card fraud detection. They used different SMOTE versions and performed undersampling and oversampling. They validated their methods using different classifiers. Randhawa et al. [2] employed a host of machine learning classifiers and designed an ensemble too using majority voting for credit card fraud classification. Vega-Márquez et al. [3] used the conditional GAN for generating synthetic data for both classes. They found that synthetic data improved the F1-score with the Xgboost classifier. They did not compare it with other synthetic data generation techniques and did not report the false positive count. Dos Santos Tanaka et al. [4] used GAN for generating minority class data in medical domain. They found that it is useful in the context of privacy preservation of sensitive data. Mottini et al. [5] proposed Cramer GAN for PNR data generation that is a combination of categorical and numerical data. They used softmax function in place of sigmoid for categorical data generation. Fiore et al. [6] has used vanilla GAN to increase the effectiveness of credit card fraud detection. Douzas et al. [7] used conditional GAN for generating the samples of the minority class containing fraudulent transactions. We propose GAN for generating the continuous data. The architecture of the generator in our proposed method is different from that of Cramer GAN.

The motivation for the present research is as follows: In credit card fraud detection, the major challenge is to obtain high sensitivity and low false positive rate simultaneously from statistical and machine learning classifiers. A supervised classifier can work properly if the data set is balanced. One way of balancing the data is to over-sample the minority class. While simple oversampling replicates the minority class observations, oversampling based on synthetic data generation does not generate data that follows the same probability distribution as that of the minority class because it is based on the nearest neighbor method. Consequently, classifiers yield high false positive rate, which in turn increases the cost, as it needs manual verification of the false positives. The motivation is to oversample minority class by using GAN. This strategy could reduce the number of false positives thereby making the fraud detection system cost effective.

The main contributions of the present paper are as follows:

- We developed a generator and a discriminator for GAN. After training, the generator of GAN can generate synthetic data from the minority class.
- We demonstrated the effectiveness of the proposed oversampling method using machine learning classifiers.
- We compared our method with the extant oversampling techniques. We could reduce the number of false positives dramatically.
- We proposed Wasserstein GAN (WGAN) as well for structured data generation. WGAN was used in literature for image data. But, here, we used it for generating the structured data of fraudulent transactions of credit card. We compared the performance of the WGAN with that of vanilla GAN.
- We performed an ablation study too, where we designed an ensemble combining the data generated using GAN and SMOTE. We compared all methods using F1-score, precision and Recall.

The rest of the paper is organized as follows: Sect. 2 presents the detail of background knowledge to understand model; Sect. 3 presents in detail our proposed model; Sect. 4 presents the dataset description and evaluation metrics; Sect. 5 presents a discussion of the results and finally Sect. 6 concludes the paper and presents future directions.

2 Background

2.1 Generative Adversarial Networks (GANs)

Of late, GAN has gained traction across the machine learning community with excellent results replicating real-world rich content such as images, languages, and music. It is inspired by game theory. It consists of two models, namely, a generator, and a discriminator, both of which compete while supporting each other and making progress together. But training GAN is not an easy task, because since Goodfellow et al. [8] proposed this concept, it has been a problem of unstable training and easy collapse. The architecture of GAN depicted in Fig. 1. The two models of GAN are as follows:

Discriminator model is responsible for predicting the probability that a sample is from a real data set. It trains on real data and the generator's generated fake data and tries to discriminate both type of data as accurately as possible, thus pointing out the inadequacy of newly generated samples. In a sense, it is like a critic which tries to discriminate generator's generated data from the real data.

Generator G. This model is responsible for synthesizing the input noise signal z into a new sample (z contains the potential real data distribution) and then feeding it to the discriminator for judgment. Its goal is to capture the true data distribution based on the output of the discriminator, making the samples it generates as realistic as possible.

These two models compete with each other during the training process: the generator G tries to "spoof" the discriminator D, and the discriminator is constantly improving itself to avoid being cheated. It is this interesting zero-sum game that has given immense strength to GAN.

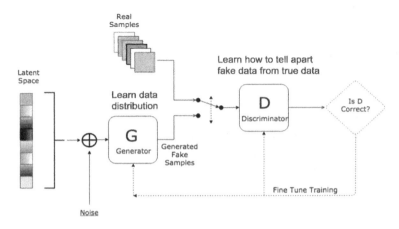

Fig. 1. Architecture of GAN with generator and discriminator

GAN [8] is a generative model that is built by combining two feed-forward neural networks. Generator component of GAN is used to generate synthetic data that looks like the original data in terms of probability distribution and quality. In the Fig. 1, z is a random input to the generator G. Discriminator D receives input as a combination of real data x and the data G(z) generated by the generator. θ_d and θ_g are parameters of discriminator and generator networks respectively. Discriminator and generator both have their respective objective functions as depicted in Fig. 2. In GAN, the generator must be a differentiable, feed-forward network. In GAN, the motive is to achieve a well trained generator so that it can generate the synthetic data that looks like the original data. Hence, optimizing the generator's weights is critical. The presence of the discriminator changed the way the generator is optimized. Discriminator of GAN works as a critic that helps in optimizing generator's weights. The goal of the discriminator is to distinguish the generated sample from the real sample as accurately as possible. That means the generator's objective is to generate synthetic samples that look so similar to the real ones that it can fool the discriminator. Therefore, the optimization of GAN is a min-max game. We optimize the weights of the generator and the discriminator alternately by freezing the weights of one of them.

$$\min_{G} \max_{D} V(D, G) = E_{x \sim P_{data(x)}}[\log(D(x)] + E_{z \sim P_z(z)}[\log(1 - D(G(z)))]$$

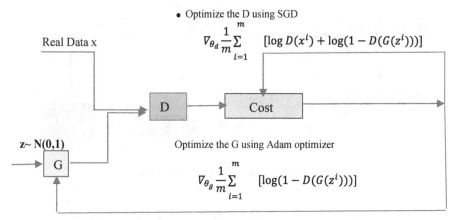

Fig. 2. Architecture of GAN with generator and discriminator objective functions.

Wasserstein GAN [9] (WGAN) employs Wasserstein distance as the loss function. Wasserstein Distance is a measure of the distance between two probability distributions. It is also called Earth Mover's (EM) distance. Wasserstein distance is better than Kullback-Leibler divergence and Jensen-Shannon divergence to measure the similarity between distributions [10].

2.2 Oversampling Methods

Random Oversampling: It simply replicates the data points of the minority class to reduce imbalance. So, no new data is generated. Due to replication, the classifier does not learn a variety of patterns of the minority class.

Synthetic Minority Over-Sampling Technique (SMOTE): Proposed in [12] SMOTE, instead of replicating the minority class, it generates synthetic data based on the position of original samples. It selects a random data point from the minority class and finds its k nearest neighbors. It then creates a synthetic point near these neighbors.

Adaptive Synthetic (ADASYN) Sampling: Proposed in [13], ADASYN is an updated version of SMOTE. This method adds a small bias to artificial points so that they are not linearly correlated to their parent data points. In this paper, to implement SMOTE and ADYSYN, we used the imbalanced-learn python library [11].

3 Proposed Model

The schematic of our proposed model is depicted in Fig. 3. We used GAN for generating the synthetic records of the fraudulent class and machine learning classifiers to validate the quality of artificially generated data and classification purpose.

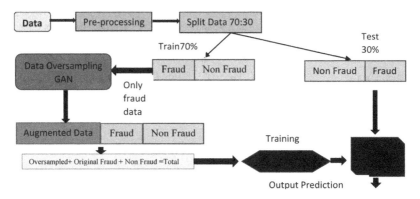

Fig. 3. Schematic diagram of the proposed method

First, we consider the whole data and perform some pre-processing like dropping the column, column standardization. We split the data using the hold-out method in the ratio of 70%:30%. Then, we oversample the training data by concentrating on the minority class of fraudulent transactions, while keeping the test data intact because the latter represents the reality.

3.1 GAN Architecture

Both generator and discriminator of GAN should be differentiable and feedforward networks [14]. As our data is a structured one, CNN and LSTM are not suitable. CNN is used for image data and LSTM is used in case of sequential data. Therefore, in our case, we used multilayer perceptron for both generator and discriminator. We used WGAN (consists of MLP as a generator) for structured data generation and to the best of our knowledge it is not attempted earlier. We used the following architectures for generator and discriminator of the vanilla GAN and WGAN. Only the objective function is different in them.

Architecture of the Generator:
Input Layer. The input layer receives randomly generated latent input of fixed length. Input data is transformed to synthetically generated data by the generator.

Hidden Layers.
- First hidden layer has 500 neurons with leaky ReLU activation [15].
- Second hidden layer has 500 neurons with leaky ReLU activation.
- Third hidden layer has 500 neurons followed by leaky ReLU activation.

Output Layer. This layer outputs generated data that has the same dimension as that of the original data. It uses the hyperbolic tangent (tanh) activation function to get non-linearity. We update the weights of this network so that generated data achieves the same distribution of as that of the original data. That update in weights is accomplished with the help of discriminator in GAN.

Architecture of the Discriminator:
Input Layer. The input layer of the discriminator receives the input vector with the same length as that of the original data.

Hidden Layers.
- First hidden layer has 500 neurons with leaky ReLU activation.
- Second hidden layer has 300 neurons with leaky ReLU activation.

Output Layer. This layer with sigmoid activation function, yields a binary output.

3.2 Classifiers

In the current work, we did not focus on the power of the classifier. We chose two traditional machine learning classifiers. We employed logistic regression (LR) with the elastic net regularization and support vector machine (SVM) with the elastic net penalty. We used Linear kernel and *SGDClassifier* [16] of *Sklearn*[1] library for SVM and LR by choosing *hinge loss* and *log loss* respectively. We trained the GAN with the minority class only. When training of GAN is completed, we generated synthetic samples from the trained generator. We then augmented the generated data with the samples of the fraudulent as well as non-fraudulent classes and used it to train the SVM and LR. The trained classifiers are then tested on the test data.

3.3 Experimental Setting

We used Adam [17] optimizer (with learning rate = 0.001) for generator and stochastic gradient descent optimizer with (learning rate = 0.001) for the discriminator. We generated 15000 data samples for each oversampling method. We trained GAN for 10,000 epochs. Input dimension of generator and discriminator is 100 and 30 respectively, while the output dimension of generator and discriminator is 30 and 1 respectively. We used Tensorflow [18] framework for deep learning and Python language for the classifiers. The combination of all the hyperparameters is obtained by a grid search.

4   Data Set Description and Evaluation Metrics

We validated the effectiveness of our proposed models on the Kaggle credit card data set [19]. This data set is highly unbalanced having 284,807 normal transactions and 492 fraudulent transactions. Thus, the positive class represents only 0.172% of the whole data. The data has 31 columns out of which *Time* and *Amount* are two named

---

[1] https://scikit-learn.org/stable/.

features and the names of *V1* to *V28* features have not been reported due to confidentiality reasons. All are continuous features. Feature *Time* represents time in seconds between transactions and feature *Amount* shows the amount value of the transaction. Last feature *Class* represents the label fraudulent or normal transaction. We divided the dataset in train and test parts in 70%:30% ratio as presented in Table 1.

Table 1. Train and test data

Data	Fraudulent samples	Normal samples	% of the whole data
Train set	338	199364	0.17% fraud
Test set	155	85443	0.18% fraud

4.1   Evaluation Metrics

The data set is highly unbalanced. Here our main intention is to reduce the count of false positives and not to measure the accuracy. We used precision, F1-score as additional performance measures. We also computed false positive, true positive, specificity and recall.

Precision = TP/Predicted Positive = TP/(TP + FP)
Recall = TP/Actual Positive = TP/(TP + FN)
Specificity = TN/Actual Negative = TN/(TN + FP)
F1-Score = 2 * (Precision * Recall)/(Precision + Recall)

Where True Positive (TP): Predicted positive and actual is also positive.
True Negative (TN): Predicted negative and actual is also negative.
False Positive (FP): Predicted positive but actual is negative.
False Negative (FN): Predicted negative but actual is positive.

5   Result and Discussion

Our main intention, in this research work, is to build a good oversampling method or synthetic data generator. We investigated the effectiveness of the proposed GAN and WGAN based oversampling methods. We compared the performance of the proposed oversampling methods with that of the existing oversampling methods using SVM and LR classifiers. The results of the classifiers on test data are presented in Tables 2 and 3 respectively. It can be seen from Table 2 that AUC scores are not good measures to check the effectiveness of the oversampling method. In fraud detection case, we would like to have high true positive count and less false positive count simultaneously. According to the Tables 2 and 3, we can say that false positive count is very high on the unbalanced data without using any oversampling method. But, compared to all oversampling methods, our proposed method performed the best in terms of controlling false positives.

Table 2. Performances comparison with SVM

Method	TP	FP	Specificity	Precision	Recall	F1-score	AUC
Plain SVM	145	2951	0.97	0.05	0.94	0.09	0.95
Random oversampling + SVM	139	1046	0.99	0.12	0.90	0.21	0.94
SMOTE + SVM	145	1595	0.98	0.08	0.94	0.15	0.96
ADASYN + SVM	145	4874	0.94	0.03	0.94	0.06	0.94
GAN + SVM	**135**	**170**	**0.99**	**0.58**	**0.85**	**0.69**	**0.93**
WGAN + SVM	**132**	**95**	**0.99**	**0.58**	**0.85**	**0.69**	**0.92**
SMOTE + GAN + SVM	**142**	**512**	**0.99**	**0.22**	**0.92**	**0.35**	**0.96**
SMOTE + WGAN + SVM	**141**	**422**	**0.91**	**0.25**	**0.91**	**0.39**	**0.95**

It is common knowledge that the fraudulent transactions are considered as positive class. Supervised machine learning classifiers misclassify non-fraudulent (normal) samples as fraudulent ones thereby increasing the false positive count. Even the true positive count is high due to soft boundary of a classifier separating the fraudulent and non-fraud datasets. Thus, even if a model yields high true positive count, it also misclassifies the normal transactions, that are near the soft boundary, as fraudulent ones. This increases the false positive count. Hence, such models are not preferred because every sample predicted as fraudulent will have to be manually verified and during the verification if they turn out to be false positives, it is a wastage of time and money. Therefore, reducing false positive count along with increasing the true positive count is the main concern nowadays.

GAN and WGAN based oversampling methods controlled the false positive count spectacularly without affecting the true positive count significantly. Precision and F1-score are very high compared to other oversampling methods. Our GAN with LR/SVM is better than plain LR/SVM because the latter, unsurprisingly, yielded high false positive count as well as high precision.

Our proposed method yielded excellent results (see Tables 2 and 3) compared to SMOTE, random oversampling and ADASYN because these oversampling methods generate the synthetic data without learning the distribution of the original class. Random oversampling does not generate any synthetic data. It replicates the existing minority class data to balance the classes. Therefore, it does not bring any variety to the data thereby afflicting the performance of the classifiers. While SMOTE and ADASYN generate new synthetic data points based on neighbors, they too do not learn the distribution of the data. Therefore, the data generated by them does not have variety.

Our proposed GAN generated data that has the same distribution as that of the minority class because the objective function of GAN is designed so as to learn the distribution There are many types of objective functions such as KL-divergence, JS-divergence used in GAN. These objective functions have a limitation in terms of learning the data distribution as follows: if the two distributions are in lower dimensional manifolds without overlaps, then KL- divergence would not perform better. We used WGAN to overcome this problem. WGAN employs Wasserstein distance that can provide meaningful and smooth representation of the distance if distributions are not

Table 3. Performance comparison with logistic regression

Method	TP	FP	Specificity	Precision	Recall	F1-score	AUC
Plain LR	145	3394	0.96	0.04	0.94	0.08	0.95
Random oversampling + LR	144	1476	0.98	0.09	0.93	0.16	0.95
SMOTE + LR	144	1454	0.98	0.09	0.93	0.16	0.95
ADASYN + LR	148	7215	0.92	0.02	0.95	0.04	0.93
GAN + LR	**132**	**120**	**0.999**	**0.52**	**0.85**	**0.65**	**0.93**
WGAN + LR	**132**	**78**	**0.999**	**0.63**	**0.85**	**0.72**	**0.92**
SMOTE + GAN + LR	**141**	**588**	**0.94**	**0.19**	**0.91**	**0.32**	**0.95**
SMOTE + WGAN + LR	**143**	**561**	**0.99**	**0.22**	**0.92**	**0.33**	**0.96**

*LR = Logistic Regression

overlapped. Reducing the distance between the distribution of artificially generated data and true data makes GAN perform better for data oversampling. WGAN outperformed GAN because WGAN has a better objective function. Training time of model is system and data dependent but after training we can use trained model for deployment and response will depend on the server. But we noticed that it is very fast (10–15 s for generating 15000 data points).

An ablation study was also conducted by taking the union of the datasets generated by both SMOTE and GAN/WGAN along with the original dataset as the new dataset and invoking classifiers on them. It is a sort of ensemble of the datasets generated by SMOTE and GAN/WGAN. Tables 2 and 3 clearly indicate that even this ensemble strategy failed to yield higher F1 score and lower false positive count compared to the GAN/WGAN based oversampling methods. Therefore, we infer that the proposed GAN/WGAN based oversampling method demonstrates its strength and power conclusively and convincingly.

6   Conclusion and Future Directions

In this paper, we proposed a GAN based minority oversampling method for credit card fraud detection. We compared GAN based oversampling method with the existing oversampling algorithms like random oversampling, SMOTE, ADASYN. We observed that the GAN based oversampling method is more effective compared to other oversampling methods in terms of reducing the false positive count. We have successfully generated a variety of data samples from the minority class after learning the distribution of the minority class using GAN and tested the quality using standard machine learning algorithms. We observed that the false positive count reduced drastically without affecting the true positive count significantly. We also proposed WGAN for data oversampling. WGAN has better objective function compared to the vanilla GAN for comparing the distribution of the generated data and with that of the original data. We found that WGAN is more effective compared to vanilla GAN. Further, an ablation study conducted involving ensembling the SMOTE and GAN/WGAN generated datasets also failed to outperform the proposed GAN/WGAN based oversampling methods in terms of F1 score and false positive count.

In the future, we would like to try different generator architecture in GAN. We will use the Variational Autoencoder (*VAE*) [20] in the generator part. We will extend the capacity of learning of GAN by using appropriate loss function. We want to investigate the effectiveness of the proposed model in another type of structured data that contain categorical, integer and numerical features. We want to use GAN in data privacy case also.

References

1. Sisodia, D.S., Reddy, N.K.: Performance evaluation of class balancing techniques for credit card fraud detection. In: 2017 IEEE International Conference on Power, Control, Signals and Instrumentation Engineering (ICPCSI), pp. 2747–2752 (2017)
2. Randhawa, K., Loo, C.K., Seera, M., Lim, C.P., Nandi, A.K.: Credit card fraud detection using adaboost and majority voting. IEEE Access **6**, 14277–14284 (2018)
3. Vega-Márquez, B., Rubio-Escudero, C., Riquelme, José C., Nepomuceno-Chamorro, I.: Creation of synthetic data with conditional generative adversarial networks. In: Martínez Álvarez, F., Troncoso Lora, A., Sáez Muñoz, J.A., Quintián, H., Corchado, E. (eds.) SOCO 2019. AISC, vol. 950, pp. 231–240. Springer, Cham (2020). https://doi.org/10.1007/978-3-030-20055-8_22
4. Dos Santos Tanaka, F.H.K., Aranha, C.: Data augmentation using GANs. CoRRabs/1904.09135 (2019). http://arxiv.org/abs/1904.09135
5. Mottini, A., Lheritier, A., Acuna-Agost, R.: Airline passenger name record generation using generative adversarial networks. arXiv preprint https://arxiv.org/abs/1807.06657 (2018)
6. Fiore, U., De Santis, A., Perla, F., Zanetti, P., Palmieri, F.: Using generative adversarial networks for improving classification effectiveness in credit card fraud detection. Inf. Sci. **479**, 448–455 (2019)
7. Douzas, G., Bacao, F.: Effective data generation for imbalanced learning using conditional generative adversarial networks. Expert Syst. Appl. **91**, 464–471 (2018)
8. Goodfellow, I., et al.: Generative adversarial nets. In: Advances in Neural Information Processing Systems, Montreal, Canada, pp. 2672–2680, December 2014
9. Arjovsky, M., Chintala, S., Bottou. L.: Wasserstein GAN. arXiv preprint https://arxiv.org/abs/1701.07875 (2017)
10. Weng, L.: From GAN to WGAN. arXiv preprint https://arxiv.org/abs/1904.08994 (2019)
11. Guillaume, L., Nogueira, F., Aridas, C.K.: Imbalanced-learn: a python toolbox to tackle the curse of imbalanced datasets in machine learning. J. Mach. Learn. Res. **18**(1), 559–563 (2017)
12. Chawla, N.V., Bowyer, K.W., Hall, L.O.: SMOTE: synthetic minority over-sampling technique. J. Artif. Intell. Res. **16**, 321–357 (2002)
13. He, H., Bai, Y., Garcia, E.A., Li, S.: ADASYN: adaptive synthetic sampling. In: 2008 IEEE International Joint Conference on Neural Networks (IEEE World Congress on Computational Intelligence), pp. 1322–1328 (2008)
14. Goodfellow, I., Bengio, Y., Courville, A.: Deep Learning. MIT Press, Cambridge (2016). http://www.deeplearningbook.org
15. Maas, A.L., Hannun, A.Y., Ng, A.Y.: Rectifier nonlinearities improve neural network acoustic models. In: ICML 2013, pp. 3–8 (2013)
16. https://scikit-learn.org/stable/modules/generated/sklearn.linear_model.SGDClassifier.html

17. Kingma, D.P., Ba, J.L.: Adam: a method for stochastic optimization. arXiv preprint https://arxiv.org/abs/1412.6980 (2014, 2017)
18. https://www.tensorflow.org/
19. Pozzolo, A.D., Caelen, O., Johnson, R.A., Bontempi, G.: Calibrating probability with undersampling for unbalanced classification. In: Proceedings - 2015 IEEE Symposium Series on Computational Intelligence, SSCI 2015, pp. 155–166 (2015)
20. Welling, M.: Auto-encoding variational Bayes. arXiv: https://arxiv.org/abs/1312.6114 (2014). ICLR 2013, vol. abs/1312.6114

Distributed Systems

An Introduction to the CellTree Paradigm (Invited Paper)

Anasuya Acharya[1]([✉]), Manoj Prabhakaran[1]([✉]), and Akash Trehan[2]([✉])

[1] IIT Bombay, Mumbai, India
{acharya,mp}@cse.iitb.ac.in
[2] Microsoft, Vancouver, Canada
aktrehan@microsoft.com

Abstract. This note is a brief introduction to CellTree, a new architecture for distributed data repositories, drawing liberally from our article which introduces the concept in greater detail [15].

A CellTree allows data to be stored in largely independent, and highly programmable *cells*, which are *"assimilated"* into a tree structure. The data in the cells are allowed to change over time, subject to each cell's own policies; a cell's policies also govern how the policies themselves can evolve. A design goal of the architecture is to let a CellTree evolve organically over time, and adapt itself to multiple applications. Different parts of the tree may be maintained by different sets of parties and the core mechanisms used for maintaining the tree can also vary across the tree and over time.

We outline the architecture of a CellTree, along with provable guarantees of liveness, correctness and consistency that can be achieved in a typical instantiation of the architecture. These properties can be guaranteed for individual cells that satisfy requisite trust assumptions, even if these assumptions don't hold for other cells in the tree. We also discuss several features of a CellTree that can be exploited by applications. Finally, we briefly outline a sample application that can be built upon the CellTree, leveraging its many features.

Keywords: Distributed data repository · CellTree · Blockchain

1 Introduction

There has been an explosion of interest in the notion of a *distributed ledger*, triggered by the popularity of Bitcoin [13]. The typical distributed ledgers today have the form of a *blockchain*, where each new block points to an earlier block. A variety of ingenious protocols have been developed to add and *immutably* maintain the blocks in such a ledger in a trustless environment. Blockchain applications today have gone well beyond that envisaged by Bitcoin (namely, a decentralized cryptocurrency transaction ledger), and have been used in supply chain management, gaming, maintaining public records, and general purpose contracts.

© Springer Nature Switzerland AG 2019
D. Garg et al. (Eds.): ICISS 2019, LNCS 11952, pp. 137–153, 2019.
https://doi.org/10.1007/978-3-030-36945-3_8

However, such blockchain technologies have several issues and – despite several proposed alternatives – many of them remain unresolved. These typically face scalability challenges, as the underlying blockchain structure is ever-growing and all the "full nodes" need to store this entire chain for fully validating *any* block. Implementation bugs in contracts, if exploited, can create irreversible effects, owing to the immutable nature of a blockchain. Another issue of note is that the proof-of-work consensus protocol used in popular blockchains has turned out to be ecologically costly.

Many recent works have proposed fixes to these – using secondary structures [1,3] to reduce the on-chain storage, alternate consensus mechanisms [2,7,9], and different graph topologies [4,14]. However, as these systems grow in scale, or when new attacks emerge, the deployments of these solutions may need revisions.

In [15], we propose a very different approach to designing a large scale, long-running system for distributed data storage. A distributed data repository is a complex system, with several constituent components, addressing several disparate sub-problems. A key philosophy of our approach is to *let different solutions coexist* in the system, and to *leave room for the system to organically evolve* over time and across applications. For this, various sub-problems are delegated to *modules*, and the overall architecture is agnostic to how each module is implemented.

An important consideration in the design is to let different users focus on different parts of the system, unencumbered by the entire system's data. Furthermore, it allows part of the whole structure to function as a smaller version of the system, complete with its security guarantees and trust assumptions. In particular, it naturally admits *multi-level confirmation* of new data, so that clients trusting lower levels in this hierarchy can get quick confirmation of the addition of data to the structure, and those who do not trust those levels can wait for a higher level of confirmation.

The CellTree Architecture. A CellTree consists of largely independent *cells*, which carries the data, as well as a (typically smaller) *nucleus* with the rules for collecting and updating data. The data can evolve subject to these policies programmed into the cell, and even these policies can evolve as they permit themselves to.

Each cell is "operated" by a *crew* selected for it and is addressed by associating it with a *node* in a binary tree. The crew is also in charge of *monitoring* the nodes in a relatively small subtree rooted at that node. Monitoring involves verifying that the evolution of a nucleus is consistent with its own policies. If so, the data is periodically *assimilated* into the tree by updating the node's hash pointer with the new cell's nucleus. This is then propagated to its ancestors and a *proof of assimilation* is propagated towards the nodes monitored. These proofs will be verified by a client accessing a cell.

The algorithms executed by the crew members operating a node (or clients accessing a node), to carry out a cell's evolution, to monitor the evolution of some other cells, and to assimilate updates and propagate assimilation signals up and down the tree are specified as *procedures*. Many tasks like selecting the next step in a cell's evolution, selecting crews for new nodes, communicating to other crews, etc. however, are left to *modules*.

Each cell's integrity and availability guarantees would depend only on (the crews of) the cells in the path from it to the root of the tree (or to any ancestor node whose crew is considered to have an honest-majority). Subtrees could be easily excised from the CellTree, or grafted to multiple locations (effectively making the structure a directed acyclic graph, rather than a tree), with little effect on cells outside the subtree.

The cell structure and the tree structure are complementary, and it is primarily the interface between them that is fixed by the CellTree architecture. The individual cells themselves can be programmed to evolve in customized ways, and the tree's protocols can also be customized using various modules at the level of nodes, edges and paths.

Organization. The rest of this paper is organized as follows. We start with a high-level discussion of various aspects taken into consideration during the design of the CellTree architecture, in Sect. 2. Section 3 outlines the architecture, including the different modules that need to be plugged into the design to instantiate a CellTree. Section 4 discusses the formal properties that can be guaranteed by the CellTree architecture. Section 5 illustrates a sample CellTree application. Section 6 sketches several features of the CellTree architecture that applications can exploit. Before concluding, we discuss a few related constructions in Sect. 7.

2   An Organic Design

The key design goals of the CellTree are to be a flexible distributed repository, where multiple solutions to various sub-problems can co-exist, and even evolve over time, to address different use-cases and attack scenarios. The framework strives to meet this by being *modular, cellular* and *evolving*, as sketched below.

Modular. There are separate processes (a) for assigning responsibilities to parties, (b) for selecting updates to be applied to the data in the system, and (c) for parties to enforce integrity and availability of the data they are responsible for. The CellTree design largely deals with (c), with support for a wide variety of options for the modules for (a) and (b). Indeed, concepts from prior blockchain constructions, like different consensus mechanisms and incentivisation, as well as relying on permissioned systems, are all possible means to achieving the goals of (a) and (b). Even in the solution for (c), various sub-tasks are left as modules, which can be implemented in a variety of ways to achieve different efficiency-robustness trade-offs.

Cellular. The notion of blocks in a blockchain is generalized to add more functionality and flexibility. For clarity, the term *cell* is used instead. The system is designed to allow cells to operate somewhat independent of each other, while retaining a cohesive structure overall:

- As time progresses more cells can be added to the system. Cells could also be excised from the system, with limited impact on the rest of the system.
- The parties hosting the distributed system can choose to focus on cells of interest to them, and ignore the remaining.
- Each cell may use its own set of mechanisms for implementing the modules mentioned above.

Evolving. Cells can be envisaged as having static addresses, but their data content could change over time. Data updates in a cell must follow an *evolution policy* associated with the cell. The evolution policy in a cell itself can evolve, and this is also dictated by the evolution policy.[1]

There is one more sense in which a CellTree can evolve: the modules used by various nodes in the tree can evolve, subject to their own evolutionary policies. However, framework for how modules are chosen and modified are also left to a module.

2.1 CellTree vs. Blockchains

The CellTree architecture and conventional blockchains have several overlapping features. Yet, the CellTree architecture differs from blockchains in several important and fundamental ways. It is instructive to contrast the two along several dimensions.

Distributed vs. Replicated. Both CellTrees and blockchains rely on a large network of participants to maintain the data in a repository. But in a typical blockchain, many participants ("the full nodes") are expected to *replicate* the entire contents of the repository. In contrast, in a CellTree no single entity is required to do so. Instead, the data is *distributed* among the participants, with each data item (i.e., contents of a cell) maintained only by a relatively small number of participants associated with it (i.e., the crews of the node hosting the cell), and cryptographically monitored by some other participants. In a large CellTree, the amount of data any party is required to maintain would be a small fraction of the entire data in the CellTree.

Multi-level Confirmation. In a CellTree, a crew operating a node can update its cell autonomously, based on its own local policies, and then have it assimilated into the tree. Unlike in a blockchain architecture, where the whole system has to approve the update, the updates within a cell are wholly determined by the crew of the node hosting the cell (subject to the policies programmed into the cell); a client that trusts the node's crew has *immediate confirmation* of the update. The purpose of assimilation and higher levels of confirmation is only to protect against (and hence disincentivize) misbehaving crews.

Reversed Hash Pointers. One of the easily spotted difference between the CellTree architecture and blockchains is that the former uses a tree topology,

---

[1] For meaningful guarantees, when a policy rewrites itself, the newly resulting policy needs to validate that the old policy is acceptable to it as a policy to evolve from.

instead of a chain. At first glance, one may view a blockchain as a *unary* Merkle Tree [11,12] (i.e., each node has a single child), while a CellTree uses a binary Merkle tree. However, this comparison is misleading. In a CellTree, the "hash pointers" point from a parent (older node) to its children (newer nodes), whereas in a blockchain, newly added nodes carry hash pointers to existing nodes.[2]

Distributed Ownership. An alternate attempt to relate the CellTree structure to a blockchain would be to compare it to a blockchain that "forks" often (and retains the forks). Though this analogy too misses the mark due to the reversed hash pointers, there is a further difference that this comparison brings to light. In a blockchain, if multiple forks have to be *permanently retained*, consensus across the entire system will be needed for each fork. In the CellTree architecture, on the other hand, each individual node is owned and operated by its own crew. Distributing the ownership of nodes to relatively small crews which can operate in parallel, vastly improves the scalability of the system.

Selecting a crew to entirely own a node, however, does raise some issues. Firstly, one needs to ensure that a sufficiently large majority of the parties selected are honest, and secondly, in the event that the crews for some nodes are compromised, the system retains as many security guarantees as possible. The first issue is left for a module to solve while the second issue is addressed by the CellTree architecture via monitoring: Even if a node's crew is corrupt, any updates to the node's cell will be assimilated into the CellTree only if they are validated and agreed upon by the crews monitoring it.

Dynamic Nodes. Crucial to implementing a Merkle tree based data structure is the ability to dynamically update the contents of previously existing nodes in the tree, so that they can assimilate newly created cells (even if the evolution of individual cells are not supported). But allowing cell data itself to evolve, in a programmable manner, brings a whole new dimension to distributed data repositories.

Though persistence is sometimes desirable, many a time it can be a burden on the system. While prior constructions have focused on the immutability or "persistence" guarantee of the blocks in a blockchain, for dynamic data we introduce a notion of *consistency*, to assure that a cell has evolved into its current form in accordance with the policies declared by the cell. These policies govern the modification of the cell's data as well as the policies themselves.

Excising Malignant Cells. A blockchain, by design, does not allow removing any blocks already accepted to be part of the chain. This (exacerbated by the need to store the entire chain) creates practical socio-legal complications when illegal data is hosted on a blockchain. A CellTree, in contrast, makes it possible to deactivate "malignant" cells, with little impact on the rest of the tree. The node containing a deactivated cell could be brought back to service (with a fresh cell in it), if all the nodes monitoring it cooperate.

---

[2] Even architectures like IOTA's Tangle [14], that do not stick to a chain structure use hash pointers in the same direction as blockchains.

3   CellTree Design

This section briefly discusses the CellTree architecture. We refer the reader to [15] for further technical details. As mentioned in Sect. 1, a CellTree has the structure of a (binary) tree, with each node associated with a cell that carries dynamic data. Below, we shall describe the expected behaviour of a cell, followed by how this behaviour is enforced by the parties that operate the CellTree.

3.1   The Cell

Each cell consists of two components: *cell-data* cdata, and a *nucleus* nuc. The cell-data contains the actual contents of the cell while the nucleus has information that constrains the trajectory of the data evolution (in the past and the future). The nucleus contains some data ndata (typically, a summary of the cell-data), in addition to some code ncode. The nuclear code consists of three algorithms that dictate cell evolution:

- chkCell: checks if its own nucleus is consistent with a given cdata.
- chkNext: checks if its own nucleus can evolve into a given (next) nucleus.
- chkPrev: checks if its own nucleus can evolve from a given (previous) nucleus.

For an update of a cell evolve from (cdata, nuc) to (cdata', nuc') to be valid, both the nuclei involved should *agree* to the evolution. This is required to enable making inferences about the past and future of a cell from the current nucleus. For efficiency purposes, nuclei should arrive at this agreement without seeing the cell data, using only the nuclear data. Furthermore, since the nucleus is available outside of the node containing the cell (to the nodes monitoring it), if the contents of the cell are to be protected, the nucleus should retain the cell's secrecy.

The machine model for the nuclear code is implemented using a module exec that, apart from standard operations, may allow references to certain external resources, like current time, cells in other nodes of this CellTree, or even data blocks or code in other blockchains.

Depending on the contents of the nuclear code, cells can emulate a variety of functionalities like static data, a blockchain ledger, a state machine, etc. Details of simple constructions for these can be found in [15].

3.2   The Tree

In order to maintain the cells in a single structure, the address space of a binary tree structure is used. Each cell will be exclusively associated with a unique node v in the tree, and will be implemented by a set of parties – called the node's *crew* (or sometimes, simply the node). Each crew member is uniquely identified by (a hash of) its verification key in a signature scheme. As time progresses, new nodes can be added to the tree and also, each node's cell may evolve as permitted by its nuclear code.

One may expect that a typical crew has a majority of honest parties. But this may not be true for every node's crew. To make the tree robust to corruption of even entire crews of some nodes, we shall have each cell's evolution monitored and certified by several other crews (specifically, by the crews of several nodes that are ancestors of the cell's node in the binary tree).

Proof of Assimilation. An updated cell is not immediately assimilated into the tree until a certification – or a *proof of assimilation* – is made available to the hosting node's crew. The proof of assimilation relies on an underlying Merkle tree structure, as described below.

When a node's cell evolves, it submits the nucleus of the cell for assimilation into the tree, to the nodes monitoring it (see Rootward Propagation, below). Along with this nucleus, the node would include fingerprints (or hashes) of its children's nuclei which it has certified for assimilation. In turn, the fingerprint of this nucleus incorporates the fingerprints of its children. These "hash pointers" form a Merkle tree (or rather, a slight generalization of Merkle trees, allowing not only leaves, but the internal nodes also to hold data).[3]

A proof of assimilation of a nucleus consists of (1) a signature on the root of a Merkle tree consisting of the node, and (2) the hashes along the path from that node to the root (which serves as a proof that the nucleus at the node was indeed accumulated into the hash at the root). The signature on the root hash would be by the crew of the root node. (The role of the root of assimilation could be played by any ancestor of the node being assimilated.)

3.3   CellTree Procedures

The core procedures of the CellTree architecture specify how data is accessed and maintained, leaving several other tasks—like choosing how to modify the data in a cell, or choosing crew members for a cell—to modules. There are four CellTree procedures: READ, EVOLVE, ROOTWARDPROPAGATION and LEAFWARDPROPAGATION. These procedures themselves rely on several modules which can be variably instantiated. The detailed specification of these procedures can be found in [15]. Below we outline their functionality.

- **Reading a Cell.** A client that wishes to read a cell in node v can invoke a procedure READ, which works as follows. First, it discovers the crew for the node v as well as for a trusted assimilation root aroot. (aroot need not necessarily be the root of the CellTree, but can be any ancestor of v in the CellTree that offers to certify the Merkle tree hashes it receives, and is considered trustworthy by the client.) Then it fetches, from v's crew, a cell along with a valid proof of assimilation signed by aroot. If the proof of assimilation (which relates to only the nucleus of the cell) verifies and if the fetched cell's

---

[3] Note that the same version of a cell may be part of multiple such Merkle trees, if for instance, an ancestor of that cell evolves through multiple versions before the cell itself evolves. This in fact, gives rise to a *Merkle Multi-Tree*, which is a collection of Merkle trees in which any two may share some subtrees.

contents match its nucleus (as checked by the program chkCell in the nucleus), then the client accepts the cell. The subtasks for discovering crews, fetching a cell from a crew, verifying the crew's signature, and executing the chkCell program are all implemented by modules (see later).

– **Cell Evolution.** To replace the current cell cell with a new cell $cell^{(+)}$ (selected using a module that achieves consensus among the crew members), a procedure EVOLVE is invoked at each crew member. The procedure use chkNext and chkPrev procedures in the nuclei of cell and $cell^{(+)}$ respectively, as well as chkCell in $cell^{(+)}$, to verify that the evolution is permissible. If so, the crew updates its storage accordingly. The tasks carried out by modules include selecting the cell, executing the verification programs, and updating the storage. (Typically, the update can be carried out locally by each crew member, without communicating with each other.)

– **Cell Assimilation.** Assimilation is carried out by propagating *assimilation signals* from cells towards the root (Rootward Propagation) and *proofs of assimilation* back from the root to all the cells (Leafward Propagation). This process is designed such that the amount of work a node needs to carry out does not grow as the tree grows. However, the amount of storage required at a node does depend on the *depth of that node*, as a version of the cell is retained at least until all proofs of assimilation for a later version are received.

  • **Rootward Propagation:** In the procedure ROOTWARDPROPAGATION, each crew member accepts and verifies a list of nuclear updates from each node it is monitoring. Here, verification involves verifying the consistency between consecutive updates (using chkNext and chkPrev methods in the two nuclei), as well as ensuring that the hash pointers included in an updated node points to valid cells that resulted from verified updates. (In case of verification failure, the previous version of the node is retained.) Then, the crew prepares a node in the Merkle multi-tree, with the current version of its cell, with hash pointers to the verified versions of the cells of its two child nodes. This information is propagated to crews monitoring it, along with a the local list of updates since the last rootward propagation. The communication between the node's crew and the crews monitoring it is accomplished through a module.

  • **Leafward Propagation:** The procedure LEAFWARDPROPAGATION is used by a crew to propagate proof of assimilation from an ancestor node aroot (possibly itself) to one or more of its subtree nodes. The procedure verifies the proof received, extends it to proofs of assimilation for its descendent nodes, and propagates the extended proofs to them. A module is used to collect the proofs, determine the set of nodes to which proofs should be propagated, and to actually communicate with those nodes.

3.4   Modules

A CellTree relies on several modules, but is oblivious to their implementation. While many of the modules are entirely local to a node's crew, some modules need to coordinate across multiple nodes.

- **Node Creation and Crew Selection.** Creating a new node and selecting a crew for it are tasks carried out collectively by the nodes which would be monitoring the new node, using a module `createNode`. This module could use, e.g., the committee selection protocol used within Algorand [7].
- **Cell Selection.** As mentioned before, cell evolution is triggered by a module `selectCell`, which is responsible for obtaining a consensus among the crew members as to the next version of a cell.
- **Propagation.** As described earlier, the modules `rootward` and `leafward` are used by crews to send and receive assimilation signals and proofs of assimilation. Typically, the `send` and `receive` methods operate in the background and would involve consensus mechanisms and secure communication protocols used within and across crews.
- **Local Storage.** The module `store` is used by each party in a crew to locally store and retrieve various values across separate invocations of the algorithms. Typically, this module requires no communication among crew members (as the consistency guarantees of values being stored are ensured by the other modules).
- **Client Access to a CellTree.** Modules `fetch` and `discover` are used by the procedure READ. These modules may implement mechanisms for access control and denial-of-service protection.
  The proofs of assimilation involve a collective signature by the crew (on a hash value). The protocol for creating such signatures and the algorithm for locally verifying them are encapsulated in the module `crewSign`.
- **Code Execution.** The machine model used to execute the nuclear code is specified as a module `exec`. The module may support multiple languages and library functions.
- **Hashing.** The hash algorithm and Merkle tree evaluation are implemented by the module `hash`. A method `hash.generateNonce` included in this module can be used to create onces that control the hash evaluation (e.g., if a timestamp in the nonce is in the future, the hash evaluation could return an error).
- **Scheduling.** The `sched` module decides when the CellTree procedures are run by the members of a crew.
- **Selection and Evolution of Modules.** The CellTree framework admits different implementations of the various modules to coexist. But the framework does not specify how modules are chosen, and possibly changed over time, instead delegating it to a module `moduleManager` (which governs its own evolution).

4   Robustness Properties

Listed here are the desirable properties for a CellTree. These properties are parametrized by a node v, since, even if parts of the tree are malfunctioning, we seek to guarantee these properties to other nodes.

- consistency(v): Let C be the set of cells returned by a set of successful invocations of READ(v) by honest clients. Then, there exists a sequence of nuclei $\mathsf{nuc}^{(0)}, \cdots, \mathsf{nuc}^{(N)}$ such that for all $i \in [1, N]$, both chkNext($\mathsf{nuc}^{(i-1)}, \mathsf{nuc}^{(i)}$) and chkPrev($\mathsf{nuc}^{(i)}, \mathsf{nuc}^{(i-1)}$) hold and further, for all cell $\in C$, there exists $i \in [0, N]$, such that cell.nuc $= \mathsf{nuc}^{(i)}$ and chkCell(cell) holds.
- correctness(v): Any cell returned by READ(v) to an honest client is equal to a cell assigned to v using the procedure EVOLVE by the crew G_v prior to that (or is the empty cell that every node is initialized with).
- liveness(v): If a cell is assigned to a node v at any point in time (by the crew G_v using the procedure EVOLVE), eventually every invocation of READ(v) by any honest client will return this cell, or a cell assigned to v subsequently.

The definitions of correctness and liveness refers to *the* crew G_v. However, the actual members in a crew are defined recursively by the opinion of its ancestor crews (using information they obtained via the module `createNode`). Also, to define a crew's opinion we need the crew to have an honest majority, and they should all agree on this opinion. A node v is considered *good* if there is a set of parties $\hat{G}$ such that (1) $\hat{G}$ has an honest majority, (2) $\hat{G}$ considers itself to be the crew of v, and (3) there is an ancestor of v that is itself good which also considers $\hat{G}$ to be the crew for v. The base case of this recursive definition is with respect to a given set of parties G_ϵ, and only the first two of the above two conditions hold. We shall require the protocol to be such that the above definition always uniquely defines a crew $\hat{G}$ for every good node v. When this is the case, the consistency, correctness and liveness properties are well-defined.

In [15], a somewhat simplistic instantiation of a CellTree architecture, called **CT₀**, is presented and consistency, correctness and liveness guarantees for each node v are provided based on assumptions regarding the goodness of the ancestors of v. Specifically, for a node v and a set of parties G_ϵ, the following assumptions were defined:

- $A_v(G_\epsilon)$ stands for the assumption that the node v is good with respect to G_ϵ.
- $A_v^i(G_\epsilon)$ stands for the assumption that in any set of i consecutive nodes in the path from the root node ϵ to v (or if no such set exists, then in the entire path) there is at least one node that is good with respect to G_ϵ.

Then it was shown that, when G_ϵ is the root node crew used by the `discover` module of **CT₀**, the following guarantees hold:

$$A_v^\ell(G_\epsilon) \Rightarrow \text{consistency}(v),$$
$$A_v(G_\epsilon) \wedge A_v^\ell(G_\epsilon) \Rightarrow \text{correctness}(v),$$
$$A_v^1(G_\epsilon) \Rightarrow \text{liveness}(v).$$

This follows from the fact that, when A_v^ℓ holds, the `discover` module of **CT₀** would indeed return the "correct" crew of v, and all updates made at v will be verified by a good node's crew. Further, the correctness of the merkle hash value propagated to the root would be verified by a chain of good nodes. These checks are enough to ensure consistency(v). correctness(v) is (and needs to be) guaranteed only when v is also a good node. The strongest assumption $A_v^1(G_\epsilon)$ is used for guaranteeing liveness(v). In $\mathbf{CT_0}$, for the sake of simplicity, a node's crew directly communicates only with the crews of its parent and its two children. Thus, for any ancestor u of v, if u's crew fails or turns corrupt (which requires a majority of the crew members to fail/turn corrupt), then v will not be able to communicate its updates towards the root, beyond u. A more sophisticated instantiation of the CellTree architecture can base liveness(v) also on a similar assumption as A_v^ℓ, rather than A_v^1.

Even so, we point out that A_v^1 is not an overly strong assumption. It requires only *the nodes in the path from the root to* v being good, which is only an exponentially small fraction of all the nodes created in the tree (assuming a well-balanced tree); also it is a set of nodes that are known at the time of creating the node v. Nodes created in the future (even descendents of v) have no effect on any of these guarantees, including liveness.

4.1   Performance Parameters

The CellTree architecture is designed to be scalable, so that a node's communication, computation and storage stay bounded even as the tree grows. The only parameter of the size of the tree that affects a node's complexity is the depth of the node itself (due to the need to store old versions of a cell until newer versions are assimilated at the root), which does not change once the node is created.

Latency: The latency for assimilation and receiving the proof of assimilation depends linearly on the length of the path from the assimilation root aroot to that node, l. During the leafward propagation step, at each node the procedure LEAFWARDPROPAGATION can be triggered right after the parent node has finished their leafward propagation procedure. Therefore, the proof of assimilation arrives at the node within time given by the sum of time differences for rootward propagation between each node and its parent, and leafward propagation between a node (bounded by ϕ) and its child for l nodes.

Storage: Each crew member of a node at depth d stores the following: (1) a nucleus for each of the nodes monitored by it, (2) the last cell (of its own node) for which a proof of assimilation was received, all the cells whose nuclei have been propagated rootwards but whose proofs of assimilation have not yet arrived, and the current cell, (3) proofs of assimilation from the root consisting of at most $O(d)$ hash values and a single crew-signature, and (4) the nuclei of all the local updates since the last rootward propagation. At steady state, the total storage needed can be bounded by the cell size β and $d\phi$ the dominant terms in latency between receiving two proof of assimilation as all the state between these need to be stored.

Communication: Typically, a crew member communicates with its peers in the crew for consensus (left to a module), as well as with members of the crews of nodes that monitor it or that it monitors. Addressing the amount of data communicated between *nodes*, it depends on the size of the messages and the number of such messages during assimilation.

During ROOTWARDPROPAGATION, assimilation signals consisting of a list of unassimilated nuclei from each monitored node is sent to the node. During LEAFWARDPROPAGATION, the proof of assimilation of size at most $O(d)$ is communicated.

5   Using a CellTree: A Banking Application

In this section we explore how the CellTree architecture can be used in a real-life application. For illustration, we consider a decentralized banking application, that allows speedy transactions between account holders (possibly from different banks).

Unlike a typical blockchain implementation, we shall not require a single ledger that holds all the transactions. Instead, it is natural in a CellTree to allocate a separate cell for each user (with the binary address of the cell in the tree playing the role of an account number). The cell holds all the relevant data related to the account, including additional information required to carry out transactions (as described below). The crews maintaining the cells can be drawn from a pool of service providers, including regulatory agencies, banks' agents and other commercial agents. The correctness, consistency and liveness conditions of the CellTree along with the programs in the cells' nuclei (described below) ensure the integrity of the account information.

We briefly sketch how a transaction is carried out between two accounts. At a high-level, the individual cells would locally update their cell information, with the monitoring cells ensuring that this is done correctly. Since different cells evolve asynchronously, the update would be carried out in a few steps.

Firstly, outside of the CellTree infrastructure, the two account holders agree on the details of the transaction – the account addresses, amount transferred, timestamps and sequence numbers, and random nonces contributed by the two parties. A transaction ID is computed by hashing these transaction details.

To evolve, the two cells play the role of an *initiator* and a *responder*. First, the initiator evolves, and after its evolution is (sufficiently) assimilated, the responder evolves. The initiator incorporates the transaction into an *outstanding transactions* list, and then the responder will evolve to incorporate this transaction into its *recently accepted transactions* list. For this to be a valid evolution for the sender (according to the programs in the nuclear code), the account balance of the sender should permit the current transaction, after subtracting all the outgoing amounts in the outstanding transactions, but not adding any of the outstanding incoming amounts (some flexibility consistent with a bank's policies could be programmed into the cell). For the responder (whether it is the sender or the receiver), it is also verified that a transaction with this transaction ID exists in the initiator's outstanding transactions list (using an appropriate `fetch` module).

Finally, the initiator's cell should evolve to close the outstanding transaction (moving it to a *recently closed transactions* list), and update its account balance. For this it is checked that the transaction ID being closed appears in the responder's recently closed transactions list. During every evolution it is also checked that there are no outstanding transactions that have *expired* (i.e., too old to be accepted); all such transactions must be closed or *canceled*, depending on whether the initiator has accepted the transaction or not. Also, the "recent" lists must be cleared of sufficiently old entries.

Note that the transaction between two accounts does not involve any action from a bank (except if there are agents of the bank involved as crew members in the transacting cells or their monitors). However, if a transaction occurs between accounts in different banks, the banks do need to carry out a transaction between each other. Such transactions are carried out periodically (say, once every day), using a similar process as above to update their balance sheets.

A customer can also carry out direct transactions with the bank, correspond- ing to deposits, withdrawals, interest payments and banking charges. The link between physical currency deposited at the bank branches or withdrawn from ATMs is established by the bank. Other instruments like cheques, demand drafts and bank transfers using other digital means (other than on the CellTree) will also require the banks to be involved in the transaction.

We rely on the CellTree for the correctness, consistency and liveness condi- tions. To ensure this, the crews have to be sufficiently trustworthy. These crews could consist of agents of the banking system as well as commercial agents that the account holders can hire. One may also use an instance of the CellTree architecture which provides better liveness guarantees than $\mathbf{CT_0}$.

Another important consideration in using a CellTree for bank accounts is that of privacy. This can be addressed using the following measures:

- The `fetch` modules will incorporate access control layers to ensure that only authorized users can read the contents of a cell.
- To facilitate transactions, crews of other cells are allowed to check if a trans- action ID is present in the outstanding transactions list of the cell. The `fetch` module will require that the transaction ID is communicated by the reader and the cell responds only with a boolean answer confirming or denying the existence of the transaction ID. Since the transaction ID itself is a hash includ- ing random nonces, an untrusted cell's crew cannot learn anything using such queries.
- The crews of an account's own cell as well as the cell's monitoring it need access to the contents of the cell or the cell nucleus. As mentioned before, these could be considered trustworthy. But for further security, the crew could use secure multi-party computation to protect against a fraction of the crew members being corrupt (we call such cells "secret cells"). Since secret cells involve more computational effort, one may consider a business model that provides crew members for a secret cell for a fee.

Finally, before such a scheme can be practically deployed, it should also include mechanisms for recovery from errors and failures. This can be accom- plished within the framework of the CellTree architecture by suitably defining the various modules.

6   Extended Features

Above and beyond the features discussed so far, a CellTree can provide richer functionality and stronger security guarantees. We discuss some of these features can be implemented using appropriate modules.

- **Improved Liveness.** The liveness guarantee of the simple construction $\mathbf{CT_0}$ from [15] requires the assumption A_v^1 (see Sect. 4). But this can be improved to hold under A_v^ℓ, by using `rootward` and `leafward` modules that allow crews to directly communicate with all the crews they monitor or which monitor them.
- **Removing the Reliance on a Single Root.** This can be done by allowing more nodes in the CellTree to perform the duties of the root: issuing proofs of assimilation, and acting as the starting point for the `discover` module.
- **Modifying the Crews.** In a realistic instantiation, provisions for adding and removing members to the crew after its formation need to be added for use in revoking the public keys of crew members, for replacing misbehaving crew members, or for resizing a crew.
- **Quality of Service.** The assimilation rate for the CellTree in our usecase is fixed by certain parameters. However, one could support different rates of assimilation to different nodes, thereby providing varying levels of quality of service in terms of efficiency. Further, different nodes could be monitored by different number of nodes, providing different levels of assurance.
- **Pruning, Grafting and Mirroring.** Subtrees can be detached (pruned) from a CellTree, or grafted on to a CellTree – possibly in multiple locations, in case of mirroring – with little effect on the other nodes (which are not monitoring any part of the subtree in question).
- **Excising Cells.** A cell's contents can be deleted, or altered without respecting its program, if *the crews of all the nodes monitoring it* cooperate.
- **Computed Reads.** It is possible to support access to a *function* of a cell's content (with proof).
- **Secret Cells.** The crew members of a node need not be aware of the contents of the cell, but can still provide authorized clients with access to the cell contents, or functions thereof, via secret-sharing or secure multiparty computation protocols.
- **Computing on Multiple Cells.** Concurrent algorithms can be designed to operate on multiple cells, working independently on each cell. This enables maintaining multiple views of a database in different nodes (e.g., in a banking application, each customer's ledger is a partial view of a bank's central ledger).
- **Saplings.** A sapling is a CellTree whose root is assimilated into another parent CellTree. While the parent's crews do not monitor a saplings nodes', they do provide commitment guarantees.
- **Higher Arity Trees.** Higher arity nodes can be easily simulated by allowing the same crew to operate a subtree instead of a single node.
- **Incentivization** The CellTree architecture is agnostic about higher level mechanisms that could be used for incentivizing parties to play the role of

crew members. Different parts of the CellTree may employ different incentivization mechanisms.

Finally, we emphasize that a major feature of the CellTree architecture is the ability for different implementations of the same modules to coexist in the tree, offering application specific features in different parts of the tree. Designing such modules and analyzing their effect on the robustness and performance guarantees of a CellTree are left for future research.

7   Related Work

Merkle trees [11,12], and succinct proofs using them [10] have been valuable tools in cryptographers' toolkit for a long time. Cryptographically authenticated blockchains and public ledgers can be traced back to the work of Haber and Scott [8], but became popular only with the advent of Bitcoin [13] and other crypto currencies that used them for recording their transactions. It is outside the scope of this work to survey all the ensuing innovations in this area.

But below we shall discuss a few distributed data repositories which deviate from the blockchain topology, and mention how the CellTree architecture is different from them in its goals and features.

The *Hashgraph* [4] is a distributed ledger with high transaction throughput as compared to blockchains. Its efficient functioning, however, requires that the set of parties involved in the protocol be aware of all the others. (This is comparable to how a single node's crew operates in a CellTree.) The blocks (or events as they are called) in the Hashgraph form a directed acyclic graph (DAG) with hashpointers as edges (unlike in a blockchain, where the graph is a single path), with new blocks pointing to old blocks (like in a blockchain). As in standard blockchains, the selection and confirmation of new blocks in the ledger are probabilistic, but the ability of all the parties to interact with each other allows the use of an efficient voting protocol (rather than one based on, say, proof-of-work). Also, as in standard blockchains, the desired guarantee is that of immutability or persistence of blocks that are confirmed.

The *Tangle* [14] is a permissionless distributed data structure which also uses a DAG structure to store the transactions, again with the goal of increasing the throughput compared to a blockchain. Tangle allows users to be aware of only parts of the entire data structure. Incidentally, the specific algorithms used for building the DAG structure and considering a node confirmed are known to be susceptible to *"parasitic chain attacks,"* and is the subject of ongoing research [6].

The above two systems store data in a graph with hashpointers as edges that has the form of a DAG (rather than a path), to increase the throughput of transactions. The CellTree architecture shares this feature, but promises even better performance when multi-level confirmation can be exploited. Also, the other differences that CellTree has with blockchains continue to apply to these systems as well.

The *Inter-Planetary File System* (IPFS) [5] is a peer-to-peer version controlled file system in which data items, with (optional links to other data items) can be stored. While different in its goals from blockchains, IPFS is also a distributed data repository, with parties storing some of the IPFS objects in local storage, and accessing others from a peer. The IPFS uses content-addressed sharing, where the address is a hash of the content (with linked objects replaced by their hashes). To detect and avoid duplication, IPFS uses deterministic hashing (no nonces used) so that the same file is hashed to the same address.

Unlike a data repository that is queried using addresses (e.g., the node address in a CellTree), IPFS does not attempt to provide any form of consensus on the "correct" data. All data items, linking to previously existing data items, are valid, and they have their own content-based address. As such, only liveness (all stored data can be retrieved) is of concern to IPFS.

8   Conclusion

A CellTree [15] is designed to be flexible and heterogeneous. It allows data and policy evolution, allows parties to focus on only parts of the repository that are of interest to them, and separates out sub-tasks into modules that can be instantiated differently in different parts of the tree. We present its formal security guarantees and discuss the parameters that bound the performance. We also illustrated how a practical application can be built on a CellTree platform.

We leave it for future work to exploit this novel architecture for more powerful applications.

References

1. Enabling blockchain innovations with pegged sidechains (2014). https://blockstream.com/sidechains.pdf
2. Cardano (2015). https://www.cardano.org
3. The bitcoin lightning network: scalable off-chain instant payments (2016). https://lightning.network/lightning-network-paper.pdf
4. Leemon, B., Mance, H., Paul, M.: Hedera: a governing council and public hashgraph network (2017). https://www.hederahashgraph.com/whitepaper
5. Benet, J.: IPFS - content addressed, versioned, P2P file system. CoRR, abs/1407.3561 (2014)
6. Cullen, A., Ferraro, P., King, C.K., Shorten, R.: Distributed ledger technology for IoT: parasite chain attacks. CoRR, abs/1904.00996 (2019)
7. Gilad, Y., Hemo, R., Micali, S., Vlachos, G., Zeldovich, N.: Algorand: scaling byzantine agreements for cryptocurrencies. In: Proceedings of the 26th Symposium on Operating Systems Principles, pp. 51–68. ACM (2017)
8. Haber, S., Stornetta, W.S.: How to time-stamp a digital document. In: Menezes, A.J., Vanstone, S.A. (eds.) CRYPTO 1990. LNCS, vol. 537, pp. 437–455. Springer, Heidelberg (1991). https://doi.org/10.1007/3-540-38424-3_32
9. Kiayias, A., Russell, A., David, B., Oliynykov, R.: Ouroboros: a provably secure proof-of-stake blockchain protocol. In: Katz, J., Shacham, H. (eds.) CRYPTO 2017. LNCS, vol. 10401, pp. 357–388. Springer, Cham (2017). https://doi.org/10.1007/978-3-319-63688-7_12

10. Kilian, J.: A note on efficient zero-knowledge proofs and arguments. In: Proceedings of the Twenty-Fourth Annual ACM Symposium on Theory of Computing, pp. 723–732. ACM (1992)
11. Merkle, R.C.: Method of providing digital signatures. US Patent 4309569 (1982)
12. Merkle, R.C.: A digital signature based on a conventional encryption function. In: Pomerance, C. (ed.) CRYPTO 1987. LNCS, vol. 293, pp. 369–378. Springer, Heidelberg (1988). https://doi.org/10.1007/3-540-48184-2_32
13. Nakamoto, S.: Bitcoin: a peer-to-peer electronic cash system (2009). http://www.bitcoin.org/bitcoin.pdf
14. Popov, S.: The tangle (2017). http://iotatoken.com/IOTA_Whitepaper.pdf
15. Prabhakaran, M., Trehan, A., Acharya, A.: CellTree: a new paradigm for distributed data repositories (2019). https://eprint.iacr.org/2019/516

Secure Information Flow Analysis Using the PRISM Model Checker

Ali A. Noroozi$^{(\boxtimes)}$, Khayyam Salehi, Jaber Karimpour, and Ayaz Isazadeh

Department of Computer Science, University of Tabriz, Tabriz, Iran
{noroozi,kh_salehi,karimpour,isazadeh}@tabrizu.ac.ir

Abstract. Secure information flow checks whether sensitive information leak to public outputs of a program or not. It has been widely used to analyze the security of various programs and protocols and guarantee their confidentiality and robustness.

In this paper, the problem of verifying secure information flow of concurrent probabilistic programs is discussed. Programs are modeled by Markovian processes and secure information flow is specified by observational determinism. Then, two algorithms are proposed to verify observational determinism in the Markovian model. The algorithms employ a trace-based approach to traverse the model and check for satisfiability of observational determinism. The proposed algorithms have been implemented into a tool called PRISM-Leak, which is constructed on the PRISM model checker. An anonymity protocol, the dining cryptographers, is discussed as a case study to show how PRISM-Leak can be used to evaluate the security of programs. The scalability of the tool is demonstrated by comparing it to the state-of-the-art information flow tools.

Keywords: Information security · Secure information flow · Observational determinism · Markovian processes · PRISM-Leak

1 Introduction

Secure information flow is an important mechanism to discover leakages in various programs and protocols [3,28]. Leakages occur when an attacker infers information about *secret* inputs of a program by observing its *public* outputs. In order to detect leakages and prevent insecure information flows, a security property needs to be defined to specify secure behavior of the program and a verification method is used to check whether the property holds or not.

Many security properties have been introduced in the literature, including *observational determinism*, which specifies secure information flow for concurrent programs. Introduced by McLean [17] and Roscoe [26] and improved by Zdancewic and Myers [32] and many others [9,12,14,15,20,21,31], observational determinism requires a concurrent program to produce traces, i.e., sequences of public values, that appear deterministic and thus indistinguishable to the

© Springer Nature Switzerland AG 2019
D. Garg et al. (Eds.): ICISS 2019, LNCS 11952, pp. 154–172, 2019.
https://doi.org/10.1007/978-3-030-36945-3_9

attacker. However, existing definitions of observational determinism are not precise enough and are rather too restrictive or too permissive. An ideal security property should be restrictive enough to reject insecure programs and permissive enough to accept secure programs. Furthermore, most of these definitions are scheduler-independent [9,12,14,15,21,31,32]. Since the security of a concurrent program depends on the choice of a scheduler and might change by modifying the scheduler, observational determinism needs to be defined scheduler-specific [20].

For verifying satisfiability of observational determinism, various methods, including type systems [31,32], logics [9,12,14] and algorithmic verification [15,20,21] have been used. Type systems are often too restrictive and non-automatic. Logic-based methods can be precise, but require a significant amount of manual effort. Algorithmic verification is automatic, but existing methods are not scalable. In fact, there is no automatic and scalable algorithmic verification tool for checking observational determinism.

In this paper, an automatic approach is proposed to specify and algorithmically verify observational determinism for concurrent probabilistic programs using the PRISM model checker. Assume a concurrent program that contains probabilistic modules with shared variables and a probabilistic scheduler that determines the execution order of statements of the modules. The program contains public, secret and possibly neutral variables. The set of public variables is denoted by L. Furthermore, assume an attacker that is able to pick a scheduler, run the program under control of the scheduler and observe the program traces. The attacker does not influence the initial values of the public variables, i.e., the program has no public input.

Considering these assumptions, we model programs using Markovian processes. Observational determinism is defined to be scheduler-specific and more precise. It contains two conditions, OD_1 and OD_2, which a program needs to satisfy both to be observationally deterministic. OD_1 requires prefix and stutter equivalence for traces of each public variable and OD_2 enforces existential stutter equivalence for traces of all public variables. To verify these conditions, two trace-based algorithms are proposed. The proposed approach has been validated by implementing the algorithms in PRISM-Leak [24], which is a tool for evaluating secure information flow of concurrent probabilistic programs. PRISM-Leak has been built upon the PRISM model checker [16] to check the security of PRISM programs. Finally, a case study is discussed and the scalability of the proposed algorithms is compared to the state-of-the-art tools of information flow analysis. The experimental results show that PRISM-Leak has the best performance among the tools that are capable of analyzing the case study.

In summary, the paper contributes to the literature by

- a formal definition of observational determinism on a Markovian program model,
- two algorithms to verify the conditions of observational determinism,
- an automatic and scalable tool to verify observational determinism for concurrent probabilistic programs defined in the PRISM language.

The paper proceeds as follows. Section 2 provides the core background on the Markovian processes, the dining cryptographers protocol and various types of information flow channels considered in this paper. Section 3 discusses the related work and their strengths and weaknesses. Section 4 presents a formal definition of observational determinism and Sect. 5 proposes two verification algorithms. In Sect. 6, the verification algorithms are evaluated and compared to the existing approaches. We conclude the paper in Sect. 7 and discuss some future work.

2   Background

2.1   Markovian Models

Markovian models allow us to define states and transitions containing enough information to extract all traces of a program that are visible to the attacker. *Markov decision processes (MDPs)* are used to model operational semantics of concurrent probabilistic programs. Furthermore, *memoryless probabilistic schedulers*, a simple but important subclass of schedulers, are used to denote schedulers of concurrent programs. When a memoryless probabilistic scheduler is applied to an MDP, a *Markov chain (MC)* is produced, which is the final model used in this paper for specifying observational determinism and verifying it. Here, the notations used throughout the paper are formally defined. For more information on how Markovian models and schedulers work, please see chapter 10 of [1].

Definition 1. *A **Markov decision process (MDP)** is a tuple $\mathcal{M} = (S, Act, \mathbf{P}, \zeta, Val_L, V)$ where S is a set of states, Act is a set of actions, $\mathbf{P} : S \times Act \times S \to [0,1]$ is a transition probability function such that $\forall s \in S. \ \forall \alpha \in Act. \ \sum_{s' \in S} \mathbf{P}(s, \alpha, s') \in \{0,1\}$, the function $\zeta : S \to [0,1]$ is an initial distribution such that $\sum_{s \in S} \zeta(s) = 1$, Val_L is the finite set of values of the public variables and $V : S \to Val_L$ is a labeling function.*

An MDP $\mathcal{M}$ is called *finite* if S, Act, and Val_L are finite. An action α is *enabled* in state s if and only if $\sum_{s' \in S} \mathbf{P}(s, \alpha, s') = 1$. Let $Act(s)$ denote the set of enabled actions in s. In our program model, actions represent the program statements.

An MDP with no action and nondeterminism is called a Markov Chain.

Definition 2. *A (discrete-time) **Markov chain (MC)** is a tuple $\mathcal{M} = (S, \mathbf{P}, \zeta, Val_L, V)$ where $\mathbf{P} : S \times S \to [0,1]$ is a transition probability function such that $\forall s \in S. \ \sum_{s' \in S} \mathbf{P}(s, s') = 1$. The other elements, i.e., S, ζ, Val_L and V are the same as MDP.*

Given a state s, a memoryless probabilistic scheduler returns a probability for each action $\alpha \in Act(s)$. This random choice is independent of what has happened in the history, i.e., which path led to the current state. This is why it is called memoryless. Let $\mathcal{D}(\mathcal{X})$ denote the set of all probability distributions over a set $\mathcal{X}$. Formally,

Definition 3. *Let $\mathcal{M} = (S, Act, \mathbf{P}, \zeta, Val_L, V)$ be an MDP. A **memoryless probabilistic scheduler** for $\mathcal{M}$ is a function $\delta : S \to \mathcal{D}(Act)$, such that $\delta(s) \in \mathcal{D}(Act(s))$ for all $s \in S$.*

As all nondeterministic choices in an MDP $\mathcal{M}$ are resolved by a scheduler δ, a Markov chain $\mathcal{M}_\delta$ is induced. Formally,

Definition 4. *Let $\mathcal{M} = (S, Act, \mathbf{P}, \zeta, Val_L, V)$ be an MDP and $\delta : S \to \mathcal{D}(Act)$ be a memoryless probabilistic scheduler on $\mathcal{M}$. The **MC of $\mathcal{M}$ induced by δ** is given by*

$$\mathcal{M}_\delta = (S, \mathbf{P}_\delta, \zeta, Val_L, V)$$

where

$$\mathbf{P}_\delta(s, s') = \sum_{\alpha \in Act(s)} \delta(s)(\alpha).\mathbf{P}(s, \alpha, s').$$

In what follows, we fix an MC $\mathcal{M}_\delta^\mathbf{P} = (S, \mathbf{P}_\delta, \zeta, Val_L, V)$ which models the executions of the concurrent probabilistic program $\mathbf{P}$ under the control of a scheduler δ. A state of $\mathcal{M}_\delta^\mathbf{P}$ indicates the current values of variables, together with the current value of the program counter that indicates the next program statement to be executed. The function V *labels* each state with values of the public variables in that state. In fact, a state label is what an attacker observes in that state.

The set of *successors* of s is defined as $Post(s) = \{s' \mid \mathbf{P}_\delta(s, s') > 0\}$. The states s with $\zeta(s) > 0$ are considered as the *initial states*. The set of initial states of $\mathcal{M}_\delta^\mathbf{P}$ is denoted by $Init(\mathcal{M}_\delta^\mathbf{P})$. To ensure $\mathcal{M}_\delta^\mathbf{P}$ is non-blocking, we include a self-loop to each state s that has no successor, i.e., $\mathbf{P}_\delta(s, s) = 1$. Then, a state s is called *final* if $Post(s) = \{s\}$. It is assumed that all final states correspond to the termination of the program.

A **path** (or execution path) π of $\mathcal{M}_\delta^\mathbf{P}$ is an infinite state sequence $s_0 s_1 \ldots s_n^\omega$ such that $s_0 \in Init(\mathcal{M}_\delta^\mathbf{P})$, $s_i \in Post(s_{i-1})$ for all $0 < i \leq n$, s_n is a final state and ω denotes infinite iteration (self-loop over s_n). The set of paths starting from a state s is denoted by $Paths(s)$. The set of all paths of $\mathcal{M}_\delta^\mathbf{P}$ is denoted by $Paths(\mathcal{M}_\delta^\mathbf{P})$.

A **trace** of a path $\pi = s_0 s_1 \ldots s_n^\omega$ is defined as $T = trace_{|L}(\pi) = V(s_0) V(s_1) \ldots V(s_n)^\omega$. We refer to n as the length of T, i.e., $length(T) = n$. The labeling function, instead of all public variables, can be restricted to just a single public variable $l \in L$, i.e., $V_{|l} : S \to Val_l$. Then, the trace of π on l is defined as $T_{|l} = trace_{|l}(\pi) = V_{|l}(s_0) V_{|l}(s_1) \ldots V_{|l}(s_n)^\omega$. Note that $T_{|L} = trace_{|L}(\pi)$. The set of traces starting from a state s is denoted by $Traces(s)$. The set of all trace of $\mathcal{M}_\delta^\mathbf{P}$ is denoted by $Traces(\mathcal{M}_\delta^\mathbf{P})$.

Two traces T and T' are **stutter equivalent**, denoted $T \triangleq T'$, if they are both of the form $A_0^+ A_1^+ A_2^+ \ldots$ for $A_0, A_1, A_2, \cdots \subseteq Val_L$ where A_i^+ is the

Kleene plus operation on A_i and is defined as $A_i^+ = \{A_i^k \mid k \in \mathbb{N}, k \geq 1\}$. A finite trace T_1 is called a prefix of T, if there exists another infinite trace T_2 such that $T_1 T_2 = T$. Two traces are **prefix and stutter equivalent**, denoted by $\triangleq_p$, if one is stutter equivalent to a prefix of another. For example, the traces $[0, 0, 0, 1, 1^\omega]$ and $[0, 1, 1, 1^\omega]$ are stutter equivalent and the traces $[0, 0, 0, 2, 1^\omega]$ and $[0, 2, 1, 1, 4, 4^\omega]$ are prefix and stutter equivalent.

A state s is **low-equivalent** to another state s', written $s =_L s'$, if $V(s) = V(s')$. Low-equivalence can also be defined on a single public variable $l \in L$: $s =_l s'$ if $V_{|l}(s) = V_{|l}(s')$. This relation corresponds to the observational power of the attacker. When two states are low-equivalent, they are the same to the attacker, even if secret values differ in these states.

DAG Structure of Markovian Models. We assume the programs always terminate and states indicate the current values of the variables and the program counter. Furthermore, loops of the program are unfolded. This implies that Markovian models of every program takes the form of a *directed acyclic graph (DAG)*, ignoring later-added self-loops of final states. Initial states of the program are represented as roots of the DAG and final states as leaves. Therefore, there is no loop in the Markovian models (except later-added self-loops) and all path lead to a final state.

2.2   Dining Cryptographers Protocol

We use the *dining cryptographers protocol* [7] as a base to compare precision of various definitions of observational determinism. It is well-known and highly-studied anonymity protocol and thus suitable for comparison purposes.

In the dining cryptographers protocol, n cryptographers are having dinner at a round table. After dinner, they are told that the dinner has been paid by their master or one of the cryptographers. They want to know whether the master has paid the dinner or not, without revealing the identity of the payer cryptographer, if the master did not pay. Hence, each cryptographer tosses an unbiased coin and shows the result only to the right cryptographer. If the two coins that a cryptographer can observe are the same, then she announces 'agree'; otherwise, announces 'disagree'. However, if she is the actual payer, then she announces 'disagree' for the same coins and 'agree' for the different ones. If n is odd, then an even number of 'agree's implies that one of the cryptographers has paid, while an odd number implies that the master has paid. The latter is reverse for an even n.

Assume an external attacker (none of the cryptographers or the master) who tries to find out the payer's identity. The external attacker can observe the announcements of the cryptographers. Two cases are assumed for the secret, i.e., the payer:

1. one of the cryptographers, i.e., $Val_{payer} = \{c_1, \ldots, c_n\}$,
2. the master (m, for short) or one of the cryptographers, i.e., $Val_{payer} = \{m, c_1, \ldots, c_n\}$.

For the first case, where the payer is one of the cryptographers, the protocol is secure and there is no leakage. But for the second case, where the master is also a candidate to be the payer, the protocol is insecure [7]. Therefore, it is expected for a security definition to classify the first case as secure and the second case as insecure.

2.3 Information Flow Channels

Information flow channels are mechanisms that transfer secret information to the attacker. There are various types of channels: *direct, indirect, possibilistic* [6], *termination behavior* [14], *internally observable timing* [27], *probabilistic* [6], and *externally observable timing* [29].

Direct channels occur when the value of a secret variable is directly assigned to a public variable. Indirect channels occur when the control structure of the program reveals secret information. Possibilistic channels occur in concurrent programs when an interleaving of the components results in a direct or indirect channel. Termination channels reveal secret information through the termination or non-termination of program execution. Internally observable timing channels happen when secret information affects the timing behavior of a module, which, through the scheduler, influences the execution order of updates to public variables. Probabilistic channels leak sensitive information through the probabilistic behavior of the program. Externally observable timing channels occur when sensitive information affect the timing behavior of the program.

3 Related Work

In this section, existing definitions of observational determinism are presented and compared to each other. We formalize all these definitions in our program model $\mathcal{M}_\delta^P$ in order to make the comparison and discussion easier. Since we assumed the attacker does not influence the initial values of the public variables, all the initial states are low-equivalent, i.e., $s_0 =_L s_0'$. A concurrent program P under a scheduler δ satisfies observational determinism, according to

- Zdancewic and Myers [32], if and only if all traces of each public variable are prefix and stutter equivalent, i.e.,

$$\forall T, T' \in Traces(\mathcal{M}_\delta^P), l \in L. \ T_{|l} \triangleq_p T_{|l}';$$

- Huisman et al. [14], iff all traces of each public variable are stutter equivalent, i.e.,

$$\forall T, T' \in Traces(\mathcal{M}_\delta^P), l \in L. \ T_{|l} \triangleq T_{|l}';$$

- Terauchi [31], iff all traces of all public variables are prefix and stutter equivalent, i.e.,

$$\forall T, T' \in Traces(\mathcal{M}_\delta^P). \ T_{|L} \triangleq_p T_{|L}';$$

- Huisman and Blondeel [12], Karimpour et al. [15] and Dabaghchian and Abdollahi [9], iff all traces of all public variables are stutter equivalent, i.e.,

$$\forall T, T' \in Traces(\mathcal{M}_\delta^\mathrm{P}). \ T_{|L} \triangleq T'_{|L};$$

- Ngo et al. [20], iff the following two conditions are satisfied:
  SSOD-1: $\forall T, T' \in Traces(\mathcal{M}_\delta^\mathrm{P}), l \in L. \ T_{|l} \triangleq T'_{|l};$
  SSOD-2: $\forall s_0, s_0' \in Init(\mathcal{M}_\delta^\mathrm{P}), \forall T \in Traces(s_0), \exists T' \in Traces(s_0'). \ T_{|L} \triangleq T'_{|L};$
- Noroozi et al. [21], iff all paths of all public variables are divergence weak low-bisimilar, i.e.,

$$\forall \pi, \pi' \in Paths(\mathcal{M}_\delta^\mathrm{P}). \ \pi \approx_L^{div} \pi',$$

where divergence weak low-bisimulation ($\approx_L^{div}$) is an equivalence relation that relates two paths that mutually mimic behavior of each other.

Note that all these definitions, except Ngo et al. [20], are scheduler-independent and consider all possible interleavings of the modules. We redefined them in our scheduler-specific model in order to make the comparison easier.

Zdancewic and Myers define observational determinism in terms of prefix and stutter equivalence of traces of each public variable. This definition correctly accepts the first case of the dining cryptographers protocol. However, it incorrectly accepts the second case too. This shows that the definition is too permissive. On the other hand, requiring stutter equivalence of traces of each public variable, as in Huisman et al. [14], is too restrictive and incorrectly rejects the first case of the protocol. Furthermore, requiring traces to agree on the updates to all public variables, as in [9,12,15,21,31], is too restrictive. For example, the first case of the dining cryptographers protocol is incorrectly rejected by all of these definitions. In our experiments with different programs, we found the definition of Ngo et al. [20] the most precise of all. However, SSOD-1 was not permissive enough. For example, it incorrectly rejected the first case of the dining cryptographers.

Observational determinism has also been defined using traces of operations that read or write on public variables, instead of traces of public values. Well-known examples of these definitions are LSOD [10] and its improvements, RLSOD [10] and iRLSOD [6]. These definitions have been implemented in a tool, named JOANA [11], which uses program dependence graphs to model JAVA programs and verify them. JOANA does not explicitly classify variables into public or secret. However, it offers the ability to classify program statements into low (public) or high (secret). Thus, a variable might contain a public value at one point of the program, but a secret value at another point. This allows JOANA to detect intermediate leakages if a statement in intermediate steps is labeled as low. The use of program dependence graphs makes JOANA a scalable tool but reduces its precision. LSOD [10] and its relaxed forms, RLSOD [10] and iRLSOD [6] incorrectly produced security violations for many examples we tried, including the first case of the dining cryptographers protocol. JOANA only works with dependencies and does not take into account concrete values of variables or explicit probability distributions, as in the dining cryptographers protocol. This is an inherent limitation for all analyses that are based on program dependence graphs.

There are probabilistic versions of observational determinism for concurrent programs, such as probabilistic noninterference [19,23,29,30]. These properties match transition probabilities, in addition to the traces. This is a rather strong condition which can detect probabilistic channels but is too restrictive for most cases and programs.

To verify observational determinism, Zdancewic and Myers [32] and Terauchi [31] use type systems, which are widely used to verify secure information flow. However, they are not extensible [2]. They can be defined compositional, but at the cost of either being too restrictive or losing automatic analysis [6].

Huisman et al. [14], Huisman and Blondeel [12], Huisman and Ngo [13] and Dabaghchian and Abdollahi [9] use logic-based methods to specify observational determinism and verify it. These methods build a self-composed model [2] of the program. Then, observational determinism is specified using a program logic, such as CTL*, modal μ-calculus, LTL or CTL. Out of these methods, Huisman and Blondeel [12] and Dabaghchian and Abdollahi [9] have verified the specified property using the model checking tools Concurrency Workbench and SPIN, respectively. In contrast to type systems and program dependence graphs, logical-based methods can specify arbitrarily precise definitions for observational determinism. Most of these methods are compositional. However, they are often non-automatic and require a significant amount of manual effort.

Ngo et al. [20], Karimpour et al. [15] and Noroozi et al. [21] use algorithmic verification methods. These methods mostly model the program as a state transitions system and specify the property using states, paths, and traces of the transition system. Ngo et al. [20] model programs using Kripke structures and use a trace-based method to verify SSOD-1. In order to verify SSOD-2, they determinize the Kripke model and compute a bisimulation quotient of the determinezed model. The time complexity of verifying SSOD-1 is linear in the size of the model, whereas verifying SSOD-2 is exponential. Karimpour et al. [15] and Noroozi et al. [21] compute a weak bisimulation quotient of the model and then verify observational determinism. Algorithmic verification methods make it possible to specify secure information flow with arbitrary precision. They are fully-automatic but generally less scalable, in comparison with type systems and program dependence graphs.

A closely-related filed to secure information flow is quantitative information flow, in which information theory is used to measure the amount of information leakage of a program. If the leakage is computed to be 0, then the program is secure. Many methods and tools are available to compute the information leakage of various programs, including LeakWatch [8], QUAIL [5], HyLeak [4] and PRISM-Leak [24]. LeakWatch [8] estimates leakage of Java programs, including multi-threaded programs and taking into account the intermediate leakages. QUAIL [5] precisely computes leakage at final states of sequential programs, written in the QUAIL imperative language. HyLeak [4] is an extension of QUAIL and combines estimation and precise methods in order to improve the scalability. Finally, PRISM-Leak [24] contains a quantitative package that uses a trace-based method [22] to precisely compute leakage of concurrent probabilistic programs, written in the PRISM language [16]. In quantifying information leakage, PRISM-Leak takes into account the intermediate leakages occurred in the intermediate steps of the program executions.

4 Specifying Observational Determinism

In this section, observational determinism is defined in the Markovian model $\mathcal{M}_\delta^P$. The definition should be able to detect direct, indirect, possibilistic, internally observable timing and termination channels. In order to detect external timing or probabilistic channels, the security property should be strengthened further. For example, to detect external timing channels, the property should require *equivalence* of traces. This makes the property too restrictive, which is the exact opposite of this paper's goal. Therefore, external timing and probabilistic channels are not considered in this paper.

As Ngo et al. [20] discuss, a concurrent program might be secure with a scheduler and insecure with another one and thus defining observational determinism to be scheduler-independent makes the definition imprecise. Therefore, we define observational determinism to be scheduler-specific. Another benefit of a scheduler-specific property is that it is able to find those schedulers that the program is insecure under control of them. This makes the property immune to refinement attacks, in which the attacker selects a scheduler in order to limit the set of possible traces of the program and infer secret information from these traces.

Observational determinism requires a concurrent program to be deterministic to the attacker and produce indistinguishable traces. It demands that low-equivalent inputs produce low-equivalent traces and thus changes in the secret inputs do not change the public behavior. Inspired by Ngo et al. [20], we define observational determinism scheduler-specific and require existential stutter equivalence for traces of all public variables. However, we relax the requirement of stutter equivalence for traces of each public variable to prefix and stutter equivalence in order to improve precision and thus reduce the number of false alarms.

Definition 5. *Let $\mathcal{M}_\delta^P$ be a Markov chain, modeling executions of a concurrent probabilistic program P under the control of a scheduler δ. Formally, P satisfies observational determinism, iff OD_1 and OD_2 hold:*

OD_1: $\forall T, T' \in Traces(\mathcal{M}_\delta^P), l \in L.\ \ T_{|l} \triangleq_p T'_{|l}$,

OD_2: $\forall s_0, s'_0 \in Init(\mathcal{M}_\delta^P), \forall T \in Traces(s_0), \exists T' \in Traces(s'_0).\ \ T_{|L} \triangleq T'_{|L}$.

OD_1 requires that traces agree on the updates to each public variable. This requirement enforces deterministic observable behavior and thus the secret data do not affect the public variables.

OD_2 requires that there always exists a matching trace of all public variables for any possible initial states. This requirement results in the independence of the relative ordering of updates to the public variables from the secret values.

Both OD_1 and OD_2 correctly recognize the first case of the dining cryptographers protocol as secure. OD_1 labels the second case secure, but OD_2 labels it insecure. Therefore, our definition of observational determinism correctly recognizes the first case as secure and the second case as insecure.

For an example of an indirect channel, consider the following program, from Huisman et al. [14]

```
P1 ≡ while h>0 do
        l1:=l1+1;
        h:=h-1
     od;
     l2:=1
```

where h is a secret variable and l1 and l2 are public variables, initially set to 0. The program is insecure, because the final value of l1 contains the initial value of h. It produces the following traces of all public variables

$$h \leq 0 \ : \ [(0,0),(0,1)^\omega],$$
$$h == 1 : \ [(0,0),(1,0),(1,1)^\omega],$$
$$h == 2 : \ [(0,0),(1,0),(2,0),(2,1)^\omega],$$
$$h == 3 : \ [(0,0),(1,0),(2,0),(3,0),(3,1)^\omega],$$
$$\vdots$$

If we consider the public variables separately, the traces $[0^\omega]$, $[0,1^\omega]$, $[0,1,2^\omega]$, $[0,1,2,3^\omega]$, ... for l1 and the traces $[0^+,1^\omega]$ for l2. Obviously, the separate traces are stutter and prefix equivalent and thus OD_1 holds for this program. However, OD_2 does not hold, because for the trace $[(0,0),(0,1)^\omega]$, for example, there does not exist a stutter equivalent trace of other initial states. Therefore, our definition of observational determinism detects the termination channel of this program.

Allowing prefixing in OD_1 makes it vulnerable to termination channels [14]. However, these channels are detected by OD_2, which requires existential stutter equivalence. For example, consider the following program, which contains a termination channel

```
P2 ≡ if h>0 then l:=1 else S1 fi
```

where

```
S1 ≡ while true do skip od
```

where l is a public variable, with the initial value of 0. The attacker can infer truth value of h>0 from termination of the program. P2 has the following traces

$$h > 0 \ : \ [0,1^\omega],$$
$$h \leq 0 \ : \ [0^\omega].$$

OD_2 does not hold and thus observational determinism detects this channel.

As an example of a possibilistic channel, consider the following program, from Ngo [18]

```
P3 ≡ [S2 || S3]
```

where

```
S2 ≡ if l=1 then l:=h else skip fi
S3 ≡ l:=1
```

and l is initially set to 0 and $||$ is the parallel operator with shared variables. The modules S2 and S3 are secure if they are run separately. However, concurrent execution of the modules under a uniform scheduler might reveal the whole value of h. P3 under a uniform scheduler has the following traces

$$S2 \text{ is executed first: } [0, 0, 1^\omega],$$
$$S3 \text{ is executed first: } [0, 1, h^\omega].$$

OD_2 does not hold and thus our definition correctly labels this program as insecure. This example also demonstrates the importance of defining observational determinism scheduler-specific. If P3 is executed by a scheduler that always picks S2 first, then the program would be secure. However, it is insecure for a uniform scheduler. Therefore, the security of a concurrent program should be discussed in the context of a given scheduler.

For internally observable timing channels, consider the following program, from Russo et al. [27]

```
P4 ≡ [S4 || S5]
```

where

```
S4 ≡ if h ≥ 0 then skip; skip
              else skip fi;
     l:=1
S5 ≡ skip; skip; l:=0
```

and l has the initial value of 0. Under a one-step round-robin scheduler that picks S5 for the first step, the following traces are produced

$$h \geq 0 : [0, 0, 0, 0, 0, 0, 1^\omega],$$
$$h < 0 : [0, 0, 0, 0, 1, 0^\omega].$$

The truth value of $h \geq 0$ is leaked into l. OD_2 does not hold and hence observational determinism detects this channel.

5   Verifying Observational Determinism

In this section, two algorithms are proposed for verifying the conditions OD_1 and OD_2. The algorithms take $\mathcal{M}_\delta^P$ as input and return true or false for the satisfaction of the conditions. Both algorithms incorporate a path exploration and trace analysis approach to traverse $\mathcal{M}_\delta^P$ and check the required conditions.

5.1   Verifying OD_1

OD_1 requires that all traces of $\mathcal{M}_\delta^P$ be prefix and stutter equivalent. To verify this, a depth-first exhaustive path exploration of $\mathcal{M}_\delta^P$ is performed and prefix and stutter equivalence is checked between the traces. Once a violation is detected, the algorithm stops the exploration and returns *false*; otherwise, it continues until the exploration is complete and returns *true*.

The detailed steps are outlined in Algorithm 1. For each $l \in L$, the algorithm uses a *witness* stutter-free trace for checking whether prefix and stutter equivalence between the traces holds or not. The witness might be changed to another stutter-free trace running the algorithm. First, an empty string is considered as a witness for each l (lines 1 and 2). Then, $\mathcal{M}_\delta^P$ is explored by a depth-first recursive function, i.e., explorePathsOD1(). In order to explore all reachable states, the function is called for each initial state (lines 4 and 5). It starts from a state and traverses all successors of that state (lines 25–26) until a final state is reached (line 11), which shows that a path has been found. When the algorithm finds a path, for each public variable l (line 12) it performs the following steps to check prefix and stutter equivalence (lines 12–23). It extracts a trace (line 13), removes stutter data from it (line 14) and picks the corresponding witness (line 15). If the witness is longer than the trace, then a prefixing test is done: if the trace is not a prefix of the witness, then a violation of OD_1 has been found and the algorithm returns *false* (lines 16–18). If the witness is shorter than the trace, then the second prefixing test is done: if the witness is not a prefix of the trace, then a violation of OD_1 has been found and the algorithm returns *false*; otherwise (the witness is a prefix of the trace), the trace is longer than the witness and it should be the witness for l (lines 19–23). This process continues until a violation is found, for which *false* is returned; or all paths are explored without finding a violation and *true* is returned.

Time Complexity. The number of possible paths of a DAG can be exponential in the number of its states. This implies that the core of Algorithm 1, i.e., finding all the possible paths using depth-first exploration takes time $O(2^n)$ in the worst case, where n is in the number of states of $\mathcal{M}_\delta^P$. Lines 13–23 for extracting the trace of a path, removing stutter steps and checking prefixing takes $O(n)$ in the worst case. These lines repeat for all $l \in L$ and take time $O(n * |L|)$. Therefore, the worst-case time complexity of Algorithm 1 is exponential in the number of states of $\mathcal{M}_\delta^P$. Note that if the program is insecure, Algorithm 1 does not traverse all the paths and stops as soon as a violation is found. Another point worthy of note is that in most of our experiments, programs had a linear number of paths and a few public variables and hence the total time complexity was linear in the size of $\mathcal{M}_\delta^P$.

Algorithm 1. Verifying OD_1

Input: finite MC $\mathcal{M}_\delta^P$
Output: *true* if the program satisfies OD_1; otherwise, *false*

    // Consider an empty string as a witness for each public variable
1: **for** l **in** L **do**
2:     Let *witnesses*$[l]$ be an empty string;
3: Let π be an empty list of states for storing a path;
4: **for** s_0 **in** $Init(\mathcal{M}_\delta^P)$ **do**
5:     result = explorePathsOD1(s_0, π, *witnesses*);
6:     **if** not result **then**
7:         **return** *false*;
8: **return** *true*;

9: **function** explorePathsOD1(s, π, *witnesses*)
10:     π.add(s); *// add state s to the current path from the initial state*
11:     **if** s is a final state **then** *// found a path stored in π*
12:         **for** l **in** L **do**
13:             $T_{|l} = trace_{|l}(\pi)$;
14:             Remove stutter data from $T_{|l}$, yielding stutter-free trace $T_{|l}^{sf}$;
15:             $T_w = witnesses[l]$;
16:             **if** $length(T_{|l}^{sf}) \leq length(T_w)$ **then**
17:                 **if** $T_{|l}^{sf}$ is not prefix of T_w **then**
18:                     **return** *false*;
19:             **else**
20:                 **if** T_w is not prefix of $T_{|l}^{sf}$ **then**
21:                     **return** *false*;
22:                 **else**
23:                     $witnesses[l] = T_{|l}^{sf}$;
24:     **else**
25:         **for** s' **in** $Post(s)$ **do**
26:             result = explorePathsOD1(s', π, *witnesses*);
27:             **if** not result **then**
28:                **return** *false*;
29:     π.pop(); *// done exploring from s, so remove it from π*
30:     **return** *true*;

5.2   Verifying OD_2

OD_2 requires that, given two initial states s_0 and s_0' of $\mathcal{M}_\delta^P$, for each trace of s_0 there exists a stutter equivalent trace of s_0'. This condition can be interpreted as requiring the initial states to have the same set of stutter-free traces:

$$OD_2 : \forall s_0, s_0' \in Init(\mathcal{M}_\delta^P). \ Traces_{sf}(s_0) = Traces_{sf}(s_0').$$

where $Traces_{sf}(s_0)$ denotes the set of stutter-free traces of s_0. To verify this, a depth-first exhaustive path exploration of $\mathcal{M}_\delta^P$ is performed to store all the

Algorithm 2. Verifying OD_2

Input: finite MC $\mathcal{M}_\delta^P$
Output: *true* if the program satisfies OD_2; otherwise, *false*

1: Let π be an empty list of states for storing a path;
2: **for** s_0 in $Init(\mathcal{M}_\delta^P)$ **do**
       // *Consider an empty set of stutter-free traces for each initial state*
3:    Let $allTraces[s_0]$ be an empty set;
4:    explorePathsOD2(s_0, π, $allTraces$);
5: **for** each pair of initial states (s_0, s_0') **do**
6:    **if** $allTraces[s_0] \; != \; allTraces[s_0']$ **then**
7:       **return** *false*;
8: **return** *true*;

9: **function** explorePathsOD2(s, π, $allTraces$)
10:    π.add(s); // *add state s to the current path from the initial state*
11:    **if** s is a final state **then** // *found a path stored in π*
12:       $T_{|L} = trace_{|L}(\pi)$;
13:       Remove stutter data from $T_{|L}$, yielding stutter-free $T_{|L}^{sf}$;
14:       $s_0 = \pi[0]$; // *initial state of π*
15:       $allTraces[s_0].add(T_{|L}^{sf})$;
16:    **else**
17:       **for** s' in $Post(s)$ **do**
18:          explorePathsOD2(s', π, $allTraces$);
19:    π.pop(); // *done exploring from s, so remove it from π*
20:    **return** ;

---

stutter-free traces of each initial state in a set and then the equivalence of the sets is checked.

Algorithm 2 shows the detailed steps. It initiates an empty set for each initial state (lines 2–3). Each set will contain stutter-free traces of the corresponding initial state. The set of traces are extracted by the function explorePathsOD2(), which recursively explores all states of $\mathcal{M}_\delta^P$. When a final state is reached (line 11), the trace of the path from the initial state to the final state is extracted (line 12), stutter removed (line 13) and stored in the corresponding set (lines 14–15). After extracting the set of stutter-free traces of all the initial states, the equivalence of the sets is checked (lines 5–7). If they are all equivalent, then the algorithm returns *true*; otherwise, *false* is returned.

Time Complexity. The core of Algorithm 2 is a depth-first exploration to find all paths of $\mathcal{M}_\delta^P$, which takes time $O(2^n)$ in the worst case. The final check for the equivalence of the sets of traces takes worst-case complexity of $O(t^2)$, where t is the number of initial states of $\mathcal{M}_\delta^P$. Therefore, the time complexity of Algorithm 2 is dominated by a depth-first exploration of paths, which is exponential in the size of $\mathcal{M}_\delta^P$. As discussed in the complexity of Algorithm 1, real-world programs in our experiments had linear time complexity and both algorithms showed a high performance in practice.

6   Experimental Evaluation

In this section, the proposed algorithms are compared to other state-of-the-art tools for information flow analysis. The algorithms have been integrated into PRISM-Leak [24], which is a tool to evaluate secure information flow of concurrent probabilistic programs, written in the PRISM language [16]. PRISM-Leak contains two packages, a qualitative package that checks observational determinism using the algorithms of this paper and a quantitative package which measures various types of information leakage using a trace-based algorithm [22].

PRISM-Leak is based on the PRISM model checker [16]. PRISM is a formal modeling and analysis tool for probabilistic and concurrent programs. It has been widely used in many application domains, including security protocols, distributed algorithms, and many others. It uses the PRISM language to describe programs and build Markovian models of them. It builds the models using binary decision diagrams and multi-terminal binary decision diagrams. PRISM-Leak accesses these data structures to create an explicit list of reachable states and a sparse matrix containing the transitions. It then traverses the model based on Algorithms 1 and 2 to check observational determinism. The source codes and binary package of PRISM-Leak are available for download at [24].

The dining cryptographers protocol is used as a comparative case study. As discussed in the related work, other definitions of observational determinism [9,12,14,15,20,31,32] are imprecise for the dining cryptographers protocol. JOANA, a scalable information flow tool, is also imprecise. The only remaining choice for runtime comparison is the quantitative tools that were introduced in the related work: LeakWatch [8], QUAIL [5], HyLeak [4] and PRISM-Leak [24]. These tools compute a leakage of 0 for the first case of the protocol and a leakage greater than 0 for the second case.

We compare the runtime of the proposed algorithms and the quantitative tools in Table 1 for the first case of the dining cryptographers protocol, where the attacker is external and the master is not a candidate of being the payer. Two columns of the table are allocated for PRISM-Leak: the first column, i.e., quantitative method, is for the quantitative package and the second column, i.e., observational determinism, is for the qualitative package which contains the algorithms of this paper. Since QUAIL and HyLeak did not support concurrency, we considered a sequential version of the dining cryptographers, which is available at [24]. Table 2 compares the runtime of the tools for the second case, where the attacker is external and the payer is the master or one of the cryptographers. These run times have been obtained on a laptop with an Intel Core i7-2640M CPU @ 2.80 GHz × 2 and 8 GB RAM.

As demonstrated by the results in both Tables 1 and 2, the proposed algorithms are faster and more scalable than LeakWatch, QUAIL, and HyLeak and comparable to the quantitative method of PRISM-Leak. In Table 1, the quantitative method of PRISM-Leak is faster than the proposed algorithms, but

Table 1. Runtime comparison of the proposed algorithms to other tools for the first case of the dining cryptographers protocol. Runtime is in seconds and timeout is set to five minutes.

n	LeakWatch [8]	QUAIL [5]	HyLeak [4]	PRISM-Leak [24]	
				Quantitative method [22]	Observational determinism
7	2	1.8	30.5	0.6	**0.7**
8	3.7	3.1	39.7	0.8	**1.2**
9	7.5	6.3	55	1.3	**1.9**
10	15	12.6	72.2	2.9	**3.9**
11	32.2	26.5	97	7.3	**9.6**
12	72.4	62.1	135.4	18.7	**25.2**
13	150.7	151.6	249.3	49.9	**66.7**
14	Timeout	Timeout	Timeout	145.7	**192.4**

in Table 2, algorithms of this paper perform a little better. Note that cores of both qualitative and quantitative packages of PRISM-Leak are the same. They both rely on PRISM to construct the Markov model and use a sparse matrix to access the model transitions. However, the quantitative method traverses the model once to compute the leakage, but the qualitative package traverses it twice (first for OD_1 and second for OD_2). In Table 2, observational determinism does not hold and as soon as the qualitative package discovers that, stops the traversal. This is why the qualitative package outperforms the quantitative method in Table 2.

Table 2. Runtime comparison of the proposed approach to other tools for the second case of the dining cryptographers protocol. Runtime is in seconds and timeout is set to five minutes.

n	LeakWatch [8]	QUAIL [5]	HyLeak [4]	PRISM-Leak [24]	
				Quantitative method [22]	Observational determinism
7	3.1	2.4	30.8	0.6	**0.6**
8	6	4.5	41.7	1	**0.9**
9	12.3	9.7	57	1.5	**1.4**
10	28.2	17.5	75.3	3.5	**3.3**
11	60.5	35	99.3	7.7	**7.4**
12	122.1	78.5	144	20.4	**20.5**
13	Timeout	156.2	277.1	60.5	**58.8**
14	Timeout	Timeout	Timeout	215	**211.8**

Runtime efficiency of PRISM-Leak mainly depends on the size of the Markovian model built by the PRISM model checker and the model size can easily get large. There are a few heuristics that can be performed when writing PRISM descriptions in order to avoid large models. For example, closely-related variables should be defined near each other; or variables that have a relationship with most of the other variables should be defined first in the PRISM descriptions. For more information on these heuristics, please see [25].

7   Conclusion

An algorithmic verification approach was proposed to check secure information flow of concurrent probabilistic programs. Observational determinism was defined as a specification of secure information flow. Comparisons to existing definitions of observational determinism demonstrated that the proposed definition is more precise. Furthermore, two algorithms were proposed to verify observational determinism. The proposed algorithms have been integrated into the PRISM-Leak tool. Experimental evaluations showed promising scalability results for PRISM-Leak.

As future work, we aim to develop symbolic algorithms based on binary decision diagrams to verify observational determinism. This can further improve the scalability of PRISM-Leak. We also aim to use PRISM-Leak to evaluate secure information flow of case studies from newer application domains.

References

1. Baier, C., Katoen, J.: Principles of Model Checking. MIT Press, Cambridge (2008)
2. Barthe, G., D'Argenio, P.R., Rezk, T.: Secure information flow by self-composition. In: Proceedings of the 17th IEEE Workshop on Computer Security Foundations, CSFW 2004, pp. 100–114. IEEE Computer Society (2004)
3. Biondi, F., Enescu, M.A., Heuser, A., Legay, A., Meel, K.S., Quilbeuf, J.: Scalable approximation of quantitative information flow in programs. In: Dillig, I., Palsberg, J. (eds.) Verification, Model Checking, and Abstract Interpretation. LNCS, vol. 10747, pp. 71–93. Springer, Cham (2018). https://doi.org/10.1007/978-3-319-73721-8_4
4. Biondi, F., Kawamoto, Y., Legay, A., Traonouez, L.-M.: HyLeak: hybrid analysis tool for information leakage. In: D'Souza, D., Narayan Kumar, K. (eds.) ATVA 2017. LNCS, vol. 10482, pp. 156–163. Springer, Cham (2017). https://doi.org/10.1007/978-3-319-68167-2_11
5. Biondi, F., Legay, A., Quilbeuf, J.: Comparative analysis of leakage tools on scalable case studies. In: Fischer, B., Geldenhuys, J. (eds.) SPIN 2015. LNCS, vol. 9232, pp. 263–281. Springer, Cham (2015). https://doi.org/10.1007/978-3-319-23404-5_17
6. Bischof, S., Breitner, J., Graf, J., Hecker, M., Mohr, M., Snelting, G.: Low-deterministic security for low-nondeterministic programs. J. Comput. Secur. **3**, 335–366 (2018)
7. Chaum, D.: The dining cryptographers problem: unconditional sender and recipient untraceability. J. Cryptol. **1**(1), 65–75 (1988)

8. Chothia, T., Kawamoto, Y., Novakovic, C.: LeakWatch: estimating information leakage from Java programs. In: Kutyłowski, M., Vaidya, J. (eds.) ESORICS 2014. LNCS, vol. 8713, pp. 219–236. Springer, Cham (2014). https://doi.org/10.1007/978-3-319-11212-1_13

9. Dabaghchian, M., Abdollahi Azgomi, M.: Model checking the observational determinism security property using promela and spin. Form. Asp. Comput. **27**(5–6), 789–804 (2015)

10. Giffhorn, D., Snelting, G.: A new algorithm for low-deterministic security. Int. J. Inf. Secur. **14**(3), 263–287 (2015)

11. Graf, J., Hecker, M., Mohr, M., Snelting, G.: Tool demonstration: JOANA. In: Piessens, F., Viganò, L. (eds.) POST 2016. LNCS, vol. 9635, pp. 89–93. Springer, Heidelberg (2016). https://doi.org/10.1007/978-3-662-49635-0_5

12. Huisman, M., Blondeel, H.-C.: Model-checking secure information flow for multi-threaded programs. In: Mödersheim, S., Palamidessi, C. (eds.) TOSCA 2011. LNCS, vol. 6993, pp. 148–165. Springer, Heidelberg (2012). https://doi.org/10.1007/978-3-642-27375-9_9

13. Huisman, M., Ngo, T.M.: Scheduler-specific confidentiality for multi-threaded programs and its logic-based verification. In: Beckert, B., Damiani, F., Gurov, D. (eds.) FoVeOOS 2011. LNCS, vol. 7421, pp. 178–195. Springer, Heidelberg (2012). https://doi.org/10.1007/978-3-642-31762-0_12

14. Huisman, M., Worah, P., Sunesen, K.: A temporal logic characterisation of observational determinism. In: Proceedings of the 19th IEEE Workshop on Computer Security Foundations, CSFW 2006. IEEE Computer Society (2006)

15. Karimpour, J., Isazadeh, A., Noroozi, A.A.: Verifying observational determinism. In: Federrath, H., Gollmann, D. (eds.) 30th IFIP International Information Security Conference (SEC). ICT Systems Security and Privacy Protection, Hamburg, Germany, Part 1: Privacy, vol. AICT-455, pp. 82–93, May 2015

16. Kwiatkowska, M., Norman, G., Parker, D.: Stochastic model checking. In: Bernardo, M., Hillston, J. (eds.) SFM 2007. LNCS, vol. 4486, pp. 220–270. Springer, Heidelberg (2007). https://doi.org/10.1007/978-3-540-72522-0_6

17. McLean, J.: Proving noninterference and functional correctness using traces. J. Comput. Secur. **1**(1), 37–57 (1992)

18. Ngo, T.M.: Qualitative and quantitative information flow analysis for multi-thread programs. Ph.D. thesis, University of Twente (2014)

19. Minh Ngo, T., Stoelinga, M., Huisman, M.: Confidentiality for probabilistic multi-threaded programs and its verification. In: Jürjens, J., Livshits, B., Scandariato, R. (eds.) ESSoS 2013. LNCS, vol. 7781, pp. 107–122. Springer, Heidelberg (2013). https://doi.org/10.1007/978-3-642-36563-8_8

20. Ngo, T.M., Stoelinga, M., Huisman, M.: Effective verification of confidentiality for multi-threaded programs. J. Comput. Secur. **22**(2), 269–300 (2014)

21. Noroozi, A.A., Karimpour, J., Isazadeh, A.: Bisimulation for secure information flow analysis of multi-threaded programs. Math. Comput. Appl. **24**(2), 64 (2019). https://doi.org/10.3390/mca24020064

22. Noroozi, A.A., Karimpour, J., Isazadeh, A.: Information leakage of multi-threaded programs. Comput. Electr. Eng. **78**, 400–419 (2019). https://doi.org/10.1016/j.compeleceng.2019.07.018. http://www.sciencedirect.com/science/article/pii/S0045790618331549

23. Noroozi, A.A., Karimpour, J., Isazadeh, A., Lotfi, S.: Verifying weak probabilistic noninterference. Int. J. Adv. Comput. Sci. Appl. **8**(10) (2017). https://doi.org/10.14569/IJACSA.2017.081026

24. Noroozi, A.A., Salehi, K., Karimpour, J., Isazadeh, A.: Prism-leak - a tool for computing information leakage of concurrent probabilistic programs (2018). https://github.com/alianoroozi/PRISM-Leak
25. Parker, D.: Implementation of symbolic model checking for probabilistic systems. Ph.D. thesis, University of Birmingham (2002)
26. Roscoe, A.W.: CSP and determinism in security modelling. In: IEEE Symposium on Security and Privacy, pp. 114–127. IEEE Computer Society (1995)
27. Russo, A., Hughes, J., Naumann, D., Sabelfeld, A.: Closing internal timing channels by transformation. In: Okada, M., Satoh, I. (eds.) ASIAN 2006. LNCS, vol. 4435, pp. 120–135. Springer, Heidelberg (2007). https://doi.org/10.1007/978-3-540-77505-8_10
28. Sabelfeld, A., Myers, A.C.: Language-based information-flow security. IEEE J. Sel. Areas Commun. **21**(1), 5–19 (2003)
29. Sabelfeld, A., Sands, D.: Probabilistic noninterference for multi-threaded programs. In: Proceedings 13th IEEE Computer Security Foundations Workshop, CSFW-13, pp. 200–214, July 2000
30. Smith, G.: Probabilistic noninterference through weak probabilistic bisimulation. In: Proceedings of the 16th IEEE Workshop on Computer Security Foundations, CSFW 2003, pp. 3–13. IEEE Computer Society (2003)
31. Terauchi, T.: A type system for observational determinism. In: Proceedings of the 21st IEEE Computer Security Foundations Symposium, CSF 2008, pp. 287–300. IEEE Computer Society (2008)
32. Zdancewic, S., Myers, A.C.: Observational determinism for concurrent program security. In: 2003 Proceedings of the 16th IEEE Computer Security Foundations Workshop, pp. 29–43, June 2003. https://doi.org/10.1109/CSFW.2003.1212703

Cryptography

Selective End-To-End Data-Sharing in the Cloud

Felix Hörandner[1][(✉)], Sebastian Ramacher[2], and Simon Roth[1]

[1] Graz University of Technology, Graz, Austria
{felix.hoerandner,simon.roth}@iaik.tugraz.at
[2] AIT Austrian Institute of Technology, Vienna, Austria
Sebastian.Ramacher@ait.ac.at

Abstract. Cloud-based services enable easy-to-use data-sharing between multiple parties, and, therefore, have been widely adopted over the last decade. Storage services by large cloud providers such as Dropbox or Google Drive as well as federated solutions such as Nextcloud have amassed millions of users. Nevertheless, privacy challenges hamper the adoption of such services for sensitive data: Firstly, rather than exposing their private data to a cloud service, users desire end-to-end confidentiality of the shared files without sacrificing usability, e.g., without repeatedly encrypting when sharing the same data set with multiple receivers. Secondly, only being able to expose complete (authenticated) files may force users to expose overmuch information. The receivers, as well as the requirements, might be unknown at issue-time, and thus the issued data set does not exactly match those requirements. This mismatch can be bridged by enabling cloud services to selectively disclose only relevant parts of a file without breaking the parts' authenticity. While both challenges have been solved individually, it is not trivial to combine these solutions and maintain their security intentions.

In this paper, we tackle this issue and introduce *selective end-to-end data-sharing* by combining ideas from proxy re-encryption and redactable signature schemes. Proxy re-encryption provides us with the basis for end-to-end encrypted data-sharing, while redactable signatures enable to redact parts and selectively disclose only the remaining still authenticated parts. We overcome the issues encountered when naively combining these two concepts, introduce a security model, and present a modular instantiation together with implementations based on a selection of various building blocks. We conclude with an extensive performance evaluation of our instantiation.

Keywords: Data-sharing · End-to-end confidentiality · Proxy re-encryption · Redactable signatures

1 Introduction

The advancement of cloud-based infrastructure enabled many new applications. One prime example is the vast landscape of cloud storage providers, such as

S. Ramacher—Work done while the author was with Graz University of Technology.

D. Garg et al. (Eds.): ICISS 2019, LNCS 11952, pp. 175–195, 2019.
https://doi.org/10.1007/978-3-030-36945-3_10

Google, Apple, Microsoft, and others, but also including many solutions for federated cloud storage, such as Nextcloud. All of them offer the same essential and convenient-to-use functionality: users upload files and can later share these files on demand with others on a per-file basis or a more coarse level of granularity. Of course, when sharing sensitive data (e.g., medical records), the intermediate cloud storage provider needs to be highly trusted to operate on plain data, or a protection layer is required to ensure the *end-to-end confidentiality* between users of the system. Additionally, many use cases rely on the *authenticity* of the shared data. However, if the authenticated file was not explicitly tailored to the final receivers, e.g., because the receivers were yet unknown at the issuing time, or because they have conflicting information requirements, users are forced to expose additional unneeded parts contained in the authenticated file to satisfy the receivers' needs. Such a mismatch in the amount of issued data and data required for a use case can prevent adoption not only by privacy-conscious users but also due to legal requirements (c.f. EU's GDPR [24]). To overcome this mismatch, the cloud system should additionally support convenient and efficient *selective disclosure* of data to share specific parts of a document depending on the receiver. E.g., even if a doctor only issues a single document, the patient would be able to selectively share the parts relevant to the doctor's prescribed absence with an employer, other parts on the treatment cost with an insurance, and again different parts detailing the diagnosis with a specialist for further treatment. Therefore, we aim to combine end-to-end confidentiality and selective disclosure of authentic data to what we call *selective end-to-end data-sharing*.

End-to-End Confidentiality. In the cloud-based document sharing setting, the naïve solution employing public-key encryption has its fair share of drawbacks. While such an approach would work for users to outsource data storage, it falls flat as soon as users desire to share files with many users. In a naïve approach based on public-key encryption, the sender would have to encrypt the data (or in a hybrid setting, the symmetric keys) separately for each receiver, which would require the sender to fetch the data from cloud storage, encrypt them locally, and upload the new ciphertext again and again. Proxy re-encryption (PRE), envisioned by Blaze et al. [6] and later formalized by Ateniese et al. [2], solves this issue conveniently: Users initially encrypt data to themselves. Once they want to share that data with other users, they provide a re-encryption key to a so-called proxy, which is then able to transform the ciphertext into a ciphertext for the desired receiver, without ever learning the underlying message. Finally, the receiver downloads the re-encrypted data and decrypts them with her key. The re-encryption keys can be computed non-interactively, i.e., without the receivers involvement. Also, proxy re-encryption gives the user the flexibility to not only forward ciphertexts after they were uploaded, but also to generate re-encryption keys to enable sharing of data that will be uploaded in the future. However, note that by employing proxy re-encryption, we still require the proxy to execute the re-encryption algorithms honestly. More importantly, it is paramount that the proxy server securely handles the re-encryption keys. While the re-encryption keys generated by a sender are not powerful enough to decrypt a ciphertext on their own, combined with the secret key of a receiver, any ciphertext of the sender could be re-encrypted and, finally, decrypted.

Authenticity and Selective Disclosure. Authenticity of the data is easily achievable for the full data stored in a file. Ideally, the issuer generates a signature only over the minimal subset of data that is later required by the receiver for a given use case. Unfortunately, the issuer would need to know all relevant use cases in advance at sign time to create appropriate signed documents for each case or later interactively re-create signatures over specified sub-sets on demand. The problem becomes more interesting when one of the desired features involves selectively disclosing only parts of an authenticated file. Naively, one could authenticate the parts of a file separately and then disclose individual parts. However, at that point, one loses the link between the parts and the other parts of the complete file. More sophisticated approaches have been proposed over the last decades, for example, based on Merkle trees, which we summarize for this work as redactable signature schemes (RSS) [27]. With RSS, starting from a signature on a file, anyone can repeatedly redact the signed message and update the signature accordingly to obtain a resulting signature-message pair that only discloses a desired subset of parts. Thereby it is guaranteed, that the redacted signature was produced from the original message and the signature does not leak the redacted parts.

Applications of Selective End-to-End Data-Sharing. Besides the use in e-health scenarios, which we use throughout this paper as an example, we believe this concept also holds value for a broader set of use cases, wherever users want to share privacy-relevant data between two domains that produce and consume different sets of data. A short selection is introduced below: (1) *Expenses:* To get a refund for travel expenses, an employee selectively discloses relevant items on her bank-signed credit card bill, without exposing unrelated payments which may contain privacy-sensitive data. (2) *Commerce:* Given a customer-signed sales contract, an online marketplace wants to comply with the GDPR and preserve its customers' privacy while using subcontractors. The marketplace redacts the customer's name and address but reveals product and quantity to its supplier, and redacts the product description but reveals the address to a delivery company. (3) *Financial statements:* A user wants to prove eligibility for a discount/service by disclosing her income category contained in a signed tax document, without revealing other tax-related details such as marriage status, donations, income sources, etc. Similarly, a user may need to disclose the salary to a future landlord, while retaining the secrecy of other details. (4) *Businesses:* Businesses may employ selective end-to-end data-sharing to securely outsource data storage and sharing to a cloud service in compliance with the law. To honor the users' right to be forgotten, the company could order the external storage provider to redact all parts about that user, rather than to download, to remove, to re-sign, and to upload the file again. (5) *Identity Management:* Given a government-issued identity document, users instruct their identity provider (acting as cloud storage) to selectively disclose the minimal required set of contained attributes for the receiving service providers. In this use case, unlinkability might also be desired.

Contribution. We propose *selective end-to-end data-sharing* for cloud systems to provide end-to-end confidentiality, authenticity, and selective disclosure.

Firstly, we formalize an *abstract model* and its associated security properties. At the time of encrypting or signing, the final receiver or the required minimal combination of parts, respectively, might not yet be known. Therefore, our model needs to support ad-hoc and selective sharing of protected files or their parts. Besides the data *owner*, we require distinct *senders*, who can encrypt data for the owner, as well as *issuers* that certify the authenticity of the data. Apart from *unforgability*, we aim to conceal the plain text from unauthorized entities, such as the proxy (i.e. *proxy privacy*), and additionally information about redacted parts from receivers (i.e. *receiver privacy*). Further, we define *transparency* to hide whether a redaction happened or not.

Secondly, we present a *modular construction* for our model by using cryptographic building blocks that can be instantiated with various schemes, which enables to tailor this construction to specific applications' needs. A challenge for combining was that RSS generally have access to the plain message in the redaction process to update the signature. However, we must not expose the plain message to the proxy. Even if black-box redactions were possible, the signature must not leak any information about the plaintext, which is not a well-studied property in the context of RSS. We avoid these problems by signing symmetric encryptions of the message parts. To ensure that the signature corresponds to the original message and no other possible decryptions, we generate a commitment on the used symmetric key and add this commitment as another part to the redactable signature.

Finally, we *evaluate three implementations* of our modular construction that are built on different underlying primitives, namely two implementations with RSS for unordered data with CL [11] and DHS [18,19] accumulators, as well as an implementation supporting ordered data. To give an impression for real-world usage, we perform the benchmarks with various combinations of part numbers and sizes, on both a PC as well as a mobile phone.

Related Work. Proxy re-encryption, introduced by Blaze et al. [6], enables a semi-trusted proxy to transform ciphertext for one user into ciphertext of the same underlying message now encrypted for another user, where the proxy does not learn anything about the plain message. Ateniese et al. [3] proposed the first strongly secure constructions, while follow-up work focused on stronger security notions [12,30], performance improvements [16], and features such as forward secrecy [20], key-privacy [1], or lattice-based instantiations [13].

Attribute-based encryption (ABE) [25,34,35] is a well-known primitive enabling fine-grained access to encrypted data. The idea is, that a central authority issues private keys that can be used to decrypt ciphertexts depending on attributes and policies. While ABE enables this fine-grained access control based on attributes, it is still all-or-nothing concerning encrypted data.

Functional encryption (FE) [7], a generalization of ABEs, enables to define functions on the encrypted plaintext given specialized private keys. To selectively share data, one could distribute the corresponding private keys where the functions only reveal parts of the encrypted data. Consequently, the ability to selectively share per ciphertext is lost without creating new key pairs.

Redactable signatures [27,37] enable to redact (i.e., black-out) parts of a signed document that should not be revealed, while the authenticity of the remaining parts can still be verified. This concept was extended for specific data structures such as trees [8,36] and graphs [29]. As a stronger privacy notion, transparency [8] was added to capture if a scheme hides whether a redaction happened or not. A generalized framework for RSS is offered by Derler et al. [22]. Further enhancements enable only a designated verifier, but not a data thief, to verify the signature's authenticity and anonymize the signer's identity to reduce metadata leakage [21]. We refer to [17] for a comprehensive overview.

Homomorphic signatures [27] make it possible to evaluate a function on the message-signature pair where the outcome remains valid. Such a function can also be designed to remove (i.e., redact) parts of the message and signature. The concept of homomorphic proxy re-authenticators [23] applies proxy re-encryption to securely share and aggregate such homomorphic signatures in a multi-user setting. However, homomorphic signatures do not inherently provide support for defining which redactions are admissible or the notion of transparency.

Attribute-based credentials (ABCs or anonymous credentials) enable to only reveal a minimal subset of authentic data. In such a system, an issuer certifies information about the user as an anonymous credential. The user may then compute presentations containing the minimal data set required by a receiver, which can verify the authenticity. Additionally, ABCs offer unlinkability, i.e., they guarantee that no two actions can be linked by colluding service providers and issuers. This concept was introduced by Chaum [14,15] and the most prominent instantiations are Microsoft's U-Prove [33] and IBM's identity mixer [9,10]. However, as the plain data is required to compute the presentations, this operation must be performed in a sufficiently trusted environment.

In our previous work [26], we have identified the need for selective disclosure in a semi-trusted cloud environment and informally proposed to combine PRE and RSS, but did not yet provide a formal definition or concrete constructions.

The cloudification of ABCs [28] represents the closest related research to our work and to filling this gap. Their concept enables a semi-trusted cloud service to derive representations from encrypted credentials without learning the underlying plaintext. Also, unlinkability is further guaranteed protecting the users' privacy, which makes it a very good choice for identity management where only small amounts of identity attributes are exchanged. However, this property becomes impractical with larger documents as hybrid encryption trivially breaks unlinkability. In contrast, our work focuses on a more general model with a construction that is efficient for both small as well as large documents. In particular, our construction (1) already integrates hybrid encryption for large documents avoiding ambiguity of the actually signed content, and (2) supports features of redactable signatures such as the transparency notion, signer-defined admissible redactions, as well as different data structures. These features come at a cost: the proposed construction for our model does not provide unlinkability.

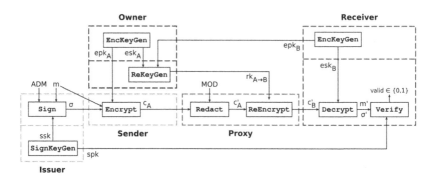

Fig. 1. Algorithms performed by actors (dashed lines denote trust boundaries)

2   Definition: Selective End-to-End Data-Sharing

We present an abstract model for selective end-to-end data-sharing and define security properties. It is our goal to formalize a generic framework that enables various instantiations.

Data Flow. As an informal overview, Fig. 1 illustrates the model's algorithms in the context of interactions between the following five actors: (1) The *issuer* signs the plain data. For example, a hospital or government agency may certify the data owner's health record or identity data, respectively. (2) The *sender* encrypts the signed data for the owner. (3) The *owner* is the entity, for which the data was originally encrypted. Initially, only this owner can decrypt the ciphertext. The owner may generate re-encryption keys to delegate decryption rights to other receivers. (4) The *proxy* redacts specified parts of a signed and encrypted message. Then, the proxy uses a re-encryption key to transform the remaining parts, which are encrypted for one entity (the owner), into ciphertext for another entity (a receiver). (5) Finally, the *receiver* is able to decrypt the non-redacted parts and verify their authenticity. Of course, multiple of these roles might be held by the same entity. For example, an owner signs her data (as issuer), uploads data (as sender), or accesses data she outsourced (as receiver).

Notation. In our following definitions, we adapt the syntax and notions inspired by standard definitions of PRE [2] and RSS [22].

Definition 1 (Selective End-to-End Data-Sharing). *A scheme for selective end-to-end data-sharing (SEEDS) consists of the PPT algorithms as defined below. The algorithms return an error symbol $\perp$ if their input is not consistent.*

SignKeyGen(1^κ) $\rightarrow$ (ssk, spk): *On input of a security parameter κ, this probabilistic algorithm outputs a signature keypair* (ssk, spk).

EncKeyGen(1^κ) $\rightarrow$ (esk, epk): *On input of a security parameter κ, this probabilistic algorithm outputs an encryption keypair* (esk, epk).

ReKeyGen(esk_A, epk_B) $\rightarrow$ $\text{rk}_{A \rightarrow B}$: *On input of a private encryption key esk_A of user A, and a public encryption key epk_B of user B, this (probabilistic) algorithm outputs a re-encryption key $\text{rk}_{A \rightarrow B}$.*

Sign(ssk, m, ADM) $\rightarrow \sigma$: *On input of a private signature key* ssk, *a message* m *and a description of admissible messages* ADM, *this (probabilistic) algorithm outputs the signature* σ. *The admissible redactions* ADM *specifies which message parts must not be redacted.*

Verify(spk, m, σ) $\rightarrow$ *valid*: *On input of a public key* spk, *a signature* σ *and a message* m, *this deterministic algorithm outputs a bit valid* $\in \{0, 1\}$.

Encrypt(epk_A, m, σ) $\rightarrow c_A$: *On input of a public encryption key* epk_A, *a message* m *and a signature* σ, *this (probabilistic) algorithm outputs the ciphertext* c_A.

Decrypt(esk_A, c_A) $\rightarrow (m, \sigma)$: *On input of a private decryption key* esk_A, *a signed ciphertext* c_A, *this deterministic algorithm outputs the underlying plain message* m *and signature* σ *if the signature is valid, and* $\perp$ *otherwise.*

Redact(c_A, MOD) $\rightarrow c'_A$: *This (probabilistic) algorithm takes a valid, signed ciphertext* c_A *and modification instructions* MOD *as input.* MOD *specifies which message parts should be redacted. The algorithm returns a redacted signed ciphertext* c'_A.

ReEncrypt($\mathsf{rk}_{A \rightarrow B}$, c_A) $\rightarrow c_B$: *On input of a re-encryption key* $\mathsf{rk}_{A \rightarrow B}$ *and a signed ciphertext* c_A, *this (probabilistic) algorithm returns a transformed signed ciphertext* c_B *of the same message.*

Correctness. The correctness property requires that all honestly signed, encrypted, and possibly redacted and re-encrypted ciphertexts can be correctly decrypted and verified.

$$
\begin{aligned}
&\forall \kappa \in N, \forall (\mathsf{ssk}, \mathsf{spk}) \leftarrow \mathsf{SignKeyGen}(1^\kappa) \\
&\forall (\mathsf{esk}_A, \mathsf{epk}_A) \leftarrow \mathsf{EncKeyGen}(1^\kappa) \\
&\forall (\mathsf{esk}_B, \mathsf{epk}_B) \leftarrow \mathsf{EncKeyGen}(1^\kappa) \\
&\forall \mathsf{rk}_{A \rightarrow B} \leftarrow \mathsf{ReKeyGen}(\mathsf{esk}_A, \mathsf{epk}_B) \\
&\forall m, \forall \mathsf{ADM} \preceq m, \forall \sigma \leftarrow \mathsf{Sign}(\mathsf{ssk}, m, \mathsf{ADM}) \\
&\forall c_A \leftarrow \mathsf{Encrypt}(\mathsf{epk}_A, m, \sigma) \\
&\forall c_B \leftarrow \mathsf{ReEncrypt}(\mathsf{rk}_{A \rightarrow B}, c_A), \\
&\forall \mathsf{MOD} \overset{\mathsf{ADM}}{\preceq} m, \forall c'_A \leftarrow \mathsf{Redact}(c_A, \mathsf{MOD}) \\
&\forall c'_B \leftarrow \mathsf{ReEncrypt}(\mathsf{rk}_{A \rightarrow B}, c'_A),
\end{aligned}
\; : \;
\begin{aligned}
&\mathsf{Decrypt}(\mathsf{esk}_A, c_A) = (m, \sigma), \\
&\mathsf{Decrypt}(\mathsf{esk}_B, c_B) = (m, \sigma), \\
&\mathsf{Verify}(\mathsf{spk}, m, \sigma) = 1, \\
&(m', \sigma') \leftarrow \mathsf{Decrypt}(\mathsf{esk}_A, c'_A), \\
&\mathsf{Verify}(\mathsf{spk}, m', \sigma') = 1, \\
&(m', \sigma'') \leftarrow \mathsf{Decrypt}(\mathsf{esk}_B, c'_B), \\
&\mathsf{Verify}(\mathsf{spk}, m', \sigma'') = 1, \\
&\text{with } m' \xleftarrow{\mathsf{MOD}} m_i.
\end{aligned}
$$

Oracles. To keep the our security experiments concise, we define various oracles. The adversaries are given access to a subset of these oracles in the security experiments. These oracles are implicitly able to access public parameters and keys generated in the security games. The environment maintains the following initially empty sets: HU for honest users, CU for corrupted users, CH for challenger users, SK for signature keys, EK for encryption keys, and Sigs for signatures.

Add User Oracle, $\text{AU}(i,t)$: Generates and tracks all key pairs for a user.

> **if** $i \in \text{HU} \cup \text{CU} \cup \text{CH}$ or $t = \text{CH}$: **return** $\bot$
> add i to set of type t
> $\text{EK}[i] \leftarrow (\text{esk}_i, \text{epk}_i) \leftarrow \text{EncKeyGen}(1^\kappa)$
> $\text{SK}[i] \leftarrow (\text{ssk}_i, \text{spk}_i) \leftarrow \text{SignKeyGen}(1^\kappa)$
> **if** $t = \text{CU}$: **return** $((\text{esk}_i, \text{epk}_i), (\text{ssk}_i, \text{spk}_i))$
> **if** $t = \text{HU}$: **return** $((\bot, \text{epk}_i), (\bot, \text{spk}_i))$

Sign Oracle, $\text{SIG}(i, m, \text{ADM})$: Signs messages for the challenge and honest users, and tracks all signatures.

> **if** $i \notin \text{CH} \cup \text{HU}$ or $\text{SK}[i][0] = \bot$: **return** $\bot$
> $\sigma \leftarrow \text{Sign}(\text{SK}[i][0], m, \text{ADM})$
> $\text{Sigs} \leftarrow \text{Sigs}$
> $\quad \cup \{ m' \mid \forall \text{MOD} \stackrel{\text{ADM}}{\preceq} m \ \forall m' \xleftarrow{\text{MOD}} m \}$
> **return** (m, σ)

Sign Encrypt Oracle, $\text{SE}(i, j, m, \text{ADM})$: Signs and encrypts messages for any user, and tracks all signatures.

> **if** $i, j \notin \text{CH} \cup \text{HU} \cup \text{CU}$: **return** $\bot$
> $\sigma \leftarrow \text{Sign}(\text{SK}[i][0], m, \text{ADM})$
> $C_A \leftarrow \text{Encrypt}(\text{EK}[j][1], m, \sigma)$
> $\text{Sigs} \leftarrow \text{Sigs}$
> $\quad \cup \{ m' \mid \forall \text{MOD} \stackrel{\text{ADM}}{\preceq} m \ \forall m' \xleftarrow{\text{MOD}} m \}$
> **return** C_A

Re-Encryption Key Generator Oracle, $\text{RKG}(i, j)$: Generates keys for re-encryptions keys except for re-encryptions from the challenge user to a corrupted user.

> **if** $i \in \text{CH}$ and $j \in \text{CU}$: **return** $\bot$
> **if** $i, j \notin \text{HU} \cup \text{CU} \cup \text{CH}$ or $i = j$: **return** $\bot$
> **return** $\text{ReKeyGen}(\text{EK}[i][0], \text{EK}[j][1])$

Re-Encrypt Oracle, $\text{RE}(i, j, c_j)$: Performs re-encryption of a ciphertext as long as the target user is not corrupted and the ciphertext is not derived from the challenge.

> **if** $i, j \notin \text{HU} \cup \text{CU} \cup \text{CH}$ or $i = j$: **return** $\bot$
> **if** c_i is not a proper 2nd level ciphertext for $\text{EK}[i][0]$: **return** $\bot$
> **if** 1) the oracle is called in the guess phase, and 2) $j \in \text{CU}$, and 3) c_i is a derivative of C^*, that is if $(m, \sigma) \leftarrow \text{Decrypt}(\text{EK}[i][0], c_i)$ and $m \subseteq m_0$ or $m \subseteq m_1$: **return** $\bot$
> $\text{rk}_{i \to j} \leftarrow \text{ReKeyGen}(\text{EK}[i][0], \text{EK}[j][1])$
> **return** $\text{ReEncrypt}(\text{rk}_{i \to j}, c_i)$.

Decrypt Oracle, $\text{D}(i, c_i)$: Decrypts a ciphertext as long as it is not derived from the challenge ciphertext.

> **if** $i \notin \text{HU} \cup \text{CU} \cup \text{CH}$: **return** $\bot$
> **if** c_i is not a proper ciphertext for $\text{EK}[i][0]$: **return** $\bot$
> **if** the oracle is called in the guess phase, and c_i is a derivative of C^*, that is if $(m, \sigma) \leftarrow \text{Decrypt}(\text{EK}[i][0], c_i)$ and $m \subseteq m_0$ or $m \subseteq m_1$: **return** $\bot$
> **return** $(m, \sigma) \leftarrow \text{Decrypt}(\text{EK}[i][0], c_i)$

Unforgeability. Unforgeability requires that it should be infeasible to compute a valid signature σ for a given public key spk on a message m without knowledge of the corresponding signing key ssk. The adversary may obtain signatures of other users and therefore is given access to a signing oracle (SIG). Of course, we exclude signatures or their redactions that were obtained by adaptive queries to that signature oracle.

Experiment $\text{Exp}^{\text{Unf}}_{\text{SEEDS}, \mathcal{A}}(1^\kappa)$

$\quad \text{CH} \leftarrow \{0\}, SK[0] \leftarrow (\text{ssk}^*, \text{spk}^*) \leftarrow \text{SignKeyGen}(1^\kappa), \mathcal{O} \leftarrow \{\text{SIG}\}, (m, \sigma) \leftarrow \mathcal{A}^{\mathcal{O}}(\text{spk}^*)$
$\quad$ **if** $\text{Verify}(\text{spk}^*, m, \sigma) = 1$ and $m \notin \text{Sigs}$, **then return** 1, **else return** 0

Experiment 1. Unforgeability Experiment for Signatures of SEEDS Schemes

Definition 2 (Unforgeability). *A* SEEDS *scheme is unforgeable, if for any PPT adversary $\mathcal{A}$ there exists a negligible function ε such that*

$$\Pr\left[\mathsf{Exp}^{\mathsf{Unf}}_{\mathsf{SEEDS},\mathcal{A}}(1^{\kappa}) = 1\right] < \varepsilon(\kappa)$$

Proxy Privacy. Proxy privacy captures that proxies should not learn anything about the plain data of ciphertext while processing them with the Redact and ReEncrypt operations. This property is modeled as an IND-CCA style game, where the adversary is challenged on a signed and encrypted message. Since the proxy may learn additional information in normal operation, the adversary gets access to several oracles: Obtaining additional ciphertexts is modeled with a Sign-and-Encrypt oracle (SE). A proxy would also get re-encryption keys enabling re-encryption operations between corrupt and honest users (RE, RKG). Furthermore, the adversary even gets a decryption oracle (D) to capture that the proxy colludes with a corrupted receiver, who reveals the plaintext of ciphertext processed by the proxy. We exclude operations that would trivially break the game, such as re-encryption keys from the challenge user to a corrupt user, or re-encryptions and decryptions of (redacted) ciphertexts of the challenge.

Experiment $\mathsf{Exp}^{\mathsf{PP}}_{\mathsf{SEEDS},\mathcal{A}}(1^{\kappa})$

   $\mathrm{SK}[0] \leftarrow (\mathsf{ssk}^*, \mathsf{spk}^*) \leftarrow \mathsf{SignKeyGen}(1^{\kappa})$, $\mathrm{EK}[0] \leftarrow (\mathsf{esk}^*, \mathsf{epk}^*) \leftarrow \mathsf{EncKeyGen}(1^{\kappa})$
   $\mathrm{CH} \leftarrow \{0\}$, $b \xleftarrow{R} \{0,1\}$, $\mathcal{O}_1 \leftarrow \{\mathsf{AU}, \mathsf{SE}, \mathsf{RKG}, \mathsf{RE}, \mathsf{D}\}$, $\mathcal{O}_2 \leftarrow \{\mathsf{SE}, \mathsf{RE}, \mathsf{D}\}$
   $(m_0, \mathsf{ADM}_0, m_1, \mathsf{ADM}_1,,) \leftarrow \mathcal{A}^{\mathcal{O}_1}(\mathsf{spk}^*, \mathsf{epk}^*)$
   if $m_0 \not\sim m_1$, or $\mathsf{ADM}_0 \not\sim \mathsf{ADM}_1$: **abort**
   $\sigma \leftarrow \mathsf{Sign}(\mathsf{ssk}^*, m_b, \mathsf{ADM}_b)$, $c^* \leftarrow \mathsf{Encrypt}(\mathsf{epk}^*, m_b, \sigma)$, $b' \leftarrow \mathcal{A}^{\mathcal{O}_2}(, c^*)$
   if $b = b'$, **then return** 1, **else return** 0

Experiment 2: Proxy Privacy Experiment for Ciphertexts of SEEDS Schemes ($X \sim Y \ldots |X| = |Y|$ and corresponding items x_i, y_i have same length)

Definition 3 (Proxy Privacy). *A* SEEDS *scheme is proxy private, if for any PPT adversary $\mathcal{A}$ there exists a negligible function ε such that*

$$\left|\Pr\left[\mathsf{Exp}^{\mathsf{PP}}_{\mathsf{SEEDS},\mathcal{A}}(1^{\kappa}) = 1\right] - 1/2\right| < \varepsilon(\kappa)$$

Receiver Privacy. Receiver privacy captures that users only want to share information selectively. Therefore, receivers should not learn any information on parts that were redacted when given a redacted ciphertext. Since receivers may additionally obtain decrypted messages and their signatures during normal operation, the adversary gets access to a signature oracle (SIG). The experiment relies on another oracle (LoRRedact), that simulates the proxy's output. One of two messages is chosen with challenge bit b, redacted, re-encrypted and returned to the adversary to guess b. To avoid trivial attacks, the remaining message parts must be a valid subset of the other message's parts. If the ciphertext leaks information about the redacted parts, the adversary could exploit this to win.

Experiment $\mathsf{Exp}^{\mathsf{RP}}_{\mathsf{SEEDS},\mathcal{A}}(1^\kappa)$	$\mathsf{LoRRedact}(i,j,m_0,\mathsf{MOD}_0,m_1,\mathsf{MOD}_1,\mathsf{ADM},b)$:
$\mathsf{SK}[0] \leftarrow (\mathsf{ssk}^*,\mathsf{spk}^*) \leftarrow \mathsf{SignKeyGen}(1^\kappa)$	**if** $i \notin \mathsf{CH}$ or $j \notin \mathsf{HU} \cup \mathsf{CU}$: **return** $\perp$
$\mathsf{EK}[0] \leftarrow (\mathsf{esk}^*,\mathsf{epk}^*) \leftarrow \mathsf{EncKeyGen}(1^\kappa)$	$\mathsf{rk}_{A\to B} \leftarrow \mathsf{ReKeyGen}(\mathsf{EK}[i][0],\mathsf{EK}[j][1])$
$\mathsf{CH} \leftarrow \{0\},\ b \xleftarrow{R} \{0,1\}$	**for** both $c \in \{0,1\}$
$\mathcal{O} \leftarrow \{\mathsf{AU},\mathsf{SIG},\mathsf{LoRRedact}(\cdots\cdots,b)\}$	$\quad \sigma_c \leftarrow \mathsf{Sign}(\mathsf{SK}[i][0],m_c,\mathsf{ADM})$
$b' \leftarrow \mathcal{A}^{\mathcal{O}}(\mathsf{spk}^*,\mathsf{epk}^*)$	$\quad c_{A,c} \leftarrow \mathsf{Encrypt}(\mathsf{EK}[i][1],m_c,\sigma_c)$
if $b = b'$, then **return** 1	$\quad c'_{A,c} \leftarrow \mathsf{Redact}(c_{A,c},\mathsf{MOD}_c)$
else return 0	$\quad c'_{B,c} \leftarrow \mathsf{ReEncrypt}(\mathsf{rk}_{A\to B},c'_{A,c})$
	$\quad (m'_c,\sigma'_c) \leftarrow \mathsf{Decrypt}(\mathsf{EK}[j][0],c'_{B,c})$
	if $m'_0 = m'_1$: **return** $c'_{B,b}$
	else: return $\perp$

Experiment 3. Receiver Privacy Experiment for SEEDS Schemes

Definition 4 (Receiver Privacy). *A* SEEDS *scheme is receiver private, if for any PPT adversary $\mathcal{A}$ there exists a negligible function ε such that*

$$\left| \Pr\left[\mathsf{Exp}^{\mathsf{RP}}_{\mathsf{SEEDS},\mathcal{A}}(1^\kappa) = 1 \right] - 1/2 \right| < \varepsilon(\kappa)$$

Transparency. Additionally, a SEEDS scheme may provide transparency. For example, considering a medical report, privacy alone might hide what treatment a patient received, but not the fact that some treatment was administered. Therefore, it should be infeasible to decide whether parts of an encrypted message were redacted or not. Again, the adversary gets access to a signature oracle (SIG) to cover the decrypted signature message pairs during normal operation of receivers. The experiment relies on another oracle (RedactOrNot), that simulates the proxy's output. Depending on the challenge bit b, the adversary gets a ciphertext that was redacted or a ciphertext over the same subset of message parts generated through the sign operation but without redaction. If the returned ciphertext leaks information about the fact that redaction was performed or not, the adversary could exploit this to win.

Experiment $\mathsf{Exp}^{\mathsf{Trans}}_{\mathsf{SEEDS},\mathcal{A}}(1^\kappa)$	$\mathsf{RedactOrNot}(i,m,\mathsf{MOD},\mathsf{ADM},b)$:
$\mathsf{SK}[0] \leftarrow (\mathsf{ssk}^*,\mathsf{spk}^*) \leftarrow \mathsf{SignKeyGen}(1^\kappa)$	**if** $i \notin \mathsf{CH}$: **return** $\perp$
$\mathsf{EK}[0] \leftarrow (\mathsf{esk}^*,\mathsf{epk}^*) \leftarrow \mathsf{EncKeyGen}(1^\kappa)$	$\sigma \leftarrow \mathsf{Sign}(\mathsf{SK}[i][0],m,\mathsf{ADM})$
$\mathsf{CH} \leftarrow \{0\},\ b \xleftarrow{R} \{0,1\}$	$c \leftarrow \mathsf{Encrypt}(\mathsf{EK}[i][1],m,\sigma)$
$\mathcal{O} \leftarrow \{\mathsf{AU},\mathsf{SIG},\mathsf{RedactOrNot}(\cdot,\cdot,\cdot,\cdot,b)\}$	$c'_0 \leftarrow \mathsf{Redact}(c,\mathsf{MOD})$
$b' \leftarrow \mathcal{A}^{\mathcal{O}}(\mathsf{esk}^*,\mathsf{epk}^*,\mathsf{spk}^*)$	$(m',\sigma') \leftarrow \mathsf{Decrypt}(\mathsf{EK}[i][0],c'_0)$
if $b = b'$, then **return** 1	$\sigma' \leftarrow \mathsf{Sign}(\mathsf{SK}[i][0],m',\mathsf{ADM})$
else: return 0	$c'_1 \leftarrow \mathsf{Encrypt}(\mathsf{EK}[i][1],m',\sigma')$
	return c'_b.

Experiment 4. Transparency Experiment for Ciphertexts of SEEDS Schemes

Definition 5 (Transparency). *A* SEEDS *scheme is transparent, if for any* PPT *adversary* $\mathcal{A}$ *there exists a negligible function* ε *such that*

$$\left| \Pr\left[\mathsf{Exp}_{\mathsf{SEEDS},\mathcal{A}}^{\mathsf{Trans}}(1^\kappa) = 1 \right] - 1/2 \right| < \varepsilon(\kappa)$$

3   Modular Instantiation

Scheme 1 instantiates our model by building on generic cryptographic mechanisms, most prominently proxy re-encryption and redactable signatures, which can be instantiated with various underlying schemes.

Signing. Instead of signing the plain message parts m_i, we generate a redactable signature over their symmetric ciphertexts c_i. To prevent ambiguity of the actually signed content, we commit to the used symmetric key k with a commitment scheme, giving (O, C), and incorporate this commitment C as another part when generating the redactable signature $\hat{\sigma}$. Neither the ciphertexts of the parts, nor the redactable signature over these ciphertexts, nor the (hiding) commitment reveals anything about the plaintext. To verify, we verify the redactable signature over the ciphertext as well as commitment and check if the message parts decrypted with the committed key match the given message.

Selective Sharing. We use proxy re-encryption to securely share (encrypt and re-encrypt) the commitment's opening information O with the intended receiver. With the decrypted opening information O and the commitment C itself, the receiver reconstructs the symmetric key k, which can decrypt the ciphertexts into message parts. In between, redaction can be directly performed on the redactable signature over symmetric ciphertexts and the hiding commitment.

Admissible Redactions. The admissible redactions ADM describe a set of parts that must not be redacted. For the redactable signature scheme, a canonical representation of this set also has to be signed and later verified against the remaining parts. In combination with proxy re-encryption, the information on admissible redactions also must be protected and is, therefore, part-wise encrypted, which not only allows the receiver to verify the message, but also the proxy to verify if the performed redaction is still valid. Of course, hashes of parts that must remain can be used to describe ADM to reduce its size. In the construction, the commitment C is added to the signature but must not be redacted, so it is internally added to ADM.

Subject Binding. The signature is completely uncoupled from the encryption, and so anyone who obtains or decrypts a signature may encrypt it for herself again. Depending on the use case, the signed data may need to be bound to a specific subject, to describe that this data is about that user. To achieve this, the issuer could specify the subject within the document's signed content. One example would be to add the owner's epk as the first message item, enabling receivers to authenticate supposed owners by engaging in a challenge-response protocol over their spk. As we aim to offer a generic construction, a concrete method of subject binding is left up to the specific application.

As public parameters, fix a proxy re-encryption scheme PRE, a symmetric encryption scheme S, a commitment scheme C with fixed parameters $cpp \leftarrow$ C.KeyGen(1^κ), and a redactable signature scheme RSS.

SignKeyGen(1^κ) $\rightarrow$ (ssk, spk): **return** RSS.KeyGen(1^κ)
EncKeyGen(1^κ) $\rightarrow$ (esk, epk): **return** PRE.KeyGen(1^κ)
ReKeyGen(esk$_A$, epk$_B$) $\rightarrow$ rk$_{A \rightarrow B}$: **return** PRE.ReKeyGen(esk$_A$, epk$_B$)

Sign(ssk, m, ADM) $\rightarrow \sigma$:
  $k \leftarrow$ S.KeyGen(1^κ)
  $c \leftarrow \{$S.Enc(k, m_i) $\mid m_i \in M\}$
  $c_{\mathsf{ADM}} \leftarrow \{c_i \in c \mid m_i \in$ ADM$\}$
  $(C, O) \leftarrow$ C.Com(k)
  $(\cdot, \hat{\sigma}) \leftarrow$ RSS.Sign(ssk, $\{C\} \cup c, \{C\} \cup c_{\mathsf{ADM}}$)
  return $\sigma \leftarrow (O, C, c, \hat{\sigma})$

Verify(spk, m, σ) $\rightarrow valid \in \{0, 1\}$:
  Parse m as $\{m_i\}_{i=1}^n$
  Parse σ as $(O, C, \{c_i\}_{i=1}^n, \hat{\sigma})$
  if the following holds, **return** 1
    RSS.Verify(spk, $\{C\} \cup c, \hat{\sigma}$) $= 1$
    $\forall i \in [1...n] : m_i =$ S.Dec(k, c_i)
    with $k \leftarrow$ C.Open(C, O)
  else: return 0

Encrypt(epk$_A$, m, σ) $\rightarrow c_A$:
  Parse σ as $(O, C, c, \hat{\sigma})$
  $O_A \leftarrow$ PRE.Enc^2(epk$_A$, O)
  return $c_A \leftarrow (O_A, C, c, \hat{\sigma})$

Decrypt(esk$_A$, c_A) $\rightarrow (m, \sigma)$:
  Parse c_A as $(O_A, C, \{c_i\}_{i=0}^n, \hat{\sigma})$
  $O \leftarrow$ PRE.Dec^j(esk$_A$, O_A),
    with j as ciphertext-level
  $k \leftarrow$ C.Open(O, C)
  $m \leftarrow \{m_i\}_{i=1}^n$, $m_i \leftarrow$ S.Dec(k, c_i)
  $\sigma \leftarrow (O, C, c, \hat{\sigma})$
  if Verify(spk, m, σ) $= 1$: **return** (m, σ)
  else: return $\perp$
  We assume that spk can always be correctly derived from any ciphertext c_A.

Redact(c_A, MOD) $\rightarrow c'_A$:
  Parse c_A as $(O_A, C, c, \hat{\sigma})$
  $(\{C\} \cup c', \hat{\sigma}') \leftarrow$
    RSS.Redact($\{C\} \cup c, \hat{\sigma}$, MOD)
  return $c'_A \leftarrow (O_A, C, c', \hat{\sigma}')$

ReEncrypt(rk$_{A \rightarrow B}$, c_A) $\rightarrow c_B$:
  Parse c_A as $(O_A, C, c, \hat{\sigma})$
  $O_B \leftarrow$ PRE.ReEnc(rk$_{A \rightarrow B}$, O_A)
  return $c_B \leftarrow (O_B, C, c, \hat{\sigma})$

Scheme 1. Modular Instantiation

Tailoring. The modular design enables to instantiate the building blocks with concrete schemes that best fit the envisioned application scenario. To support the required data structures, a suitable RSS may be selected. Also, performance and space characteristics are a driving factor when choosing suitable schemes. For example, in the original RSS from Johnson et al. [27] the signature grows with each part that is redacted starting from a constant size, while in the (not optimized) RSS from Derler et al. [22, Scheme 1], the signature shrinks with each redaction. Further, already deployed technologies or provisioned key material may come into consideration to facilitate migration. This modularity also becomes beneficial when it is desired to replace a cryptographic mechanism with a related but extended concept. For example, when moving from "classical" PRE to conditional PRE [38] that further limits the proxy's power.

Theorem 1. *Scheme 1 is unforgeable, proxy-private, receiver-private, and transparent, if the used* PRE *is IND-RCCA2 secure,* S *is IND-CPA secure,* C *is binding and hiding, and* RSS *is unforgeable, private, and transparent.*

The proof is given in Appendix A.

4   Performance

We evaluate the practicability of Scheme 1 by developing and benchmarking three implementations that differ in the used RSS and accumulator schemes. To give an impression for multiple scenarios, we test with various numbers of parts and part sizes, ranging from small identity cards with 10 attributes to 100 measurements à 1 kB and from documents with 5 parts à 200 kB to 50 high-definition x-ray scans à 10 MB.

Implementations. Our three implementations of Scheme 1 aim for 128 bit security. Table 1 summarizes the used cryptographic schemes and their parametrization according to recommendations from NIST [5] for factoring-based and symmetric-key primitives. The groups for pairing-based curves are chosen following recent recommendations [4,31]. These implementations were developed for the Java platform using the IAIK-JCE and ECCelerate libraries[1]. We selected the accumulators based on the comparison by Derler et al. [18].

Table 1. Cryptographic building blocks for our three implementations

	Impl. 1: Sets & CL	Impl. 2: Sets & DHS	Impl. 3: Lists & CL
PRE	Chow et al. [16], 3072bit		
S	AES-CBC, 128bit		
C	Hash Commitment (SHA3), 256bit		
Hash	SHA3, 256bit		
RSS	DPSS [22, Scheme 1]	DPSS [22, Scheme 1]	DPSS [22, Scheme 2]
Accu.	CL [11], 3072bit	DHS [19, Scheme 3], 384bit	CL [11], 3072bit
DSS	RSA, 3072bit	ECDSA, 256bit	RSA, 3072bit

Evaluation Methodology. In each benchmark, we redact half of the parts. While Redact and ReEnc are likely to be executed on powerful computers, for example in the cloud, the other cryptographic operations might be performed by less powerful mobile phones. Therefore, we performed the benchmarks on two platforms: a PC as well as an Android mobile phone. Table 2 summarizes the execution times of the different implementations for both platforms, where we

---

[1] https://jce.iaik.tugraz.at/.

took the average of 10 runs with different randomly generated data. Instead of also performing the signature verification within the Dec algorithm, we list Verify separately. We had to skip the 500 MB test on the phone, as memory usage is limited to 192 MB for apps on our Google Pixel 2.

General Observations. The growth of execution times is caused by two parameters: the number of parts and the size of the individual parts. Sign symmetrically encrypts all parts and hashes the ciphertexts, so that the RSS signature can then be generated independently of the part sizes. Verify not only hashes the ciphertexts of all remaining parts to verify them against the RSS signature but also symmetrically decrypts the ciphertexts to match them to the plain message. Redact shows very different characteristics in the individual implementations. In contrast, the times for Enc and ReEnc respectively are almost identical, independent of both parameters, as they only perform a single PRE operation on the commitment's opening information from which the symmetric key can be reconstructed. Dec again depends on the number and size of (remaining) parts, as besides the single PRE decryption, all remaining parts are symmetrically decrypted.

Table 2. Execution times (in milliseconds) of three implementations for Scheme 1 (Dec* denotes decryption without additional signature verification)

#	Size	Impl. 1: Sets & CL						Impl. 2: Sets & DHS						Impl. 3: Lists & CL					
		Sign	Enc	Redact	ReEnc	Dec*	Verify	Sign	Enc	Redact	ReEnc	Dec*	Verify	Sign	Enc	Redact	ReEnc	Dec*	Verify
PC (Intel i7-4790, 3.6 GHz, 16GB RAM)																			
10x	1kB	26	1	12	1	1	13	13	2	<1	2	1	47	37	1	36	1	1	18
25x	1kB	54	1	28	1	1	28	19	2	<1	1	1	89	97	1	129	1	1	43
100x	1kB	179	1	97	1	1	89	63	2	<1	1	1	302	852	1	1591	1	1	265
5x	200kB	23	1	6	1	3	16	12	1	<1	1	4	38	28	1	16	1	3	18
25x	1MB	142	1	39	1	40	85	101	1	<1	1	33	143	189	1	151	1	33	111
50x	10MB	1871	1	393	1	749	1100	1777	1	<1	1	752	1216	2310	1	905	1	733	1285
Mobile Phone (Google Pixel 2)																			
10x	1kB	198	13	112	7	21	121	716	13	<1	6	20	2327	212	11	204	6	19	153
25x	1kB	360	12	199	6	22	211	1171	12	<1	6	21	4649	451	12	623	6	20	258
100x	1kB	1194	12	695	6	24	607	3578	12	1	6	27	15982	2631	12	6835	6	27	973
5x	200kB	177	12	73	6	28	106	657	12	<1	6	28	1896	188	12	92	6	24	110
25x	1MB	777	12	370	6	111	480	1654	12	<1	7	111	4936	893	11	808	6	111	533

Impl. 1 for Sets Using CL Accumulators. Impl. 1 provides the best overall performance for verification. For the first implementation, we use an RSS scheme for sets [22, Scheme 1] with CL accumulators [11], where we hash the message parts before signing. With this accumulator, it is possible to optimize the implementation, as described in [22], to generate a batch witness against which multiple values can be verified at once. These batch operations are considerably more efficient than generating and verifying witnesses for each part. However, with this optimization, it becomes necessary to update the batch witness during the Redact operation. As only a single witness needs to be stored and transmitted, the RSS signature size is constant.

Impl. 2 for Sets Using DHS Accumulators. In the second implementation, we use the same RSS scheme for sets [22, Scheme 1] but move towards elliptic curves by instantiating it with ECDSA signatures and DHS accumulators [19, Scheme 3] (extended version of [18]), which is a variant of Nguyen's accumulator [32]. This accumulator does not allow for the optimization used in the first implementation. Consequently, Redact is very fast, as no witnesses need to be updated. Instead, a witness has to be generated and verified per part. On the PC, Sign is slightly faster compared to the first implementation, as signing with ECDSA, evaluating a DHS accumulator, and creating even multiple witnesses is overall more efficient. However, the witness verification within Verify is more costly, which causes a significant impact with a growing number of parts. Interestingly, phones seem to struggle with the implementation of this accumulator, resulting in far worse times than the otherwise observed slowdown compared with the PC. Considering space characteristics, while it is necessary to store one witness per part instead of a single batch witness, each DHS witness is only a single EC point which requires significantly less space than a witness from the CL scheme. Assuming 384-bit EC (compressed) points per witness and an EC point for the DHS accumulator, compared to one 3072-bit CL accumulator and batch witness, the break-even point lies at 15 parts.

Impl. 3 for Lists Using CL Accumulators. For the third implementation, we focused on supporting ordered data by using an RSS scheme for lists [22, Scheme 2], while otherwise the same primitives as in our first implementation are used. Of course, with a scheme for sets, it would be possible to encode the ordering for example by appending an index to the parts. However, after redaction, a gap would be observable, which breaks transparency. Achieving transparency for ordered data comes at a cost: Scheme 2 of Derler et al. [22] requires additional accumulators and witnesses updates to keep track of the ordering without breaking transparency, which of course leads to higher computation and space requirements compared to the first implementation. Using CL accumulators again allows for an optimization [22] around batch witnesses and verifications. This optimization also reduces the RSS signature size from $\mathcal{O}(n^2)$ to $\mathcal{O}(n)$.

5   Conclusion

In this paper, we introduced selective end-to-end data-sharing, which covers various issues for data-sharing in honest-but-curious cloud environments by providing end-to-end confidentiality, authenticity, and selective disclosure. First, we formally defined the concept and modeled requirements for cloud data-sharing as security properties. We then instantiated this model with a proven-secure modular construction that is built on generic cryptographic mechanisms, which can be instantiated with various schemes allowing for implementations tailored to the needs of different application domains. Finally, we evaluated the performance characteristics of three implementations to highlight the practical usefulness of our modular construction and model as a whole.

Acknowledgments. This work was supported by the H2020 EU project CREDENTIAL under grant agreement number 653454.

A   Proof of Theorem 1

We prove Theorem 1 by proving Lemma 1–4 to show the properties unforgeability, proxy privacy, receiver privacy, and, finally, transparency. For proofs using a sequence of games, we denote the event that an adversary wins game i by S_i.

Lemma 1. *If* RSS *is unforgeable and* C *is binding, then Scheme 1 is unforgeable.*

Proof. We prove this lemma using a sequence of games.

Game 0: The original SEEDS unforgeability game.
Game 1: We adapt Game 0 to also abort when the signatures were generated by SIG.

SIG($i, m,$ ADM):
  if $i \notin$ CH $\cup$ HU or SK$[i][0] = \perp$: return $\perp$
  $\sigma \leftarrow$ Sign(SK$[i][0], m,$ ADM)
  $\boxed{\text{Parse } \sigma \text{ as } (O, C, c, \hat{\sigma})}$
  $\overline{\text{Sigs} \leftarrow \text{Sigs}}$
    $\cup \{m' \mid \forall \text{MOD} \overset{\text{ADM}}{\preceq} m \; \forall m' \xleftarrow{\text{MOD}} m\}$
  $\boxed{\text{Coms} \leftarrow \text{Coms} \cup \{C\}}$
  return (m, σ)

Game 1:
  $(ssk^*, spk^*) \leftarrow$ SignKeyGen(1^κ)
  CH $\leftarrow \{0\}$, $SK[0] \leftarrow (ssk^*, spk^*)$
  $\mathcal{O} \leftarrow \{SIG\}$
  $(m, \sigma) \leftarrow \mathcal{A}^{\mathcal{O}}(spk^*)$
  $\boxed{\text{Parse } \sigma \text{ as } (O, C, c, \hat{\sigma})}$
  $\boxed{\text{if } C \in \text{Coms: return } 0}$
  if Verify(spk^*, m, σ) $= 1$ and $m \notin$
  Sigs, then **return** 1, **else return** 0

Transition $0 \Rightarrow 1$: Game 1 behaves the same as Game 0 unless $\mathcal{A}$ returned a valid pair (m, σ) where the included RSS signature $\hat{\sigma}$ on $\{C\} \cup c$ was generated by SIG. We denote this failure event as F, thus $|\Pr[S_0] - \Pr[S_1]| \leq \Pr[F]$. In this case, since C, c, and $\hat{\sigma}$ are fixed, two different messages can only be obtained, by decrypting with different keys k_1 and k_2. From the fixed C, different keys can only be recovered with different opening informations O_1 and O_2. To achieve this, the adversary would have to break the binding property of C, therefore $\Pr[F] = \epsilon_C^{Bind}(\kappa)$.

Finally, we build an efficient adversary $\mathcal{B}$ from an adversary $\mathcal{A}$ winning Game 1 for the unforgeability of RSS in $\mathcal{R}_{\text{RSS}}^{Unf} \rightarrow G_1$. We can simulate SIG except for $i = 0$, where we obtain the RSS signatures using its signing oracle. Note that all values are consistently distributed. Now, if we obtain a forgery (m, σ) from $\mathcal{A}$, then parse σ as $(O, C, c, \hat{\sigma})$ and forward $\{C\} \cup c, \hat{\sigma}$ as a forgery. Therefore, $\Pr[S_1] = \epsilon_{\text{RSS}}^{Unf}(\kappa)$, resulting in $\Pr[S_0] = \epsilon_C^{Bind}(\kappa) + \epsilon_{\text{RSS}}^{Unf}(\kappa)$, which is negligible.

Reduction $\mathcal{R}_{\text{RSS}}^{Unf} \rightarrow G_1(pk)$:
  $(m, \sigma) \leftarrow \mathcal{A}^{\text{SIG}}(pk)$
  Parse σ as $(O, C, C, \hat{\sigma})$
  return $(\{C\} \cup c, \hat{\sigma})$

SIG($0, m,$ ADM):
  $k \leftarrow$ S.KeyGen(1^κ)
  $c \leftarrow \{$S.Enc$(k, m_i) \mid m_i \in M\}$
  $c_{\text{ADM}} \leftarrow \{c_i \mid c_i \in c, m_i \in$ ADM$\}$
  $\sigma \leftarrow (O, C, c, \mathcal{O}^{Sign}(\underline{sk}, \{C\} \cup c, \{C\} \cup c_{\text{ADM}}))$
  Sigs $\leftarrow$ Sigs $\cup \{m' \mid \forall \text{MOD} \overset{\text{ADM}}{\preceq} m \; \forall m' \xleftarrow{\text{MOD}} m\}$
  Coms $\leftarrow$ Coms $\cup \{C\}$
  return (m', σ)

Lemma 2. *If the* PRE *is IND-RCCA-2 secure,* C *is hiding,* S *is IND-CPA secure, and* RSS *is unforgeable, then Scheme 1 is proxy private.*

Proof. We prove proxy privacy using a sequence of games.

Game 0: The original SEEDS proxy privacy game.

Game 1: We restrict the decryption oracles to ciphertexts that contain messages signed by the signature oracle. Therefore, we adapt SE as SIG in Lemma 1 to track the generated commitments, $\boxed{\text{Coms} \leftarrow \text{Coms} \cup \{C\}}$. Also, we adapt D to $\boxed{\text{parse } c_i \text{ as } (O_A, C, c, \hat\sigma)}$ and $\boxed{\text{if } C \notin \text{Coms: return } \bot}$.

Transition 0 $\Rightarrow$ 1: The two games proceed identically unless the adversary submits a valid signature to D. In that case the adversary produced a forgery, i.e. $|\Pr[S_0] - \Pr[S_1]| \leq \epsilon_{\mathsf{SEEDS}}^{Unf}(\kappa)$.

Game 2: In the used Encrypt algorithm, we replace the opening information with a random r from the same domain, and simulate the oracles accordingly:

Encrypt:
> Parse σ as $(O, C, c, \hat\sigma)$
> $\boxed{r \xleftarrow{R} Domain(\mathsf{C}_O)}$
> $O_A \leftarrow \mathsf{PRE.Enc}^2(\mathsf{epk}_A, \boxed{r})$
> $\boxed{\mathsf{Map} \leftarrow \mathsf{Map} \cup \{(O_A, C, O)\}}$
> **return** $c_A \leftarrow (O_A, C, c, \hat\sigma)$.

$\mathsf{RE}(i, j, k, c_j)$:
> Parse c_j as $(O_A, C, c, \hat\sigma)$
> Look up $(O_A, C, O) \in \mathsf{Map}$
> **if** not contained: run RE unmodified
> **else**
>> $O_B \leftarrow \mathsf{PRE.ReEnc}(\mathsf{rk}_{i \to j}, O_A)$
>> $\mathsf{Map} \leftarrow \mathsf{Map} \cup \{(O_B, C, O)\}$
>> **return** $(O_B, C, c, \hat\sigma)$

$\mathsf{D}(i, c_i)$:
> Parse c_i as $(O_A, C, c, \hat\sigma)$
> Lookup $(O_A, C, O) \in \mathsf{Map}$
> **if** not contained: run D unmodified.
> **else**
>> $k \leftarrow \mathsf{C.Open}(O, C)$
>> $m \leftarrow \{\mathsf{S.Dec}(k, c_l) \mid c_l \in c\}$
>> $\sigma \leftarrow (O, C, c, \hat\sigma)$
> **if** $\mathsf{Verify}(\mathsf{spk}, m, \sigma) \neq 1$ or m is a subset of chosen/forwarded m_0, m_1:
>> **return** $\bot$
> **return** (m, σ)

Transition 1 $\Rightarrow$ 2: From a distinguisher $\mathcal{D}^{1 \to 2}$, we build an IND-RCCA-2 adversary against the PRE scheme. Indeed, let $\mathcal{C}$ be an IND-RCCA-2 challenger. We modify Encrypt in the following way: Simulate everything honestly, but sample $\boxed{r}$ uniformly at random from the domain of openings of C and run $\boxed{O_A \leftarrow \mathcal{C}(O, r)}$, where $c \leftarrow \mathcal{C}(m_0, m_1)$ denotes a challenge ciphertext with respect to m_0 and m_1. The RE oracle calls the challenger's RE oracle instead of PRE.ReEnc. Consequently, $|\Pr[S_1] - \Pr[S_2]| \leq \epsilon_{\mathsf{PRE}}^{IND-RCCA-2}(\kappa)$.

Game 3: For the signature contained in the challenge ciphertext, we commit to a random value, i.e., we set $\boxed{r \xleftarrow{R} Domain(\mathsf{S}_k)}$ and $(C, O) \leftarrow \mathsf{C.Com}(\boxed{r})$.

Transition $2 \Rightarrow 3$: From a distinguisher $\mathcal{D}^{2 \to 3}$, we obtain a hiding adversary against C. Let $\mathcal{C}$ be a hiding challenger. We modify Sign in the following way: Simulate everything honestly, but choose $\boxed{r}$ uniformly at random from the same domain as the S keys and run $\boxed{C \leftarrow \mathcal{C}(k, r)}$, where $C \leftarrow \mathcal{C}(m_0, m_1)$ denotes a challenge commitment with respect to m_0 and m_1. Therefore, $|\Pr[S_2] - \Pr[S_3]| \leq \epsilon_{\mathcal{C}}^{Hide}(\kappa)$.

Game 4: In the challenge ciphertext, we replace the message parts with random values drawn from an identical domain with the same corresponding lengths, i.e. $\boxed{\text{for } i \in [1..|M|]:\ r_i \xleftarrow{R} Domain(m)}$ and $c \leftarrow \{\mathsf{S.Enc}(k, \boxed{r_i}) \mid m_i \in m\}$.

Transition $3 \Rightarrow 4$: A distinguisher $\mathcal{D}^{3 \to 4}$ is a (hybrid) IND-CPA adversary against S. Let $\mathcal{C}$ be an IND-CPA challenger. We modify Sign in the following way: Simulate everything honestly, but for each message part choose $\boxed{r_i}$ uniformly at random from the message space and run $\boxed{c_i \leftarrow \mathcal{C}(m_i, r_i)}$, where $c \leftarrow \mathcal{C}(m_0, m_1)$ denotes a challenge ciphertext with respect to m_0 and m_1. Therefore, $|\Pr[S_4] - \Pr[S_3]| \leq |m| \cdot \epsilon_{\mathsf{S}}^{IND-CPA}(\kappa)$, with $|m|$ polynomial in the security parameter κ.

Finally, we have that $\Pr[S_4] = 1/2$, since the adversary now cannot do better than guessing. Combining the claims, we see that the following is negligible:

$$|\Pr[S_0] - 1/2| \leq \epsilon_{\mathsf{SEEDS}}^{Unf}(\kappa) + \epsilon_{\mathsf{PRE}}^{IND-RCCA-2}(\kappa) + \epsilon_{\mathsf{C}}^{Hide}(\kappa) + |m| \cdot \epsilon_{\mathsf{S}}^{IND-CPA}(\kappa)$$

Lemma 3. *If RSS is private, then Scheme 1 is receiver private.*

Proof. Assuming there is an efficient adversary $\mathcal{A}$ against the receiver privacy of Scheme 1, we build an adversary $\mathcal{B}$ against the privacy of RSS:

Reduction $\mathcal{R}_{\mathsf{RSS}}^{Priv} \to_{\mathsf{SEEDS}}^{RP}$ (pk):
  $(esk^*, epk^*) \leftarrow \mathsf{SEEDS.EncKeyGen}(1^\kappa)$
  $\mathsf{CH} \leftarrow \{0\}$
  $\mathsf{EK}[0] \leftarrow (esk^*, epk^*),\ \mathsf{SK}[0] \leftarrow (\bot, \mathsf{pk})$
  $\mathcal{O} \leftarrow \{\mathsf{AU}, \mathsf{SIG}, \mathsf{LoRRedact}(\cdots\cdots, b)\}$
  return $b^* \leftarrow \mathcal{A}^{\mathcal{O}}(\mathsf{pk}, epk^*)$

  $\mathsf{AU}(i, t)$: This oracle is simulated honestly.

  $\mathsf{SIG}(i, m, \mathsf{ADM})$: For $i \in \mathsf{HU}$ and $i \in \mathsf{CU}$ everything is computed honestly, while we use $\mathcal{O}^{Sign}$ for $i \in \mathsf{CH}$ as in Lemma 1.

$\mathsf{LoRRedact}(i, j, m_0, \mathsf{MOD}_0, m_1, \mathsf{MOD}_1, \mathsf{ADM}, b)$:
  For $i \neq 0$ or $j \notin \mathsf{HU} \cup \mathsf{CU}$ everything is computed honestly, otherwise we run:
    $rk \leftarrow \mathsf{ReKeyGen}(\mathsf{EK}[i][0], \mathsf{EK}[j][1])$
    $k \leftarrow \mathsf{S.KeyGen}(1^\kappa; \omega)$
    $(C, O) \leftarrow \mathcal{C}.\mathsf{Com}(k)$
    $O_B \leftarrow \mathsf{PRE.ReEnc}(rk, \mathsf{PRE.Enc}(\mathsf{EK}[i][1], O))$
    for both $c \in \{0, 1\}$:
      $c_c \leftarrow \{\mathsf{S.Enc}(k, m_i) \mid m_i \in m_c\}$
      $c_{\mathsf{ADM}, c} \leftarrow \{c_i \mid c_i \in c_c, m_i \in \mathsf{ADM}\}$
    $X \leftarrow \mathcal{O}^{\mathsf{LoRRedact}}(\underline{\mathsf{sk}}, \underline{\mathsf{pk}},$
      $(\{C\} \cup c_c, \{C\} \cup c_{\mathsf{ADM},c}, \mathsf{MOD}_c)_{c \in \{0,1\}}, \underline{b})$
    if $X = \bot$: **return** $\bot$
    Parse X as $(\{C\} \cup c_{b'}, \hat{\sigma}'_b)$
    return $(O_B, C, c'_b, \hat{\sigma}'_b)$

The reduction extends the RSS public key to a SEEDS public key, and forwards it to $\mathcal{A}$. The oracle LoRRedact sets up everything honestly and obtains signatures from LoRRedact of RSS. All values are distributed consistently, and $\mathcal{B}$ wins the privacy experiment of RSS with the same probability as $\mathcal{A}$ breaks the SEEDS receiver privacy of Scheme 1.

Lemma 4. *If* RSS *is transparent, then Scheme 1 is transparent.*

Proof. Assuming there is an efficient adversary $\mathcal{A}$ against the transparency of Scheme 1, we construct an adversary $\mathcal{B}$ against the transparency of the RSS:

Reduction $\mathcal{R}_{\mathsf{RSS}}^{Trans} \to_{\mathsf{SEEDS}}^{Trans}$ (pk):
  $(\mathsf{esk}^*, \mathsf{epk}^*) \leftarrow \mathsf{SEEDS.EncKeyGen}(1^\kappa)$
  $\mathsf{CH} \leftarrow \{0\}$
  $\mathsf{EK}[0] \leftarrow (\mathsf{esk}^*, \mathsf{epk}^*), \mathsf{SK}[0] \leftarrow (\bot, \mathsf{pk})$
  $\mathcal{O} \leftarrow \{\mathsf{AU}, \mathsf{SIG}, \mathsf{RedactOrNot}\}$
  return $b' \leftarrow \mathcal{A}^{\mathcal{O}}(\mathsf{esk}^*, \mathsf{epk}^*, \mathsf{pk})$

$\mathsf{AU}(i,t)$: This oracle is simulated honestly.

$\mathsf{SIG}(i, m, \mathsf{ADM})$: For $i \in \mathsf{HU}$ and $i \in \mathsf{CU}$ everything is computeed honestly, while we use $\mathcal{O}^{Sign}$ for $i \in \mathsf{CH}$ as in Lemma 1.

$\mathsf{RedactOrNot}(i, m, \mathsf{MOD}, \mathsf{ADM}, b)$: For $i \neq 0$ everything is computed honestly, otherwise we run the following:
  $k \leftarrow \mathsf{S.KeyGen}(1^\kappa; \omega)$
  $(C, O) \leftarrow \mathsf{C.Com}(k)$
  $O_A \leftarrow \mathsf{PRE.Enc}(\mathsf{EK}[i][1], O)$
  $c \leftarrow \{\mathsf{S.Enc}(k, m_i) \mid m_i \in m\}$
  $c_{\mathsf{ADM}} \leftarrow \{c_i \mid c_i \in c, m_i \in \mathsf{ADM}\}$
  $(\{C\} \cup c', \hat{\sigma}') \leftarrow \mathcal{O}^{Sign/Redact}(\underline{\mathsf{sk}}, \underline{\mathsf{pk}},$
      $\{C\} \cup c, \mathsf{MOD}, \{C\} \cup c_{\mathsf{ADM}}, \underline{b})$
  return $c'_{A,b} \leftarrow (O_A, C, c', \hat{\sigma}')$

The reduction extends the RSS public key to a SEEDS public key honestly, and forwards it together with the secret encryption key to $\mathcal{A}$. Similarly, RedactOrNot sets up everything honestly and queries the RSS oracle $\mathcal{O}^{Sign/Redact}$ to obtain the signature. Finally, it outputs a consistent ciphertext, hence, $\mathcal{B}$ wins with the same probability as $\mathcal{A}$.

References

1. Ateniese, G., Benson, K., Hohenberger, S.: Key-private proxy re-encryption. In: Fischlin, M. (ed.) CT-RSA 2009. LNCS, vol. 5473, pp. 279–294. Springer, Heidelberg (2009). https://doi.org/10.1007/978-3-642-00862-7_19
2. Ateniese, G., Fu, K., Green, M., Hohenberger, S.: Improved proxy re-encryption schemes with applications to secure distributed storage. In: NDSS. The Internet Society (2005)
3. Ateniese, G., Fu, K., Green, M., Hohenberger, S.: Improved proxy re-encryption schemes with applications to secure distributed storage. ACM Trans. Inf. Syst. Secur. **9**(1), 1–30 (2006)
4. Barbulescu, R., Duquesne, S.: Updating key size estimations for pairings. J. Cryptol. **32**(4), 1298–1336 (2019)
5. Barker, E.: SP 800-57. Recommendation for Key Management, Part 1: General (Rev 4). Technical report, National Institute of Standards & Technology (2016)
6. Blaze, M., Bleumer, G., Strauss, M.: Divertible protocols and atomic proxy cryptography. In: Nyberg, K. (ed.) EUROCRYPT 1998. LNCS, vol. 1403, pp. 127–144. Springer, Heidelberg (1998). https://doi.org/10.1007/BFb0054122
7. Boneh, D., Sahai, A., Waters, B.: Functional encryption: definitions and challenges. In: Ishai, Y. (ed.) TCC 2011. LNCS, vol. 6597, pp. 253–273. Springer, Heidelberg (2011). https://doi.org/10.1007/978-3-642-19571-6_16
8. Brzuska, C., et al.: Redactable signatures for tree-structured data: definitions and constructions. In: Zhou, J., Yung, M. (eds.) ACNS 2010. LNCS, vol. 6123, pp. 87–104. Springer, Heidelberg (2010). https://doi.org/10.1007/978-3-642-13708-2_6

9. Camenisch, J., Herreweghen, E.V.: Design and implementation of the idemix anonymous credential system. In: ACM CCS, pp. 21–30. ACM (2002)

10. Camenisch, J., Lysyanskaya, A.: An efficient system for non-transferable anonymous credentials with optional anonymity revocation. In: Pfitzmann, B. (ed.) EUROCRYPT 2001. LNCS, vol. 2045, pp. 93–118. Springer, Heidelberg (2001). https://doi.org/10.1007/3-540-44987-6_7

11. Camenisch, J., Lysyanskaya, A.: Dynamic accumulators and application to efficient revocation of anonymous credentials. In: Yung, M. (ed.) CRYPTO 2002. LNCS, vol. 2442, pp. 61–76. Springer, Heidelberg (2002). https://doi.org/10.1007/3-540-45708-9_5

12. Canetti, R., Hohenberger, S.: Chosen-ciphertext secure proxy re-encryption. In: ACM CCS, pp. 185–194. ACM (2007)

13. Chandran, N., Chase, M., Liu, F.-H., Nishimaki, R., Xagawa, K.: Re-encryption, functional re-encryption, and multi-hop re-encryption: a framework for achieving obfuscation-based security and instantiations from lattices. In: Krawczyk, H. (ed.) PKC 2014. LNCS, vol. 8383, pp. 95–112. Springer, Heidelberg (2014). https://doi.org/10.1007/978-3-642-54631-0_6

14. Chaum, D.: Untraceable electronic mail, return addresses, and digital pseudonyms. Commun. ACM **24**(2), 84–88 (1981)

15. Chaum, D.: Security without identification: transaction systems to make big brother obsolete. Commun. ACM **28**(10), 1030–1044 (1985)

16. Chow, S.S.M., Weng, J., Yang, Y., Deng, R.H.: Efficient unidirectional proxy re-encryption. In: Bernstein, D.J., Lange, T. (eds.) AFRICACRYPT 2010. LNCS, vol. 6055, pp. 316–332. Springer, Heidelberg (2010). https://doi.org/10.1007/978-3-642-12678-9_19

17. Demirel, D., Derler, D., Hanser, C., Pöhls, H.C., Slamanig, D., Traverso, G.: PRISMACLOUD D4.4: overview of functional and malleable signature schemes. Technical repoet, H2020 PRISMACLOUD (2015)

18. Derler, D., Hanser, C., Slamanig, D.: Revisiting cryptographic accumulators, additional properties and relations to other primitives. In: Nyberg, K. (ed.) CT-RSA 2015. LNCS, vol. 9048, pp. 127–144. Springer, Cham (2015). https://doi.org/10.1007/978-3-319-16715-2_7

19. Derler, D., Hanser, C., Slamanig, D.: Revisiting cryptographic accumulators, additional properties and relations to other primitives. IACR ePrint 2015, 87 (2015)

20. Derler, D., Krenn, S., Lorünser, T., Ramacher, S., Slamanig, D., Striecks, C.: Revisiting proxy re-encryption: forward secrecy, improved security, and applications. In: Abdalla, M., Dahab, R. (eds.) PKC 2018. LNCS, vol. 10769, pp. 219–250. Springer, Cham (2018). https://doi.org/10.1007/978-3-319-76578-5_8

21. Derler, D., Krenn, S., Slamanig, D.: Signer-anonymous designated-verifier redactable signatures for cloud-based data sharing. In: Foresti, S., Persiano, G. (eds.) CANS 2016. LNCS, vol. 10052, pp. 211–227. Springer, Cham (2016). https://doi.org/10.1007/978-3-319-48965-0_13

22. Derler, D., Pöhls, H.C., Samelin, K., Slamanig, D.: A general framework for redactable signatures and new constructions. In: Kwon, S., Yun, A. (eds.) ICISC 2015. LNCS, vol. 9558, pp. 3–19. Springer, Cham (2016). https://doi.org/10.1007/978-3-319-30840-1_1

23. Derler, D., Ramacher, S., Slamanig, D.: Homomorphic proxy re-authenticators and applications to verifiable multi-user data aggregation. In: Kiayias, A. (ed.) FC 2017. LNCS, vol. 10322, pp. 124–142. Springer, Cham (2017). https://doi.org/10.1007/978-3-319-70972-7_7

24. European Commission: Regulation (EU) 2016/679 on the protection of natural persons with regard to the processing of personal data and on the free movement of such data, and repealing Directive 95/46/EC (General Data Protection Regulation). Official Journal of the European Union L119/59, May 2016
25. Goyal, V., Pandey, O., Sahai, A., Waters, B.: Attribute-based encryption for fine-grained access control of encrypted data. In: ACM CCS, pp. 89–98. ACM (2006)
26. Hörandner, F., Krenn, S., Migliavacca, A., Thiemer, F., Zwattendorfer, B.: CREDENTIAL: a framework for privacy-preserving cloud-based data sharing. In: ARES, pp. 742–749. IEEE Computer Society (2016)
27. Johnson, R., Molnar, D., Song, D., Wagner, D.: Homomorphic signature schemes. In: Preneel, B. (ed.) CT-RSA 2002. LNCS, vol. 2271, pp. 244–262. Springer, Heidelberg (2002). https://doi.org/10.1007/3-540-45760-7_17
28. Krenn, S., Lorünser, T., Salzer, A., Striecks, C.: Towards attribute-based credentials in the cloud. In: Capkun, S., Chow, S.S.M. (eds.) CANS 2017. LNCS, vol. 11261, pp. 179–202. Springer, Cham (2018). https://doi.org/10.1007/978-3-030-02641-7_9
29. Kundu, A., Bertino, E.: Privacy-preserving authentication of trees and graphs. Int. J. Inf. Sec. 12(6), 467–494 (2013)
30. Libert, B., Vergnaud, D.: Unidirectional chosen-ciphertext secure proxy re-encryption. In: Cramer, R. (ed.) PKC 2008. LNCS, vol. 4939, pp. 360–379. Springer, Heidelberg (2008). https://doi.org/10.1007/978-3-540-78440-1_21
31. Menezes, A., Sarkar, P., Singh, S.: Challenges with assessing the impact of NFS advances on the security of pairing-based cryptography. In: Phan, R.C.-W., Yung, M. (eds.) Mycrypt 2016. LNCS, vol. 10311, pp. 83–108. Springer, Cham (2017). https://doi.org/10.1007/978-3-319-61273-7_5
32. Nguyen, L.: Accumulators from bilinear pairings and applications. In: Menezes, A. (ed.) CT-RSA 2005. LNCS, vol. 3376, pp. 275–292. Springer, Heidelberg (2005). https://doi.org/10.1007/978-3-540-30574-3_19
33. Paquin, C., Zaverucha, G.: U-prove cryptographic specification v1.1 (revision 3). Technical report, Microsoft, December 2013
34. Pirretti, M., Traynor, P., McDaniel, P.D., Waters, B.: Secure attribute-based systems. In: ACM CCS, pp. 99–112. ACM (2006)
35. Sahai, A., Waters, B.: Fuzzy identity-based encryption. In: Cramer, R. (ed.) EUROCRYPT 2005. LNCS, vol. 3494, pp. 457–473. Springer, Heidelberg (2005). https://doi.org/10.1007/11426639_27
36. Samelin, K., Pöhls, H.C., Bilzhause, A., Posegga, J., de Meer, H.: Redactable signatures for independent removal of structure and content. In: Ryan, M.D., Smyth, B., Wang, G. (eds.) ISPEC 2012. LNCS, vol. 7232, pp. 17–33. Springer, Heidelberg (2012). https://doi.org/10.1007/978-3-642-29101-2_2
37. Steinfeld, R., Bull, L., Zheng, Y.: Content extraction signatures. In: Kim, K. (ed.) ICISC 2001. LNCS, vol. 2288, pp. 285–304. Springer, Heidelberg (2002). https://doi.org/10.1007/3-540-45861-1_22
38. Weng, J., Deng, R.H., Ding, X., Chu, C., Lai, J.: Conditional proxy re-encryption secure against chosen-ciphertext attack. In: AsiaCCS, pp. 322–332. ACM (2009)

Cloud Data Sharing and Device-Loss Recovery with Hardware-Bound Keys

Felix Hörandner$^{(\boxtimes)}$ and Franco Nieddu

Graz University of Technology, Graz, Austria
{felix.hoerandner,franco.nieddu}@iaik.tugraz.at

Abstract. Cloud-based storage services, such as Dropbox, Google Drive, or NextCloud, are broadly used to share data with others or between the individual devices of one user due to their convenience. Various end-to-end encryption mechanisms can be applied to protect the confidentiality of sensitive data in a not fully trusted cloud environment. As all such encryption mechanisms require to store keys on the client's device, losing a device (and key) might lead to catastrophic consequences: Losing access to all outsourced data. Strategies to recover from key-loss have various trade-offs. For example, storing the key on a flash drive burdens the user to keep it secure and available, while encrypting the key with a password before uploading it to the cloud requires users to remember a complex password. These strategies also require that the key can be extracted from the device's hardware, which risks the confidentiality of the key and data once a curious person finds a lost device or a thief steals it.

In this paper, we propose and implement a cloud-based data sharing system that supports recovery after key-loss while binding the keys to the devices' hardware. By using multi-use proxy re-encryption, we build a network of re-encryption keys that enables users to use any of their devices to access data or share it with other users. In case of device-loss, we amend this network of re-encryption keys – potentially with the help of one or more user-selected recovery users – to restore data access to the user's new device. Our implementation highlights the system's feasibility and underlines its practical performance.

Keywords: Cloud data sharing · Key-loss recovery · Hardware-protected keys

1 Introduction

Cloud storage services have seen broad adoption due to their convenience: These services enable users to store their data in the cloud, to access these data from any of their multiple devices (e.g., laptop, phone, tablet, etc.), and to share them with others. To also support sensitive data (e.g., medical records or company secrets), such services employ cryptographic mechanisms to ensure end-to-end confidentiality, for example, in the form of hybrid encryption or more elaborate

© Springer Nature Switzerland AG 2019
D. Garg et al. (Eds.): ICISS 2019, LNCS 11952, pp. 196–217, 2019.
https://doi.org/10.1007/978-3-030-36945-3_11

lockbox-constructions [9,10,18]. With such cryptography, sharing access to data boils down to managing and distributing keys.

Employing cryptography to achieve secure data sharing requires to store the involved key material on the users' devices. If these devices (and their keys) are lost, broken or stolen, users face dire consequences, i.e., losing access to their important data. Therefore, applications that rely on client-side keys need to employ a strategy to recover from device- or key-loss. In data sharing scenarios where users own multiple devices, the loss of one device can be compensated as the user's other devices still have access. However, not all users own multiple devices, and, thus, a single-device recovery option has to be offered as well.

Approaches for recovery from key-loss have different trade-offs: Key material can be stored on a flash drive or printed as a QR code, which requires a secure location that stays available as well as confidential. Password-based encryption [17,21] or biometric encryption [8,16] can protect the key before storing it on a cloud service. Such approaches rely on limited entropy, which could be brute-forced by powerful attackers given sufficient time. Alternatively, secret sharing [23] enables to split the key into parts, distribute these parts across various semi-trusted entities, and reconstruct the key from a subset. This splitting requires a trust decision but enables a user-defined trade-off between confidentiality and availability.

However, all of these approaches for key distribution and recovery require that the key can be extracted, which leaves users vulnerable if one device is lost or stolen. Instead, we aim for a system which enables to bind the per-device keys to the devices' hardware with technologies such as Intel's SGX [15] or ARM's TrustZone [2] so that they cannot be extracted by attackers.

Our Proposed System. In this work, we build a cloud-based data sharing system, which supports multiple devices per user with keys bound to the hardware but also offers recovery from device- and key-loss for users with only one device. Highlighted features of our system are: (1) recovery with a threshold of users that enables a better trade-off between availability to confidentiality for single-device users, (2) improved key security through hardware protection, and (3) consequently immediate full access after recovery without the need for manual re-keying.

As a *basis*, we leverage proxy re-encryption (PRE) [3,5] and in particular its multi-use property. When using PRE instead of traditional public key encryption, the user generates re-encryption keys, which enable a proxy (i.e., the cloud storage service) to transform ciphertexts encrypted for the data owner into ciphertexts encrypted for an intended receiver. Multi-use PRE (MU-PRE) [6] allows to further re-encrypt ciphertexts that were already re-encrypted.

To *support multiple devices per user*, we propose to build and maintain a set of re-encryption keys, which enables to re-encrypt a user's ciphertexts for any of her (authorized) devices. With the multi-use property, any connected device of the user may generate re-encryption keys to other users' devices, which effectively shares access to her ciphertexts, as these ciphertexts can be successively re-encrypted. Building and maintaining such a network of re-encryption keys enables full access and sharing capabilities on each device.

Recovery from key-loss not only needs to be supported for the trivial case where the user owns a second device with access to all data, but also for users who only own a single device: Single-device users select a sufficiently trusted recovery user who is willing to assist in case recovery becomes necessary. This recovery user is responsible for identifying and authenticating users who request recovery to ensure that only new devices of legit users get access. Users need to convince their recovery users to generate a re-encryption key for their new devices. With that re-encryption key, the cloud storage service re-encrypts the user's data for the recovery user and further for the user's new device, making it accessible again. As the cloud storage service does not expose intermediate ciphertexts, recovery users do not get access to the data. Recovery requires little effort on the user's side to make all data immediately available (i.e., generate re-encryption keys).

Our approach also enables us to *bind the keys to the devices' hardware*. The data sharing and recovery processes are designed so that private key material does not have to be extracted from the devices' hardware. Therefore, we are able to bind the keys to the device's hardware and only unlock them for authorized users. As attackers (e.g., thieves) are not able to extract and steal the keys, time-consuming re-keying and re-distribution of keys is not necessary.

Implementation and Discussion. Additionally, we evaluate the feasibility and performance of our system through a proof-of-concept implementation. In particular, we give details on the implementation of the used MU-PRE scheme and estimate costs of deployment on Amazon Web Services (AWS). Finally, we discuss the recovery effort from the user's perspective, elaborate on the performance results in the data sharing setting, and argue the benefits of hardware-bound keys as such approaches require no re-keying on the users' devices.

2　Background and Related Work

Cloud Data Storage. Cloud storage services employ cryptography to achieve end-to-end confidentiality for data that are handled in a not fully trusted cloud environment. With hybrid encryption, the data is symmetrically encrypted, while the used symmetric key is encrypted with a public key encryption scheme for one or more intended receivers. Fu's Cepheus [9] expands on hybrid encryption and introduces the concept of a lockbox: A lockbox contains the key to access a user's data. As the lockbox is protected (e.g., public key encrypted), it can be stored in public, and only authorized people are able to open it. Plutus [18] and SiRiUS [10] further expand on this idea.

Encryption for Data Sharing. With hybrid encryption or lockbox-constructions, *public key encryption* can be used to share access to a file by distributing access to the symmetric content encryption key.

Proxy Re-Encryption (PRE) [3,5] can be used instead of public key encryption to share access to the symmetric keys or lockboxes. PRE extends asymmetric encryption by enabling a semi-trusted proxy to transform ciphertext encrypted for one user into ciphertext encrypted for another user, without learning the underlying plaintext in an intermediate step. The user controls the sharing process by generating re-encryption keys towards other users, which the proxy requires in the transformation process. Ateniese et al. [3] applied PRE to data sharing: Users encrypt their files for themselves and generate re-encryption keys for intended receivers. Given those re-encryption keys, the cloud storage service (i.e., proxy) transforms the user's data for authorized receivers, who are then able to decrypt the ciphertext with their own key material. Previous work (e.g., [12]) has focused on single-use PRE schemes, where ciphertexts can be re-encrypted once, but already re-encrypted ciphertext cannot be further transformed.

Attribute-Based Encryption (ABE) [11] represents another alternative to share access to data. With ABE, data is encrypted for attributes rather than for specific public keys (i.e., identities). Everyone with key material matching the ciphertext's attributes is able to decrypt. Such keys are issued by a trusted third party, which entails high trust requirements, as this party can decrypt any ciphertext.

Recovery from Key-Loss. The above-described encryption mechanisms either rely on per-user master keys or individual keys per device. We summarize approaches to recovery in case the device holding such keys breaks or is lost.

Password-based encryption can be used to wrap the user's key before uploading it to a cloud storage. This wrapped key is retrieved either by the user's other devices or on a new device once recovery becomes necessary. Such encryption relies on keys generated from the user's password through a key derivation function (e.g., PKDF2 [17], scrypt [21]). Increasing the derivation costs propagates directly to attackers. Consequently, this approach offers little protection against cloud attackers with plenty of resources and sufficient time to brute-force the password.

When employing *biometric cryptosystems* (BCSs), e.g., based on fuzzy extractors [8] or biohashing [16], the users' biometric templates (e.g., fingerprints) are used to protect the keys. After storing these protected keys at a cloud service, they can be downloaded and decrypted on any device where the user inputs her biometric template. Unfortunately, BCSs require additional data to generate stable, high-entropy keys [19], which again need to be kept available and confidential.

With *secret sharing* [23], users split their keys into multiple shares, hand these shares to different trusted parties, and are later able to reconstruct the key from a threshold of shares. For example, Huang et al. [14] propose to apply secret sharing on keys in a cloud data sharing setting. However, they do not suggest any authentication mechanisms to ensure that only authorized parties obtain shares.

Password-Protected Secret Sharing [4, 7] introducing password-based authentication for secret sharing where entities holding the shares are able to verify the user's password but do not learn it. For example, Hörandner et al. [13] have applied this concept to split the keys over a hierarchy of trusted services.

However, secret sharing, as well as the previous key recovery mechanisms, require that the users' keys can be extracted from the devices' hardware.

Hardware-Protection for Keys. We are interested in technologies that bind the keys to the devices' hardware and only unlock them for authorized users.

On phones with ARM's TrustZone [2] technology, the CPU switches between a less trusted and a more trusted state (so-called world), while preventing unintended information leakage between them. The more trusted world has access to secrets and is typically used to execute security code, while the less trusted world runs the operating system and applications. Such technologies can be used to establish a secure boot chain, which ensures that a valid version of the operating system is loaded on the device. Such a valid operating system only unlocks the protected key material after the user has been authenticated. Devices with hardware support for key protection are widely deployed: All devices shipped with Android Nougat or newer are required to have such hardware protections. That are >38%[1] of 2.5 Billion devices[2] as of Juli 2019, when conservatively only counting devices with Oreo and Pie, as devices rarely receive more than one major-version upgrade. iPhone 5S and later also support hardware-bound keys.

On PCs and servers, Intel's SGX [15] introduces new instruction codes that enable to deploy code in a private memory region, a so-called enclave. The memory contents cannot be read by any other process even if the operating system is malicious. SGX employs on-the-fly encryption and integrity verification in the CPU. This technology has been introduced with Intel's Skylake CPUs in 2015.

Building Block. *Multi-Use Proxy Re-Encryption* (MU-PRE) [6] not only allows to re-encrypt once but multiple times in succession, i.e., to re-encrypt ciphertexts that have already been re-encrypted. We focus on unidirectional, non-interactive MU-PRE schemes as a fundamental building block of our concept.

Definition 1 (MU-PRE). *A multi-use proxy re-encryption (MU-PRE) scheme with message space $\mathcal{M}$ consists of the following PPT algorithms:*

$\mathsf{KeyGen}(1^{\kappa}) \rightarrow (\mathsf{sk}, \mathsf{pk})$: *On input of a security parameter κ, the algorithm outputs a secret and public key $(\mathsf{sk}, \mathsf{pk})$.*

$\mathsf{Enc}(\mathsf{pk}, M) \rightarrow C^1$: *On input of a public key pk and a message $M \in \mathcal{M}$, the algorithm outputs a level-1 ciphertext C^1.*

$\mathsf{Dec}(\mathsf{sk}, C^l) \rightarrow M$: *On input of a secret key sk and level-l ciphertext C^l, the algorithm outputs $M \in \mathcal{M}$ or $\{\bot\}$.*

$\mathsf{RKGen}(\mathsf{sk}_A, \mathsf{pk}_B) \rightarrow \mathsf{rk}_{A \rightarrow B}$: *On input of a secret key sk_A of user A and a public key pk_B of user B, the algorithm outputs a re-encryption key $\mathsf{rk}_{A \rightarrow B}$.*

$\mathsf{ReEnc}(\mathsf{rk}_{A \rightarrow B}, C_A^l) \rightarrow C_B^{l+1}$: *Given a re-encryption key $\mathsf{rk}_{A \rightarrow B}$ and a level-l ciphertext C_A^l for A, the algorithm returns a l+1-level ciphertext C_B^{l+1} for B.*

---

[1] https://developer.android.com/about/dashboards/.

[2] Announced at Google I/O 2019.

3   System Model

This section introduces the actors of our system, their main interactions, and trust assumptions. Figure 1 illustrates our data sharing setting.

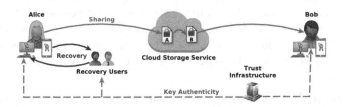

Fig. 1. System model

Actors and Data Flow. *Multiple users* want to store and share their data securely. Every user has *one primary device* and possibly *multiple secondary devices*. Each of those devices has its own key pair, where the private key is stored in a secure environment (e.g., hardware-protected). The users instruct their devices to encrypt the data before uploading it to the *cloud storage service*. Of course, they may download that data again and decrypt it with appropriate key material. To also share data with other users, the data owner generates a re-encryption key towards the data receiver and hands that key to the cloud storage service. Then, the cloud storage service can transform ciphertext of the data owner into data encrypted for the intended receiver on demand. Our system is based on multi-use proxy re-encryption to set up a network of proxy re-encryption keys between the devices owned by a user as well as devices of other users.

Such a network of re-encryption keys not only enables our system to support convenient data sharing between different users and different devices of one user, but also offers user-friendly strategies to recover from device- and key-loss. Strategies to recover from key-loss might also require one (or more) trusted *recovery users*, which support the recovering user and thus accept further responsibility.

Additionally, a *trust infrastructure* can be used to ensure the authenticity of key material, which simplifies establishing the identity of data receivers.

Trust Assumptions. The user trusts the *cloud storage service* to operate honestly, while it might be curious to learn about the data it handles (e.g., curious insiders or cloud platform operators). To protect the data's confidentiality, the system employs end-to-end encryption (in our case, MU-PRE).

The user *trusts her devices' hardware* to protect her keys and only unlock them after successful authentication. Such hardware-protection for keys thwarts two attacks: Neither malicious applications nor unauthorized people with physical access to the device (e.g., thieves) are able to steal the user's keys and data. The user also trusts the sharing system's client application running on her devices.

Users with access permissions must not collude with the cloud storage service. Otherwise, the service re-encrypts the user's data and the corrupted receivers can decrypt it. Data owners select receivers with this trust requirement in mind.

Likewise, *recovery users* must not collude with the cloud storage service. While they might be curious, recovery users alone are not able to read another user's plain data, as honest cloud storage services do not expose the data. Recovery users are required to be willing and able to cooperate when recovery becomes necessary. As the development of users is hard to predict when selecting these recovery users, we also enable to distribute the risk over a threshold of users.

4   Concept Employing Multi-use Proxy Re-encryption

In this section, we introduce our concept for cloud-based data sharing that employs multi-use proxy re-encryption. First, we elaborate on how our concept builds a network of re-encryption keys between the devices of a user and – to enable data sharing – the devices of other users. Next, we give details on how to amend the network of re-encryption keys to recover from key-loss if devices are not available anymore, e.g., when they break. Also, this section considers the authenticity of keys, outlines operations per process, and suggests performance improvements.

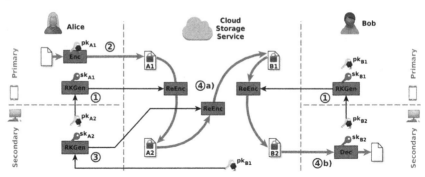

Fig. 2. Concept for data sharing

4.1   Setup and Multi-device Data Sharing

Figure 2 illustrates the processes to store data at the cloud storage service, to share the data with other devices and users, and, finally, to download and decrypt the data. We describe the processes below and summarize them in Protocol 1.

⓪ **Setup.** When setting up an account, the user generates a key pair on her primary device and registers the public key at the cloud storage service. Additional steps to ensure the authenticity of her key are discussed in Sect. 4.3.

① **Register Secondary Device.** To add a new secondary device, in addition to performing the above-described setup, the user approves this device by generating a new re-encryption key from her primary device A1 to this secondary device A2: The secondary device sends its public key to the primary

---

⓪ Setup: on primary device A1
1. generate key pair: $(\mathsf{sk}_{A1}, \mathsf{pk}_{A1}) \leftarrow \mathsf{KeyGen}(1^\kappa)$
2. certify authenticity of public key pk_{A1}
3. install public key pk_{A1} at cloud storage service

① Register Secondary Device:
on secondary device A2
1. generate key pair: $(\mathsf{sk}_{A2}, \mathsf{pk}_{A2}) \leftarrow \mathsf{KeyGen}(1^\kappa)$
2. certify authenticity of public key pk_{A2}
3. install public key pk_{A2} at cloud storage service
4. send public key pk_{A2} to primary device
on primary device A1
5. verify authenticity of public key pk_{A2}
6. if user accepts, generate re-encryption key towards secondary device:
   $\mathsf{rk}_{A1 \to A2} \leftarrow \mathsf{RKGen}(\mathsf{sk}_{A1}, \mathsf{pk}_{A2})$
7. install re-encryption key at cloud storage service

② Upload Data: on any device
1. encrypt data for primary device A1: $C_{A1}^1 \leftarrow \mathsf{Enc}(\mathsf{pk}_{A1}, M)$
2. upload ciphertext C to cloud storage service

③ Grant Access:
on any device B∗ of requester (User B)
1. send request for access to data owner with pk_{B1}
on any device A∗ of data owner (User A)
2. verify authenticity of the public key of B's primary device pk_{B1}
3. let data owner review and accept request
4. generate re-encryption key from current device to B's primary device:
   $\mathsf{rk}_{A* \to B1} \leftarrow \mathsf{RKGen}(\mathsf{sk}_{A*}, \mathsf{pk}_{B1})$
5. install re-encryption key at cloud storage service

④ Download Data:
on any device B∗ of requester
1. request download for ciphertext C at cloud storage service
on cloud storage service
2. find chain of re-encryption keys from data owner's primary device to requesting
   device: $(\mathsf{rk}_{0 \to 1}, ..., \mathsf{rk}_{n-1 \to n})$
3. re-encrypt ciphertext along this chain (usually 0-3 re-encryptions):
   $C^{i+1} \leftarrow \mathsf{ReEnc}(\mathsf{rk}_{i \to i+1}, C^i)$
on device B∗ of requester
4. decrypt ciphertext with device's private key sk_{B*}: $M \leftarrow \mathsf{Dec}(\mathsf{sk}_{B*}, C)$

Protocol 1. Setup and Data Sharing

device, e.g., through a push notification or by showing a QR code at one device and scanning it at the other. After the user reviewed and accepted the request on her primary device, the primary device generates a re-encryption key $\mathsf{rk}_{A1 \to A2} \leftarrow \mathsf{RKGen}(\mathsf{sk}_{A1}, \mathsf{pk}_{A2})$ and registers this key at the cloud storage service.

② Upload Data (and Download for Data Owner). All devices of a user, as well as other users, always encrypt the data for the primary device of a user, i.e. for the primary's public key.

Besides the primary device, the user's secondary devices are also able to access the encrypted data: Upon request, the cloud storage service uses the re-encryption key $rk_{A1 \to A2}$, which was generated during registration, to transform the encrypted data C_{A1} for the secondary device, resulting in C_{A2}. This ciphertext C_{A2} can then be decrypted at the secondary device with its private key sk_{A2}.

③ **Grant Access.** Data sharing with other users can be initiated by the data owner A, or requested by a receiver B, e.g., through a push notification. To grant access, the public key of the receiver's primary device pk_{B1} is required. This key is registered at the cloud storage service or can be sent with the receiver's request. After verifying the key's authenticity, A's device generates a re-encryption key for B's primary device. Let us assume the more complex case, where A is using her secondary device, giving $rk_{A2 \to B1} \leftarrow \mathsf{RKGen}(sk_{A2}, pk_{B1})$. Next, A's device installs this re-encryption key at the cloud storage service along with an access control policy.

④ **Download Shared Data.** On request from B, the cloud storage service re-encrypts A's ciphertext C_{A1} up to three times in the default case as shown in Fig. 2: These re-encryption operations use (1) the re-encryption key towards A's secondary device ($C_{A2} \leftarrow \mathsf{ReEnc}(rk_{A1 \to A2}, C_{A1})$), (2) the cross-user re-encryption key towards B's primary device ($C_{B1} \leftarrow \mathsf{ReEnc}(rk_{A2 \to B1}, C_{B1})$), and (3) the re-encryption key towards B's secondary device ($C_{B2} \leftarrow \mathsf{ReEnc}(rk_{B1 \to B2}, C_{B1})$). Finally, the receiver B decrypts C_{B2} by $M \leftarrow \mathsf{Dec}(sk_{B2}, C_{B2})$. Thus, users can initiate sharing from any of their devices, while receivers can access that data from any owned device. Recovery may increase the re-encryption chain's length.

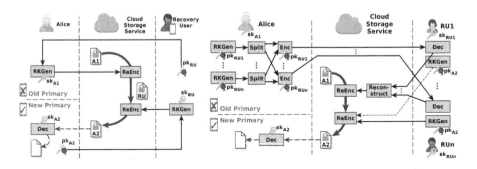

Fig. 3. Recovery with rec. user

Fig. 4. Recovery with threshold of rec. users

4.2 Recovery from Key-Loss

If a user's device is not available anymore (e.g., lost or broken), the user aims to regain access to her data and sharing capabilities. In our heterogeneous environment, some users own secondary devices, while others do not, and users transition between these groups over time when buying or losing devices. Thus, our recovery mechanisms also need to be seamlessly compatible with each other. Protocol 2 details three recovery mechanisms: (1) We show recovery with a secondary device as the simplest and most convenient solution. (2) Users without a secondary device may recover with the help of one recovery user. (3) We wish to highlight our third mechanism, where users recover with the support of a threshold of recovery users, and thereby improve their trade-off between availability and confidentiality.

(R1) **Recovery with Secondary Device.** With one or more registered secondary devices, the user simply selects one of those secondary devices as her new primary device. As new data will be encrypted for this new primary device, old secondary devices or receivers would not have access to this data through the existing network of re-encryption keys. To amend the network, the new primary device re-generates all outgoing re-encryption keys from the old device, i.e., keys that can transform ciphertexts from the primary device to other devices or users.

(R2) **Recovery with Recovery User.** As some users might not own a secondary device, they may rely on the support of a trusted recovery user (e.g., a family member) in the recovery process, as shown in Fig. 3. During registration, the user selects another trusted user (i.e., recovery user), generates a re-encryption key from her primary device to that recovery user ($rk_{A1 \to RU}$), and stores this key at the cloud storage service. Once the primary device's key material is not available anymore, the user convinces the recovery user to generate a new re-encryption key to the user's new primary device ($rk_{RU \to A1'}$). With this key, the cloud storage service can re-encrypt the user's data (encrypted for her old primary device) for the recovery user and then re-encrypt it again for her new primary device. Trusted (commercial) services might also offer to act as recovery user. Relying on a single recovery user poses an availability risk in case that user is no longer willing or able to help in recovery. This risk can be reduced by using multiple independent recovery users, which, however, increases the risk that one of these users colludes with the cloud storage service to access data.

(R3) **Recovery with Threshold of Recovery Users.** We propose to rely on a threshold of recovery users by employing secret sharing mechanisms [23], as shown in Fig. 4. This process allows users to select a more favorable trade-off between availability and confidentiality risks. The user initially selects a list of n recovery users RU_i and generates a re-encryption key towards each of them. Instead of handing these keys directly to the cloud storage service, the user splits each of these keys into n shares, takes the ith share of different keys, and encrypts these i^{th} shares for the corresponding i^{th} recovery user. To complete the setup, the user uploads the resulting n ciphertexts to the cloud storage service.

Once recovery becomes necessary, the user convinces a threshold of recovery users to download their ciphertexts, decrypt them, and return the decrypted shares to the cloud storage service. With those shares, the cloud storage service can reconstruct at least one re-encryption key towards one of the recovery users ($rk_{A1 \to RU_i}$). When also given a re-encryption from that recovery user to the user's new primary device ($rk_{RU_i \to A2}$), the cloud storage service is again able to transform the user's data for her new primary device.

(R1) **Recover with Secondary Device:** on secondary device A2
1. select a secondary device A2 as new primary and inform cloud storage service
2. re-generate and replace all outgoing re-encryption keys $rk_{A1 \to *}$ of old device: $rk_{A2 \to *} \leftarrow \mathsf{RKGen}(sk_{A2}, pk_*)$

(R2) **Recover with Recovery User:**
on old primary device A1, during setup/registration
1. select a recovery user RU
2. generate re-encryption key to recovery user: $rk_{A1 \to RU} \leftarrow \mathsf{RKGen}(sk_{A1}, pk_{RU})$
3. install this re-encryption key at the cloud storage service for recovery purposes
on new primary device A1', during recovery
4. send recovery request to recovery user via cloud storage service with $pk_{A1'}$
on any device of recovery user RU
5. perform out-of-band authentication of the device requesting recovery
6. generate a re-encryption key to new device: $rk_{RU \to A1'} \leftarrow \mathsf{RKGen}(sk_{RU}, pk_{A1'})$
7. install this key at the cloud storage service
on new primary device A1'
8. re-generate and replace all outgoing re-encryption keys of the old device

(R3) **Recover with Threshold of Recovery Users:**
on old primary device A1, during setup/registration
1. select a list of recovery users $\{RU_i\}$
2. for each recovery user RU_i
   (a) generate a re-encryption key: $rk_{A1 \to RU_i}$
   (b) split re-encryption key: $(s_{i,1}, ..., s_{i,n}) \leftarrow \mathsf{Split}(t, n, rk_{A1 \to RU_i})$
   (c) encrypt i^{th} shares of different keys: $\mathsf{RInfo}_i \leftarrow \mathsf{Enc}(pk_{RU_i}, \{s_{1,i}, ..., s_{n,i}\})$
   (d) upload RInfo_i to cloud storage service
on new primary device A1', during recovery
3. send recovery request to recovery users via cloud storage service with $pk_{A1'}$
on any device of each recovery user RU
4. perform out-of-band authentication of the device requesting recovery
5. generate re-encryption key to new device: $rk_{RU \to A1'} \leftarrow \mathsf{RKGen}(sk_{RU}, pk_{A1'})$
6. decrypt RInfo_i: $\{s_{1,i}, ..., s_{n,i}\} \leftarrow \mathsf{Dec}(sk_{RU}, \mathsf{RInfo}_i)$
7. send re-encryption key and decrypted RInfo_i to cloud storage service
on cloud storage service
8. reconstruct one $rk_{A1 \to RU_i} \leftarrow \mathsf{Reconstruct}(\{s_{i,1}, ..., s_{i,t}\})$
9. take the corresponding $rk_{RU_i \to A1'}$ to close the re-encryption chain
on new primary device A1'
10. re-generate and replace all outgoing re-encryption keys of the old device

Protocol 2. Recovery from Key-Loss

4.3 Key Authenticity

When users operate on keys from other devices or users (e.g., registering a device, encrypting, or sharing data), they rely on the authenticity of these keys. A key's authenticity can be established manually by comparing the received key's fingerprint with the key's owner, e.g., via a call, or shown on the owner's screen. The process to establish can be simplified by relying on trusted infrastructure. In this section, we give an example solution based on public key infrastructure

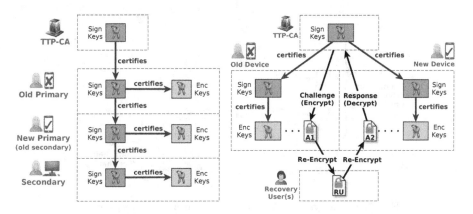

Fig. 5. Certification chain

Fig. 6. Certification with recovery users

(PKI), but approaches employing decentralized PKI mechanisms can also be conceived.

General Use. As shown in Fig. 5, we build a certificate hierarchy, where the primary device and secondary devices act as intermediate certificate authorities (CAs). We introduce an additional signing key pair per device, which certifies the device's encryption pk. During account setup, the primary device's signing key is certified by a trusted third party CA (TTP-CA) for the user's human-readable identifier. This CA must ensure that it issues a certificate for a given identifier only once and that it does not accept similar identifiers, e.g., prevents homoglyph attacks. When registering a secondary device, the secondary device sends its signing pk to the primary device, which – acting as intermediate CA – certifies the secondary's signing pk given the user's consent. If the signing pk was transmitted by showing and scanning a QR code, the user's consent is given implicitly in this process. Other less direct communication mechanisms (e.g., push notifications) might require additional verification, for example showing the pk's fingerprint on both devices to be compared by the user. Before operating on foreign keys (e.g., as a reaction to a sharing request), the receiving device traverses the certificate chain to find and display the identifier of the owner. This identifier serves as a basis for users to accept or deny the operation.

When Recovering with Secondary Devices. These authenticity measures are directly compatible with our recovery process relying on a secondary device: Any secondary device that has become the new primary device can act again as intermediate CA to certify the keys of new secondary devices. Consequently, the length of the certification chain increases by one.

When Recovering with Recovery Users. In case the user did not register a secondary device, the problem becomes more interesting, as no such device can be used as a link in a chain to ensure authenticity. Naively, the signing keys of the old primary device could be extracted from hardware and backed up to

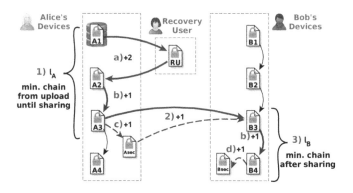

Fig. 7. Re-encryption chain for data sharing after recovery

allow for certifying the new devices key, which however would lead us back to the initial problem of having keys that are not bound to hardware. Instead, we propose a process to convince the TTP-CA to issue another certificate for the new device of the same user, as shown in Fig. 6. The TTP-CA uses the same trust mechanism as for decryption rights and outsources the authorization check to the user's selected recovery user(s): First, the TTP-CA picks a challenge and encrypts this challenge for the (certified) encryption key of the user's old primary device. If the recovery user(s) were convinced that the recovery request and new device are legitimate, they help the new device to regain decryption capabilities for the user. Thus, the new device can decrypt the challenge and present the response to the TTP-CA, which then issues a certificate for the new signing keys.

4.4 Operations

To elaborate on the performance of our concept, Tables 1 and 2 list the underlying operations required in the processes of Protocols 1 and 2. We focus on MU-PRE and secret sharing operations as they reflect the novelty of our concept and – depending on the scheme – might consume the most time. Pairing this list of operations with times of used schemes allows estimating the overall times for the processes. The tables refer to n users, t as threshold, o outgoing re-encryption keys from the old device, as well as l_A and l_B re-encryption steps (c.f. Fig. 7).

Re-encryption Chain Length. A chain of multiple re-encryption operations might be necessary to download data, as shown in Fig. 7. While there might be multiple re-encryption chains for a requested file, we are interested in the shortest chain, i.e. shortest path in a graph of re-encryption keys. Such a chain consists of (1) l_A re-encryption steps between the devices of the data owner, and – in case of sharing – (2) 1 re-encryption step between the owner and the requester, as well as (3) l_B steps on the side of another user. In the default case, the requested data were not subject to a prior recovery operation. If the data

Table 1. Operations for setup and data sharing

Setup and data sharing	Client	Cloud Service
⓪ Setup (once)	1 KeyGen	-
① Register Secondary Device (rarely)	1 KeyGen + 1 RKGen	-
② Grant Access (sometimes)	1 RKGen	-
③ Upload Data (frequently)	1 Enc	-
④ Download Data (frequently)		
requester owns data	1 Dec$^{l_A+1}$	l_A ReEnc
requester does not own data	1 Dec$^{l_A+l_B+2}$	$(l_A + l_B + 1)$ ReEnc

Table 2. Operations for recovery

Recovery (rarely)	Registration	During Recovery		
	Client	Client	Other Client	Cloud Service
ⓡ1 Secondary Device	-	o RKGen	-	-
ⓡ2 Recovery User	1 RKGen	o RKGen	1 RKGen	-
ⓡ3 Threshold t of n Users	n RKGen	o RKGen	1 RKGen	1 Reconstruct
	+ n Split		+ t Dec	
	+ n Enc			

owner requests such data from her primary device, no re-encryption is necessary ($l_A = 0$). The sub-chains increase in length (a) by +2 each time the data was recovered with the help of recovery users, (b) by +1 each time the data was involved in recovery via a secondary device, (c) by +1 if the data is shared by a secondary device, and (d) by +1 if the data is accessed by a secondary device.

4.5 Performance Improvements

After recovery, the added re-encryption steps have an impact on performance: (a) the cloud storage service has to perform more re-encryption operations, which lead to (b) ciphertexts at a higher re-encryption level that – depending on the use MU-PRE scheme – usually take longer to decrypt. Therefore, in this section, we discuss performance improvements, namely pre-computing and caching cryptographic operations, updating the network of re-encryption keys, and reducing the ciphertexts' re-encryption level. Updating keys and data trades an initial effort for a reduced subsequent effort. The actors may adaptively decide on when and where it is beneficial to apply refresh operations (e.g., on frequently used data).

Caching and Pre-computing. Instead of re-encrypting data for the requester on demand, the cloud storage service may pre-compute the re-encryption operations to reduce the response time. Such pre-computation entails a higher initial computational effort and requires more storage space for the different ciphertext versions of the same data. Thus, pre-computation pays off for data that is frequently requested by the same users. This can be achieved by caching re-encryptions and deleting the least used when the cache grows too large.

The same approach may be applied for decryption: Clients pre-compute the decryption operation in the background or cache results for frequently used data to hide the computation costs from the users. We only apply this pre-computation or caching for the symmetric content encryption keys as the symmetric cryptography on the content is very efficient anyway. By wrapping the content encryption keys with a hardware-protected key, they can be securely stored on the user's device.

Re-generating Re-encryption Keys. Next, we consider re-generating re-encryption keys that were connected to the old device of a user who went through recovery. These keys can be (a) outgoing, i.e., they transform ciphertext from the recovered user to other users, or (b) incoming, i.e., they transform ciphertext from other users to the recovered user. Outgoing re-encryption keys of an old device are re-generated during recovery by the new device with its sk to also make new data that are encrypted for the new device accessible for the original receivers.

The problem is more interesting for incoming re-encryption keys to the old device: We need to convince the other user's device (i.e., source) to use its sk to generate a new re-encryption key towards the recovered user's new device. One possibility would be to prompt the source user to manually check if a re-encryption key (and thus decryption rights) may be generated for the requesting user. Instead, we suggest that the source user's device relies on the key authenticity mechanisms described in Sect. 4.3 to identify the key's owner, which enables to authorize requests without user interaction by comparing with previous decisions. Such re-generated incoming keys reduce the re-encryption chain's length, as data can be transformed directly rather than via links generated for recovery.

Refreshing Ciphertext Level. Added re-encryption steps due to recovery also increase ciphertext levels. MU-PRE schemes where the decryption time grows with the ciphertext level benefit from resetting this ciphertext level. When using hybrid encryption, the user's device decrypts the wrapped key and newly encrypts it as first level ciphertext, before uploading it. While the transmitted data size of wrapped keys is rather small, the MU-PRE operations on the client side might be more significant. However, these operations can be performed in the background by multiple threads invisible to the user. Nevertheless, the cloud storage service and user's device might wish to negotiate for which ciphertexts a refresh pays off.

5   Implementation

To validate and evaluate our proposed system, we first describe our proof of concept instantiation. Next, we discuss the MU-PRE scheme's implementation details and benchmark its performance. Finally, we estimate the costs of deploying our system in the cloud and elaborate on the binding of keys to the hardware.

Table 3. Execution times of our MU-PRE implementation (in Milliseconds)

	Level l	KeyGen	RKGen	Enc $M \to C^l$	ReEnc $C^l \to C^{l+1}$	Dec $C^l \to M$
	1	0.10	4.52	3.31	11.42	4.58
	2	-	-	-	15.84	7.53
Cloud Server	3	-	-	-	16.15	10.72
(AWS c5.xlarge)	4	-	-	-	16.45	13.91
	5	-	-	-	16.76	17.10
	6	-	-	-	-	20.29
	1	1.10	47.22	34.35	118.53	47.85
	2	-	-	-	164.27	78.30
Mobile Phone	3	-	-	-	168.24	111.97
(OnePlus 6T)	4	-	-	-	170.20	146.01
	5	-	-	-	171.99	181.09
	6	-	-	-	-	211.37

5.1 Instantiation

We have developed the cloud storage service as a Java web server, which we deployed on a cloud server (AWS c5.xlarge). An Android app acts as the client for both primary and secondary devices to enable users to conveniently interact with the data sharing and recovery capabilities. This app runs on a OnePlus 6T. During registration of secondary devices, these apps communicate through displaying and scanning QR codes. The apps employ push notifications via Google's Firebase for further communication between devices of one or different users. Finally, we extended and deployed a CAPSO[3] server as certification authority.

5.2 Cryptography Implementation

In this section, we describe our selection criteria for a MU-PRE scheme, give implementation details, and present performance measurements.

Scheme Selection. We selected the MU-PRE scheme by Cai and Liu [6], as it satisfies our requirements: Their scheme is unidirectional, non-interactive, collusion-safe, and CCA-secure. Unidirectional means that a re-encryption key from A to B can only be used to transform ciphertexts in that direction but not vice versa, which – as opposed to bidirectional schemes – does not force users to share decryption right in order to get access to the other users' data. In non-interactive schemes, a user can generate re-encryption keys towards another user by herself with her sk and the other user's pk. Collusion safeness captures that

---

[3] https://ca.iaik.tugraz.at/.

even if the proxy and receiver collude, they are not able to derive the sender's sk from the proxy's re-encryption key and receiver's key pair. Finally, their scheme is CCA-secure, which also covers processes where others encrypt data for a user and write it to her account with appropriate permissions.

Implementation. We implemented the MU-PRE scheme by Cai and Liu [6] with parameters chosen according to NIST's recommendations [20] for 128 bit security. While Cai and Liu have defined their scheme for type-1 pairings, we have rewritten the scheme for more complex but also more efficient type-3 pairings. Our C implementation of the rewritten scheme builds on the RELIC toolkit [1] for their bilinear pairings on elliptic curves. We use the Java Native Interface (JNI) to integrate the compiled binaries into the server's and phone's Java environment.

Performance. Table 3 presents the benchmark results of our MU-PRE implementation, where a 128 bit AES key is encrypted, repeatedly re-encrypted, and finally decrypted. Without previous recovery, ciphertexts are re-encrypted up to 3 times resulting in ciphertexts for level 1 to 4. The benchmark has been performed on both a cloud server (AWS c5.xlarge) as well as a mobile phone (One-Plus 6T). The presented times are an average of 100 runs on the phone and 10k runs on the server. Note that the currently single-threaded implementation only makes use of one core during the benchmark. For operations on different ciphertext levels, we observe the following: ReEnc on first-level ciphertexts is faster than on higher levels. The ReEnc time remains almost constant from second-level ciphertexts onward. The time to perform Dec grows linearly for each level. Using the least square method to fit a line to our measurements for Dec, we arrive at $1.31 + 3.16l$ ms on the server and $13.43 + 33.14l$ ms on the phone.

5.3   Deployment Cost Estimation

In Table 4, we evaluate the additional costs required to integrate our advanced cryptography into existing storage services, which includes storing/retrieving ciphertexts and re-encryption keys as well as re-encrypting the ciphertexts.

Costs Factors. When employing hybrid encryption, the symmetric encryption of the payload usually introduces little space overhead. Thus, we ignore the payload and focus on the symmetric key which is encrypted and transformed by MU-PRE as C^l. To store at AWS DynamoDB, we consider \$1.525/1M requests and \$0.306/1 GB-month for first-level ciphertexts (3×384 bit EC points $= 144$B) and re-encryption keys (5×384 bit EC points $= 240$B), while incoming traffic is free. To get data, we consider three aspects: Firstly, we have \$0.305 per 1M requests and per 1kB block to obtain the ciphertext and $l - 1$ relevant re-encryption keys. Secondly, to transform the ciphertext multiple times, we add \$0.194/h to run AWS EC2 c5.xlarge machines. Running multiple of our single-threaded re-encryption operations in parallel (on 10k ciphertexts across all ciphertext levels) shows that 2.15 times more operations can be performed by utilizing both cores and Intel's Hyperthreading technology on the AWS machine.

Table 4. Deployment costs on Amazon Web Services (for 100M items in $)

	DynamoDB		EC2 (c5.xlarge)		Traffic	Example Scenario		
	C^1	rk	l	$C^1 \to C^l$	C^l	#C	#rk	Costs
Store	156.91	159.84	-	-	*free*	*100.0M*	*10.0M*	172.89
Get	30.50	30.50	*1*	-	1.30	*50.0M*	-	15.90
	30.50	30.50	*2*	14.28	4.32	*25.0M*	*25.0M*	19.90
	30.50	30.50	*3*	34.11	7.34	*12.5M*	*25.0M*	16.62
	30.50	30.50	*4*	54.32	10.37	*12.5M*	*37.5M*	23.34

$248.64

We use this scaling factor on the measurements presented in Table 3. Finally, we add $0.09/1 GB to return the re-encrypted ciphertexts, which have a size of $144 + (l-1) \cdot 336B$. Our estimation is based on AWS prices for the EU-Frankfurt region in Oct 2019.

Example Scenario. We estimate the added costs of 1M users, who each upload 100 files and share their data using 10 re-encryption keys (100M C^1, 10M rk). Further, we consider that of these 100M files, 50% are downloaded by the same primary device ($l = 1$), and 25% by a secondary device or another user's primary device ($l = 2$), while the remaining downloads use an even longer re-encryption chain (12.5% with $l = 3$ and with $l = 4$). Table 4 estimates a total of $248.64.

5.4   Hardware-Binding of Keys

In this section, we give details on how to bind MU-PRE keys to a device's hardware.

Mobile phones with technologies such as ARM's TrustZone [2] set up a trusted computing base by establishing a secure boot chain and eventually verifying the operating system's validity. In Android and iOS, the hardware-based protection for keys is integrated with the operating system's key chain, which ensures that the keys are only unlocked to be used in cryptographic operations for authenticated and authorized users. As these operating systems do not allow to run custom cryptographic code directly in the trusted execution environment, we follow a hybrid approach: We use hardware-protected keys for traditional cryptographic schemes to wrap our MU-PRE key material before storing them in the phone's file system. This MU-PRE key material is temporarily unwrapped for individual operations of our MU-PRE implementation. This approach is sufficient for our use case: Unauthorized people with physical access (e.g., thieves) are not able to authenticate to unlock or extract the keys needed for the unwrapping procedure. Further, a valid operating system sufficiently separates user-installed apps, so that malicious apps do not learn the user's data.

On PCs or servers supporting Intel's SGX [15], the cryptographic code can be deployed in a secure enclave, which protects (i.e., seals) the key material. We further need to perform user authentication inside the enclave before offering cryptographic operations on the protected key to prevent unauthorized access. Enclaves do not protect against malware on the operating system's level, as SGX was not designed to establish a secure boot chain that leads to a valid system. Therefore, malware could try to sniff and replay authentication data, e.g., by corrupting the drivers for the keyboard or fingerprint reader. Ruan [22] describes a mechanism to prevent such attacks by achieving secure input via secure output: The user is presented with a randomized keypad on her screen (via secure output). After clicking, the click coordinates can be passed without any further protection to the enclave for verification, as eavesdroppers cannot learn which keys were pressed due to their randomized position.

6   Discussion

Recovery with Threshold. Strategies to recovery from key-loss entail a trade-off between availability and confidentiality. When employing a strategy that relies on one piece of information, there is a risk that this information is not available when recovery becomes necessary. Distributing the recovery information to multiple locations increases the chances that it will be available for recovery, but leads to a higher risk that one location becomes corrupted. The same argument applies for trusted recovery users, as they might no longer be willing or able to help, or might even collude with the cloud storage service to decrypt data.

We presented a recovery mechanism that enables users to choose a more favorable trade-off for themselves: The user selects a set of recovery users and specifies a threshold of how many recovery users need to cooperate in order to recover successfully. This threshold also defines how many recovery users need to betray the user by colluding with the cloud storage service to decrypt her data.

Recovery Effort for Users. The effort to recover from key-loss depends on the users' recovery mechanism: If the user owns two or more devices, she can recover from the loss of one device by herself. A user who only owns a single device needs support from at least one other (recovery) user. After device- or key-loss, the user authenticates out-of-band to the recovery user (e.g., via a phone call) and convinces her to generate a re-encryption key for the user's new device. To reduce availability requirements, a user can also recruit multiple recovery users so that only a subset of these users need to be convinced to cooperate for recovery.

Data Sharing Performance. Our implementation of the MU-PRE scheme demonstrates the practical efficiency of the proposed system.

Cloud storage services perform re-encryption operations to make data accessible. Re-encrypting 1st to 4th-level ciphertexts takes an accumulated ≈ 44 ms on our benchmark server, while significantly more powerful machines are available in cloud environments. Response times can be further reduced by adaptively caching or pre-computing re-encryptions.

For *clients* on both PCs and phones, our implementation is sufficiently fast for all operations. On our phone, re-encryption keys can be generated in ≈ 50 ms, while encryption needs $\approx$35 ms. To decrypt ciphertexts with levels ranging from 1st to 4th, our phone takes between $\approx$50 ms and $\approx$150 ms. These ciphertext levels depend on which devices are used to share and access the data. Besides optimizing the MU-PRE implementation or using more powerful phones, these times can be further improved by (a) pre-computing and caching the decryption of the small symmetric content encryption keys and storing the results securely on the device given hardware-protection for keys, or (b) resetting the ciphertext levels of ciphertexts that went through recovery in the background.

Improved Key Security. The data sharing and recovery mechanisms in our concept were designed so that the involved client-side key material does not have to be extracted from the client devices' hardware at any point. Therefore, we are able to employ technologies that bind the keys to the devices' hardware and only unlock the keys for authorized users. Consequently, attackers and malicious apps are also not to obtain the user's key material.

Fast Recovery without Re-keying. Without hardware-bound keys, device-loss also implies potential key-compromise, e.g., if the device storing the key was stolen or has been lost and found. As unprotected keys can be extracted from the device, re-keying of all related ciphertexts becomes necessary. For a "naive" storage system using hybrid encryption, re-keying requires that wrapped symmetric keys for all ciphertexts are downloaded, decrypted, encrypted anew, and again uploaded. This causes substantial computation and communication effort for both the client as well as the cloud storage service. Until this costly process is completed, affected user might not be able to fully use the system and access their data. As our solution relies on hardware-binding, the keys cannot easily be extracted, and, therefore, no re-keying is necessary. Instead of the high re-keying effort, only re-encryption keys need to be generated, after which all access and data sharing capabilities are immediately restored.

7   Conclusion

In this paper, we proposed and implemented a cloud-based data sharing system, which (1) supports multiple devices per user, (2) offers three mechanisms to recover from device- and key-loss, and (3) enables to bind the keys to the device's hardware.

Our concept is based on multi-use proxy re-encryption to achieve end-to-end confidentiality. Users are not only able to store sensitive data at a semi-trusted storage service that is operated in the cloud, but can also share these data with authorized receivers via the cloud service. As users may own multiple devices, our concept enables them to access data and initiate sharing from each device.

The proposed strategies to recover from device-loss protect users from losing access to their encrypted data. While recovery is simple given a second device with full access, we also present mechanisms to recover with the help of one or more user-selected recovery users. We wish to highlight recovery with a threshold of multiple recovery users, as it reduces the risk of recovery users who – over time – become no longer willing or able to participate in the recovery process. The recovery mechanisms require little effort from the users: A user initially selects her recovery user(s) and later convinces them to aid her in the recovery process.

As our concept does not require to extract the devices' keys, these keys can be bound to the hardware. Hardware security features prevent thieves and malicious apps from extracting keys and form using them to access the users' data. This leads to another benefit: If a device is lost, it is no longer necessary to suspend access to the user's data while performing time-consuming and communication-intense re-keying of all ciphertexts on the user's client.

The concrete instantiation of our concept demonstrates its feasibility. Benchmarks of our MU-PRE implementation based on Cai and Liu's scheme [6] as well as our deployment cost estimation underline the concept's practical efficiency.

References

1. Aranha, D.F., Gouvêa, C.P.L.: RELIC is an Efficient LIbrary for Cryptography. https://github.com/relic-toolkit/relic. Accessed 04 July 2019
2. ARM: TrustZone. https://developer.arm.com/ip-products/security-ip/trustzone. Accessed 28 June 2019
3. Ateniese, G., Fu, K., Green, M., Hohenberger, S.: Improved proxy re-encryption schemes with applications to secure distributed storage. In: NDSS. The Internet Society (2005)
4. Bagherzandi, A., Jarecki, S., Saxena, N., Lu, Y.: Password-protected secret sharing. In: ACM Conference on Computer and Communications Security, pp. 433–444. ACM (2011)
5. Blaze, M., Bleumer, G., Strauss, M.: Divertible protocols and atomic proxy cryptography. In: Nyberg, K. (ed.) EUROCRYPT 1998. LNCS, vol. 1403, pp. 127–144. Springer, Heidelberg (1998). https://doi.org/10.1007/BFb0054122
6. Cai, Y., Liu, X.: A multi-use CCA-secure proxy re-encryption scheme. In: DASC, pp. 39–44. IEEE Computer Society (2014)
7. Camenisch, J., Lysyanskaya, A., Neven, G.: Practical yet universally composable two-server password-authenticated secret sharing. In: ACM Conference on Computer and Communications Security, pp. 525–536. ACM (2012)
8. Dodis, Y., Reyzin, L., Smith, A.: Fuzzy extractors: how to generate strong keys from biometrics and other noisy data. In: Cachin, C., Camenisch, J.L. (eds.) EUROCRYPT 2004. LNCS, vol. 3027, pp. 523–540. Springer, Heidelberg (2004). https://doi.org/10.1007/978-3-540-24676-3_31
9. Fu, K.E.: Group sharing and random access in cryptographic storage file systems. Ph.D. thesis, Massachusetts Institute of Technology (1999)
10. Goh, E., Shacham, H., Modadugu, N., Boneh, D.: SiRiUS: securing remote untrusted storage. In: NDSS. The Internet Society (2003)
11. Goyal, V., Pandey, O., Sahai, A., Waters, B.: Attribute-based encryption for fine-grained access control of encrypted data. In: ACM Conference on Computer and Communications Security, pp. 89–98. ACM (2006)
12. Hörandner, F., Krenn, S., Migliavacca, A., Thiemer, F., Zwattendorfer, B.: CREDENTIAL: a framework for privacy-preserving cloud-based data sharing. In: ARES, pp. 742–749. IEEE Computer Society (2016)

13. Hörandner, F., Rabensteiner, C.: Horcruxes for everyone - a framework for key-loss recovery by splitting trust. In: TrustCom/BigDataSE. IEEE (2019)
14. Huang, Z., Li, Q., Zheng, D., Chen, K., Li, X.: YI Cloud: improving user privacy with secret key recovery in cloud storage. In: SOSE, pp. 268–272. IEEE Computer Society (2011)
15. Intel: Software Guard Extensions. https://software.intel.com/en-us/sgx. Accessed 28 June 2019
16. Jin, A.T.B., Ling, D.N.C., Goh, A.: Biohashing: two factor authentication featuring fingerprint data and tokenised random number. Pattern Recogn. 37(11), 2245–2255 (2004)
17. Kaliski, B.: PKCS #5: Password-Based Cryptography Specification Version 2.0. RFC 2898, pp. 1–34 (2000)
18. Kallahalla, M., Riedel, E., Swaminathan, R., Wang, Q., Fu, K.: Plutus: scalable secure file sharing on untrusted storage. In: FAST. USENIX (2003)
19. Nagar, A., Nandakumar, K., Jain, A.K.: Biometric template transformation: a security analysis. In: Media Forensics and Security. SPIE Proceedings, vol. 7541, p. 75410O. SPIE (2010)
20. National Institute of Standards & Technology: SP 800-57. Recommendation for Key Management, Part 1: General (Rev 4). Technical report, NIST (2016)
21. Percival, C.: Stronger key derivation via sequential memory-hard functions (2009)
22. Ruan, X.: Intel identity protection technology: the robust, convenient, and cost-effective way to deter identity theft. In: Ruan, X., et al. (eds.) Platform Embedded Security Technology Revealed, pp. 211–226. Apress, Berkeley (2014). https://doi.org/10.1007/978-1-4302-6572-6_10
23. Shamir, A.: How to share a secret. Commun. ACM 22(11), 612–613 (1979)

Item-Based Privacy-Preserving Recommender System with Offline Users and Reduced Trust Requirements

Pranav Verma[✉], Anish Mathuria[✉], and Sourish Dasgupta[✉]

Dhirubhai Ambani Institute of Information and Communication Technology, Gandhinagar, India
{pranav_verma,anish_mathuria,sourish_dasgupta}@daiict.ac.in

Abstract. Safeguarding privacy of ratings assigned by users is an important issue for recommender systems. There are several existing protocols that allow a server to generate recommendations from homomorphically encrypted ratings, thereby ensuring privacy of rating data. After collecting the encrypted ratings, the server may require further interaction with each user, which is problematic in case some users were to go offline. To solve the offline user problem previous solutions use additional semi-honest third parties. In this paper, we propose a privacy-preserving recommender system that does not suffer from the offline user problem. Unlike previous works, our proposal does not require any additional third party. We demonstrate with the help of experiments that the time required to generate recommendations is efficient for practical applications.

Keywords: Recommender system · Offline users · Homomorphic encryption · Privacy · ElGamal encryption · Group key

1 Introduction

Recommendation systems (RS) are widely used by online retailers to help customers find interesting products and thereby increase sales. To generate recommendations, the service providers ask users to rate items. In general, the more a service provider knows about users' interests the better is the accuracy of the recommendations. However, users may be concerned about sharing their personal information with a service provider. For example, a person may not wish to disclose his political opinions or religious beliefs to anyone. This threat becomes more severe when a service provider shares data collected from various users with third parties for financial gain or some other reasons. To mitigate the risks, there have been many proposals for recommender systems aimed at achieving privacy. The goal of a privacy preserving recommender system (PPRS) is to ensure that both the items rated by a user and the recommended items are kept confidential from the service provider and other users.

© Springer Nature Switzerland AG 2019
D. Garg et al. (Eds.): ICISS 2019, LNCS 11952, pp. 218–238, 2019.
https://doi.org/10.1007/978-3-030-36945-3_12

Following the definition in [25] we define the recommendation problem as follows. Let there be a set of n users $U = \{u_1, \ldots, u_n\}$, set of m items $I = i_1, \ldots, i_m$ and a recommendation server. Users' ratings are stored at server in a $n \times m$ matrix referred to as rating matrix $M = (R_1, \ldots, R_n)^T$, where $R_i = (r_{i,1}, r_{i,2}, \ldots, r_{i,m})$ is a rating vector from user i. The value $r_{i,j}$ represents user i's rating to item j which can be real or integer from a specified range defined by the system.

Definition 1. *Each user u rates a subset of items from I, $I_u = \{i_{j_1}, i_{j_2}, \ldots, i_{j_k}\}$, where $k < m$. Given a user u and an item i which user has not rated already, the job of a recommendation server is to predict $r_{u,i}$. The items having highest predicted ratings are shown to u as recommendations.*

In PPRS, users' ratings and generated recommendations must be kept private to them. For a user, the availability of recommendations should not be dependent on status of other users being online or offline.

Three approaches are commonly used to achieve privacy in recommender systems: perturbation [24], differential privacy [18] and encryption [2,10]. The first two approaches add randomness to hide users' data. There is an inherent problem with these approaches in that there is a trade-off between recommendation accuracy and privacy. Encryption based approaches use homomorphic schemes to allow computations over encrypted data. These approaches can generate accurate predictions and provide strong privacy, but they can be computationally costly. Many existing PPRS schemes which use homomorphic encryption based protocols require all users to be online while generating recommendations.

A user of a RS is said to be offline when there is no active session between the user and the server. Ideally, a recommender system should be able to provide accurate recommendations even if some users are offline. To solve the offline user problem several approaches have been proposed. Their main drawback is that they rely on an additional third party between users and the recommendation server.

Adomavicius and Tuzhilin [1] classified RS into three types: content based filtering (CBF), collaborative filtering (CF) and hybrid. There are two variations in CF: item-based CF and user-based CF. Item-based CF uses item-item similarity for recommendation whereas, user-based CF utilizes similarity between user profiles. Sarwar, Karypis, Konstan and Riedl [21] showed with experimental results that item-based CF approach can produce better rating predictions for some applications. In general, the above two approaches are complementary with some advantages over each other.

The offline user problem, which we focus on in this paper, is applicable to both approaches. There are existing solutions which address this problem, but in all of them the underlying CF approach is user-based CF [3,11,16].

Table 1. Notations

n	Total number of users
m	Total number of items
u_i	i^{th} user
i_j	j^{th} item
$r_{i,j}$	Item rating given by user u_i to item i_j
$f_{i,j}$	Item flag value based on rating $r_{i,j}$
$\alpha_{i,j}$	Ephemeral key of u_i used to encrypt $r_{i,j}$
$\beta_{i,j}$	Ephemeral key of u_i used to encrypt $f_{i,j}$
T	Size of plaintext message space
$E_{pk}(x)$	Encryption of x using public key pk
$\bar{r}_j$	Average rating for an item j
$s(i_j, i_k)$	Similarity score between items j and k
q	Large prime number
G	Cyclic group
g	Generator of G
x_i	User i's private key
y_i	User i's public key
Y	Common public key
$RP_{i,k}$	Predicted rating for user i for item k

1.1 Contributions

In this work, we propose a privacy-preserving protocol for item based CF that does not require users to remain active while generating recommendations. The main features of the scheme are:

- Our work is the first (as far as we know) to propose an item-based PPRS that solves the offline user problem.
- It does not require any additional trusted (or semi-trusted) third party, unlike the existing schemes for user-based PPRS. Since fewer parties have access to data (encrypted or otherwise), it reduces the trust requirement for users and recommender server.
- Unlike a previous approach by Jeckmans [16], our protocol generates recommendations using inputs from entire user-base of the system.
- The time for recommendation generation is efficient for practical applications.

1.2 Organization

The remainder of this paper is organized as follows. In Sect. 2 we review the previous literature related to our work. In particular, we review Badsha, Yi and Khalil's protocol (BYK) [2] based on the additive homomorphic variant of

ElGamal encryption scheme. The protocol suffers from the offline user problem, but we have adapted their architecture to build a solution described in Sect. 3. In Sect. 3 we propose a protocol that allows a user to obtain recommendations without requiring all users to interact with the recommendation server during the generation process. Section 4 contains the privacy analysis of the protocol. Section 5 gives a performance analysis in terms of computation and communication costs. Section 6 presents the experimental results. Section 7 concludes the paper. Notations used in the paper are listed in Table 1.

2 Related Work

In the following, we briefly review four existing protocols proposed by: Erkin et al. [10,11], Badsha, Yi, Khalil and Bertino [3] and Jeckmans [16].

2.1 Erkin-Veugen-Toft-Lagendijk Protocols

In the first protocol proposed by Erkin et al. [10], a user requests recommendations by encrypting his rating vector and sending it to the server. The server broadcasts the received vector to all users. Each user homomorphically computes the similarity of the received vector with his own rating vector. The result is sent to the server, which uses a threshold to filter out those users whose interests are very similar to the user requesting recommendations. They also proposed protocols to compute similarity and generate recommendations homomorphically using Paillier [19] and Brakerski and Vaikuntanathan [6] schemes.

The drawback of the above protocol is that all users must be online to participate in the recommendation generation process. In a subsequent work [11], they proposed a solution where users are not required to be online all the time. The protocol requires a semi-trusted third party namely privacy service provider (PSP). Once the users upload their encrypted rating data onto the server, the server along with PSP performs homomorphic operations to generate recommendations. The online presence of all users is not necessary while generating the recommendations.

2.2 Badsha-Yi-Khalil-Bertino Protocol

In [3] authors adapted the architecture used in [11], using data server (DS) in place of PSP. They proposed a privacy-preserving user-based collaborative filtering protocol using Boneh, Goh and Nissim (BGN) [5] homomorphic encryption. Here the target user sends encrypted ratings to the recommender server (RS) and receives encrypted ratings of other users. The target user then computes similarity with other users locally and sends the encrypted similarity score to RS. RS computes recommendations, permutes those values and sends them to DS which after decrypting recommendations forwards to the user. The user receives permuted recommendations from DS and permutation order from RS. Finally, the user retrieves the actual recommendations in the correct order.

The similarity computation at the user side can be computationally expensive if the user base of the recommender system is vast. DS and RS are assumed to be semi-honest parties. The DS learns nothing about a user's recommendations, assuming there is no collusion between DS and RS.

2.3 Arjan's Protocol

Arjan proposed forming groups of users based on friendship among them. Each user u provides its list of friends to the server and how much their opinion matters to u. In the literature [14,15,17,22] it is shown that the recommendation for items like movies, songs, books, etc. a familiarity measure can be used instead of computing user similarity. A user can define his familiarity by assigning a 'weight' to other users (friends); the ratings of these friends will be more relevant than other users. Arjan's proposal uses a proxy re-encryption server [4] to solve the offline user problem. It uses an additive secret sharing scheme [13]. Each user sends one share of its rating to the recommender server (encrypted with the server's public key) and another share to the proxy re-encryption server (encrypted with the user's public key). When a user needs recommendations, he collects one-half of his friends' ratings from the proxy server and sends them to the recommender server after encrypting them with his key. The server and user then jointly compute the recommendations. The protocol has the following drawbacks:

- The recommendations are generated using the ratings given by a limited number of users, which may not be as accurate as the recommendation generated using the entire rating matrix.
- A friend is assigned a constant weight for all items; it is possible that two friends have the same interest in mobile phones but very different liking on computer hardware. This will decrease the recommendation accuracy.
- It assumes that all the friends of a user are using the same recommender service.

2.4 Badsha, Yi and Khalil Protocol

This protocol uses the ElGamal encryption scheme [9], which is proven IND-CPA secure under the decisional Diffie-Hellman (DDH) assumption [23]. The IND-CPA security guarantees that the ciphertext reveals nothing about the message. There is a small change from the original ElGamal scheme: for a message m the public key $y = g^x$, where x is the private key, the ciphertext is defined by the pair: $(C_1, C_2) = (g^r, g^m y^r)$, where r is a random number. The original ElGamal scheme is multiplicative homomorphic, whereas the modified scheme has the additive homomorphic property, namely for all messages m_1, m_2, $E_y(m_1 + m_2) = E_y(m_1)E_y(m_2)$.

The BYK protocol assumes that the users and server have agreed on a common public key $y = \prod_{i=1}^{n} y_i$, where $y_i = g^{x_i}$ is the public key of user u_i and x_i is

PARAMETERS: U is set of n users: $u_1, \ldots, u_n$, P is set of m items: $p_1, \ldots, p_m$, S is the server, common public key: y, user i's private key: x_i.
INPUT: Each user i rates every item j as $r_{i,j}$ and sets corresponding flag $f_{i,j}$ as 0 or 1
OUTPUT: Average rating of item θ: $\bar{p}_\theta$
PROTOCOL:

1. All users send their respective encrypted ratings and flags to S.
   - $u_i \to S : \left(g^{\alpha_{i,\theta}}, g^{r_{i,\theta}} y^{\alpha_{i,\theta}} \right)$
   - $u_i \to S : \left(g^{\beta_{i,\theta}}, g^{f_{i,\theta}} y^{\beta_{i,\theta}} \right)$
2. Server performs the following:
   - Compute: $\left(g^{\sum_{i=1}^n \alpha_{i,\theta}}, g^{\sum_{i=1}^n r_{i,\theta}} y^{\sum_{i=1}^n \alpha_{i,\theta}} \right)$
   - Compute: $\left(g^{\sum_{i=1}^n \beta_{i,\theta}}, g^{\sum_{i=1}^n f_{i,\theta}} y^{\sum_{i=1}^n \beta_{i,\theta}} \right)$
   - Server broadcasts the following values:

   $$S \to u_i : g^{\sum_{i=1}^n \alpha_{i,\theta}}, g^{\sum_{i=1}^n \beta_{i,\theta}}$$

3. All users raise the received values with their private key and send result to S:
   - $u_i \to S : \left(g^{\sum_{i=1}^n \alpha_{i,\theta}} \right)^{x_i}, \left(g^{\sum_{i=1}^n \beta_{i,\theta}} \right)^{x_i}$
4. S decrypts the aggregate values, and then computes the average rating for p_θ:
   - Compute: $g^{\sum_{i=1}^n r_{i,\theta}} = \dfrac{\left(g^{\sum_{i=1}^n r_{i,\theta}} y^{\sum_{i=1}^n \alpha_{i,\theta}} \right)}{\left(g^{\sum_{i=1}^n \alpha_{i,\theta}} \right)^{\sum_{i=1}^n x_i}}$

   - Compute: $g^{\sum_{i=1}^n f_{i,\theta}} = \dfrac{\left(g^{\sum_{i=1}^n f_{i,\theta}} y^{\sum_{i=1}^n \beta_{i,\theta}} \right)}{\left(g^{\sum_{i=1}^n \beta_{i,\theta}} \right)^{\sum_{i=1}^n x_i}}$

   - Compute: $\sum_{i=1}^n r_{i,\theta}$ and $\sum_{i=1}^n f_{i,\theta}$ using Pollard's algorithm and computes $\bar{p}_\theta$

Algorithm 1. BYK protocol

the private key. The protocol has three phases: average rating, similarity and recommendation computation. We will discuss the first phase of the BYK protocol which computes the average rating for each item. Let $U = \{u_1, u_2, \ldots, u_n\}$ be a set of users and let $P = \{p_1, p_2, \ldots, p_n\}$ be a set of items. Each user encrypts the ratings and corresponding flags; the flag value is 1 if a user has rated the item, otherwise it is 0. Set of users' ratings for the items is $R = \{r_{i,j} | i \in U, j \in P\}$ and the corresponding set of flags is $F = \{f_{i,j} | i \in U, j \in P\}$. To compute average rating for a single item, the server and users execute the protocol shown in Algorithm 1.

Notice that the minimum and maximum values for the sum of ratings (respectively, sum of flags) is known a priori. When x lies within a relatively small interval, there are efficient algorithms available to solve for x given g^x. The server can compute the values $\sum_{i=1}^n r_{i,\theta}$ and $\sum_{i=1}^n f_{i,\theta}$. Therefore, at the end of the protocol, the server learns the average rating for item θ. The protocol requires each user to be available online.

Table 2 summarizes the various approaches that we discussed.

Table 2. Comparison of homomorphic encryption based protocols

Protocol	HE scheme	CF type	Solves offline users	Required TTP
Erkin et al. (2011)	Paillier, ElGamal	User-based	✗	✗
Erkin et al. (2012)	Paillier, DGK	User-based	✓	✓
Arjan's protocol (2014)	Brakerski and Vaikunthnathan	User-based	✓	✓
BYK protocol (2016)	ElGamal	Item-based	✗	✗
Badsha et al. (2017)	Boneh, Goh and Nissim (BGN)	User-based	✓	✓

3 Our Privacy-Preserving Protocol with Offline Users

We extend the architecture of Badsha et al. [2] to construct our protocol. Their protocol is based on item-item similarity and it suffers from offline user problem. Our proposal on the other hand, addresses the problem without introducing additional party for computations and without putting significant computation overhead on users.

3.1 Adversarial Model

In our settings, the users are assumed to be semi-honest: users do not collude with each other or with recommender server. The server too is assumed to be semi-honest; it may try to gain some knowledge about a user's ratings or recommended items. However, the server does not deviate from the protocol. We assume the communication channel between the users and the server is secure.

3.2 Group Key Protocol

In our scheme, the set of users is divided into groups by the server. Users belonging to the same group, unlike in [16], are not required to be familiar with each other. Each user in the group contributes to generating a group private key. The group private key is known to every user belonging to that group, so any user from the group can act on behalf of the entire group during the recommendation generation step. There is no need for a leader or cluster head. The group public keys are used by the server to generate the common key Y, which is used by all users to encrypt their ratings.

To generate a public and private key pair for each group, we use the Burmester-Desmedt (BD) protocol [7]. The BD protocol assumes that all parties form a circle and communicate over authenticated links. It is provably secure against a passive adversary under the DDH assumption [8]. In our setting, the clients do not know each other; therefore the server acts as a mediator to help users communicate. For a group consisting of z users, the protocol proceeds as follows:

- Each user u_i chooses at random an ephemeral private key a_i and computes an ephemeral public key as $t_i = g^{a_i}$. At the time of registration users send respective t_i to server.

- Server maintains a table with user id and corresponding t_i. It sends t_{i+1} and t_{i-1} to u_i, where the group ids are cyclic meaning for a group of 100 users $u_{101} = u_1$.
- Each user then computes $W_i = \left(\frac{t_{i+1}}{t_{i-1}}\right)^{a_i}$ and sends it to server.
- Server sends the required values to each user so that they can compute the group private key X as:

$$X = \left(t_{i-1}^{a_i}\right)^z W_i^{z-1} W_{i+1}^{z-2} \cdots W_z^{i-1} W_1^{i-2} \cdots W_{i-2}$$
$$= g^{a_1 a_2 + a_2 a_3 + \cdots + a_{z-1} a_z + a_z a_1}$$

Here the server can not compute the group private key of any group since it requires knowledge of a_i, which is private to respective users. The group public key is sent to the server and the group private keys are known only to the group members. In the group key generation phase, the server does not perform any computation, it simply forwards the messages to intended users.

3.3 Group-Oriented Average Computation

First, the server randomly divides all registered users into arbitrary size groups. All the members of a group G_k, run the above group key generation protocol to establish a group private key as X_k, where k denotes the group number. Each user computes the group public key $Y_k = g^{X_k}$.

Any one user who is available online from each group sends the group public key to the server, and the server generates a common public key Y as: $Y = \prod_{i=1}^{k} Y_i$. Server broadcasts this common public key Y to all users. Each user encrypt its ratings using Y and sends the resulting ciphertexts to the server.

Algorithm 2 shows the proposed protocol for computing the average rating for item θ (the remaining phases are described in Appendixes A, B and C). The first two steps are the same as that of BYK protocol. The main difference in the remaining steps is that they do not require every user to be present as long as at least one member of each group is online.

3.4 Adding New Users

The user base of a recommender system is dynamic. Thus, there could be some existing users leaving the system and some new users joining. We define *new users* as the users who join the system after the common public key Y has been set up. To add users to one of the existing groups G_k, the new user should learn the respective X_k, Y_k and Y. Here only X_k is private to the group members of G_k. This can be done using any public key encryption technique. Both users first share their public keys via server and then u_{old} sends X_k to u_{new} via server only. Since the server is semi-honest, it can eavesdrop but cannot retrieve X_k.

If there are very few groups when the recommender system is set up, the server can create additional new groups. This will require re-computation of Y, which will be an overhead on every user.

PARAMETERS: U is set of n users: $u_1, \ldots, u_n$, P is set of m items: $p_1, \ldots, p_m$, S is the server, common public key: Y, group private key: X_i

INPUT: Each user i rates every item j as $r_{i,j}$ and sets corresponding flag $f_{i,j}$ as 0 or 1

OUTPUT: Average rating of item θ: $\bar{p}_\theta$

PROTOCOL:

Server first divides users into groups, those users generate group public and private key pairs as: X_i, Y_i, then server generates common key Y and broadcasts to all users.

1. All users send their respective encrypted ratings and flags to S. (This time they encrypt using Y)
   - $u_i \rightarrow S : (g^{\alpha_{i,\theta}}, g^{r_{i,\theta}} y^{\alpha_{i,\theta}})$
   - $u_i \rightarrow S : \left(g^{\beta_{i,\theta}}, g^{f_{i,\theta}} y^{\beta_{i,\theta}}\right)$
2. Server sends following values to the user $u_{\omega,k}$. Here $u_{\omega,k}$ denotes any one user ω from group G_k who is online.
   - $S \rightarrow u_{\omega,k} : g^{\sum_{i=1}^n \alpha_{i,\theta}}, g^{\sum_{i=1}^n \beta_{i,\theta}}$
3. Every user receiving the above value, raises it with the corresponding group private key and returns result to S:

$$u_{\omega,k} \rightarrow S : \left(g^{\sum_{i=1}^n \alpha_{i,\theta}}\right)^{X_k}, \left(g^{\sum_{i=1}^n \beta_{i,\theta}}\right)^{X_k}$$

4. Server now decrypts the aggregate values:

   - Compute: $g^{\sum_{i=1}^n r_{i,\theta}} = \dfrac{\left(g^{\sum_{i=1}^n r_{i,\theta}} Y^{\sum_{i=1}^n \alpha_{i,\theta}}\right)}{\left(g^{\sum_{i=1}^n \alpha_{i,\theta}}\right)^{\sum_{i=1}^k X_i}}$

   - Compute: $g^{\sum_{i=1}^n f_{i,\theta}} = \dfrac{\left(g^{\sum_{i=1}^n f_{i,\theta}} Y^{\sum_{i=1}^n \beta_{i,\theta}}\right)}{\left(g^{\sum_{i=1}^n \beta_{i,\theta}}\right)^{\sum_{i=1}^k X_i}}$

   - Compute: $\sum_{i=1}^n r_{i,\theta}$ and $\sum_{i=1}^n f_{i,\theta}$ using Pollard's algorithm and computes $\bar{p}_\theta$

Algorithm 2. Proposed protocol for computing average rating

4 Privacy Analysis

We model our protocol as a secure two-party computation protocol. We assume that all users collectively form one party and their inputs are encrypted ratings. Recommendation server is the other party, both parties jointly compute the average rating of an item which only the server learns. Recall that the server is a semi-honest party.

To prove that the protocol protects users' privacy in presence of a semi-honest server we adapt the privacy definition by Goldreich [12]. It states that a computation protocol is privacy-preserving if the view of each party during protocol execution can be simulated by a polynomial-time algorithm knowing only the input and output. In our setup only server's view needs to be simulated as users are assumed to be honest. A *view* includes inputs, outputs and a security parameter k for the party.

$$View_{ideal/real} : \{input, output, k\}$$

Definition 2. *The proposed protocol securely computes the average rating of an item in the presence of a semi-honest server, if the server or simulator cannot infer any information from their respective views.*

Theorem 1. *By assuming the semantic security of the encryption system E, the proposed protocol is secure.*

Proof. We assume that the encryption system $E()$ is semantically secure (IND-CPA secure). We denote the server's real and ideal world views by $View_{real}$ and $View_{ideal}$, respectively.

$$View_{real} = \{(g, P_u, P_G, E_{pk}(r_{i,j})), (sum_r, sum_f, (C_j, C'_j), (D_j, D'_j)), k\}$$

Here input g is the generator, P_u is set of users' public keys, P_G is set of groups' public keys, $E_{pk}(r_{i,j})$ is the encrypted rating submitted by the user. The outputs that server computes are sum_r and sum_f as sum of ratings and flags respectively, (C_j, C'_j) and (D_j, D'_j) are the encrypted sum of ratings and flags respectively and k it the security parameter.

Now we can design a simulator to represent server in the ideal world as $View_{ideal}$. Here we assume the presence of a trusted party (TP) which always returns the correct computation outputs. The simulated values are represented using bar ($^-$) over them. The values g, P_u and P_G are available to server as input. TP generates $2n$ random numbers representing n ratings and n flags from the specified range provided in the protocol and encrypts them using public key Y. These values are sent to the server. Now server computes

$$(\bar{C}_j, \bar{C}'_j) = \left(\prod_{i=1}^{n} g^{\alpha_{i,j}}, \prod_{i=1}^{n} g^{r_{i,j}} Y^{\alpha_{i,j}} \right)$$

$$(\bar{D}_j, \bar{D}'_j) = \left(\prod_{i=1}^{n} g^{\beta_{i,j}}, \prod_{i=1}^{n} g^{f_{i,j}} Y^{\beta_{i,j}} \right)$$

Next server sends values of $\bar{C}_j$ and $\bar{D}_j$ to TP and it returns $(\bar{C}_j)^{x_i}$, $(\bar{D}_j)^{x_i}$ to the server. Server then computes sum'_r and sum'_f as shown in the protocol. At this point server's view is:

$$View_{ideal} = \{g, P_u, P_G, sum'_r, sum'_f, (\bar{C}_j, \bar{C}'_j), (\bar{D}_j, \bar{D}'_j), k\}$$

The difference between $View_{real}$ and $View_{ideal}$ is in output part i.e. $(sum_r, sum_f, (C_j, C'_j), (D_j, D'_j)$ along with k and $(sum'_r, sum'_f, (\bar{C}_j, \bar{C}'_j), (\bar{D}_j, \bar{D}'_j))$. In ideal world the simulator does not learn anything about individual rating from the decrypted aggregate values. Further, the ratings given as inputs by TP are encrypted which does not leak any information since $E()$ is IND-CPA.

We have shown that the real world semi-honest server can be simulated in ideal world and the users' privacy is maintained, hence from Definition 2 the claim is proved. $\square$

Table 3. Computation cost for each phase. enc, exp, mul shows encryption, exponentiation and multiplication costs, $\sqrt{T}enc$ is cost to solve discrete logarithm. Values shown inside { } are additionally required by any one user from the group

Computation	User	Server
Group key generation	$(b+1)\ exp + (b-1)\ mul$	–
Average rating	$2m\ enc,\ \{2m\ exp\}$	$4m(n-1)\ mul + 2\sqrt{T}m\ enc$
Similarity	$\dfrac{m(m+1)}{2}\ enc,\ \left\{\dfrac{m(m+1)}{2}\right\}\ exp$	$\dfrac{2m-1}{2}(n+k-1)\ mul + \dfrac{m(m+2)}{2}\sqrt{T}\ enc$
CBF prediction	$(2m+2)\ exp$	$2(m-1)\ mul + 2\ exp$
CF prediction	$2m\ exp$	$m\ mul + 6\ exp$

In above proof we have not modeled the step-3 and step-4 of the protocol, where server decrypts the aggregate values. In these steps server computes $C_j^{x_1+\cdots+x_n}$ and $D_j^{x_1+\cdots+x_n}$. If a semi-honest server can find value of $x_1+\cdots+x_n$ from these values, then it can read all individual ratings and flags in plaintext. In the Sect. 3.2 it is shown that

$$x_i = g^{a_1a_2 + a_2a_3 + \cdots + a_{z-1}a_z + a_za_1}$$

where a_is are chosen randomly from a large prime group. In this space discrete logarithm is unsolvable using any polynomial-time algorithm. Hence the server can decrypt the aggregate rating and flags but cannot retrieve individual's private information.

Next we show that the aggregate values available to server in plaintext does not compromise users' private information, if there are more than one user.

Theorem 2. *If the number of users is more than one, then a semi-honest server cannot compute the ratings given by an individual user after the protocol run.*

Proof. Let i_θ be an arbitrary but fixed item. At the end of the protocol run, the server receives *sum of ratings* and *sum of flags* in plaintext. For n users, the server will have sum of ratings s for i_θ as: $s = r_{1,\theta} + r_{2,\theta} + \cdots + r_{n,\theta}$. From this equation, the server cannot determine what rating a user has given to i_θ as there are multiple unknowns and only one equation. Hence, the claim holds.   □

5   Efficiency Evaluation

We evaluate the computation and communication costs for a single user, as the steps performed by each user are identical. In the average rating phase, we evaluate the costs per user and m items. In the similarity computation phase, costs shown are again per user and m items which makes $^mC_2$ pairs. The costs of CBF and CF phases are evaluated assuming the prediction for a user is computed only once.

Table 4. Communication cost for each phase (in bits)

Computation	User	Server
Group key generation	$len(t_i) + len(X_i)$	$2n + n(n-1)len(X_i)$
Average rating	$4ml,$	$2kml$
Similarity	$\{4m + 2m\}l$ $\dfrac{m(m+1)}{2}l, \left\{\dfrac{m(m+1)}{2}l\right\}$	$2kml$
CBF prediction	$2(m+2)l$	$2(m+2)l$
CF prediction	$2(m+2)l$	$2(m+2)l$

5.1   Computation Cost

We evaluate the computation costs for server and users for each phase of the protocol. Here we only consider the key generation and average rating computation phases. The key generation is a one-time computation. As in the protocol, there will be any one user from each group who will share the group key with the server and any one who will act in step-2. So there will be a difference in computation cost between all other users in the group and those users who participate during run of the protocol. In Table 3 in *user* column, the values written inside { } are with additional communication required by any one user from the group.

Group Key Generation. We assume that server has divided the users into groups and every user knows their group members. The group-wide communication is required only once to generate the group public and private key pair. Assume there are b users in each group, each user will have ephemeral key r_i and corresponding public key $t_i = g^{r_i}$.

Each user computes $X_i = \left(\dfrac{t_{i-1}}{t_{i+1}}\right)^{r_i}$ which requires one division and one exponentiation operation. Each user then computes the group private key as:

$$GK = \left(t_{i+1}^{r_i}\right)^b X_i^{b-1} X_{i+1}^{b-2} \cdots X_b^{i-1} X_1^{i-2} \cdots X_{i-2}$$

This requires b exponentiations and $b-1$ multiplications.

Average Rating. In step-1, each user performs two encryptions (including flag) and in step-3, only one user has to compute two exponentiations per item.
Total: for all users except one: $2m$ enc. For the user who acts during step-3 it will be: $2m$ enc $+2m$ exp.
For n users and m items in step-2 the server performs: $2m(n-1)$ multiplications, whereas in step-3: $2m(n-1)$ multiplications $+ m$ divisions $+ m$ discrete logarithm solutions.

5.2   Communication Cost

We evaluate the communication cost for the server and each user. Here we only consider key generation and average rating computation phases. As mentioned above any one user will have different cost in comparison to the rest of the group members. We evaluate the amount of data that is communicated by users and server while executing the different phases of the protocol. In Table 4 we assume that each of the ciphertexts C_1, C_2 is of length l bits.

Group Key Generation. Say that there are b users in a group, they all have r_i and t_i as their respective ephemeral input and ephemeral public key respectively. Each user sends t_i and X_i to server. Thus, the total cost for each user: $len(t_i) + len(X_i)$ bits. Server forwards messages to all users in the group, total cost for the server: $2b + (b(b-1) * len(X_i))$ bits.

Average Rating. Each user sends the encrypted rating and flag for each item to server in step-1: $4m(l)$ bits.
Any one user from each group will take part in step-3: $2(l)$ bits.
Total: $4m(l)$ bits for all users and additional $2(l)$ bits for one user from each group.
For each item the server will send k (total number of groups) values for ratings and flags in step-2: $2km(l)$ bits.

5.3   Comparison with Existing Protocols

The most recent work on the offline user problem is by Badsha et al. [3] so we compare our protocol's performance with it. To this end, we assume the cost of encryption operation as *enc* irrespective of the scheme used. n and m denote the number of users and items respectively, k denotes the number of groups present in the proposed protocol.

User. In [3], the cost for a user u_i at initialization stage is $2m$ enc. Whereas during the similarity computation phase, for every other user the target user u_i has to perform $(m-1)$ multiplication and m encryption. Computing similarity with all other users u_i will take $(n-1)((m-1)mul + menc)$ i.e. $\mathcal{O}(mn)$.
   On the other hand, in our proposal, as shown in Table 3, total cost for a user u_i is: $(2m + n + 1)exp + (n-1)mul + \left(\dfrac{m^2 + 5m}{2}\right)$ enc i.e. $\mathcal{O}(m^2)$.

Server. In [3], there are two servers, recommender server and data server and both the servers are used during recommendation phase only. The recommender server first computes bilinear pairing between ratings and similarity value. This has to be done $(n-1)$ times for a target user u_i. Finally, to generate recommendation for one item, server multiplies $(n-1)$ pairings which takes $(n-1)p + (n-2)mul$ time, where p is the cost of pairing. There are m items so

Table 5. Computation and communication cost of protocols supporting offline users

Protocol	Computation cost			Communication cost		
	User	Server	TTP	User	Server	TTP
Erkin et al.	$\mathcal{O}(m)$	$\mathcal{O}(mn)$	$\mathcal{O}(mn)$	$\mathcal{O}(m)$	$\mathcal{O}(mn)$	$\mathcal{O}(mn)$
Arjan	$\mathcal{O}(fm)$	$\mathcal{O}(fm)$	$\mathcal{O}(f)$	$\mathcal{O}(m)$	$\mathcal{O}(m)$	$\mathcal{O}(f)$
Badsha et al.	$\mathcal{O}(mn)$	$\mathcal{O}(mn)$	$\mathcal{O}(m)$	$\mathcal{O}(mn)$	$\mathcal{O}(mn)$	$\mathcal{O}(m)$
Our proposal	$\mathcal{O}(m^2)$	$\mathcal{O}(mn)$	–	$\mathcal{O}(m^2)$	$\mathcal{O}(km)$	–

the total cost: $m((n-1)p + (n-2)mul)$. Data server decrypts the recommendations and solves discrete logarithm for each item which takes enc and $\sqrt{T}(enc)$ time, where T is the size of the message space.

Total server side computation cost is: $m(n-1)p + m(n-1)mul + \sqrt{T}m$ enc, i.e. $\mathcal{O}(mn)$.

In the proposed protocol only recommender server is used and its total computation cost is $\mathcal{O}(mn)mul + \mathcal{O}(m^2)\sqrt{T}(enc) + 8$ exp, i.e. $\mathcal{O}(m^2)$.

Our scheme incurs higher computational cost than [3]. In [3] to compute similarity, each user has to perform some computations ($\mathcal{O}(mn)$ encryptions) when it requires the recommendations. This computation has to be done on the fly while the user is online, the time required for this depends on the number of users. In our proposal, the cost is higher in the similarity phase, but those computations can be performed offline, computations for CBF and CF phases shown in Table 3 are the online costs i.e., $\mathcal{O}(m)$ exponentiations. A comparison of the overall costs of various protocols is shown in Table 5.

Below are some observations from the comparisons:

- In Arjan's protocol f denotes the total number of friends in the group, where $f \ll n$. In our proposal the group size is denoted by k where $k \ll n$.
- In evaluating the communication cost for the server in our proposed protocol, we have not included the cost of generating group key as it is a one-time task. Once the group keys are generated, they can be used over a long period.
- As noted in [3] the weighted sum approach is more efficient than simple average ratings of similar users which was used in [11]. Our proposed protocol too uses the weighted sum approach.
- In both [3] and [11], a user has access to encrypted ratings provided by the other users which is avoided in our protocol.

6   Experimental Results

We evaluated our scheme on a virtual machine with Intel-i5 processor and 3 GB RAM. We used the Sagemath library in Python to implement cryptographic operations. We used a publicly available Movielens data set which contains 1 million records collected from 6040 users for about 3900 movies [20]. For our

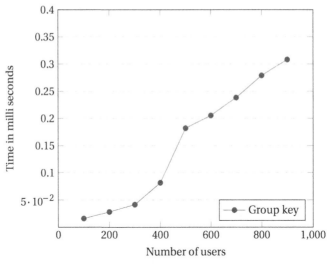

(a) Group key generation time

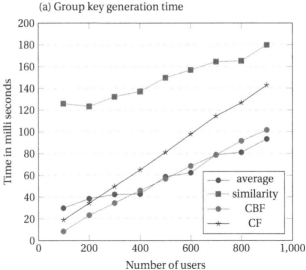

(b) Recommendation generation time

Fig. 1. Experimental results

experiments, we reduced the dataset by randomly choosing 900 users and 900 items. In our setting, we choose the size of the group G to be 2^{160}, and the length of the ephemeral keys α and β to be 80 bits. To compute one modular exponentiation, it took 0.13 ms while for multiplication it took 0.0019 μsec on average. To compute the group key generation time, we took the varying number of users and computed how much time it takes for one user to generate the group key. Since we do not consider communication time. Further, we assume that all the information required for computation is available to the user as input.

User: In the average computation phase, each user encrypts ratings and flag values for each item and sends it to the server. We take 900 items, so each user encrypts 900 ratings and flags.

Server: In step-2 server receives the ratings and flags from each user for every item, we compute time taken to find the average rating for one item. There are 900 users, so the server will have 900 encrypted ratings and 900 encrypted flags. These encrypted messages are of the form (C_1, C_2), thus the server has to perform 1800 modular multiplications for ratings and flags separately. In step-4 server has to perform 900 multiplications for rating and same for flags, then server computes two discrete logarithms, and finally computes the average rating of an item. The group key generation cost is shown for a group of 100 users. This is only the computation time required without communication delays. In similarity computation, we measure the time taken by a user to encrypt required values for 900 items whereas, on the server side we measured the time taken to find similarity between one pair. In CBF and CF phases, we have shown the time required to generate rating prediction for one item.

Figure 1(a) shows the time required to generate the group key for a varying number of users. For a group of 900 users, it takes 0.3082 ms of computation time which can be acceptable for real applications. Figure 1(b) shows how computation time required for different phases of the protocol grows with an increase in the total number of users. In the experiment, we have kept the number of items constant at 900 items. We measure the time taken for each phase as the time required to do computations while the server is online as some steps can be executed offline. For example, the server can compute similarity and store them in a similarity matrix once it has received the required information from the user groups. A user can generate ephemeral keys in advance since a user is unlikely to rate every item, its rating will contain most of the entries as encryption of zero, which user can prepare offline. The graph shows that the computation time for similarity computations is comparatively more; this can be reduced as servers used in real-world applications will have higher computational power. The group key generation time, average rating computation and similarity computation times need not be computed each time a user asks for recommendations. These computations can be done periodically, only CF and CBF phases are required to generate recommendations that take a fairly short time and can be used in practical applications.

7 Conclusion

In this paper we considered a scenario where the server does not require participation of all users after it receives the ciphertexts of the ratings from the users. This scenario has been studied in the literature, but existing solutions use third party. In this paper, we proposed an approach that does not require any additional third party. We have shown with the privacy analysis of the protocol that it meets the defined privacy goals. Experimental results show that the protocol can be implemented in practical applications as the computation cost for recommendation generation is small and should be acceptable in practice.

One interesting research challenge is how to ensure that there is at least one online user in every group at all times. To satisfy this requirement, the server can dynamically adjust the group membership. We leave this as future work.

A   Similarity Computation

Cosine similarity is used here to show the similarity between two items. It computes similarity between rating vectors of two items using cosine of angle between the vectors, smaller angle represents more similarity.

Algorithm 3 shows the similarity computation phase. Before executing these phases, the users would have been divided into groups and generated group keys for respective groups. The common key Y is available to all users. The server has computed the average rating of all items.

The similarity between two items θ and θ' is computed as:

$$s\left(\theta, \theta'\right) = \frac{\sum_{i=1}^{n} r_{i,\theta} r_{i,\theta'}}{\sqrt{\sum_{i=1}^{n} r_{i,\theta}^2} \sqrt{\sum_{i=1}^{n} r_{i,\theta'}^2}}$$

B   CBF-Based Recommendation

To generate recommendations, the server computes predicted ratings for all items and send them to the user. At the user end items with the highest ratings are shown to the user as recommended items list. The server sends predicted ratings encrypted under the target user's public key so these predictions can be seen by the intended user only. In CBF-Based recommendations, for a user u the rating for item θ is computed as:

$$RP_{u,\theta} = \frac{\sum_{j=1}^{m} r_{u,\theta} s\left(p_j, p_\theta\right)}{\sum_{j=1}^{m} s\left(p_j, p_\theta\right)}$$

The user sends its encrypted ratings to the server, and the server computes numerator and denominator values of rating predictions for all items, encrypts them using the target user's public key and sends back to the user. The user decrypts all predicted ratings and receives the recommendations. Algorithm 4 shows the detailed steps.

C   CF-Based Recommendation

To generate recommendations using CF-based technique, the data flow is similar to that of CBF-based technique with following equation for prediction:

$$RP_{u,\theta} = \frac{\bar{p}_\theta \sum_{j=1}^{m} s\left(p_\theta, p_j\right) + \sum_{j=1}^{m} \left(r_{u,j} - \bar{p}_j\right) s\left(p_\theta, p_j\right)}{\sum_{j=1}^{m} s\left(p_\theta, p_j\right)}$$

Detailed steps are shown in Algorithm 5.

PARAMETERS: U is set of n users: $u_1, \ldots, u_n$, P is set of m items: $p_1, \ldots, p_m$, S is the server, common public key: Y, group private key: X_i

INPUT: Each user i rates every item j as $r_{i,j}$ and sets corresponding flag $f_{i,j}$ as 0 or 1

OUTPUT: Similarity between two items θ and θ': $s(\theta, \theta')$

PROTOCOL:

1. All users send three values to S, encrypted using Y: $r_{i,\theta}^2, r_{i,\theta'}^2, r_{i,\theta} r_{i,\theta'}$

   - $u_i \to S : \left(g^{\alpha_{i,\theta}}, g^{r_{i,\theta}^2} y^{\alpha_{i,\theta}} \right)$

   - $u_i \to S : \left(g^{\beta_{i,\theta'}}, g^{r_{i,\theta'}^2} y^{\beta_{i,\theta'}} \right)$

   - $u_i \to S : \left(g^{\gamma_{i,\theta\theta'}}, g^{r_{i,\theta\theta'}^2} y^{\gamma_{i,\theta\theta'}} \right)$

   - Server gets encrypted $\sum_{i=1}^{n} r_{i,\theta}^2, \sum_{i=1}^{n} r_{i,\theta'}^2, \sum_{i=1}^{n} r_{i,\theta} r_{i,\theta'}$ as:

     - Compute: $\left(g^{\sum_{i=1}^{n} \alpha_{i,\theta}}, g^{\sum_{i=1}^{n} r_{i,\theta}^2} Y^{\sum_{i=1}^{n} \alpha_{i,\theta}} \right)$

     - Compute: $\left(g^{\sum_{i=1}^{n} \beta_{i,\theta'}}, g^{\sum_{i=1}^{n} r_{i,\theta'}^2} Y^{\sum_{i=1}^{n} \beta_{i,\theta'}} \right)$

     - Compute: $\left(g^{\sum_{i=1}^{n} \gamma_{i,\theta\theta'}}, g^{\sum_{i=1}^{n} r_{i,\theta} r_{i,\theta'}} Y^{\sum_{i=1}^{n} \gamma_{i,\theta\theta'}} \right)$

   Now, if some users from each group are offline, then in order to decrypt these values server sends following values the user $u_{\omega,k}$. Here $u_{\omega,k}$ denotes any one user ω from group G_k who is online.

$$S \to u_{\omega,k} : \left(g^{\sum_{i=1}^{n} \alpha_{i,\theta}}, \; g^{\sum_{i=1}^{n} \beta_{i,\theta'}} \; g^{\sum_{i=1}^{n} \gamma_{i,\theta\theta'}} \right)$$

2. Users receiving above value raises it with group private key and returns result to S:

$$u_{\omega,k} \to S : \left(g^{\sum_{i=1}^{n} \alpha_{i,\theta}} \right)^{X_k}, \; \left(g^{\sum_{i=1}^{n} \beta_{i,\theta'}} \right)^{X_k}, \; \left(g^{\sum_{i=1}^{n} \gamma_{i,\theta\theta'}} \right)^{X_k}$$

3. Server now decrypts the aggregate values:

   - Compute: $g^{\sum_{i=1}^{n} r_{i,\theta}^2} = \dfrac{\left(g^{\sum_{i=1}^{n} r_{i,\theta}^2} Y^{\sum_{i=1}^{n} \alpha_{i,\theta}} \right)}{\left(g^{\sum_{i=1}^{n} \alpha_{i,\theta}} \right)^{\sum_{i=1}^{k} X_i}}$

   - Compute: $g^{\sum_{i=1}^{n} r_{i,\theta'}^2} = \dfrac{\left(g^{\sum_{i=1}^{n} r_{i,\theta'}^2} Y^{\sum_{i=1}^{n} \beta_{i,\theta'}} \right)}{\left(g^{\sum_{i=1}^{n} \beta_{i,\theta'}} \right)^{\sum_{i=1}^{k} X_i}}$

   - Compute: $g^{\sum_{i=1}^{n} r_{i,\theta} r_{i,\theta'}} = \dfrac{\left(g^{\sum_{i=1}^{n} r_{i,\theta} r_{i,\theta'}} Y^{\sum_{i=1}^{n} \gamma_{i,\theta\theta'}} \right)}{\left(g^{\sum_{i=1}^{n} \gamma_{i,\theta\theta'}} \right)^{\sum_{i=1}^{k} X_i}}$

   - Compute: $\sum_{i=1}^{n} r_{i,\theta}^2, \sum_{i=1}^{n} r_{i,\theta'}^2$ and $\sum_{i=1}^{n} r_{i,\theta} r_{i,\theta'}$ using Pollard's algorithm

   - Compute similarity $(s_{\theta,\theta'})$ between items θ and θ' using cosine similarity:

$$s(\theta, \theta') = \frac{\sum_{i=1}^{n} r_{i,\theta} r_{i,\theta'}}{\sqrt{\sum_{i=1}^{n} r_{i,\theta}^2} \sqrt{\sum_{i=1}^{n} r_{i,\theta'}^2}}$$

Algorithm 3. Proposed protocol to compute item-item similarity

PARAMETERS: U is set of n users: $u_1, \ldots, u_n$, P is set of m items: $p_1, \ldots, p_m$, S is the server, common public key: Y, group private key: X_i
INPUT: Each user i rates every item j as $r_{i,j}$ and sets corresponding flag $f_{i,j}$ as 0 or 1
OUTPUT: Encrypted rating predictions for all items
PROTOCOL:

1. The user sends encrypted ratings for all items to S:
   $$u_i \rightarrow S : (g^{\alpha_{i,j}}, g^{r_{i,j}} t^{\alpha_{i,j}})$$

2. Server computes encrypted numerator using homomorphic operation as:
   $$(A, B) = \prod_{j=1}^{m} E_t (g^{r_{i,j}})^{s(p_k, p_j)}, \text{ where } k = 1, \ldots, m$$

   Server computes the denominator encrypted under user i's public key for all items:
   $$E_t \left(g^{\sum_{j=1}^{m} s(p_k, p_j)} \right)$$
   Server sends these numerator and denominator values for items to the user.
3. User now decrypts the received values corresponding to each item and solves discrete logarithm to obtain $\sum_{j=1}^{m} r_{u,\theta} s(p_j, p_\theta)$ and $\sum_{j=1}^{m} s(p_j, p_\theta)$.
   Now user has the
   predicted ratings for all items.

Algorithm 4. Proposed protocol to compute CBF-Based recommendation

PARAMETERS: U is set of n users: $u_1, \ldots, u_n$, P is set of m items: $p_1, \ldots, p_m$, S is the server, common public key: Y, group private key: X_i
INPUT: Each user i rates every item j as $r_{i,j}$ and sets corresponding flag $f_{i,j}$ as 0 or 1
OUTPUT: Encrypted rating predictions for all items
PROTOCOL:

1. The user sends encrypted ratings for all items to S:
   $$u_i \rightarrow S : (g^{\alpha_{i,j}}, g^{r_{i,j}} t^{\alpha_{i,j}})$$

2. The server has average ratings of all items and similarity between every two items.
   To compute encrypted numerator:
   - compute: $E_t \left(g^{\bar{p}_\theta \sum_{j=1}^{m} s(p_\theta, p_j)} \right)$ and $E_t \left(g^{\bar{p}_\theta} \right)$
   - compute: $(A, B) = E_t \left(g^{\bar{p}_\theta \sum_{j=1}^{m} s(p_\theta, p_j)} \right) \prod_{j=1}^{m} \left(\frac{E_t(g^{r_{u,j}})}{E_t(g^{\bar{p}_j})} \right)^{s(p_\theta, p_j)}$

   Next, server computes denominator as:
   - $(A', B') = E_t \left(g^{\sum_{j=1}^{m} s(p_\theta, p_j)} \right)$
3. User decrypts the received values corresponding to each item and solves discrete logarithm to obtain
   $\bar{p}_\theta \sum_{j=1}^{m} s(p_\theta, p_j) + \sum_{j=1}^{m} (r_{u,j} - \bar{p}_j) s(p_\theta, p_j)$ and $\sum_{j=1}^{m} s(p_\theta, p_j)$ Now user has the predicted ratings for all items.

Algorithm 5. Proposed protocol to compute CF-Based recommendation

References

1. Adomavicius, G., Tuzhilin, A.: Toward the next generation of recommender systems: a survey of the state-of-the-art and possible extensions. IEEE Trans. Knowl. Data Eng. **6**, 734–749 (2005)

2. Badsha, S., Yi, X., Khalil, I.: A practical privacy-preserving recommender system. Data Sci. Eng. **1**(3), 161–177 (2016)
3. Badsha, S., Yi, X., Khalil, I., Bertino, E.: Privacy preserving user-based recommender system. In: 2017 IEEE 37th International Conference on Distributed Computing Systems (ICDCS), pp. 1074–1083. IEEE (2017)
4. Blaze, M., Bleumer, G., Strauss, M.: Divertible protocols and atomic proxy cryptography. In: Nyberg, K. (ed.) EUROCRYPT 1998. LNCS, vol. 1403, pp. 127–144. Springer, Heidelberg (1998). https://doi.org/10.1007/BFb0054122
5. Boneh, D., Goh, E.-J., Nissim, K.: Evaluating 2-DNF formulas on ciphertexts. In: Kilian, J. (ed.) TCC 2005. LNCS, vol. 3378, pp. 325–341. Springer, Heidelberg (2005). https://doi.org/10.1007/978-3-540-30576-7_18
6. Brakerski, Z., Vaikuntanathan, V.: Fully homomorphic encryption from ring-LWE and security for key dependent messages. In: Rogaway, P. (ed.) CRYPTO 2011. LNCS, vol. 6841, pp. 505–524. Springer, Heidelberg (2011). https://doi.org/10.1007/978-3-642-22792-9_29
7. Burmester, M., Desmedt, Y.: A secure and efficient conference key distribution system. In: De Santis, A. (ed.) EUROCRYPT 1994. LNCS, vol. 950, pp. 275–286. Springer, Heidelberg (1995). https://doi.org/10.1007/BFb0053443
8. Burmester, M., Desmedt, Y.: A secure and scalable group key exchange system. Inf. Process. Lett. **94**(3), 137–143 (2005)
9. ElGamal, T.: A public key cryptosystem and a signature scheme based on discrete logarithms. IEEE Trans. Inf. Theory **31**(4), 469–472 (1985)
10. Erkin, Z., Beye, M., Veugen, T., Lagendijk, R.L.: Efficiently computing private recommendations. In: ICASSP, pp. 5864–5867 (2011)
11. Erkin, Z., Veugen, T., Toft, T., Lagendijk, R.L.: Generating private recommendations efficiently using homomorphic encryption and data packing. IEEE Trans. Inf. Forensics Secur. **7**(3), 1053–1066 (2012)
12. Goldreich, O.: Secure multi-party computation (1998)
13. Goldreich, O., et al.: Foundations of cryptography-a primer. Found. Trends® Theor. Comput. Sci. **1**(1), 1–116 (2005)
14. Groh, G., Ehmig, C.: Recommendations in taste related domains: collaborative filtering vs. social filtering. In: Proceedings of the 2007 International ACM Conference on Supporting Group Work, pp. 127–136. ACM (2007)
15. Guy, I., Zwerdling, N., Carmel, D., Ronen, I., Uziel, E., Yogev, S., Ofek-Koifman, S.: Personalized recommendation of social software items based on social relations. In: Proceedings of the Third ACM Conference on Recommender Systems, pp. 53–60. ACM (2009)
16. Jeckmans, A.J.P.: Cryptographically-enhanced privacy for recommender systems. University of Twente (2014)
17. Lerman, K.: Social networks and social information filtering on Digg. arXiv preprint cs/0612046 (2006)
18. McSherry, F., Mironov, I.: Differentially private recommender systems: building privacy into the Netflix Prize contenders. In: Proceedings of the 15th ACM SIGKDD International Conference on Knowledge Discovery and Data Mining, pp. 627–636. ACM (2009)
19. Paillier, P.: Public-key cryptosystems based on composite degree residuosity classes. In: Stern, J. (ed.) EUROCRYPT 1999. LNCS, vol. 1592, pp. 223–238. Springer, Heidelberg (1999). https://doi.org/10.1007/3-540-48910-X_16
20. Resnick, P., Iacovou, N., Suchak, M., Bergstrom, P., Riedl, J.: GroupLens: an open architecture for collaborative filtering of netnews. In: Proceedings of the 1994 ACM Conference on Computer Supported Cooperative Work, pp. 175–186. ACM (1994)

21. Sarwar, B.M., Karypis, G., Konstan, J.A., Riedl, J.: Item-based collaborative filtering recommendation algorithms. In: Proceedings of the Tenth International World Wide Web Conference, WWW 2010, Hong Kong, China, 1–5 May 2001, pp. 285–295 (2001). https://doi.org/10.1145/371920.372071
22. Sinha, R.R., Swearingen, K., et al.: Comparing recommendations made by online systems and friends. In: DELOS Workshop: Personalisation and Recommender Systems in Digital Libraries, vol. 106 (2001)
23. Tsiounis, Y., Yung, M.: On the security of ElGamal based encryption. In: Imai, H., Zheng, Y. (eds.) PKC 1998. LNCS, vol. 1431, pp. 117–134. Springer, Heidelberg (1998). https://doi.org/10.1007/BFb0054019
24. Yakut, I., Polat, H.: Arbitrarily distributed data-based recommendations with privacy. Data Knowl. Eng. **72**, 239–256 (2012)
25. Zhang, F., et al.: Privacy-aware smart city: a case study in collaborative filtering recommender systems. J. Parallel Distrib. Comput. **127**, 145–159 (2019)

Wip: Degree Evaluation of Grain-v1

Deepak Kumar Dalai and Santu Pal[(⊠)]

National Institute of Science Education and Research, HBNI,
Bhubaneswar 752050, India
{deeepak,santu.pal}@niser.ac.in

Abstract. In this paper, we initiated a degree evaluation technique for the NFSR based stream cipher like Grain family where the degree of the NFSR update bits is higher than the degree of the output function. Here, we have applied the technique on Grain-v1 to evaluate degree NFSR update bit and output bit during key scheduling phase of reduced round. We are trying to improve this technique and correctness for the full paper.

Keywords: Cryptanalysis · Stream cipher · Grain-v1 · Degree evaluation

1 Introduction

Most of the cryptographic primitives, specially NFSR based ciphers, consist of by a Boolean functions, which take private (i.e., key) and public (i.e. IV) bits as inputs. By exploiting the degree of the Boolean function, one can find out the weaknesses of the primitives. The correct estimation of degree of a NFSR based stream cipher is a challenging job. There are few tools such as statistical analysis, symbolic computation etc. to estimate the algebraic degree. By estimating the algebraic degree, one can exploit so many attack like cube attacks, integral attacks, algebraic attacks, higher order differential attacks etc.

The theories of estimating degree are based on the two ideas, first one uses the Walsh spectrum [2–4] and second one uses the simple fact. Our work follows the later. At CRYPTO 2017, Liu [9] has described an algorithm to find out the upper bounds on the degrees of NFSR based cipher by using a new concept, called "Numeric mapping". A degree evaluation technique for Trivium like cipher was designed and shown that the estimated bound is close to its original value for maximum cases. They have used their degree estimation technique to identify the number of rounds where the key and IV bits are mixed properly or not, and further it is used for the distinguishing purpose as a cube tester. Our work is similar to this work. After that, Ye et al. [13] have presented an algorithm to find the exact super polynomial of a cube and also proved that it is not a zero sum distinguisher for 838 rounds of Trivium given by Liu. To find the super polynomial, they first compute the ANF of the output function by a backward method iteratively and the ANF of the involved bits in the output function z up to some manageable rounds and then compute the super polynomial.

© Springer Nature Switzerland AG 2019
D. Garg et al. (Eds.): ICISS 2019, LNCS 11952, pp. 239–251, 2019.
https://doi.org/10.1007/978-3-030-36945-3_13

At CRYPTO 2018, Fu et al. [6] considered the output function z as $P_1P_2+P_3$, where P_1 should be selected by (a) frequency of P_1 is high in higher degree term (b) P_1 has low degree (c) minimum number of key guessing in P_1. The right key guessing of P_1 gives a simple polynomial as $(1+P_1)z = (1+P_1)P_3$ and wrong one gives $(1 + P_1')z = (1 + P_1')(P_1P_2 + P_3)$. Finally they have calculated the degree of $(1 + P_1)z = (1 + P_1)P_3$ as d by using their proposed algorithm and used $d+1$ dimensional cube as distinguisher. There are other literature [14], where degrees of NFSR based cryptosystem are discussed.

In this paper, we have simplified the h function of Grain-v1 by using some static variables and then calculated the maximum degree over initial state bits up to some round of Grain-v1. Our aim is to find out at which round the feedback bit and output can achieve the highest degree and to claim that at this round the key bits and IV bits mix properly.

1.1 Our Contribution

Our aim is to evaluate the degree of the feedback bits of NFSR and LFSR the and output bit over the initial state bits (which includes the bits of key, IV and nonce bits). In this paper, we have initiated a work to evaluate the degree of the said bits using difference of involved tap points in the NFSR and the output functions. The degree of NFSR update terms in Grain-v1 is higher than the degree of its output function. To control the degree of output function we have put some conditions on IV bits. Therefore, our degree evaluation is subjected to some conditions on IV bits. We have followed the following steps to evaluate the degree.

1. The differences between the state bits involved in the NFSR update function.
2. The common bits with shifted bits according to the differences.
3. Calculating the degree of the quadratic terms.
4. Common bits according to the difference trail.
5. The possibility of degrees of NFSR update terms.

We could calculate the degrees of the NFSR update bits up to 54 rounds i.e., the degree of feedback bits b_{80+t}, l_{80+t} and output bit z_{80+t} for $0 \leq t \leq 54$. We have verified the degree up to 42 round by SAGE.

1.2 Organization of Paper

In first section, we introduce the degree evaluation techniques for NFSR based stream cipher and present our aim and contribution. The main work is contained in Sect. 2, where we present all steps and tools for the degree evaluation. In Sect. 3, we apply the technique to evaluate the degrees in Grain-v1. In last section, we conclude the paper with future work.

2   Degree Evaluation of Grain-v1

Grain-v1 [7] is a hardware based stream cipher consisting of an 80-bit NFSR, an 80-bit LFSR and a nonlinear filter function h of 5 variables, where $b_i, s_i, 0 \leq i \leq 79$ are the state bits of the NFSR and LFSR respectively. The state update functions of LFSR and NFSR are presented in Eq. 1 and Eq. 2 respectively.

$$s_{t+80} = s_{t+62} + s_{t+51} + s_{t+38} + s_{t+23} + s_{t+13} + s_t, \text{ for } t \geq 0. \tag{1}$$

$$\begin{aligned}
b_{t+80} = {} & s_t + b_{t+62} + b_{t+60} + b_{t+52} + b_{t+45} + b_{t+37} + b_{t+33} \\
& + b_{t+28} + b_{t+21} + b_{t+14} + b_{t+9} + b_t + b_{t+63}b_{t+60} + \\
& b_{t+37}b_{t+33} + b_{t+15}b_{t+9} + b_{t+60}b_{t+52}b_{t+45} + b_{t+33}b_{t+28}b_{t+21} + \\
& b_{t+63}b_{t+45}b_{t+28}b_{t+9} + b_{t+60}b_{t+52}b_{t+37}b_{t+33} + b_{t+63}b_{t+60}b_{t+21} \\
& b_{t+15} + b_{t+63}b_{t+60}b_{t+52}b_{t+45}b_{t+37} + b_{t+33}b_{t+28}b_{t+21}b_{t+15}b_{t+9} \\
& + b_{t+52}b_{t+45}b_{t+37}b_{t+33}b_{t+28}b_{t+21}, \text{ for } t \geq 0. \tag{2}
\end{aligned}$$

The algebraic normal form of the nonlinear filter function h is given by

$$\begin{aligned}
h(s_{t+3}, s_{t+25}, s_{t+46}, s_{t+64}, b_{t+63}) = {} & s_{t+25} + b_{t+63} + s_{t+3}s_{t+64} + s_{t+46}s_{t+64} + \\
& s_{t+64}b_{t+63} + s_{t+3}s_{t+25}s_{t+46} + s_{t+3}s_{t+46}s_{t+64} + s_{t+3}s_{t+46}b_{t+63} + \\
& s_{t+25}s_{t+46}b_{t+63} + s_{t+46}s_{t+64}b_{t+63}. \tag{3}
\end{aligned}$$

The keystream bit z_t of the cipher is calculated by combining the output of the nonlinear filter function and some state bits of the NFSR. The algebraic expression of the keystream bit at t-th round is

$$\begin{aligned}
z_t = {} & b_{t+1} + b_{t+2} + b_{t+4} + b_{t+10} + b_{t+31} + b_{t+43} + b_{t+56} \\
& + h(s_{t+3}, s_{t+25}, s_{t+46}, s_{t+64}, b_{t+63}), \text{ for } t \geq 0. \tag{4}
\end{aligned}$$

The NFSR is loaded with key bits and LFSR is loaded with 64 bits IV and rest of the sixteen bits are padded as all one pattern. Then the cipher runs the KSA (key scheduling algorithm) for 160 rounds, without generating any keystream bit as output bit. Instead, these keystream bits are added with the feedback bit of the NFSR and LFSR. After running 160 rounds of KSA the cipher starts the PRGA (pseudorandom bit generation algorithm), where the cipher produces keystream bits as output.

We see that during KSA, both the LFSR and NFSR feedback have a term z_t. Hence the degree of LFSR bits is dominated by the degree of z_t. As the NFSR has nonlinear terms, the degree of NFSR bits may not be dominated by the degree of z_t in all rounds. From Eq. 4, it is clear that the highest degree term of z_t (i.e., 3-degree terms) comes from h. So we vanish those 3-degree terms of h by imposing some restrictions on IV bits for few initial rounds as following.

It can be seen from Eq. 3 that s_{t+46} is present in all 3-degree terms (and one 2-degree term) in h. If the value of state bits s_{46} to s_{63} are equal to 0 (i.e., the last 18 bits of IV), then all 3-degree terms of h are vanished for first 18 rounds. The equation of h for $0 \leq t \leq 17$ becomes

$$h(s_{t+3}, s_{t+25}, 0, s_{t+64}, b_{t+63}) = s_{t+25} + b_{t+63} + s_{t+3}s_{t+64} + s_{t+64}b_{t+63}.$$

As during the key loading the LFSR bits from s_{64} to s_{79} are set 1 as padding bits, h contains only two linear bits for first 16 rounds as the equation of h is

$$h(s_{t+3}, s_{t+25}, 0, 1, b_{t+63}) = s_{t+25} + s_{t+3} \text{ for } 0 \leq t \leq 15.$$

As round increases the conditions set (i.e., $s_{46} = \cdots = s_{63} = 0$ and $s_{64} = \cdots = s_{79} = 1$), the conditions shifted to other state bits in the LFSR. Therefore, the equation of h is simplified for higher rounds (i.e., $t \geq 16$). The equation of h is presented in Table 1 for first 77 rounds (i.e., $0 \leq t \leq 76$).

Table 1. ANF of h function of Grain-v1 at different rounds

Static bit	h function	Rounds
$s_{t+46} = 0, s_{t+64} = 1$	$h = s_{t+3} + s_{t+25}$	$0-15$
$s_{t+46} = 0$	$h = s_{t+25} + b_{t+63} + s_{t+3}s_{t+64} + s_{t+64}b_{t+63}$	16
$s_{t+46} = 0$	$h = s_{t+25} + b_{t+63} + s_{t+3}s_{t+64} + s_{t+64}b_{t+63}$	17
$s_{t+46} = 1$	$h = s_{t+25} + b_{t+63} + s_{t+64} + s_{t+3}s_{t+25} + s_{t+3}b_{t+63} + s_{t+25}b_{t+63}$	$18-20$
$s_{t+25} = 0, s_{t+46} = 1$	$h = b_{t+63} + s_{t+64} + s_{t+3}b_{t+63}$	$21-32$
$s_{t+25} = 0$	$h = b_{t+63} + s_{t+3}s_{t+64} + s_{t+46}s_{t+64} + s_{t+64}b_{t+63} + s_{t+3}s_{t+46}s_{t+64} + s_{t+3}s_{t+46}b_{t+63} + s_{t+46}s_{t+64}b_{t+63}$	$33-38$
$s_{t+25} = 1$	$h = 1 + b_{t+63} + s_{t+3}s_{t+64} + s_{t+46}s_{t+64} + s_{t+64}b_{t+63} + s_{t+3}s_{t+46} + s_{t+3}s_{t+46}s_{t+64} + s_{t+3}s_{t+46}b_{t+63} + s_{t+46}b_{t+63} + s_{t+46}s_{t+64}b_{t+63}$	$39-42$
$s_{t+3} = 0, s_{t+25} = 1$	$h = 1 + b_{t+63} + s_{t+46}s_{t+64} + s_{t+64}b_{t+63} + s_{t+46}b_{t+63} + s_{t+46}s_{t+64}b_{t+63}$	$43-54$
$s_{t+3} = 0$	$h = s_{t+25} + b_{t+63} + s_{t+46}s_{t+64} + s_{t+64}b_{t+63} + s_{t+25}s_{t+46}b_{t+63} + s_{t+46}s_{t+64}b_{t+63}$	$54-60$
$s_{t+3} = 1$	$h = s_{t+25} + b_{t+63} + s_{t+64} + s_{t+64}b_{t+63} + s_{t+25}s_{t+46} + s_{t+46}b_{t+63} + s_{t+25}s_{t+46}b_{t+63} + s_{t+46}s_{t+64}b_{t+63}$	$61-76$

Grain-v1 is prone to be attacked by different way. There are several literature [1,5,8,10–12,15,16] on this. Interested reader can go through this.

2.1   Calculating Repeated Bits

In Grain-v1, the set of state bits $B = \{b_9, b_{15}, b_{21}, b_{28}, b_{33}, b_{37}, b_{45}, b_{52}, b_{60}, b_{63}\}$ are involved in the non-linear terms of the state update relation of NFSR (see Eq. 2). We enumerate the differences between each pair of these state bits. The differences can be computed using the following recursion.

Definition 1. *Let there is a ordered set of n integers $S = \{a_1, a_2, \cdots, a_n\}$. For $1 \le k \le n-1$, the kth order difference of S is defined as $\Delta^k S = \{a_{k+1}-a_1, a_{k+2}-a_2, \cdots, a_n - a_{n-k}\}$ and $\Delta^0 S = S$. The i-th element of $\Delta^k S$ (i.e, $a_{k+i} - a_i$) is denoted as $\Delta^k S_i$ for $1 \le i \le n-k$.*

It can be easily checked that $\Delta^k S$ can be recursively computed as the following.

Lemma 1. *For $2 \le k \le n-1$, $\Delta^k S_i = \Delta^{k-1} S_i + \Delta^1 S_{k+i-1}$ for $1 \le i \le n-k$.*

For the Grain-v1 case, let take the set S as the index of the bits involved in the nonlinear terms of the state update relation of NFSR i.e., in set B. Then Table 2 presents the order difference of the indices of these state bits where the differences and repeated indices can be identified. The value of the term $\Delta^k S_i$

Table 2. Order difference Δ^k of the indices

Bits	b_9	b_{15}	b_{21}	b_{28}	b_{33}	b_{37}	b_{45}	b_{52}	b_{60}	b_{63}
Order (k)										
0	9	15	21	28	33	37	45	52	60	63
1		6	6	7	5	4	8	7	8	3
2			12	13	12	9	12	15	15	11
3				19	18	16	17	19	23	18
4					24	22	24	24	27	26
5						28	30	31	32	30
6							36	37	39	35
7								43	45	42
8									51	48
9										54

represents that in Grain-v1 the state value of $(k+i)$-th nonlinear bit in ordered set S is shifted to i-th state after $\Delta^k S_i$ rounds. For example, $\Delta^2 S_3 = 12$ in Table 2 represents that the state value of the 33-th state (i.e., b_{33}) is shifted to 21-th state (i.e., b_{21}) in the NFSR after 12 rounds.

The sorted list of differences (from Table 2) and the pair of bits where the difference is occurred are present in Table 3.

When two terms multiplied, the degree of final term is lesser than the sum of the individual terms if there are some common variables between the terms.

Table 3. Table of Common bits according to differences

Difference	Between pair of bits	Difference	Between pair of bits	Difference	Between pair of bits
3	(b_{60}, b_{63})	16	(b_{21}, b_{37})	31	(b_{21}, b_{52})
4	(b_{33}, b_{37})	17	(b_{28}, b_{45})	32	(b_{28}, b_{60})
5	(b_{28}, b_{33})	18	$(b_{15}, b_{33}), (b_{45}, b_{63})$	35	(b_{28}, b_{63})
6	$(b_9, b_{15}), (b_{15}, b_{21})$	19	$(b_9, b_{28}), (b_{33}, b_{52})$	36	(b_9, b_{45})
7	$(b_{21}, b_{28}), (b_{45}, b_{52})$	23	(b_{37}, b_{60})	37	(b_{15}, b_{52})
8	$(b_{37}, b_{45}), (b_{52}, b_{60})$	22	(b_{15}, b_{37})	39	(b_{21}, b_{60})
9	(b_{28}, b_{37})	24	$(b_9, b_{33}), (b_{21}, b_{45}), (b_{28}, b_{52})$	42	(b_{21}, b_{63})
11	(b_{52}, b_{63})	26	(b_{37}, b_{63})	43	(b_9, b_{52})
12	$(b_9, b_{21}), (b_{21}, b_{33}), (b_{33}, b_{45})$	27	(b_{33}, b_{60})	45	(b_{15}, b_{60})
13	(b_{15}, b_{28})	28	(b_9, b_{37})	48	(b_{15}, b_{63})
15	$(b_{37}, b_{52}), (b_{45}, b_{60})$	30	$(b_{15}, b_{45}), (b_{33}, b_{63})$	51	(b_9, b_{60})
				54	(b_9, b_{63})

The following theorem presents the degree of the multiplication of two nonlinear terms in the case of feedback shift registers.

Theorem 1. *Let denote B_k and C_k be two nonlinear terms at the k-th round (i.e., multiplication of some state bits in a feedback shift register at k-th round). Further denote that b_i is i-th state bit in k-th round. If b_i is a variable in B_k and b_{i-j} is a variable in C_k for some $0 \leq j \leq i$ then $\deg(B_k C_{k+j}) < \deg(B_k) + \deg(C_{k+j})$. If there are exactly m such pairs of b_i and b_{i-j} in B_k and C_k respectively, then $\deg(B_k C_{k+j}) = \deg(B_k) + \deg(C_{k+j}) - m$.*

For an example, consider B_k and C_k as the highest degree term of the NFSR in Grain-v1 i.e., $B_k = C_k = b_{52} b_{45} b_{37} b_{33} b_{28} b_{21}$. Since b_{37} is in B_k and $b_{33} = b_{37-4}$ is in C_k, the $\deg(B_k C_{k+4}) = \deg(B_k) \deg(C_k) - 1 = 11$. For a demonstration, Table 4 represents the degrees of $B_k C_{k+j}, k \geq 80$ for those shifts j for the terms $B_k = C_k = b_{52} b_{45} b_{37} b_{33} b_{28} b_{21}$.

Table 4. Table of degrees of $B_k C_{k+j}, i \geq 80$

Shift(j)	Deg($B_k C_{k+j}$)	Bits in B_k, C_k	Shifts(j)	Deg($B_k C_{k+j}$)	Bits in B_k, C_k
4	11	b_{37}, b_{33}	15	11	b_{52}, b_{37}
5	11	b_{33}, b_{28}	16	11	b_{37}, b_{21}
7	10	$b_{28}, b_{21}; b_{52}, b_{45}$	17	11	b_{45}, b_{28}
8	11	b_{45}, b_{37}	19	11	b_{52}, b_{33}
9	11	b_{37}, b_{28}	24	10	$b_{45}, b_{21}; b_{52}, b_{28}$
12	10	$b_{33}, b_{21}; b_{45}, b_{33}$	31	11	b_{52}, b_{21}

Further, if there is a common bit in m terms, then the degree of the multiplication of m terms reduced by $m - 1$ from the sum of the degrees of m terms because of the $m - 1$ times of repetition of the bit. Since we are checking common terms between a pair of terms at a time, the repetition is subtracted $\binom{m}{2}$ times (instead of $m - 1$) from the sum of degree as in Theorem 1. This can be settled by adding $\binom{m-1}{2}$ common repetition again for correct degree calculation.

Observation 1. *Let a bit b be present in m terms of a multiplication of n terms where $n \geq m$. The common bit b comes in $\binom{m}{2}$ pairs of terms and each time the degree is subtracted by 1 as in Theorem 1. As a result, the actual degree of the multiplication is reduced by $\binom{m-1}{2}$, which is the number of repeated counting of the common bit b. Hence the number $\binom{m-1}{2}$ needs to be added to the final degree for the correct degree calculation.*

By exploiting Observation 1, it is possible to make a list of trails of three differences (i.e., $i - j - (i + j)$) with respect to a set (say B) such that a bit is common in three terms. That is, if a bit b_{k+i+j}, b_{k+i} and b_k are present in the terms X_k, Y_k and Z_k respectively, then the terms X_k, Y_{k+j}, Z_{k+i+j} contains a

Table 5. Table of Repeated Common bit with difference Trail

Difference Trail	Common bit-Via bit-Shift bit	Difference Trail	Common bit-Via bit-Shift bit	Difference Trail	Common bit-Via bit-Shift bit
$6 - 6 - 12$	$b_9 - b_{15} - b_{21}$	$27 - 3 - 30$	$b_{33} - b_{60} - b_{63}$	$6 - 18 - 24$	$b_9 - b_{15} - b_{33}$
$7 - 5 - 12$	$b_{21} - b_{28} - b_{33}$	$28 - 8 - 36$	$b_9 - b_{37} - b_{45}$	$6 - 16 - 22$	$b_{15} - b_{21} - b_{37}$
$4 - 8 - 12$	$b_{33} - b_{37} - b_{45}$	$30 - 7 - 37$	$b_{15} - b_{45} - b_{52}$	$7 - 17 - 24$	$b_{21} - b_{28} - b_{45}$
$7 - 8 - 15$	$b_{45} - b_{52} - b_{60}$	$31 - 8 - 39$	$b_{21} - b_{52} - b_{60}$	$19 - 5 - 22$	$b_9 - b_{28} - b_{33}$
$12 - 7 - 19$	$b_9 - b_{21} - b_{28}$	$32 - 3 - 35$	$b_{28} - b_{60} - b_{63}$	$4 - 23 - 27$	$b_{33} - b_{37} - b_{60}$
$13 - 5 - 18$	$b_{15} - b_{28} - b_{33}$	$36 - 7 - 43$	$b_9 - b_{45} - b_{52}$	$8 - 18 - 26$	$b_{37} - b_{45} - b_{63}$
$12 - 4 - 16$	$b_{21} - b_{33} - b_{37}$	$37 - 8 - 45$	$b_{15} - b_{52} - b_{60}$	$6 - 22 - 28$	$b_9 - b_{15} - b_{37}$
$9 - 8 - 17$	$b_{28} - b_{37} - b_{45}$	$39 - 3 - 42$	$b_{21} - b_{60} - b_{63}$	$6 - 24 - 30$	$b_{15} - b_{21} - b_{45}$
$12 - 7 - 19$	$b_9 - b_{21} - b_{28}$	$43 - 8 - 51$	$b_9 - b_{52} - b_{60}$	$7 - 24 - 31$	$b_{21} - b_{28} - b_{52}$
$15 - 8 - 23$	$b_{37} - b_{52} - b_{60}$	$45 - 3 - 48$	$b_{15} - b_{60} - b_{63}$	$5 - 27 - 32$	$b_{28} - b_{33} - b_{60}$
$15 - 3 - 18$	$b_{45} - b_{60} - b_{63}$	$6 - 7 - 13$	$b_{15} - b_{21} - b_{28}$	$4 - 26 - 30$	$b_{33} - b_{37} - b_{63}$
$19 - 5 - 24$	$b_9 - b_{28} - b_{33}$	$5 - 4 - 9$	$b_{28} - b_{33} - b_{37}$	$6 - 30 - 36$	$b_9 - b_{15} - b_{45}$
$18 - 4 - 22$	$b_{15} - b_{33} - b_{37}$	$8 - 7 - 15$	$b_{37} - b_{45} - b_{52}$	$6 - 31 - 37$	$b_{15} - b_{21} - b_{52}$
$16 - 8 - 24$	$b_{21} - b_{37} - b_{45}$	$8 - 3 - 11$	$b_{52} - b_{60} - b_{63}$	$7 - 32 - 39$	$b_{21} - b_{28} - b_{60}$
$17 - 7 - 24$	$b_{28} - b_{45} - b_{52}$	$6 - 13 - 19$	$b_9 - b_{15} - b_{28}$	$5 - 30 - 35$	$b_{28} - b_{33} - b_{63}$
$19 - 8 - 27$	$b_{33} - b_{52} - b_{60}$	$6 - 12 - 18$	$b_{15} - b_{21} - b_{33}$	$6 - 37 - 43$	$b_9 - b_{15} - b_{52}$
$23 - 3 - 26$	$b_{37} - b_{60} - b_{63}$	$7 - 9 - 16$	$b_{21} - b_{28} - b_{37}$	$6 - 39 - 45$	$b_{15} - b_{21} - b_{60}$
$24 - 4 - 28$	$b_9 - b_{33} - b_{37}$	$5 - 12 - 17$	$b_{28} - b_{33} - b_{45}$	$7 - 35 - 42$	$b_{21} - b_{28} - b_{63}$
$22 - 8 - 30$	$b_{15} - b_{37} - b_{45}$	$4 - 15 - 19$	$b_{33} - b_{37} - b_{52}$	$6 - 45 - 51$	$b_9 - b_{15} - b_{60}$
$24 - 7 - 31$	$b_{21} - b_{45} - b_{52}$	$8 - 15 - 23$	$b_{37} - b_{45} - b_{60}$	$6 - 42 - 48$	$b_{15} - b_{21} - b_{63}$
$24 - 8 - 32$	$b_{28} - b_{52} - b_{60}$	$7 - 11 - 18$	$b_{45} - b_{52} - b_{63}$		

common term b_{k+i+j}. As our aim is to find out maximum degree, we need to find the terms when the degree of their multiplication does not reduce. Hence, it will be easier to find out such possible terms looking from the list of trails. Table 5 presents the list of trails with respect to the set B (i.e., the bits involved in the nonlinear terms of NFSR of Grain-v1).

Example 1. If the bits b_{37}, b_{33} and b_{28} are present in the terms X_{28}, Y_{28} and Z_{28} respectively, then there is difference trail $5 - 4 - 9$ between b_{28} and b_{37}. So the terms $X_{28}, Y_{28+4}, Z_{28+5+4}$ contains a common term $b_{28+5+4} = b_{37}$.

The NFSR update function of Grain-v1 contains the terms of degree 6 and less. Expecting the higher degree terms contribute for the highest degree term in NFSR, we have taken terms of degree $6, 5$ or 4. The terms are $b_{21}b_{28}b_{33}b_{37}b_{45}b_{52}$, $b_{37}b_{45}b_{52}b_{60}b_{63}$, $b_9b_{15}b_{21}b_{28}b_{33}$, $b_9b_{28}b_{45}b_{63}$, $b_{33}b_{37}b_{52}b_{60}$ and $b_{15}b_{21}b_{60}b_{63}$. Hence, there are 36 possibilities of pair wise multiplications among them self. Each possibility will show the number of common bits and the differences. Based on those differences we can estimate that which pair of terms give the maximum degree of NFSR update bits. Table 6 contains all 36 possibilities, where one can find the number of common bits and the differences of bits between each pair. To explain the contents of the table, let consider the entry between the row containing the term $n_k = b_{15}b_{21}b_{60}b_{63}$ and the column containing the term $m_k = b_{33}b_{37}b_{52}b_{60}$. $b_{33} : 27$ implies that the multiplication $m_{k+27}n_k$ contains a common bit $b_{33+27} = b_{60}$. Similarly the multiplication $m_{k+30}n_k$ contains a common bit $b_{33+30} = b_{63}$ and other 5 cases.

In the following section, we present the algorithm to find the degree of NFSR function (b_{80+t}), LFSR function (s_{80+t}) and output function (z_t).

3   Calculating the Degree of Feedback and Output Bits

In key scheduling phase, the output bit z_t is added with the NFSR function for the feedback. Here, the degree of the NFSR update function is 6 and degree of output function is 3. As round increases the degree of output bit z_t increases. If the degree of output bit z_t can be resisted to increase it (using the conditional equations in Table 1), then the degree of NFSR update bits are dominated by NFSR update functions for some more rounds. We present a correct degree estimation technique of NFSR update bit (b_{80+t}) and output bit (z_t) of Grain like cipher in Algorithm 1.

Example 2. We evaluate the degree of $b_{117} = b_{80+37}$ at round $t = 37$.

1. There are six terms of $\mathbf{b}_{117}$ of degree $4, 5$ or 6. For the example we considered the term, say $T_5 = b_{100}b_{97}b_{89}b_{82}b_{74}$ which gives the maximum degree.
2. There are differences of the indices of bits (which are greater than or equal to 80) are $3, 8, 7, 11, 15, 18$ using Table 2. Further b_{100} contain some terms. For this example, we replace b_{100} by $b_{83}b_{80}b_{72}b_{65}b_{57}$ and for other high degree terms it can be done similar way. The term can be rewritten as

Table 6. Table of differences (i) between terms m_{k+i} and n_k contain a common bit

$m_k \rightarrow$ $n_k \downarrow$	$b_{15}b_{21}$ $b_{60}b_{63}$	$b_{33}b_{37}$ $b_{52}b_{60}$	b_9b_{28} $b_{45}b_{63}$	b_9b_{15} $b_{21}b_{28}b_{33}$	$b_{37}b_{45}$ b_{52} $b_{60}b_{63}$	$b_{21}b_{28}b_{33}$ $b_{37}b_{45}b_{52}$
$b_{15}b_{21}$ $b_{60}b_{63}$	$b_{15}: 6,45$ 48 $b_{21}: 39,42$ $b_{60}: 3$	$b_{33}: 27,30$ $b_{37}: 23,26$ $b_{52}: 8,11$ $b_{60}: 3$	$b_9: 6,12,$ 51,54 $b_{28}: 32,35$ $b_{45}: 15,18$	$b_9: 6,12,51,54$ $b_{15}: 6,45,48; b_{21}$ $: 39,42; b_{28}: 32$,35; $b_{33}: 27,30$	$b_{37}: 23,26$ $b_{45}: 15,18$ $b_{52}: 8,11$ $b_{60}: 3$	$b_{21}: 39,42; b_{28}:$ $32,35; b_{33}: 27,30$ $b_{37}: 23,26; b_{45}:$ $15,18; b_{52}: 8,11$
$b_{33}b_{37}$ $b_{52}b_{60}$	$b_{15}: 18,22,$ 37,45 $b_{21}: 12,16,$ 31,39	$b_{33}: 4,19,$ 27 $b_{37}: 15,23$ $b_{52}: 8$	$b_9: 24,28$ 43,51 $b_{28}: 5,9,$ 24,32 $b_{45}: 7,15$	$b_9: 24,28,43,51$ $b_{15}: 18,22,37,45$ $b_{21}: 12,16,31,39$ $b_{28}: 5,9,24,32$ $b_{33}: 4,19,27$	$b_{37}: 15,23$ $b_{45}: 7,15$ $b_{52}: 8$	$b_{21}: 12,16,31,39$ $b_{28}: 5,9,24,32$ $b_{33}: 4,19,27$ $b_{37}: 15,23$ $b_{45}: 7,15; b_{52}: 8$
b_9b_{28} $b_{45}b_{63}$	$b_{15}: 13,30,$ 48 $b_{21}: 7,24,$ 42; $b_{60}: 3$	$b_{33}: 12,30$ $b_{37}: 8,26$ $b_{52}: 11$ $b_{60}: 3$	$b_9: 19,36,$ 54 $b_{28}: 17,35$ $b_{45}: 18$	$b_9: 19,36,54; b_{15}:$ $13,30,48; b_{21}: 7,$ $24,42; b_{28}: 17,35$ $b_{33}: 12,30$	$b_{37}: 8,26$ $b_{45}: 18$ $b_{52}: 11$ $b_{60}: 3$	$b_{21}: 7,24,42; b_{28}$ $: 17,35; b_{33}: 12,$ $30; b_{37}: 8,26$ $b_{45}: 18; b_{52}: 11$
b_9b_{15} b_{21} $b_{28}b_{33}$	$b_{15}: 6,30,$ 18 $b_{21}: 7,12$		$b_9: 6,12,$ 19,24 $b_{28}: 5$	$b_9: 6,12,19,24$ $b_{15}: 6,30,18; b_{21}$ $: 28,12; b_{28}: 5$		$b_{21}: 7,12$ $b_{28}: 5$
$b_{37}b_{45}$ b_{52} $b_{60}b_{63}$	$b_{15}: 22,30,$ 37,45,48 $b_{21}: 16,24,$ 31,39,42 $b_{60}: 3)$	$b_{33}: 4,12,$ 19,27,30 $b_{37}: 8,15$ 23,26 $b_{52}: 8,11$ $b_{60}: 3)$	$b_9: 28,36,$ 43,51,54 $b_{28}: 9,17,$ 24,32,35 $b_{45}: 7,15,$ 18	$b_9: 28,36,43,51,$ $54; b_{15}: 22,30,37$,45,48; $b_{21}: 16,24$,31,39,42; $b_{28}: 9,$ $17,24,32,35; b_{33}:$ $4,12,19,27,30$	$b_{37}: 8,15,$ 23,26 $b_{45}: 7,15,$ 18 $b_{52}: 8,11$ $b_{60}: 3$	$b_{21}: 16,24,31,39,$ $42; b_{28}: 9,17,24,$ $32,35; b_{33}: 4,12,$ $19,27,30; b_{37}: 8,$ $15,23,26; b_{45}: 7,$ $15,18; b_{52}: 8,11$
$b_{21}b_{28}$ $b_{33}b_{37}$ $b_{45}b_{52}$	$b_{15}: 6,13,$ 18,22,30 ,37 $b_{21}: 7,12,$ 16,24,31	$b_{33}: 4,12,$ 19 $b_{37}: 8,15$	$b_9: 12,19,$ 24,28,36 43 $b_{28}: 5,9,$ 17,24 $b_{45}: 7$	$b_9: 12,19,24,,28,$ $36,43; b_{15}: 6,13,$ $18,22,30,37; b_{21}:$ $7,12,16,24,31$ $b_{28}: 5,9,17,24$ $b_{33}: 4,12,19$	$b_{37}: 8,15$ $b_{45}: 7$	$b_{21}: 7,12,16,24$ $,31; b_{28}: 5,9,17$ $24; b_{33}: 4,12,19$ $b_{37}: 8,15; b_{45}: 7$

$T = b_{97}b_{89}b_{83}b_{82}b_{80}b_{74}b_{72}b_{65}b_{57}$. Now we will find out the degree of T. Since last four bits are of degree one, for sake of simplicity, we consider T as $b_{97}b_{89}b_{83}b_{82}b_{80}$. Now we apply step 4 of the algorithm.

3. As per the step 4 in Algorithm 1, the rows of the difference table as Table 2 are $8, 6, 1, 2; 14, 7, 3; 15, 9; 17$.
4. The differences of the pair of bits are found from Table 3: $(b_9, b_{15}), (b_{21}, b_{28}), (b_{28}, b_{45}), (b_{37}, b_{52}), (b_{45}, b_{52}), (b_{45}, b_{60}), (b_{15}, b_{21}),$ $(b_{28}, b_{37}), (b_{37}, b_{45}), (b_{45}, b_{52}), (b_{52}, b_{60}), (b_{60}, b_{63})$.

Algorithm 1. Algorithm for max degree of NFSR bits of Grain-v1.

 Input : Round t
 Output: A highest degree term of b_{80+t}
1 List the high degree terms $T_1, T_2, \cdots, T_n$ in b_{80+t};
2 Set $DEG_i = 0, 1 \le i \le n$ and let $T_i = b_{t+i_1} b_{t+i_2} \cdots b_{t+i_k}$;
3 **for** i *from 1 to n* **do**
4 | Construct a difference table as Table 2 using the bits in T_i.;
5 | Find out differences of the pair from Table 3.;
6 | Find the terms involved in each bit b_{t+i_j} in T_i, which gives highest degree
    using Table 6. Let the terms are $Q_{t+i_1}, Q_{t+i_2}, \cdots, Q_{t+i_k}$;
7 | Set $DEG_i = Deg(Q_{t+i_1}) + \cdots + Deg(Q_{t+i_k})$.;
8 | Find out pairwise common key bits according to the difference of the bits
    in the terms Q_{t+i_j} using Table 3 and count the number, say l.;
9 | Set $DEG_i = DEG_i - l$.;
10 | Count repeated common bits from Table 5, say m.;
11 | Set $DEG_i = DEG_i + m$.;
12 **end**
13 Set $DEG = MAX(DEG_i)$.;
14 **return** DEG.;

---

5. Consider the pair (b_9, b_{15}). This pair indicates that b_9 is in b_{89} and b_{15} in b_{83}, which is a common bit of both. We write such information of all pairs as $b_{89} : b_9$ and $b_{83} : (b_{15})$ in step 1 in Table 7.

6. Now we select the suitable terms for each bit of $b_{80}, b_{82}, b_{83}, b_{89}, b_{97}, b_{100}$ step by step (Step 2 to Step 5 in Table 7 respectively). As example, for b_{80} : (b_{37}, b_{45}, b_{63}), we will try to find the term from Table 6 where b_{37}, b_{45}, b_{63} are not involved or are least involved. So we set $b_{80} = b_{33} b_{28} b_{21} b_{15} b_9$ and corresponding pairs of b_{80} with others are deleted. Here, b_{28} is removed from b_{97}, b_{89} and b_{60} is removed from b_{83} in step 2 in Table 7.

7. The last step of Table 7 performs step 7 to step 9 of Algorithm 1, where the degrees of all terms are added in step 7. Then we see from the step 8 that b_{28} is a common bit between b_{89} and b_{82}, so $l = 1$. Hence $DEG(b_{117}) = Deg b_{97} + Deg b_{89} + Deg b_{83} + Deg b_{82} + Deg b_{80} + Deg b_{74} + Deg b_{72} + Deg b_{65} + Deg b_{57} = 5 + 6 + 6 + 5 + 5 + 1 + 1 + 1 + 1 - 1 = 30$.

We used Algorithm 1 to calculate the degrees of the NFSR, LFSR update bits and the output bit up to some rounds. Table 8 presents the degrees of these bits. The degree of terms up to first 42 rounds in Table 8 are verified using the software SAGE.

Table 7. Table of Calculating Degrees of NFSR bit b_{117}

Step 1:$b_{100} : b_{45}, b_{52}, b_{60}.$ $\quad b_{97} : b_{28}, b_{37}, b_{45}, b_{52}(b_{63}).$ $\quad b_{89} : b_9, b_{15}, b_{21}, b_{28}, b_{45}.$ $\quad\quad (b_{45}, b_{60}, b_{63}).$ $\quad b_{83} : b_{60}(b_{15}, b_{21}).$ $\quad b_{82} : (b_{28}, b_{52}, b_{60}, b_{63}).$ $\quad b_{80} : (b_{37}, b_{45}, b_{63}).$	**Step 2:**$b_{100} : b_{45}, b_{52}, b_{60}.$ $\quad b_{97} : b_{37}, b_{45}, b_{52}(b_{63}).$ $\quad b_{89} : b_9, b_{15}, b_{21}, b_{45}. \ (b_{45}, b_{60}, b_{63}).$ $\quad b_{83} : (b_{15}, b_{21}).$ $\quad b_{82} : (b_{28}, b_{52}, b_{60}, b_{63}).$ $\quad b_{80} = b_{33}b_{28}b_{21}b_{15}b_9.$
Step 4:$b_{100} : b_{60}.$ $\quad b_{97} : \mathbf{b_{37}}, (b_{63}).$ $\quad b_{89} = b_{52}b_{45}b_{37}b_{33}b_{28}b_{21}(\mathbf{b_{21}}).$ $\quad (b_{45}).$ $\quad b_{83} :.$ $\quad b_{82} = b_{33}b_{28}b_{21}b_{15}b_9(\mathbf{b_{28}}).$ $\quad b_{80} = b_{33}b_{28}b_{21}b_{15}b_9.$	**Step 3:**$b_{100} : b_{60}.$ $\quad b_{97} : b_{37}, b_{52}(b_{63}).$ $\quad b_{89} : b_9, b_{15}, \mathbf{b_{21}}. \ (b_{45}, b_{60}, b_{63}).$ $\quad b_{83} : (b_{15}, b_{21}).$ $\quad b_{82} = b_{33}b_{28}b_{21}b_{15}b_9(\mathbf{b_{28}}).$ $\quad b_{80} = b_{33}b_{28}b_{21}b_{15}b_9.$
Step 5:$b_{100} :.$ $\quad b_{97} = b_{33}b_{28}b_{21}b_{15}b_9.$ $\quad b_{89} = b_{52}b_{45}b_{37}b_{33}b_{28}b_{21}(\mathbf{b_{21}}).$ $\quad b_{83} = b_{52}b_{45}b_{37}b_{33}b_{28}b_{21}.$ $\quad b_{82} = b_{33}b_{28}b_{21}b_{15}b_9(\mathbf{b_{28}}).$ $\quad b_{80} = b_{33}b_{28}b_{21}b_{15}b_9.$	$Deg(b_{117}) = Deg(b_{100}b_{97}b_{89}b_{82}) + 1.$ $\quad = Deg(b_{97}b_{89}b_{83}b_{82}b_{80}) + 3 + 1.$ $\quad = Deg(b_{97}b_{89}b_{83}b_{82}) + 5 + 3 + 1.$ $\quad = Deg(b_{97}b_{89}b_{83}) + 5 + 5 + 3 + 1.$ $\quad = Deg(b_{97}b_{89}b_{83}) + 6 + 5 + 5 + 4.$ $\quad = 5 + 6 + 6 + 5 + 5 + 4 - 1 = 30.$

Table 8. Table of Degrees of different non-linear functions

Rounds (i)	Degree of b_{80+i}	Degree of z_{80+i}	Degree of s_{80+i}	Rounds (i)	Degree of b_{80+i}	Degree of z_{80+i}	Degree of s_{80+i}
0–15	6	1	1	42	33	22	22
16	6	2	2	43	34	22	22
17–19	10	7	7	44	34	22	22
20–27	15	7	7	45	38	26	26
28–33	19	7	7	46	38	26	26
34	23	18	18	47	38	26	26
35	26	18	18	48	38	26	26
36	26	18	18	49	38	26	26
37	30	22	22	50	38	34	34
38	31	22	22	51	45	39	39
39	31	22	22	52	47	41	41
40	32	22	22	53	47	45	45
41	32	22	22	54	51	48	48

4 Conclusion and Future Scope

In this paper, we are aiming to develop a degree evaluation technique for feedback and output bits of the NFSR based stream cipher. Using our technique we are able to calculate the degree of the said bits during the key scheduling algorithm of Grain-v1 of reduced round. As in work in progress form, our aim is to a concrete work which can evaluate the degree of feedback and output bits of NFSR based stream ciphers. As a result, we will able to claim that how many iterations are required for a proper mix of NFSR and LFSR bits of Grain like cipher. Further, we can find out the degrees of the IV bits (key bits are taken as a constant) such that one can mount a cube attack on Grain like cipher.

References

1. Bjørstad, T.E.: Cryptanalysis of grain using time/memory/data tradeoffs (2008). http://www.ecrypt.eu.org/stream
2. Boura, C., Canteaut, A.: On the influence of the algebraic degree of f^{-1} on the algebraic degree of G ∘ F. IEEE Trans. Inf. Theory **59**(1), 691–702 (2013)
3. Boura, C., Canteaut, A., De Cannière, C.: Higher-order differential properties of KECCAK and *Luffa*. In: Joux, A. (ed.) FSE 2011. LNCS, vol. 6733, pp. 252–269. Springer, Heidelberg (2011). https://doi.org/10.1007/978-3-642-21702-9_15
4. Canteaut, A., Videau, M.: Degree of composition of highly nonlinear functions and applications to higher order differential cryptanalysis. In: Knudsen, L.R. (ed.) EUROCRYPT 2002. LNCS, vol. 2332, pp. 518–533. Springer, Heidelberg (2002). https://doi.org/10.1007/3-540-46035-7_34
5. Ding, L., Jin, C., Guan, J., Zhang, S., Li, J., Wang, H., Zhao, W.: New state recovery attacks on the grain v1 stream cipher. China Commun. **13**(11), 180–188 (2016)
6. Fu, X., Wang, X., Dong, X., Meier, W.: A key-recovery attack on 855-round trivium. In: Shacham, H., Boldyreva, A. (eds.) CRYPTO 2018. LNCS, vol. 10992, pp. 160–184. Springer, Cham (2018). https://doi.org/10.1007/978-3-319-96881-0_6
7. Hell, M., Johansson, T., Meier, W.: Grain: a stream cipher for constrained environments. Int. J. Wirel. Mob. Comput. **2**(1), 86–93 (2007)
8. Knellwolf, S., Meier, W., Naya-Plasencia, M.: Conditional differential cryptanalysis of NLFSR-based cryptosystems. In: Abe, M. (ed.) ASIACRYPT 2010. LNCS, vol. 6477, pp. 130–145. Springer, Heidelberg (2010). https://doi.org/10.1007/978-3-642-17373-8_8
9. Liu, M.: Degree evaluation of NFSR-based cryptosystems. In: Katz, J., Shacham, H. (eds.) CRYPTO 2017. LNCS, vol. 10403, pp. 227–249. Springer, Cham (2017). https://doi.org/10.1007/978-3-319-63697-9_8
10. Mihaljević, M.J., Gangopadhyay, S., Paul, G., Imai, H.: Internal state recovery of grain-v1 employing normality order of the filter function. IET Inf. Secur. **6**(2), 55–64 (2012)
11. Mihaljević, M.J., Sinha, N., Gangopadhyay, S., Maitra, S., Paul, G., Matsuura, K.: An improved cryptanalsis of lightweight stream cipher grain-v1. In: Cryptacus: Workshop and MC meeting (2017)
12. Siddhanti, A.A., Maitra, S., Sinha, N.: Certain observations on ACORN v3 and grain v1–implications towards TMDTO attacks. J. Hardw. Syst. Secur. **3**(1), 64–77 (2019)

13. Ye, C., Tian, T.: Deterministic cube attacks: a new method to recover superpolies in practice. IACR Cryptology ePrint Archive **2018**, 1082 (2018)

14. Ye, C., Tian, T.: A new framework for finding nonlinear superpolies in cube attacks against trivium-like ciphers. In: Susilo, W., Yang, G. (eds.) ACISP 2018. LNCS, vol. 10946, pp. 172–187. Springer, Cham (2018). https://doi.org/10.1007/978-3-319-93638-3_11

15. Zhang, B., Li, Z., Feng, D., Lin, D.: Near collision attack on the grain v1 stream cipher. In: Moriai, S. (ed.) FSE 2013. LNCS, vol. 8424, pp. 518–538. Springer, Heidelberg (2014). https://doi.org/10.1007/978-3-662-43933-3_27

16. Zhang, B., Xu, C., Meier, W.: Fast near collision attack on the grain v1 stream cipher. In: Nielsen, J.B., Rijmen, V. (eds.) EUROCRYPT 2018. LNCS, vol. 10821, pp. 771–802. Springer, Cham (2018). https://doi.org/10.1007/978-3-319-78375-8_25

Online Social Networks

A Novel *k*-Anonymization Approach to Prevent Insider Attack in Collaborative Social Network Data Publishing

Bintu Kadhiwala$^{(\boxtimes)}$ and Sankita J. Patel

Sardar Vallabhbhai National Institute of Technology,
Surat 395007, Gujarat, India
bintukadhiwala@gmail.com, sankitapatel@gmail.com

Abstract. Social network data analysts can retrieve improved results if mining operations are performed on collaborative social network data instead of independent social network data. The collaborative social network can be constructed by joining data of all social networking sites. This data may contain sensitive information about individuals in its original form and sharing of such data, as it is, may violate individual privacy. Hence, various techniques are discussed in literature for privacy preserving publishing of social network data. However, these techniques suffer from the *insider attack*, performed by colluding data provider(s) to breach the privacy of the social network data contributed by other data providers. In this paper, we propose an approach that offers protection against the *insider attack* in the collaborative social network data publishing scenario. Experimental results demonstrate that our approach preserves data utility while protecting collaborated social network data against the *insider attack*.

Keywords: Collaborative social network data publishing · Insider attack · *m*-privacy · *k*-anonymity

1 Introduction

A social network can be viewed as a mapping of relationships between various organizations, individuals, groups, and other information processing entities [30,35,38]. Formally, it is represented as an undirected graph $G = (N,E,A)$, where N is a set of nodes representing people, E is a set of edges showing relationships between nodes and A is a set of attributes associated with people. Typically, in social network analysis, data from such a social network is published and subsequently analysed [25,28,38]. However, in practice, multiple social networking sites work in collaboration to publish their data and perform data analysis on aggregated data to retrieve improved data analysis results and reduce overall data processing cost [8]. Such a setup is termed collaborative social network data publishing and processing.

© Springer Nature Switzerland AG 2019
D. Garg et al. (Eds.): ICISS 2019, LNCS 11952, pp. 255–275, 2019.
https://doi.org/10.1007/978-3-030-36945-3_14

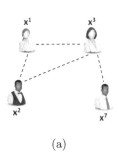
(a)

(b)

Fig. 1. (a) social network of employees from company P_1 and (b) social network of employees from company P_2.

Table 1. Attribute information dataset T_1 of employees from company P_1.

Name	Node	Age	Zip	Gender	Salary
Ada	X^1	25	41076	Male	8000
Gladys	X^2	25	41075	Male	8000
Cathy	X^3	27	41076	Male	7000
George	X^7	30	41099	Male	7000

Table 2. Attribute information dataset T_2 of employees from company P_2.

Name	Node	Age	Zip	Gender	Salary
Dell	X^4	35	41099	Male	8000
Henry	X^5	38	48201	Female	7000
Fred	X^6	36	41075	Female	5000
George	X^7	30	41099	Male	7000
Harry	X^8	28	41099	Male	7000
Irene	X^9	33	41075	Female	6000

To have an insight, consider an example of two social networks of employees from companies P_1 and P_2 (Fig. 1(a) and (b)) respectively. The datasets T_1 (Table 1) and T_2 (Table 2) show attribute information of employees for P_1 and P_2 respectively where Name is an identifier, {Age, Zip, Gender} is a quasi-identifier, and Salary is a sensitive attribute.

The executives of each company use this data to prepare classification model to estimate the approximate salary for new employees. For accurate estimation, data from a single social network may not be sufficient. Hence, executives may collaborate with other companies and perform data estimation from the aggregated data. However, concerning data privacy, companies do not agree to share their data [23]. Hence, companies are required to aggregate their data in a way that gives maximum data utility and preserves individuals' privacy. As a consequence, companies share their data with the trusted data publisher (Fig. 2). The corresponding collaborative social network for companies and attribute information at the trusted data publisher are shown in Fig. 3 and Table 3 respectively.

The data publisher then releases data to data recipients after applying privacy-preserving approach(es) on the union of the collected data [10]. In literature, several Privacy Preserving Data Publishing (PPDP) approaches viz. k-anonymity [24,26], l-diversity [21], t-closeness [19] and differential privacy [6,9] are discussed. However, to apply these approaches on collaborative social network data (as discussed above) along with preserving individuals' privacy and ensuring data utility is a challenging task. For the above example, we assume that the publisher applies *k*-anonymity ($k = 2$) privacy-preserving mechanism on the aggregated data and then publishes it. The published 2-anonymous collaborative social network data and its attribute information are shown in Fig. 4 and Table 4 respectively.

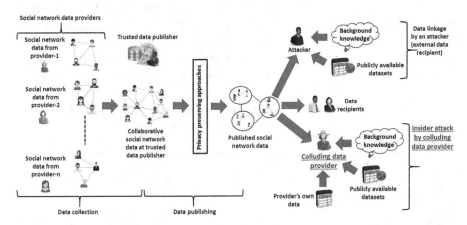

Fig. 2. *Insider attack* in privacy-preserving collaborative social network data publishing.

1.1 Problem Formulation

The problem of inferring sensitive information from published data has been studied in-depth in [10]. From literature, we observe that existing PPDP approaches are based on a key assumption that attackers are among the data recipients only, whose intention is to uncover sensitive information about individuals [1,10]. However, we believe that, in the above discussed collaborative data publishing scenario, data provider(s) may also be colluding. These colluding data providers can compromise the privacy of individuals whose data records are shared by other data providers as shown in Fig. 2. This situation may lead to an *insider attack* - a type of attack by colluding data provider(s). In an attack, the colluding data provider(s) may use their own data records, in addition to the published data and background knowledge, to infer the data records shared by other data providers.

Formally, if n is a set of collaborative data providers and m is a set of colluding data providers, where $m \subset n$ and $|m| < |n|$, then the *insider attack* can be carried out by a single or a group of up to m colluding data providers out of total n data providers. Such m colluding data providers are also known as an m-adversary.

Table 3. Union of datasets T_1 and T_2 after collaboration at trusted data publisher.

Fig. 3. The collaborative social network at trusted data publisher.

Provider	Name	Node	Age	Zip	Gender	Salary
P_1	Ada	X^1	25	41076	Male	8000
P_1	Gladys	X^2	25	41075	Male	8000
P_1	Cathy	X^3	27	41076	Male	7000
P_2	Dell	X^4	35	41099	Male	8000
P_2	Henry	X^5	38	48201	Female	7000
P_2	Fred	X^6	36	41075	Female	5000
P_1,P_2	George	X^7	30	41099	Male	7000
P_2	Harry	X^8	28	41099	Male	7000
P_2	Irene	X^9	33	41075	Female	6000

gen(cl_1) = {[30-35], 41099, male}
cl_1 = {x^4, x^7}
gen(cl_2) = {[25-27], 41076, male}
cl_2 = {x^3, x^1}

(2, 1) —1— (2, 1)

3   1   2

(3, 1)   (2, 0) cl_3 = {x^2, x^8}
gen(cl_3) = {[25-28], 410**, male}

cl_4 = {x^5, x^6, x^9}
gen(cl_4) = {[33-38], *****, female}

Fig. 4. 2-anonymous social network of Fig. 3.

Table 4. 2-anonymous attribute information of social network of Fig. 4.

Provider	Name	Node	Age	Zip	Gender	Salary	EQ
P_2	Dell	X^4	[30–35]	41099	Male	8000	EQ1
P_1, P_2	George	X^7	[30–35]	41099	Male	7000	
P_1	Cathy	X^3	[25–27]	41076	Male	7000	EQ2
P_1	Ada	X^1	[25–27]	41076	Male	8000	
P_1	Gladys	X^2	[25–28]	410**	Male	8000	EQ3
P_2	Harry	X^8	[25–28]	410**	Male	7000	
P_2	Henry	X^5	[33–38]	*****	Female	7000	
P_2	Fred	X^6	[33–38]	*****	Female	5000	EQ4
P_2	Irene	X^9	[33–38]	*****	Female	6000	

In the aforementioned example of two companies, if the data provider P_1 is colluding, then as depicted in Fig. 2, using the published dataset, he/she can compromise Harry's privacy by deriving his sensitive attribute "salary". This can be done with the help of background knowledge after removing all other records from EQ3 of the published data (Table 4). The challenge is to publish collaborative social network data to resist against this *insider attack* - the threat introduced by m-adversary while preserving data utility.

The m-privacy notion [12–14] is utilized to protect the published social network data against m-adversary. To offer such protection, the in-built data knowledge of m-adversary and the data records they jointly contribute is taken into account by the m-privacy notion while applying privacy-preserving mechanism(s). As a result, m-privacy promises that each generated equivalence group satisfies privacy constraint even after excluding records owned by an m-adversary.

1.2   Contribution

Our main contributions in this paper are as follows:

- We introduce the *insider attack* in collaborative social network data publishing scenario and emphasize the motivation for prevention of the same.
- We integrate m-privacy [12–14] to prevent *insider attack* in the clustering based social network anonymization approach for collaborative social network data publishing scenario.
- We present design and analysis of trusted third-party based m-privacy anonymization approach for privacy preservation of collaborative social network data against external data recipients and also against up to m colluding data providers out of total n collaborative social network data providers.

1.3 Organization

The rest of the paper is structured as follows: Sect. 2 reviews the existing work related to the problem domain. Section 3 discusses the social network privacy model and other basic preliminaries in brief. The proposed approach for *insider attack* prevention is described in Sect. 4. Section 5 presents the analysis of the proposed approach. Section 6 discusses the obtained experimental results and also highlights the key findings. Finally, Sect. 7 draws concluding remarks and provides directions for future work.

2 Related Work

The replacing of the identifier attributes of individual users by meaningless attributes or the removal of these attributes is not sufficient to provide privacy when the social network data is to be published [2]. In this case, the privacy of victim(s) can be breached by an adversary using his/her background knowledge and the published social network data. To protect data against such attack, Sweeney and Samarati proposed an anonymization approach known as the k-anonymity model [26] that can be utilized for preserving privacy.

The anonymization approaches for privacy-preserving publishing of social network data are classified into three categories. The aim of these approaches is to prevent adversaries from identifying the existence of any target victim or the target link between nodes.

In [4,15,17,32–34], the authors proposed the approaches that randomly modifies the social network structure with the help of edge switching, addition or deletion operations. These randomized graph modification approaches introduce perturbation in a way that satisfies privacy requirement and also optimizes the data utility objectives.

In [20,31,37], the authors discussed the approaches that anonymize a social network via a deterministic procedure of insertion and/or deletion of vertices and/or edges for ensuring indistinguishability. These greedy graph modification approaches assume that the adversary has background knowledge of its target node and hence modify the graph structure in order to satisfy the privacy constraint, for example, k-anonymity constraint and data utility objectives.

In [7,16,36], the authors proposed approaches that group vertices and edges into a cluster of size at least k, where k is the anonymity parameter instead of modifying the graph structure as in the approaches of previous two categories. Then, the generated cluster of vertices and edges is anonymized into a super-vertex by generalizing quasi identifiers of all nodes in that cluster. In this way, the social network user's attribute information is protected. The various clustering-based approaches can further be divided into edge clustering approaches, vertex clustering approaches, vertex and edge clustering approaches, and vertex-attribute mapping clustering approaches [38].

Graph modification approaches may not be faithful to the original data as the additions and/or deletions of edges and/or vertices by these approaches perturb the graph structure to a large extent. Clustering based approaches cause less damage to the graph structure as compared to graph modification approaches. In addition, clustering based approaches for social network anonymization proposed in [7,27] consider both node attribute descriptive information and structural information. Sufficient privacy can only be provided to social network users, if the privacy-preserving approach preserves the privacy of both the descriptive information and the structural information. The graph modification approaches provide privacy to structural information only without taking into account the user's descriptive information. Hence, in our work, we focus on clustering-based anonymization approaches for privacy-preserving publishing of social network data.

In [36], the authors proposed the first clustering based anonymization approach for social networks that considers relationship between users in addition to node attribute information. This works in two steps. In the first step, the approach anonymizes node attribute information without taking into consideration the relationship information. In the next step, it considers the relationship information and provides privacy to it with the help of edge removal operations in a controlled manner.

In [7], the authors proposed clustering based a Social Network Greedy Anonymization approach that also protects both structural information and node descriptive information. This approach anonymizes the descriptive information and the structural information simultaneously instead of anonymizing both one after another in two steps.

These existing clustering based privacy preserving approaches can be adopted for publishing of collaborative social network data. However, these approaches do not protect the published social network data against an *insider attack* with respect to the collaborative social network data publishing scenario. In [12–14], the notion of m-privacy is discussed to protect anonymized data against the *insider attack* for tabular data. It can be utilized using either a Trusted Third Party based method or a Secure Multiparty Computation based method for a collaborative data publishing scenario. In [11], the authors discussed the Trusted Third Party (TTP) based method in which m-privacy is verified by a trusted data publisher at a centralized place. In [12,13], the authors discussed Secure

Multiparty Computation (SMC) based method in which m-privacy is verified using cryptographic operations.

Looking at the complexities of both methods, time taken by the SMC based method is higher than the TTP based method. Furthermore, as per our observation, the computation cost of SMC based method increases when the number of collaborative parties in the distributed scenario increases. As a result, for an application scenario in which number of collaborative parties is more, TTP based method is preferable to use. In addition, both methods guarantee that there is no intermediate disclosure of information during the anonymization process.

Hence, the main aim of our work in this paper is *insider attack* prevention for collaborative social network data publication by incorporating the Trusted Third Party based m-privacy with a clustering based anonymization approach.

3 Preliminaries

3.1 Social Network Privacy Model

A social network can be modeled as an undirected graph $G = (N,E,A)$, where N is a set of vertices represents individual entities, $E \subseteq N \times N$ is a set of edges representing a relationship between two entities and A is a set of corresponding tuples of the vertices containing identifier attributes, quasi-identifier attributes, and sensitive attributes [7,29].

Definition (Masked Social Network): Given an initial social network modeled as a graph $G = (N,E,A)$, and a partition $S = \{cl_1, cl_2,..., cl_v\}$ of the nodes set N, $\bigcup_{j=1}^{v} cl_j = N$, $cl_i \cap cl_j = \phi$, $i, j = 1...v$, $i \neq j$, then the masked social network MG is defined as, $MG = (MN,ME,MA)$ [7,29], where:

- $MN = \{Cl_1, Cl_2, ..., Cl_v\}$, Cl_i is a node corresponding to the cluster $cl_j \in S$ that is described by the "tuple" $gen(cl_j)$ - the generalization information of cl_j, w.r.t. quasi-identifier attribute set and the intra-cluster generalization pair $(|cl_j|, |E_{cl_j}|)$;
- $ME \subseteq MN \times MN$; $(Cl_i, Cl_j) \in ME$ iif $Cl_i, Cl_j \in MN$ and $\exists X \in cl_i, \exists Y \in cl_j$, such that $(X, Y) \in E$. Each generalized edge is labeled with the inter-cluster generalization value $|E_{cl_i,cl_j}|$;
- MA is the set of corresponding tuples of the clusters' vertices containing generalized quasi-identifier attributes and sensitive attributes.

Definition (k-anonymous Masked Social Network): The masked social network $MG = (MN,ME,MA)$, where $MN = \{Cl_1, Cl_2, ..., Cl_v\}$, and $Cl_j = [gen(cl_j), (|cl_j|, |E_{cl_j}|)]$, $j = 1,..., v$ is said to be k-anonymous iff $|cl_j| \geq k$ for all $j = 1,..., v$. That is, each cluster formed from the initial partition should contain at least k vertices.

3.2   m-Privacy

Given n data providers, a set of records T, and an anonymization mechanism A, an adversary I is a coalition of m (m < n) providers that jointly contribute a set of records T_I. The anonymized dataset $T^* = A(T)$ is said to satisfy m-privacy with respect to a privacy constraint C iff any anonymized superset of records $A(T')$ from non-colluding providers satisfies C, i.e.,

$$\forall I \subset P, |\ I\ |= m, \forall T' : T\backslash T_I \subseteq T' \subseteq T, C(A(T')) = true \tag{1}$$

It requires that each equivalence group must satisfy C after excluding any records provided by an m-adversary.

3.3   Information Loss Measures

In [7,29], two types of information loss measures - the generalization information loss and the structural information loss are discussed.

Generalization Information Loss. The generalization information loss measure quantifies descriptive data loss resulting from quasi-identifier attribute generalization [5,7,29].

Definition (Generalization Information Loss (GIL)): Let cl be a cluster, $gen(cl)$ be its generalization information and $QI = \{N_1, N_2, .., N_s, C_1, C_2, .., C_t\}$ be the set of quasi-identifier attributes. The generalization information loss resulting from quasi-identifier attributes generalization of the cl tuples to $gen(cl)$ is given by:

$$GIL(cl) = |cl| \cdot \left(\sum_{j=1}^{s} \frac{size(gen(cl)[Nj])}{size\left(\min_{X \in N}(X[N_j]), \max_{X \in N}(X[N_j])\right)} + \sum_{j=1}^{t} \frac{height(\wedge(gen(cl)[Cj]))}{height(H_{C_j})} \right) \tag{2}$$

Where, size($[i_1, i_2]$) is the size of the interval $[i_1, i_2]$, $|cl|$ denotes the cardinality of cluster cl, $\wedge(w)$, $w \in H_{C_j}$ denotes the subhierarchy of H_{C_j} rooted at w and the height of the tree hierarchy H_{C_j} is denoted by $height(H_{C_j})$.

Definition (Total Generalization Information Loss): Total generalization information loss, denoted by $GIL(G,S)$, can be obtained after masking the graph G based on the clusters $S = \{cl_1, cl_2, .., cl_v\}$. It is the sum of the generalization information loss measure for each of the clusters in S and is given by:

$$GIL(G, S) = \sum_{j=1}^{v} GIL(cl_j) \tag{3}$$

Definition (Normalized Generalization Information Loss): The normalized generalization information loss, denoted by $NGIL(G,S)$, is given by:

$$NGIL(G, S) = \frac{GIL(G, S)}{n \cdot (s + t)} \qquad (4)$$

Where, s denotes total number of numeric quasi-identifier attributes, t denotes total number of categorical quasi-identifier attributes and n denotes total number of tuples.

Structural Information Loss. The structural information loss measure quantifies the probability of error when trying to reconstruct the structure of the original social network from its anonymized version [7,29]. We use two components of the structural information loss for the social network privacy model - the intra-cluster structural information loss and the inter-cluster structural information loss.

Definition (Intra-cluster Structural Information Loss): The intra-cluster structural information loss *(intraSIL)* is quantified as the probability of wrongly identifying a pair of nodes in *cl* as an unconnected pair or as an edge and is calculated using:

$$intraSIL(cl) = 2 \cdot |E_{cl}| \cdot \left(1 - \frac{|E_{cl}|}{\binom{|cl|}{2}} \right) \qquad (5)$$

Where, $|cl|$ denotes the cardinality of cluster *cl* and $|E_{cl}|$ denotes total number of edges in the cluster *cl*.

Definition (Inter-cluster Structural Information Loss): The inter-cluster structural information loss *(interSIL)* is quantified as the probability of wrongly labeling a pair of nodes *(X, Y)*, where $X \in cl_1$ and $Y \in cl_2$, as an unconnected pair or as an edge between two clusters and is calculated using:

$$interSIL(cl_1, cl_2) = 2 \cdot |E_{cl_1, cl_2}| \cdot \left(1 - \frac{|E_{cl_1, cl_2}|}{|cl_1| \cdot |cl_2|} \right) \qquad (6)$$

Where, $|cl_1|$ and $|cl_2|$ denote the cardinality of clusters cl_1 and cl_2 respectively and $|E_{cl_1, cl_2}|$ denotes total number of edges between clusters cl_1 and cl_2.

Definition (Total Structural Information Loss): The total structural information loss, denoted by *SIL(G,S)*, can be obtained when masking the graph *G* based on the clusters $S = \{cl_1, cl_2, .., cl_v\}$. It is the sum of all inter-cluster and intra-cluster structural information loss values and is given by:

$$SIL(G, S) = \sum_{j=1}^{v} (intraSIL(cl_j)) + \sum_{i=1}^{v} \sum_{j=i+1}^{v} (interSIL(cl_i, cl_j)) \qquad (7)$$

Definition (Normalized Structural Information Loss): The normalized structural information loss, denoted by *NSIL(G,S)*, is calculated using:

$$NSIL(G, S) = \frac{SIL(G, S)}{(n \cdot (n - 1)/4)} \tag{8}$$

We cannot compute the structural information loss during the cluster creation process, until the entire cluster partitioning is known. Therefore, the *dist* measure is introduced in [7,29]. This measure quantifies the extent to which the neighborhoods of two social network nodes are similar to each other. In addition, this measure is also used to calculate the structural distance between a node and a cluster.

Definition (distance between two nodes): The distance between two nodes $(X^i$ and $X^j)$ of the collaborative social network, denoted by $dist(X^i, X^j)$, is described by their associated n-dimensional boolean vectors B_i and B_j and is given by:

$$dist(X^i, X^j) = \frac{\left|\left\{ l | l = 1...n \wedge l \neq i, j; b_l^i \neq b_l^j \right\}\right|}{n - 2} \tag{9}$$

An n-dimensional boolean vector $B_i = (b_1^i, b_2^i, ..., b_n^i)$ is used to represent the neighbourhood of each node X^i. Here, b_j^i denotes the jth component of this vector, which is 1 if there is an edge $(X^i, X^j) \in E$, and is 0 otherwise, $\forall j = 1, ..., n$ and $j \neq i$. The value of b_i^i is considered to be undefined and hence, not equal to 0 or 1.

Definition (distance between a node and a cluster): The distance between a node X of the collaborative social network and a cluster cl, denoted by $dist(X, cl)$, is defined as the average distance between the node X and each and every node from cl and is calculated using:

$$dist(X, cl) = \frac{\sum_{X^j \in cl} dist(X, X^j)}{|cl|} \tag{10}$$

Where, $|cl|$ denotes the cardinality of cluster cl.

4   Proposed Approach

In Algorithm 1, we show the process of collaborative social network data anonymization that provides m-privacy against the *insider attack*. Given a social network graph $G = (N,E,A)$, this algorithm generates a set S of clusters that ensures both k-anonymity and m-privacy. The algorithm consists of two main phases - cluster formation phase and cluster dispersing phase.

Algorithm 1. The proposed algorithm.

INPUT: $G = (N, E, A)$ - a collaborative social network, k - the parameter for k-anonymity, m - the parameter for m-privacy, α - the parameter for GIL, β - the parameter for SIL, $\alpha + \beta = 1$

OUTPUT: a set S of clusters that ensures k-anonymity with m-privacy

1: $S \leftarrow \phi$;
2: $i \leftarrow 1$;
3: **repeat**
4:    $X^{seed} \leftarrow$ a node with maximum degree from N;
5:    $cl_i \leftarrow X^{seed}$;
6:    $N \leftarrow N - X^{seed}$; // N keeps track of nodes that are not distributed to clusters
7:    **repeat**
8:       $X^* \leftarrow argmin_{X \in N}(\alpha \cdot NGIL(G_1, S_1) + \beta \cdot dist(X, cl_i))$; // X^* is the node from N (unselected nodes) that produces the minimal information loss growth when added to the cluster cl_i. G_1 is the subgraph induced by $cl \cup \{X\}$ in G. S_1 is a partition with one cluster $cl \cup \{X\}$.
9:       $cl_i \leftarrow cl_i \cup \{X^*\}$;
10:      $N \leftarrow N - X^*$;
11:   **until** $(((cl_i$ has k elements) and (m-privacy is satisfied)) or $(N == \phi))$;
12:   **if** $(((|cl_i| < k)$ or $((|cl_i| == k)$ and (m-privacy is not satisfied)))$ **then**
13:      DisperseCluster(S, cl_i);
14:   **else if** $((|cl_i| > k)$ and (m-privacy is not satisfied))$ **then**
15:      DisperseCluster1(S, cl_i);
16:   **else**
17:      $S \leftarrow S\ U\ \{cl_i\}$;
18:      $i \leftarrow i + 1$;
19:   **end if**
20: **until** $(N == \phi)$;

In cluster formation phase, a node with the maximum degree that is not allocated to any cluster is selected as a seed for the new cluster (lines from 4 to 6). The next node that needs to be allocated to this cluster is selected from the remaining nodes in such a way that the inclusion of this node into the cluster results in minimum increase in the information loss of that cluster (line 8). The information loss growth of the cluster is quantified as a weighted measure that combines both NGIL and distance measure. The user-defined parameters α and β are used for the nodes' attribute data and the nodes' neighborhoods information respectively (line 8). The clusters are created one at a time and the current cluster grows with one node at each step (lines 9 and 10). This process is repeated until both the desired k-anonymity and m-privacy constraints are satisfied (line 11). The same process (lines from 8 to 11) is repeated unless each and every node from N is allocated to the clusters. During this cluster formation process, there are two possible cases with respect to the last constructed cluster. First, the last constructed cluster may contain less than k nodes or it may contain exactly k nodes but not satisfy the m-privacy condition (line 12). Second, the last constructed cluster may contain greater than k nodes but not satisfy m-

privacy condition (line 14). For these cases, it is required to disperse the last constructed cluster one node at a time into the previously constructed clusters.

Algorithm 2. The DisperseCluster algorithm for dispersing the cluster.

INPUT: S - a set of clusters, cl - a cluster that is to be dispersed
1: **for** every $X \in cl$ **do**
2:     $cl_u \leftarrow$ FindBestCluster(X, S);
3:     $cl_u \leftarrow cl_u \cup \{X\}$;
4: **end for**

Algorithm 3. The DisperseCluster1 algorithm for dispersing the cluster.

INPUT: S - a set of clusters, cl - a cluster that is to be dispersed
1: **for** every $X \in cl$ **do**
2:     $cl_u \leftarrow$ FindBestCluster(X, S);
3:     $cl_u \leftarrow cl_u \cup \{X\}$;
4:     $cl \leftarrow cl - \{X\}$;
5:     **if** $((|cl| \geq k)$ and $(m$-privacy is satisfied)) **then**
6:         **return** cl;
7:     **end if**
8: **end for**

Algorithm 4. The FindBestCluster algorithm for finding the best cluster.

INPUT: X - a node from the cluster that is to be dispersed, S - a set of clusters
OUTPUT: The cluster cl_j
1: bestCluster $\leftarrow$ NULL;
2: $infoLoss \leftarrow \infty$;
3: **for** every $cl_j \in S$ **do**
4:     **if** $(((\alpha \cdot NGIL(G_1, S_1) + \beta \cdot dist(X, cl_j)) < infoLoss)$ and $(m$-privacy is satisfied)) **then**
5:         $infoLoss \leftarrow \alpha \cdot NGIL(G_1, S_1) + \beta \cdot dist(X, cl_j)$;
6:         bestCluster $\leftarrow cl_j$;
7:     **end if**
8: **end for**
9: **return** bestCluster;

In cluster dispersing phase, the last constructed cluster is dispersed using either DisperseCluster algorithm (line 13) for the first case or DisperseCluster1 algorithm (line 15) for the second case. During the cluster dispersing, each node of the last constructed cluster is moved into the cluster from already generated clusters. This cluster is determined using FindBestCluster algorithm (line 2, Algorithms 2 and 3) such that this node shifting results in minimum information loss increase and also satisfies m-privacy condition. For the second case, it is possible that after removal of one node from the cluster, the conditions for k-anonymity and m-privacy may be satisfied. Hence, for the second case, every time after removal of one node from the cluster, the conditions for k-anonymity and m-privacy are checked during the disperse process (line 5, Algorithm 3). If both conditions are satisfied, then the process of dispersing cluster is terminated at that step by returning the cluster with remaining nodes (line 6, Algorithm 3).

5 Security Analysis

The threat model, privacy analysis and complexity analysis of our proposed approach is as follows:

5.1 Threat Model

The data publisher is fully trusted in our proposed approach. At a trusted data publisher site, the collaborative social network of total N nodes is constructed from the social network data of n collaborative parties out of which m $(m < n)$ number of parties may be colluding. External data recipients may use only the published data and the background knowledge to breach the privacy of the data records. The colluding data providers may use their own data records also to breach the privacy of the data records contributed by other data providers in addition to the published data and the background knowledge.

5.2 Privacy Analysis

Theorem 1. *The anonymous dataset T_k obtained from the collaborative dataset T through generalization satisfies m-privacy with respect to k-anonymity constraint if and only if for all tuples, $t' \in T_k$, $Prob\left[t' \rightarrow (t \in T)\right] \leq \frac{1}{k}$ where, m represents the number of colluding data providers and $x \rightarrow y$ represents that x is generalized from y.*

Proof. $\Rightarrow$ Assume that the anonymous dataset T_k satisfies m-privacy with respect to k-anonymity. For the generalized values t', if $t' \in T_k$, then from the definition of m-privacy with respect to k-anonymity there must a set S having identical values $t'_i \in T_k$, such that the total number of tuples in S is at least k after excluding the tuples if any that belongs to colluding data providers and $t' = t'_i$. Each tuple t'_i in S is generalized from the tuple t of collaborated dataset T that is, $(t'_i \in S) \rightarrow (t \in T)$. As we cannot distinguish among the values of t'_i and also the size of S is greater or equal to k, $|S| \geq k$, the probability that we have a particular tuple t'_i is given by $\frac{1}{|S|} \leq \frac{1}{k}$. As a consequence, the probability of t' that is generalized from a specific t_i is given by, $Prob\left[t' \rightarrow t_i\right] = Prob\left[t' = t'_i\right] \leq \frac{1}{k}$.

$\Leftarrow$ Assume that $Prob\left[t' \rightarrow (t \in T)\right] \leq \frac{1}{k}$ and t' be the tuple in T_k with the highest probability obtained through generalization from t. The generalization is done according to a generalization hierarchy and therefore tuple t must be generalized to a uniquely determined single node in each hierarchy. This hierarchy defines the only allowed values for t'. Thus, from initial assumption, for $\forall t'_i \in T_k, Prob\left[t'_i \rightarrow t\right] = Prob\left[t' \rightarrow (t \in T)\right] \leq \frac{1}{k}$. As the tuple t is uniquely generalized to one of the t'_i, the sum of all probabilities must be equal to 1. Thus, there must be at least k tuples in T_k, i.e. $k \cdot t'_i \in T_k$ that are identical to t' after excluding the tuples if any that belongs to colluding data providers. Hence, we can say that m-privacy with respect to k-anonymity holds for t'.

5.3 Complexity Analysis

The proposed approach is a greedy algorithm as this approach selects a solution from the search space, that is, the set of all partitions of N nodes consisting of subsets of k or more nodes, based on local optimum value of the two criterion measures - the total generalization information loss (the α parameter) and the total structural information loss (the β parameter). Our approach finds a good feasible solution to the anonymization problem that may not be the optimal solution. In fact, an efficient method for finding the optimal solution of the k-anonymization problem for microdata is not known and has been proven to be *NP-hard* problem [22]. The privacy preserving collaborative social network data publishing problem with respect to k-anonymity constraint is identical to this problem except only one difference that is we have to minimize two information loss measures of the data. Thus, the time complexity of the clustering based social network data anonymization operation is $O(n^2)$ as it is a greedy algorithm.

In addition, for the k-anonymity constraint, the m-privacy checking operation sequentially generates all possible $\binom{n}{m}$ combination of m-adversaries out of total n collaborative data providers and then checks privacy of the corresponding remaining records. The complexity in this case is determined by $\binom{n}{m}$. In the worst case scenario, when $m = \frac{n}{2}$, the number of possible checks are equal to the central binomial coefficient $\binom{n}{n/2}$. As a result, the average time-complexity for m-privacy checking is $O(2^n/n)$.

6   Experimental Evaluation

We perform experiments on a real dataset to estimate the performance of our proposed approach with respect to information loss measures. In addition, the data utility of the anonymized data is also measured and compared in terms of classification accuracy using the ID3 classification algorithm.

6.1 Experimental Setup

The proposed approach is implemented in Python. All experiments are performed on an unloaded PC running Windows 7 OS with an Intel Core i5 CPU

2.67 GHz with 4 GB main memory. We perform experiments on the social network with 300 nodes randomly selected from the Adult dataset available at the UC Irvine Machine Learning Repository [3]. The edge set of the social network is generated randomly with an average vertex degree of 12.5. We uniformly distribute 300 nodes among six data providers in order to consider this social network as a collaborative social network. The set of 300 nodes is referred to as an N in the proposed approach. Each node is described by the attributes node ID, age, workclass, native-country, sex, race, marital-status and providerID.

We consider a set of six attributes: age, workclass, native-country, sex, race and marital-status as a quasi-identifier attribute in all experiments. The number of distinct values for the six quasi-identifier attributes are as follows: age - 56, workclass - 6, native-country - 19, sex - 2, race - 5 and marital-status - 7. The quasi-identifier attributes workclass, native-country, sex, race and marital-status are categorical attributes and age is only the numerical attribute. We use hierarchy-free generalization for the numerical quasi-identifier attribute [18]. The heights of the generalization hierarchies of five categorical quasi-identifier attributes for their corresponding value are as follows: workclass - 2, native-country - 3, sex - 1, race - 1 and marital-status - 1. The configurations used in the experiments are shown in Table 5.

Table 5. Experimental configurations.

No.	Experiment	Parameter settings
1	Varied α-value and β-value	k-value = 5, n (no. of data providers) = 6, m (no. of colluding insiders) $\in \{0,1,2\}$, $|QIDs| = 6$, $(\alpha, \beta) \in \{(1,0),(0.5,0.5),(0,1)\}$
2	Varied *k*-value	k-value $\in \{2, 3, 4, 5, 6, 7, 9, 10\}$, n (no. of data providers) = 6, m (no. of colluding insiders) $\in \{0,2\}$, $|QIDs| = 6$, $(\alpha, \beta) \in \{(0.5, 0.5)\}$
3	Varied m (no. of colluding insiders)	k-value = 5, n (no. of data providers) = 6, m (no. of colluding insiders) $\in \{0,1,2,3,4\}$, $|QIDs| = 6$, $(\alpha, \beta) \in \{(0.5, 0.5)\}$

6.2 Experimental Results

For both existing and proposed approaches, Fig. 5 shows the effect of varied α and β, varied *k*-value and varied *m*-value on NGIL and NSIL. Furthermore, Figs. 6, 7 and 8 summarizes the utility of the anonymized data in terms of classification accuracy for the different split ratio of training data and testing data for varied α-value and β-value, varied k-value, varied m-value configurations respectively.

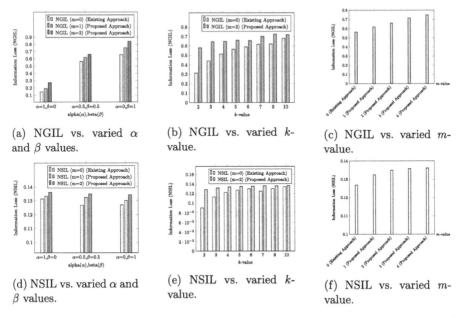

(a) NGIL vs. varied α and β values.

(b) NGIL vs. varied k-value.

(c) NGIL vs. varied m-value.

(d) NSIL vs. varied α and β values.

(e) NSIL vs. varied k-value.

(f) NSIL vs. varied m-value.

Fig. 5. Experimental results with respect to NGIL and NSIL for three experimental configurations.

6.3   Experimental Analysis

Our key findings are as follows based on the analysis of the obtained results:

For all three configurations (Fig. 5), the anonymization performed by the proposed approach results in minimum increase in both NGIL and NSIL as compared to the existing approach [7]. This is due to the increase in the size of the equivalence group while satisfying m-privacy constraint along with k-anonymity constraint.

The value of NGIL increases gradually with gradual decrease in the α parameter value (Fig. 5(a)) and the value of NSIL decreases gradually with gradual increase in the β parameter value (Fig. 5(d)) for both the existing approach and the proposed approach. The reason is that α parameter and β parameter is used to control generalization information loss and structural information loss respectively.

The pair $(\alpha, \beta) = (1, 0)$ guides the algorithm towards minimizing the generalization information loss without giving any importance to the structural information loss during cluster formation process. For real-time applications, such as study of the correlation between the age of the terrorist and related threat

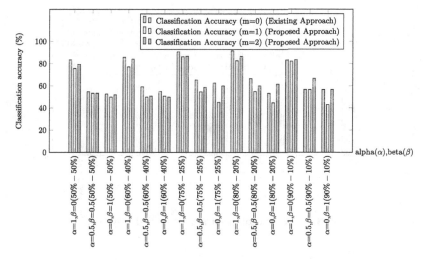

Fig. 6. Classification accuracy vs. varied α and β values.

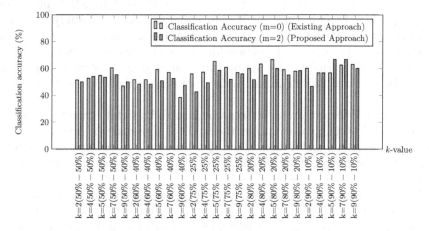

Fig. 7. Classification accuracy vs. varied k-value.

from multi-site terrorism data, preserving generalization information is more important than preserving structural information. Hence, for such application scenarios, the user can set the value of α to 1 and β to 0.

The pair $(\alpha, \beta) = (0, 1)$ guides the algorithm towards minimizing the structural information loss while giving no consideration to the generalization information loss. For real-time application scenarios, such as to prepare the classification model for the estimation of the approximate salary to be given to the newly joined employee without link re-identification from collaborative social network of company employees, preserving structural information is more important than preserving generalization information. Hence, for such application scenarios, the user can set the value of α to 0 and β to 1.

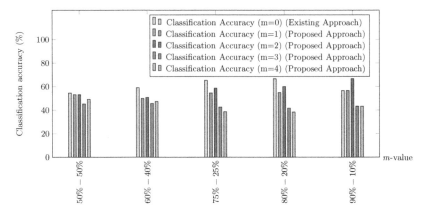

Fig. 8. Classification accuracy vs. varied m-value.

The pair $(\alpha, \beta) = (0.5, 0.5)$ indicates the request to the algorithm to give equal importance to both information loss components during the cluster formation process. For real-time application scenarios, such as to study the correlation of a person's age with the specific disease from self-help OSN in which the person's medical records and relationships between persons are both sensitive, preserving both attribute information and structural information is important. Hence, for such application scenarios, the user can set the value of α to 0.5 and β to 0.5.

In general, if the structural information is more important than the attribute information, it is mandatory to set the value of β parameter greater than the value of α parameter and if the attribute information is more important than the structural information, it is mandatory to set the value of α parameter greater than the value of β parameter.

The variation in the classification accuracy w.r.t. different split ratio of training and testing data is due to the variation in the anonymized results we receive by the existing approach and the proposed approach for all three configurations (Figs. 6, 7 and 8). That is, the same node anonymized in one configuration may be differently anonymized in another configuration. As a result, for all configurations, the training data used for building the decision tree of ID3 classification and the testing data used for accuracy checking are different. Hence, we get the variation in the accuracy values. However, this difference is in an acceptable range.

7   Conclusions

In this paper, we propose an approach that incorporates m-privacy with the clustering based approach for a new type of attack - *insider attack* - prevention with respect to collaborative social network data publishing scenario. From the experimental results, we conclude that using our approach we can achieve the privacy of collaborative social network data against the *insider attack* with the help of the *m*-privacy notion. However, we observe that, the protection against the *insider attack* is achieved by our approach with an increase in information loss values. In fact, there is always a natural trade-off between data utility and data privacy. Hence, the increase in the information loss can be accepted because our proposed approach gives protection against the *insider attack* while existing approaches do not.

This work can be extended to protection against the homogeneity attack together with *insider attack* by taking into consideration the sensitive attributes in addition to quasi-identifier attributes and relations for a collaborative social network data publishing scenario. Another extension can be devising an approach that considers actual value of the information loss measure during each cluster formation step while providing protection against *insider attack*.

References

1. Ayala-Rivera, V., McDonagh, P., Cerqueus, T., Murphy, L., et al.: A systematic comparison and evaluation of k-anonymization algorithms for practitioners. Trans. Data Priv. **7**(3), 337–370 (2014)
2. Backstrom, L., Dwork, C., Kleinberg, J.: Wherefore art thou R3579X?: Anonymized social networks, hidden patterns, and structural steganography. In: Proceedings of the 16th International Conference on World Wide Web, pp. 181–190. ACM (2007)
3. Blake, C.: UCI repository of machine learning databases (1998). http://www.ics.uci.edu/~mlearn/MLRepository.html
4. Bonchi, F., Gionis, A., Tassa, T.: Identity obfuscation in graphs through the information theoretic lens. Inf. Sci. **275**, 232–256 (2014)
5. Byun, J.-W., Kamra, A., Bertino, E., Li, N.: Efficient *k*-anonymization using clustering techniques. In: Kotagiri, R., Krishna, P.R., Mohania, M., Nantajeewarawat, E. (eds.) DASFAA 2007. LNCS, vol. 4443, pp. 188–200. Springer, Heidelberg (2007). https://doi.org/10.1007/978-3-540-71703-4_18
6. Dwork, C.: Differential privacy: a survey of results. In: Agrawal, M., Du, D., Duan, Z., Li, A. (eds.) TAMC 2008. LNCS, vol. 4978, pp. 1–19. Springer, Heidelberg (2008). https://doi.org/10.1007/978-3-540-79228-4_1
7. Campan A, Truta, T.M.: A clustering approach for data and structural anonymity in social networks. In: 2nd ACM SIGKDD International Workshop on Privacy, Security, and Trust in KDD, PinKDD 2008 (2008)
8. Cavoukian, A.: Data mining: staking a claim on your privacy. Information and Privacy Commissioner's Report, Ontario, Canada (1997)
9. Dwork, C.: A firm foundation for private data analysis. Commun. ACM **54**(1), 86–95 (2011)
10. Fung, B., Wang, K., Chen, R., Yu, P.S.: Privacy-preserving data publishing: a survey of recent developments. ACM Comput. Surv. (CSUR) **42**(4), 14 (2010)
11. Goryczka, S., Xiong, L., Fung, B.C.M.: *m*-privacy for collaborative data publishing. In: 7th International Conference on Collaborative Computing: Networking, Applications and Worksharing (CollaborateCom), pp. 1–10, October 2011. https://doi.org/10.4108/icst.collaboratecom.2011.247094

12. Goryczka, S., Xiong, L., Fung, B.C.M.: m-privacy for collaborative data publishing. IEEE Trans. Knowl. Data Eng. **26**(10), 2520–2533 (2014). https://doi.org/10.1109/TKDE.2013.18
13. Goryczka, S., Xiong, L., Fung, B.: Secure distributed data anonymization and integration with m-privacy (2013)
14. Goryczka, S., Xiong, L., Fung, B.C.M.: m-privacy for collaborative data publishing. Citeseer (2012)
15. Hanhijärvi, S., Garriga, G.C., Puolamäki, K.: Randomization techniques for graphs. In: Proceedings of the 2009 SIAM International Conference on Data Mining, pp. 780–791. SIAM (2009)
16. Hay, M., Miklau, G., Jensen, D., Towsley, D., Weis, P.: Resisting structural re-identification in anonymized social networks. Proc. VLDB Endow. **1**(1), 102–114 (2008)
17. Hay, M., Miklau, G., Jensen, D., Weis, P., Srivastava, S.: Anonymizing social networks. Computer science Department Faculty Publication Series, p. 180 (2007)
18. LeFevre, K., DeWitt, D.J., Ramakrishnan, R.: Mondrian multidimensional k-anonymity. In: 22nd International Conference on Data Engineering, ICDE 2006, p. 25, April 2006. https://doi.org/10.1109/ICDE.2006.101
19. Li, N., Li, T., Venkatasubramanian, S.: t-closeness: privacy beyond k-anonymity and l-diversity. In: IEEE 23rd International Conference on Data Engineering, ICDE 2007, pp. 106–115. IEEE (2007)
20. Liu, K., Terzi, E.: Towards identity anonymization on graphs. In: Proceedings of the 2008 ACM SIGMOD International Conference on Management of Data, pp. 93–106. ACM (2008)
21. Machanavajjhala, A., Kifer, D., Gehrke, J., Venkitasubramaniam, M.: l-diversity: privacy beyond k-anonymity. ACM Trans. Knowl. Discov. Data (TKDD) **1**(1), 3 (2007)
22. Meyerson, A., Williams, R.: On the complexity of optimal k-anonymity. In: Proceedings of the Twenty-Third ACM SIGMOD-SIGACT-SIGART Symposium on Principles of Database Systems, pp. 223–228. ACM (2004)
23. Rubenfeld, J.: The end of privacy. Stanford Law Rev. **61**, 101 (2008)
24. Samarati, P.: Protecting respondents identities in microdata release. IEEE Trans. Knowl. Data Eng. **13**(6), 1010–1027 (2001)
25. Scott, J.: Social Network Analysis: A Handbook. SAGE Publications (2000). https://books.google.co.in/books?id=Ww3_bKcz6kgC
26. Sweeney, L.: k-anonymity: a model for protecting privacy. Int. J. Uncertain. Fuzziness Knowl.-Based Syst. **10**(05), 557–570 (2002)
27. Tassa, T., Cohen, D.J.: Anonymization of centralized and distributed social networks by sequential clustering. IEEE Trans. Knowl. Data Eng. **25**(2), 311–324 (2013)
28. Wang, D.W., Liau, C.J., Hsu, T.S.: Privacy protection in social network data disclosure based on granular computing. In: 2006 IEEE International Conference on Fuzzy Systems, pp. 997–1003. IEEE (2006)
29. Wang, R., Zhang, M., Feng, D., Fu, Y.: A clustering approach for privacy-preserving in social networks. In: Lee, J., Kim, J. (eds.) ICISC 2014. LNCS, vol. 8949, pp. 193–204. Springer, Cham (2015). https://doi.org/10.1007/978-3-319-15943-0_12
30. Wellman, B.: For a social network analysis of computer networks: a sociological perspective on collaborative work and virtual community. In: Proceedings of the 1996 ACM SIGCPR/SIGMIS Conference on Computer Personnel Research, pp. 1–11. ACM (1996)

31. Wu, W., Xiao, Y., Wang, W., He, Z., Wang, Z.: K-symmetry model for identity anonymization in social networks. In: Proceedings of the 13th International Conference on Extending Database Technology, pp. 111–122. ACM (2010)
32. Ying, X., Wu, X.: Randomizing social networks: a spectrum preserving approach. In: Proceedings of the 2008 SIAM International Conference on Data Mining, pp. 739–750. SIAM (2008)
33. Ying, X., Wu, X.: Graph generation with prescribed feature constraints. In: Proceedings of the 2009 SIAM International Conference on Data Mining, pp. 966–977. SIAM (2009)
34. Ying, X., Wu, X.: On link privacy in randomizing social networks. Knowl. Inf. Syst. **28**(3), 645–663 (2011)
35. Zhan, J., Blosser, G., Yang, C., Singh, L.: Privacy-preserving collaborative social networks. In: Yang, C.C., Chen, H., Chau, M., Chang, K., Lang, S.-D., Chen, P.S., Hsieh, R., Zeng, D., Wang, F.-Y., Carley, K., Mao, W., Zhan, J. (eds.) ISI 2008. LNCS, vol. 5075, pp. 114–125. Springer, Heidelberg (2008). https://doi.org/10.1007/978-3-540-69304-8_13
36. Zheleva, E., Getoor, L.: Preserving the privacy of sensitive relationships in graph data. In: Bonchi, F., Ferrari, E., Malin, B., Saygin, Y. (eds.) PInKDD 2007. LNCS, vol. 4890, pp. 153–171. Springer, Heidelberg (2008). https://doi.org/10.1007/978-3-540-78478-4_9
37. Zhou, B., Pei, J.: Preserving privacy in social networks against neighborhood attacks (2008)
38. Zhou, B., Pei, J., Luk, W.: A brief survey on anonymization techniques for privacy preserving publishing of social network data. ACM SIGKDD Explor. Newslett. **10**(2), 12–22 (2008)

Images and Cryptography

WiP: Security Enhanced Size Invariant Visual Cryptography with Perfect Reconstruction of White Pixels

T. E. Jisha[1($\boxtimes$)] and Thomas Monoth[2($\boxtimes$)]

[1] Department of Information Technology, Kannur University, Kannur 670 567, Kerala, India
jishatevinoy@gmail.com
[2] Department of Computer Science, Mary Matha Arts & Science College, Kannur University, Mananthavady, Wayanad 670 645, Kerala, India
tmonoth@yahoo.com

Abstract. Visual Cryptography is an image encryption technique which reconstructs the image using human visual system. Presently used size invariant visual cryptography schemes (VCS) does not preserves both security and contrast conditions. In this paper we proposed a new method for size invariant block wise encoding VCS based on perfect reconstruction of white pixels which provides perfect security and retains the contrast. Here we have discussed an outline of size invariant VCS based on random basis column pixel expansion, block wise encoding and random basis VCS with perfect reconstruction of white pixels (PRWP) which have been demonstrated based on various research studies. We have also discussed the demerits of the existing models and made an experimental analysis between previous models and the proposed model. From the analysis we proved that the proposed method enhances the security and maintain the contrast.

Keywords: Visual Cryptography Scheme · Size invariant · Contrast · Security · Pixel expansion

1 Introduction

Image secret sharing scheme known as Visual Cryptography (VC) was introduced by Naor and Shamir. Visual Cryptography is one of the most powerful cryptographic techniques for image security. In (k, n) Visual Cryptography Scheme, the secret image is separated into n shares from which any k or greater than k shares decrypts the original secret image. The main goal of the VCS is that decryption can be done without any computation. Due to the speedy decoding or recovering properties and perfect cipher, VC plays an inevitable role in multimedia and information security. But the three confronting concerns in VC are: the decrypted image's contrast, pixel expansion and its security [1–3]. The disquiets stated above appeared in the VCS require additional consideration.

To surmount the pixel expansion problems many Size Invariant (without pixel expansion) VCS were proposed. In this scheme, the size of the original secret image,

© Springer Nature Switzerland AG 2019
D. Garg et al. (Eds.): ICISS 2019, LNCS 11952, pp. 279–289, 2019.
https://doi.org/10.1007/978-3-030-36945-3_15

the shares and the decrypted image are equal. The security and decrypted image's contrast are the two barriers remain in the size invariant VCS. The crucial objective of the proposed system is to produce a size invariant VCS which improves the security and retains contrast of the overlapped image. We used block wise encryption of pixels which contains manifold pixels rather than a single pixel. Also we introduced block wise encoding size invariant VCS with perfect reconstruction of white pixels instead of black pixels [4, 5, 15, 17]. The upcoming sections of the paper are as follows. Sector 2 describes different size invariant VCSs. In Sect. 3 we have demonstrated the relevance of VCS with perfect reconstruction of white pixels. Section 4 draws the proposed model, the experimental results and analysis of various schemes. The final section draws the conclusion.

2 Size Invariant Visual Cryptography

In conventional VCS each pixel is expanded into m pixels, where m is the pixel expansion. The size of the decrypted image is m times larger than the original image. The quality of the recovered image is degraded due to the pixel expansion. But in size invariant VCS the size of the secret image, share images and the decoded image are similar. In this scheme the pixel expansion $m = 1$. Mainly size invariant VCS can be categorized into two: random basis column pixel expansion and block wise encoding [4, 6, 14, 16].

2.1 Size Invariant VCS with Random Basis Column Pixel Expansion

In this method, shares with consistent share size are generated using random basis column pixel expansion technique. The size of the secret image, the shares and the reconstructed image are identical in this scheme. The 2-out-of-2 image size invariant VCS with 4-subpixel layout can be demonstrated with the random basis column pixel expansion technique. To implement this method, the following basis matrices B^w and B^b are used, where

$$B^w = \begin{bmatrix} 1 & 0 & 1 & 0 \\ 1 & 0 & 1 & 0 \end{bmatrix}, B^b = \begin{bmatrix} 1 & 0 & 1 & 0 \\ 0 & 1 & 0 & 1 \end{bmatrix}$$

For encrypting white pixels and black pixels one of the columns is randomly chosen from B^w and B^b. The column vector $V = [v_i]$

$$V = \begin{bmatrix} v1 \\ v2 \end{bmatrix}$$

The ith element represents the color of the pixel in the ith share image, the v_1 and v_2 are the pixels in the first and second share images respectively. In 2-out-of-2 image size invariant VCS, to share a black pixel, one of the columns in B^b is chosen at random. Suppose the chosen column vector from B^b is:

$$V = \begin{bmatrix} 1 \\ 0 \end{bmatrix}$$

The element 1 represents the black pixel in the first share image, and element 0 represents the white pixel in the second share image. Similarly, to share a white pixel, one of the columns in B^w is chosen at random. The different column matrices from the basis matrices B^w and B^b of a *2-out-of-2* image size invariant VCS with four subpixels are:

$$B^w = \{ \begin{bmatrix} 1 \\ 1 \end{bmatrix}, \begin{bmatrix} 0 \\ 0 \end{bmatrix}, \begin{bmatrix} 1 \\ 1 \end{bmatrix}, \begin{bmatrix} 0 \\ 0 \end{bmatrix} \}$$

$$B^b = \{ \begin{bmatrix} 1 \\ 0 \end{bmatrix}, \begin{bmatrix} 0 \\ 1 \end{bmatrix}, \begin{bmatrix} 1 \\ 0 \end{bmatrix}, \begin{bmatrix} 0 \\ 1 \end{bmatrix} \}$$

These column matrices can be used to construct the image size invariant VCS [3, 6]. An example of *(2, 2)* size invariant random basis column pixel expansion is shown in Fig. 1.

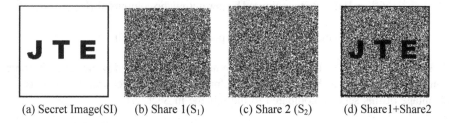

(a) Secret Image(SI)   (b) Share 1(S_1)   (c) Share 2 (S_2)   (d) Share1+Share2

Fig. 1. (a) Secret Image (SI) (b) Share 1 (S_1) (c) Share 2 (S_2) (d) Share1+Share2

The column vectors chosen from the basis matrices in this scheme violated the security clause of conventional VCS. The security clause of the conventional VCS is illustrated as follows:

For any set

$$\{r_1, r_2, \ldots, r_t\} \subset \{1, 2, \ldots, n\} \tag{1}$$

with $t < k$, the $t \times m$ matrices obtained by restricting B^w and B^b to rows $r_1, r_2, \ldots, r_t$ are not distinguishable [7, 8, 13].

The column vectors from B^w and B^b in this scheme are:

$$V_w = \begin{bmatrix} 1 \\ 1 \end{bmatrix} \text{ and } V_b = \begin{bmatrix} 1 \\ 0 \end{bmatrix}$$

From these vector elements we noticed that the rows are distinguishable. Referring to Table 2(a) we found that the number of black and white pixels in share 1 and share 2 are not equal. Hence this scheme do not preserves the security condition. This is the main drawback of this scheme. To overcome this defect we can use size invariant VCS with block wise encoding.

2.2 Size Invariant VCS with Block Wise Encoding

In this scheme, the encryption is performed on a block contains multiple pixels instead of pixel basis encryption. Each block holds equal number of pixels and adopts a threshold. If the number of black pixels in the block is greater than the accepted threshold, the pixel block is encrypted using the black pixel layout which is randomly chosen from the collection of matrices C^b, otherwise using the white pixel layout randomly chosen from the collection of matrices C^w. Usually the adopted threshold is the total number of pixels in the block divided by two [4, 9–11]. The basis matrices for the 2×2 block are:

$$B^w = \begin{bmatrix} 1 & 0 & 1 & 0 \\ 1 & 0 & 1 & 0 \end{bmatrix}, \quad B^b = \begin{bmatrix} 1 & 0 & 1 & 0 \\ 0 & 1 & 0 & 1 \end{bmatrix}$$

$$C^w = \{\text{all matrices acquired by permuting the columns of } B^w\}$$

$$C^b = \{\text{all matrices acquired by permuting the columns of } B^b\}$$

Referring to Table 2(a) we found that the number of black and white pixels in share 1 and share 2 are equal. Hence this scheme preserves the perfect security. This is the advantage of this scheme compared to the scheme in Sect. 2.1.

3   VCS with Perfect Reconstruction of White Pixels

The perfect reconstruction of black pixels is performed in the conventional VCS. While considering the binary images, usually the number of white pixels is higher than the black pixels. Few studies have been concentrated on the size invariant VCS with perfect reconstruction of white pixels based on random basis column pixel expansion. In traditional VCS, black pixels are represented by 1 and white pixels by 0. Then the basis matrix for the black pixel in conventional VCS becomes the basis matrix for the white pixel in VCS with PRWP and vice versa [5, 12]. The basis matrices for VCS with PRWP are:

$$BW^w = \begin{bmatrix} 1 & 0 & 1 & 0 \\ 0 & 1 & 0 & 1 \end{bmatrix}, \quad BW^b = \begin{bmatrix} 1 & 0 & 1 & 0 \\ 1 & 0 & 1 & 0 \end{bmatrix}$$

Referring to Table 2(b) we found that the number of black and white pixels in share 1 and share 2 are not equal. But this scheme enhances the visual quality of the reconstructed image and not maintains the perfect security. Hence we need to construct a VCS which enhances the security and retains the contrast.

4   The Proposed Model: Size Invariant VCS with Block Wise Encoding and PRWP

The proposed model enhances the security and retains the contrast of the recovered image. In this scheme we combined the perfect security feature of the size invariant VCS with block wise encoding and enhanced visual quality feature of the VCS with PRWP. The original image is encrypted into two non expanded shares. Here we considered a block of pixels for encryption rather than a single pixel in an image. All blocks should contain the same number of pixels. Here we took a block with the order of 1×2 or 1×4 or 2×2 (2 or 4 pixels).

The pixel layout of the block with four pixels may be: Block with 3 white pixels and 1 black pixel, block with 3 black pixels and 1 white pixel, block with 2 white and 2 black pixels, block with 4 black pixels and block with 4 white pixels. The possible pixel layouts are illustrated in Fig. 2.

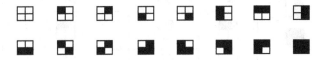

Fig. 2. Four pixel layouts in a block

In the proposed method the image can be represented with two $n \times m$ binary basis matrices,

$$BW^b = \begin{bmatrix} 1 & 0 & 1 & 0 \\ 1 & 0 & 1 & 0 \end{bmatrix}, \quad BW^w = \begin{bmatrix} 1 & 0 & 1 & 0 \\ 0 & 1 & 0 & 1 \end{bmatrix}$$

The C^b and C^w are the collection of basis matrices by permuting the columns of BW^b and BW^w respectively where block size = 4.

$$C^w = \{ \text{all matrices acquired by permuting the columns of } \begin{bmatrix} 1 & 0 & 1 & 0 \\ 1 & 0 & 1 & 0 \end{bmatrix} \}$$

$$C^b = \{ \text{all matrices acquired by permuting the columns of } \begin{bmatrix} 1 & 0 & 1 & 0 \\ 0 & 1 & 0 & 1 \end{bmatrix} \}$$

Here 0 denotes black and 1 denotes white. We have calculated the total number of black pixels and white pixels in a block. If the number of white pixels is higher or equal to the number of black pixels in a block, the block is considered as white block, if not black block. The pixels in this block are encrypted with the pixel configuration in a white block which is randomly chosen from the C^w, otherwise chosen from the C^b [4, 5]. The pixel layout for the proposed size invariant block wise encoding scheme with PRWP is shown in Table 1.

4.1 Experimental Results

Consider an image with $m \times n$ size (here m and n are *200*) and it can be divided into blocks with 4 pixels. The construction of size invariant VCS with block wise encoding and PRWP can be demonstrated with a *(2, 2)* VCS. Using the pixel layouts in Table 1 the image can be encrypted into two shares. Overlapping of these two shares can reveal the secret image. The experimental results are illustrated in Fig. 3. It shows that the size of the original secret image, share 1, share 2 and decrypted image are similar.

Table 1. The pixel layouts for proposed *(2, 2)* VCS with block wise encoding and PRWP

Original Pixel	Share 1	Share 2	(Share1 + Share 2)

The major advantages of this scheme are:

- The scheme is size invariant.
- Encryption can be done on a block of pixels rather than a single pixel.
- The scheme provides perfect security.
- It uses the PRWP scheme which retains the contrast of the reconstructed image.

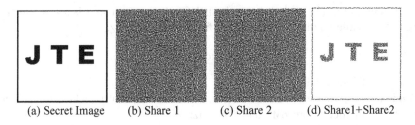

| (a) Secret Image | (b) Share 1 | (c) Share 2 | (d) Share1+Share2 |

Fig. 3. (a) Secret Image (b) Share 1 (c) Share 2 (d) Share1+Share2

4.2 Analysis of Experiment Results

We analyzed the security and contrast of various schemes like size invariant VCS based on random basis column pixel expansion which can be performed with conventional VCS or with PRWP and block wise encoding size invariant VCS with conventional VCS or with PRWP on different images. The analysis is depicted on Table 2(a) and (b). On analysis we found that size invariant VCS based on random basis column pixel expansion with conventional VCS or with PRWP contains different number of black and white pixels in the encrypted shares. This disobeys the security condition. We stated that this scheme does not preserve perfect security. But in the block wise encoding size invariant VCS with conventional VCS preserves the security but the contrast of the reconstructed image is degraded compared to the size invariant VCS with PRWP. Our scheme is optimum for both security and contrast.

Table 2. Analysis of various VCSs

(a) Conventional VCS (Perfect Reconstruction of Black Pixels)

Scheme		Secret Image		Share 1		Share 2		Share 1+Share 2		PSNR
		White	Black	White	Black	White	Black	White	Black	
Random Basis	Image 1	35438	4562	19984	20016	20096	19904	17679	22321	50.7139
	Image 2	20226	19774	20035	19965	20075	19925	10058	29942	49.4386
Block wise	Image 1	35438	4562	20000	20000	20000	20000	18152	21848	50.7969
	Image 2	20226	19774	20000	20000	20000	20000	10986	29314	49.5563

(b) VCS with PRWP

Scheme		Secret Image		Share 1		Share 2		Share1+Share 2		PSNR
		White	Black	White	Black	White	Black	White	Black	
Random Basis	Image 1	35438	4562	19889	20111	20071	19929	37699	2301	60.6443
	Image 2	20226	19774	19853	20147	19947	20053	30013	9987	54.2789
Proposed Scheme	Image 1	35438	4562	20000	20000	20000	20000	38152	1848	59.8365
	Image 2	20226	19774	20000	20000	20000	20000	30686	9314	53.8415

According to Eq. (1), in the random basis VCS the $t \times m$ matrix is a 1×1 matrix, where $t < k$. While taking 1×1 matrices from B^b and B^w viz:

$$B^b = [1] \text{ and } B^w = [0]$$

the rows are distinguishable.

But in the proposed scheme the $t \times m$ matrix is a 1×4 matrix, where $t < k$. While taking 1×4 matrices from BW^b and BW^w viz:

$$BW^w = \begin{bmatrix} 1 & 0 & 1 & 0 \end{bmatrix} \text{ and } BW^b = \begin{bmatrix} 1 & 0 & 1 & 0 \end{bmatrix}$$

the rows are indistinguishable.

For calculating the relative difference α and contrast β using the Eqs. (2) and (3).

$$\alpha = \left(\omega_H(BW^w) - \omega_H(BW^b) \right) / m \tag{2}$$

$$\beta = \alpha \times m \tag{3}$$

Where $(\omega_H(BW^w)$ and $\omega_H(BW^b)$ are the hamming weight (number of Ones) of the basis matrices BW^w and BW^b respectively.

Table 3. Decrypted images of various schemes

Scheme	Image 1	Image 2
Random Basis		
Block wise		
Random Basis With PRWP		
Proposed Scheme		

While calculating α and β in the proposed scheme:

$$\alpha = (4-2)/1 = 2, \text{ where } m = 1 \text{ and}$$
$$\beta = 2 \times 1 = 2.$$

The scheme enhances security and retains the contrast compared to other existing schemes while considering security clause in Eq. (1), the relative difference α and contrast β in Eqs. (1) and (2).

The output of the different decrypted images based on various VCSs from the experiments is shown in Table 3. From the Table we confirmed that VCS with PRWP have more contrast in the decrypted images with respect to the conventional VCS. The graphical representation of the existing schemes and our scheme with respect to the number of black and white pixels is shown in Fig. 4. This shows that the number of black and white pixels in the Share 1 and Share 2 are different in VCS with random basis column pixel expansion approach. But in the proposed scheme, the number of pixels is same and it proved the perfect security.

Figure 5 shows the graphical representation of the PSNR (Peak Signal to Noise Ratio) value between the secret image and decrypted image. From this figure we found that the contrast of the Random Basis (RB) column pixel expansion and Block Wise (BW) encoding schemes based on conventional VCS is extremely low compared to the VCS with PRWP. Also we stated that our scheme with PRWP retains the contrast compared to the size invariant random basis VCS with PRWP.

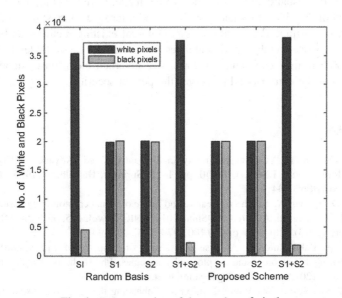

Fig. 4. Representation of the number of pixels

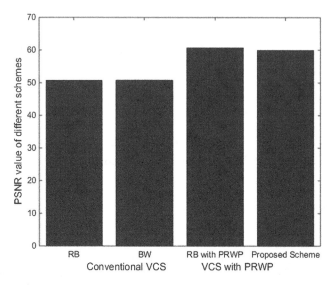

Fig. 5. PSNR value between the original image and reconstructed image

5 Conclusion

This paper presents a new method for size invariant VCS which enhances the security and preserves the visual quality of the decrypted image. Here we combined the perfect security facet of the block wise encoding VCS and improved contrast facet of the VCS with perfect reconstruction of white pixels. Different existing methods and proposed method are illustrated with experimental results and analyzed by tables and graphs. Future research in this realm can develop a size invariant block wise encoding VCS which enhances the contrast and preserves the perfect security.

References

1. Naor, M., Shamir, A.: Visual cryptography. In: De Santis, A. (ed.) Advances in Cryptology – EUROCRYPT 1994. LNCS, vol. 950, pp. 1–12. Springer, Heidelberg (1995). https://doi.org/10.1007/BFb0053419
2. Pandey, D., Kumar, A., Singh, Y.: Feature and future of visual cryptography based schemes. In: Singh, K., Awasthi, A.K. (eds.) QShine 2013. LNICST, vol. 115, pp. 816–830. Springer, Heidelberg (2013). https://doi.org/10.1007/978-3-642-37949-9_71
3. Monoth, T., Babu Anto, P.: Analysis and design of tamperproof and contrast-enhanced secret sharing based on visual cryptography schemes, Ph. D thesis, Kannur University, Kerala, India (2012). http://shodhganga.inflibnet.ac.in
4. Chow, Y.-W., Susilo, W., Wong, Duncan S.: Enhancing the perceived visual quality of a size invariant visual cryptography scheme. In: Chim, T.W., Yuen, T.H. (eds.) ICICS 2012. LNCS, vol. 7618, pp. 10–21. Springer, Heidelberg (2012). https://doi.org/10.1007/978-3-642-34129-8_2

5. Monoth, T., Babu Anto, P.: Contrast-enhanced visual cryptography schemes based on perfect reconstruction of white pixels and additional basis matrix. In: Senthilkumar, M., Ramasamy, V., Sheen, S., Veeramani, C., Bonato, A., Batten, L. (eds.) Computational Intelligence, Cyber Security and Computational Models. AISC, vol. 412, pp. 361–368. Springer, Singapore (2016). https://doi.org/10.1007/978-981-10-0251-9_34

6. Ito, R., Kuwakado, H., Tanaka, H.: Image size invariant visual cryptography. IEICE Trans. Fundam. Electron. Commun. Comput. Sci. **82**(10), 2172–2177 (1999)

7. Jisha, T.E., Monoth, T.: Research advances in black and white visual cryptography schemes. Int. J. Adv. Intell. Syst. Comput. Springer (Accepted). http://www.springer.com/series/11156

8. Liu, F., Guo, T., Wu, C., Qian, L.: Improving the visual quality of size invariant visual cryptography scheme. J. Vis. Commun. Image Represent. **23**(2), 331–342 (2012). https://doi.org/10.1016/j.jvcir.2011.11.003

9. Chen, Y.-F., Chan, Y.-K., Huang, C.-C., Tsai, M.-H., Chu, Y.-P.: A multiple-level visual secret-sharing scheme without image size expansion. Inf. Sci. **177**(21), 4696–4710 (2007)

10. Lin, T.H., Shiao, N.S., Chen, H.H., Tsai, C.S.: A new non-expansion visual cryptography scheme with high quality of recovered image. In: IET International Conference on Frontier Computing Theory, Technologies and Applications. IEEE Xplore (2010). https://doi.org/10.1049/cp.2010.0571

11. Huang, Y.-J., Chang, J.-D.: Non-expanded visual cryptography scheme with authentication. In: IEEE 2nd International Symposium on Next-Generation Electronics (ISNE). IEEE (2013). https://doi.org/10.1109/isne.2013.6512319

12. Mohan, A., Binu, V.P.: Quality improvement in color extended visual cryptography using ABM and PRWP. In: International Conference on Data Mining and Advanced Computing (SAPIENCE). IEEE Xplore (2016) https://doi.org/10.1109/SAPIENCE.2016.7684159

13. Yan, B., Xiang, Y., Hua, G.: Improving the visual quality of size-invariant visual cryptography for grayscale images. An analysis-by-synthesis (AbS) approach. IEEE Trans. Image Process. **28**(2) (2019). https://doi.org/10.1109/tip.2018.2874378

14. Yan, B., et al.: Size-invariant extended visual cryptography with embedded watermark based on error diffusion. Multimed. Tools Appl. **75**(18), 11157–11180 (2016)

15. Singh, P., Raman, B., Misra, M.: A (n, n) threshold non-expansible XOR based visual cryptography with unique meaningful shares. Sig. Process. **142**, 301–319 (2018)

16. Ou, D., Sun, W., Wu, X.: Non-expansible XOR-based visual cryptography scheme with meaningful shares. Sig. Process. **108**, 604–621 (2015). https://doi.org/10.1016/j.sigpro.2014.10.011

17. Sharma, R., Agrawal, N.K., Khare, A., Pal, A.K.: An improved size invariant n, n extended visual cryptography scheme. Int. J. Bus. Data Commun. Netw. **12**(2), 80–88 (2016)

A New High Capacity and Reversible Data Hiding Technique for Images

Eram Fatima(ID) and Saiful Islam(✉)(ID)

Department of Computer Engineering,
Zakir Husain College of Engineering and Technology,
Aligarh Muslim University, Aligarh 202002, UP, India
{eramfatima,saifulislam}@zhcet.ac.in

Abstract. The growth in the internet has paved the way for an increase in digital communication. Cryptography and data hiding provide security of the data being communicated. In cryptography, the fact that the information is hidden is not concealed, whereas, in data hiding, it is hard to tell if a cover media contains embedded information. Data hiding can be used for covert communication, or to embed extra information about the image. Often the original cover image cannot be restored once the embedded data has been extracted. However, for certain applications like those belonging to medical and military, the data hiding process cannot distort the cover image. Medical images contain important diagnostic information, and military images serve some legal purpose. Any change in these images can lead to negative consequences. Therefore, a data hiding mechanism is needed for applications in which both the image as well as the data being hidden are important to hide data in such a way which will enable the extraction of embedded data and also restore the original image. Reversible data hiding (RDH) techniques have been proposed to embed data in such sensitive images. In this paper, we discuss a histogram shifting based two pass RDH scheme. Experimental results illustrate that the proposed technique, other than being reversible provides fairly high quality marked image along with high embedding capacity.

Keywords: Reversible data hiding · Histogram modification · Image blocks

1 Introduction

Covert/secret communication has been around for as long as communication. Its first application can be traced back to Greeks when a famous Greek tyrant, Histiaeus, used the head of his most trusted servant to write the message by first shaving his head, then writing the message and waiting for the hair to come back before sending him to his son-in-law. Invisible inks have always been used as a common tool for hidden communication. The onset of computer age gave rise to new applications of secret communication, and as a result, many new information hiding techniques were developed [1].

© Springer Nature Switzerland AG 2019
D. Garg et al. (Eds.): ICISS 2019, LNCS 11952, pp. 290–304, 2019.
https://doi.org/10.1007/978-3-030-36945-3_16

Data hiding helps in secure communication just like cryptography, but in data hiding an innocent looking cover image is used to carry the information and the fact that the cover image contains secret data is concealed, whereas cryptography changes the structure of the message and the presence of secret data is known.

Often doctors need to share the status of their patients' health with other experts; for this, they need to send the images along with the reports. The report may contain information that is personal to a patient; therefore, there should be a way to communicate both the report and the images in a secure manner [2,3]. This can be done by embedding the report in the image by a process known as data hiding. Traditional data hiding methods often distort the cover image. However, in certain applications, like medical and military, the cover image contains important information, and even minor distortion can lead to negative consequences. Therefore, to embed information in sensitive images, reversible data hiding (RDH) was proposed. In RDH, along with embedded information, the exact cover image is also restored. Embedding the information in images eliminates the need to store it separately, thereby reduces memory requirement. Embedding the information in the media also makes it safe for transmission. Another application of RDH can be to embed metadata into a cover image such that the original cover image is easily restored once the metadata has been extracted.

Barton was the first to propose a reversible data hiding algorithm in a 1997 US patent [4]. In his technique, authentication information is embedded in a cover medium, and only authorized users were able to obtain the embedded information and verify the authenticity of the received medium.

RDH techniques consist of two stages, embedding and extraction stages, as shown in Fig. 1. In the first stage, secret information is hidden in a cover media at the sender side. The media containing embedded information is known as stego file. Then in the second stage, the embedded data is extracted, and the original cover media is restored.

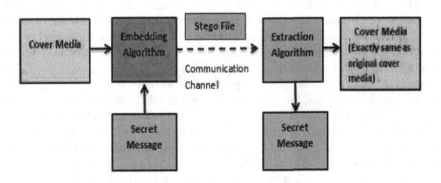

Fig. 1. Overview of RDH system.

Watermarking is another application of data hiding in which a watermark (image or information) is embedded in the cover media. Watermarks can be used for fraud detection, copyright protection, and image authentication [5,6]. In the case of physical documents and artworks, like paintings, authenticity can be verified by sophisticated techniques. A digital document, on the other hand, is a collection of bits and a perceptible watermark in the corner of the image can be easily altered. Even the details stored in the header of an image can be modified or removed. Therefore to provide authenticity to digital documents/images, the watermark cannot be just appended. Watermarking proves to be a better alternative in this situation since in watermarking the information is not appended but embedded directly into the image. The embedded information will be imperceptible to the human eye and will only be available through an extraction algorithm along with a secret key.

Current RDH techniques can be categorized into transform domain and spatial domain methods. In methods belonging to the spatial domain, data is embedded by altering the pixel values [7–9].

Most popular RDH techniques in the spatial domain are difference expansion (DE) based schemes and histogram shifting based schemes. Both methods have their advantages and disadvantages, methods belonging to the former kind can provide a higher capacity while the ones in latter are known to produce a better quality embedded image.

The DE-based technique was introduced by Tian [7] and he proposed to embed the data by expanding the difference between adjacent pixels. Ni et al. [10] were the first to propose the histogram shifting based scheme, in which, they have first shifted the histogram bins between the peak point and the zero point and then used the peak point to embed the data. Their technique was able to give a good quality marked image, but the embedding capacity was low, and the values of peak and zero points have to be transmitted to the receiver for successful retrieval of the embedded data and to restore the image. Lee et al. [11] further extended the technique by proposing to use the difference histogram as it was sharper. Tai et al. [12] further tried to solve the problem of sharing multiple peak points with the receiver by using a binary tree structure in which the number of elements at a particular level of the tree determines the number of peak points used. In this case, the sender only has to transmit the level of the tree used during data embedding. Pan et al. [13] proposed a histogram shifting based technique which eliminates the overhead of transmitting peak points to the receiver. They do this by using peak point as a reference and embedding data in neighboring bins. Since the peak is not used for embedding, it can be easily located at the receiver side, and data can be efficiently retrieved.

Multilevel histogram modification was introduced to utilize block redundancy. Zhao et al. [14] calculated the difference of adjacent pixels by scanning the image in an inverse "S" order. Fu et al. [15] used prediction error histogram to increase the concentration of differences near zero. He et al. [16] were able to improve the PSNR of the marked image by reducing the number of to be shifted pixels. In this paper, we propose a novel two-pass multilevel histogram modification based RDH technique. In this scheme, we embed the data by using minimum and maximum gray values of a block as reference points in the first and second pass, respectively. In the first pass, we take the minimum gray value of the block as a reference point, so the histogram is shifted to the left, and in the second pass when we embed using the pixel with the maximum gray level in the block, the histogram is shifted to the right. All the histogram bins which were only shifted to make space for embedding in the first pass and were not used for embedding are shifted back to their original values in the second pass. Therefore, only the pixels which are used for embedding data are altered, and the rest of the pixels remain the same. This helps to maintain the quality of the marked image.

The rest of the paper is outlined as follows. In Sect. 2 we have briefly described W. He et al.'s scheme. Section 3 deals with the proposed scheme in detail. Section 4 describes experimental results and discussions followed by Sect. 5 which concludes the paper along with directions to future work.

2   Multilevel Histogram Modification

In this section we have described multilevel histogram modification with the help of W. He et al.'s technique [16].

2.1   W. He et al.'s Scheme

They have proposed the concept of pixel value grouping, using which the pixel values of all blocks are first put in a group, according to their distribution and then reference pixels are obtained. Based on the status of the pixel value grouping, the blocks are classified into four categories and have used multilevel histogram modification of the difference histogram of blocks to embed data. The difference of reference pixels and the rest of the pixels in a group are calculated using Eq. (1) and a difference histogram is generated.

$$d_k = p_k - p_{ref} \tag{1}$$

After generating the differences, a difference histogram is constructed, and its bins are emptied before data embedding using the following equation

$$d_k^w = \begin{cases} d_k + (EL + 1), \text{if } d_k > EL \\ d_k + (EL + 1), \text{if } d_k < -EL \end{cases} \tag{2}$$

After this, the data is embedded in the histogram bins by repeating Eqs. (2, 3) for L = EL, EL − 1, ... , 0

$$d_k^w = \begin{cases} d_k + (L + w), \text{if } d_k = L \\ d_k - (L + w), \text{if } d_k = -L \end{cases} \tag{3}$$

Figure 2 illustrates the difference histogram modification for $EL = 2$

3   Proposed Work

In this section, we describe a novel two-pass multilevel histogram modification based RDH technique. RDH is carried out in two steps; the embedding step and extraction step. The embedding step comprises scanning an image block twice. In the first pass, secret bits are embedded by considering the minimum gray value of a block as a reference, and in the second pass, bits are embedded by taking the maximum gray value of the block as a reference. Since lesser pixels are associated with the min and max gray values, using them instead of using peak as reference wastes fewer pixels since the pixels associated with the reference gray value are not used for embedding. Since the min and max of a block do not change after embedding, they can be easily obtained at the decoding end.

3.1   Embedding Process

w is taken to as the data which is to be embedded and for our experiments we have taken it to be a pseudorandom sequence of bits. The data is embedded by processing and then modifying the histograms of all the blocks of an image.

Step 1: Divide the image. Partition the image I, into $m \times n$ sized blocks.
Step 2: Generate histogram.

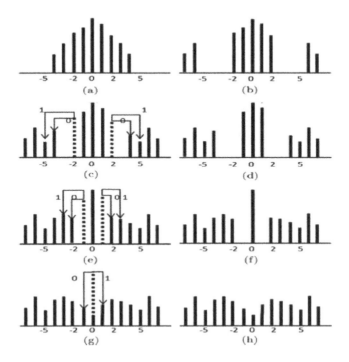

Fig. 2. Difference histogram modification for $EL = 2$.

Step 3: Find the minimum. Find the minimum gray value (the left-most bin of the histogram) of the block and assign it to min. This value will be used as a reference for data embedding.

Step 4: Empty histogram bins. Depending on the embedding level EL), histogram bins are shifted to the left by EL to make space for embedding.

$$E(i,j) = I(i,j) + EL \quad \text{if } I(i,j) - min > EL \tag{4}$$

where I(i, j) describes grayscale value of the pixel in the original image at position (i, j) and E(i, j) describes the value of the pixel at position (i, j) of the embedded image.

Step 5: Data Embedding. Bins adjacent to min are used to embed data by using Eq. (5). The number of bins used will be equal to EL.

$$E(i,j) = I(i,j) + (I(i,j) - min) - w \quad \text{if } I(i,j) - min \le EL \tag{5}$$

where E(i, j) is the pixel value obtained after embedding data using min as reference.

Once data has been embedded in all the blocks, the obtained image is again divided into $m \times n$ sized blocks. In the next pass of embedding, we take the maximum value (the right-most bin of the histogram) of a block as a reference.

Step 6: Empty bins by shifting histogram to the right to create space for embedding using the following equation,

$$E_n(i,j) = E(i,j) - EL \quad \text{if } E(i,j) - max < -EL \tag{6}$$

Step 7: Bins adjacent to max are used to embed data by using Eq. (7). The number of bins used will be equal to EL.

$$E_n(i,j) = E(i,j) - (E(i,j) - max) - w \quad \text{if } E(i,j) - max \ge -EL \tag{7}$$

where $E_n(i,j)$ denotes the final embedded image.

3.2 Example

Let $w =$ "1001010" be the data to be embedded. Figure 3 explains all the steps that are carried out to embed data using min as reference (for $EL = 2$). The pixels in the block are traversed in raster scan order. All the pixel values which are modified at each step have been shaded. All the image blocks are scanned again, and data is embedded using maximum (max = 167) gray value of the block as a reference. Let $w =$ "0101" be the data to be embedded. The final embedded block, along with the histogram, is illustrated in Fig. 4.

3.3 Extraction Process

The data extraction and image recovery process is inverse of the data embedding process and comprises of the steps as described below.

161	161	163	163
160	160	163	164
161	161	160	165
162	162	161	165

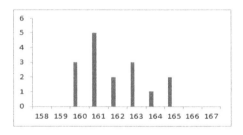

(a) Block of image Lena and its corresponding histogram.

161	161	*165*	*165*
160	160	*165*	*166*
161	161	160	*167*
162	162	161	*167*

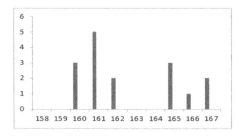

(b) Two bins (163 and 164) are emptied by shifting bins to the right by 2 (since EL=2). The shaded blocks contain the values which had to be incremented to make space for embedding.

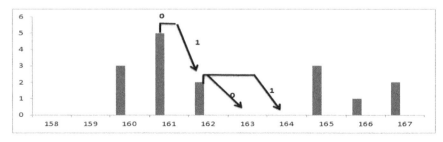

(c) Embedding data in the emptied bins. Arrows point to the value into which a specific value changes after being embedded by a data bit specified on the arrow.

161	*162*	165	165
160	160	165	166
162	*161*	160	167
164	*163*	*162*	167

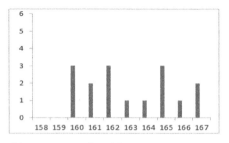

(d) Block after embedding and its corresponding histogram.

Fig. 3. Embedding data using min as reference.

159	160	*163*	*164*
158	158	*163*	*166*
160	159	158	167
162	161	160	167

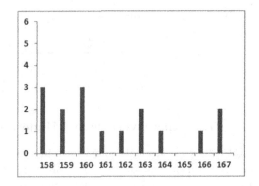

Fig. 4. Final embedded block and its corresponding histogram.

Step 1: Divide the image. Partition the image I, into $m \times n$ sized blocks.

Step 2: Generate histogram.

Step 3: Find the maximum. Since in the final marked image max was used as a reference, the maximum gray values of the block are not altered and can be easily obtained at the decoder side.

Step 4: Extract the secret bits. If $abs(E_n(i, j) - max \geq -2 * EL)$

$$w = \begin{cases} 0, \text{if } abs(E_n(i, j) - max) = even \\ 1, \text{otherwise} \end{cases} \qquad (8)$$

Step 5: Restore the image as,

$$E(i, j) = E_n(i, j) + floor(\frac{abs(E_n(i, j) - max)}{2}) \quad \text{if } E_n(i, j) - max \geq -2 * EL \quad (9)$$

$$E(i, j) = E_n(i, j) + EL \quad \text{if } E_n(i, j) < -2 * EL \qquad (10)$$

Once the data embedded using max as reference have been extracted, and the image has been restored, the value of min can be obtained with the help of which the data embedded by using min as reference are extracted, and image restoration is done to get back original cover image.

Following equations are applied on all the blocks to obtain the original image.

Step 6: Divide the image. Partition the image I, into mxn sized blocks.

Step 7: Generate histogram.

Step 8: Find the minimum. Obtain the minimum gray value of the block and use it as a reference to extract the data and restore the image.

Step 9: Extract the secret bits.
   If $abs(E(i, j) - min \leq 2 * EL)$

$$w = \begin{cases} 0, \text{if } abs(E(i, j) - min) = even \\ 1, \text{otherwise} \end{cases} \qquad (11)$$

Step10: Restore the image as,

$$I(i,j) = E(i,j) - floor(\frac{abs(E(i,j) - min)}{2}) \quad \text{if } E(i,j) - min \leq 2*EL \quad (12)$$

$$I(i,j) = E(i,j) - EL \quad \text{if } E(i,j) > 2*EL \quad (13)$$

3.4   Preventing Overflow and Underflow

Pixel values in grayscale images are in the range of 0 to 255. During histogram modification, it is possible to get values out of this range. Therefore, the blocks that contain pixel values which on modification will give values out of the range have to be skipped. In the proposed method, all the blocks with pixel values greater than 255-EL and less than EL have been skipped to prevent over/underflow. We have used a location map to record all the blocks that have not been used for data embedding.

The data embedding process is described below:

Step 1: Partition the image.

Step 2: Construct location map. Scan the blocks, and for any block Bi containing a value greater than 255-EL or less than EL set $LM(i)$ as 1, otherwise set $LM(i)$ as 0. The location map is losslessly compressed using run-length encoding.

Step 3: Embed secret data. Embed the secret data bits and store the position of the last data carrying block (denoted as $Pend$).

Step 4: Embed auxiliary information and location map. Select the first few pixels of the image in a random order and record the least significant bits of first $14 + 2\lceil log_2 N \rceil + Lclm$ image pixels (denoted as $Slsb$), where $Lclm$ is the length of the compressed location map. Auxiliary information and the $Lclm$ are embedded by replacing these LSBs. Auxiliary information consists of
- block size m (4 bits) and n (4 bits)
- embedding level EL (6 bits),
- end position $Pend$ ($\lceil log_2 N \rceil$ bits)
- length of compressed location map $Lclm$ ($\lceil log_2 N \rceil$ bits)

The binary sequence $Slsb$ is finally embedded in the rest of the blocks to obtain the embedded image.

The random order in which the pixels are selected is generated using a key. Using the key, the same random order can be generated at the decoding end. The pixel value at the first position of the image is used as the key in our experiments. At the decoding end, the first few LSBs of the marked image are first retrieved to get the auxiliary information and the location map. The compressed location map is then losslessly decompressed to generate the location map. After that, we extract the recorded LSB ($Slsb$) and replace the LSB of the first few pixel values with these LSB, then the secret data is extracted, and finally, the image is restored.

4   Experimental Results and Discussions

In this section, we describe the results of evaluating our technique based on embedding capacity and quality of the image obtained after embedding.

The size of all the images used to test this scheme was 512×512 and were downloaded from the USC-SIPI image database. All the images are shown in Fig. 5.

4.1   Embedding Capacity and Quality of Embedded Image

Embedding capacity (EC) provides a measure of the amount of data (pure payload) that can be hidden in an image. Another factor used to measure the performance is the quality of the embedded image. Quality can be measured by calculating the PSNR of the embedded image and original image. Schemes which obtain higher PSNR with the same embedding capacity are considered to be better.

In our scheme, we have used a random binary sequence as the data to be embedded. The sequence was obtained by the pre-defined function, randi() in MATLAB. From Fig. 6, it is evident that block size effects embedding performance. It is observed that PSNR is high for larger block sizes and when EL is not high. However, the maximum EC for larger sized blocks is lower. After carrying out the experiment for various block sizes, it was found that maximum EC was obtained for a block size of 4×4.

We have also tested our algorithm on the BOSSbase dataset. We were able to successfully embed and extract data as well as restore the original images for 9,841 images out of 10,000 images. The contrast of the rest of the 159 images was very low, which increased the size of the location map. Due to the lesser number of embeddable pixels in these low contrast images, the location map could not be embedded.

4.2   Comparison with Other Schemes

Table 1 compares the results obtained by our scheme and W. He et al.'s. For 4×4 block size, we have calculated the maximum embedding capacity and PSNR for each EL.

From Table 1 we can see that our scheme provides better PSNR for the same EC. For example, in case of image Boat for $EL = 1$, EC for both the schemes is same (0.06), but our scheme provides better PSNR (55.54) as compared to W. He et al.'s PSNR (50.13). Even for higher EL, for example in image Elaine when $EL = 5$, the EC provided by both the schemes is same, but our scheme provides a PSNR of 40.29 whereas W. He et al.'s scheme provides a PSNR of 39.59.

For larger EL, a greater number of bins are used for embedding, and only very few, and sometimes even none of the bins are to-be-shifted bins. In such cases, all the pixel values are modified because all bins are used to carry data. Our scheme maintains PSNR by eliminating the shift caused in the to-be-shifted bins (which are only shifted to make space for embedding and are not used for

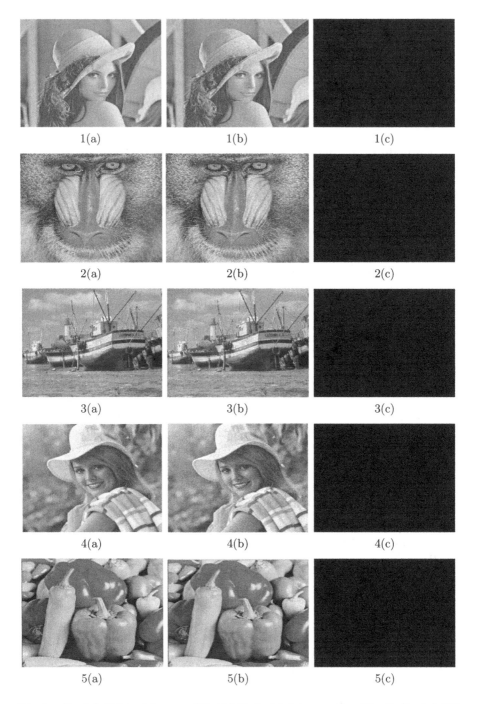

1(a)   1(b)   1(c)

2(a)   2(b)   2(c)

3(a)   3(b)   3(c)

4(a)   4(b)   4(c)

5(a)   5(b)   5(c)

Fig. 5. (1a–5a) Original images, (1b–5b) Embedded images for $EL = 9$, (1c–5c) Difference of original and restored images.

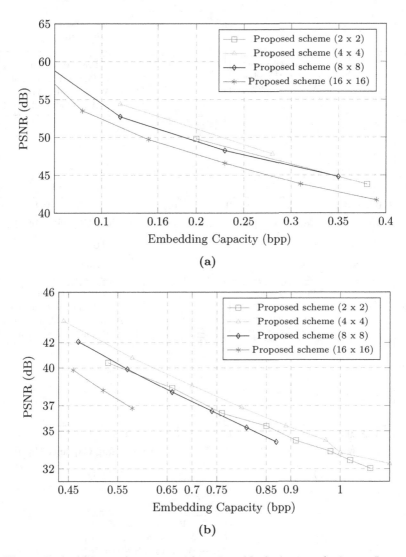

Fig. 6. Embedding performance with various block sizes on the image Lena.

embedding). Therefore, the PSNR is lower for higher *EL*. This is a limitation of our scheme.

Comparison of our scheme with various other schemes [13,16,17] has been illustrated in Fig. 7.

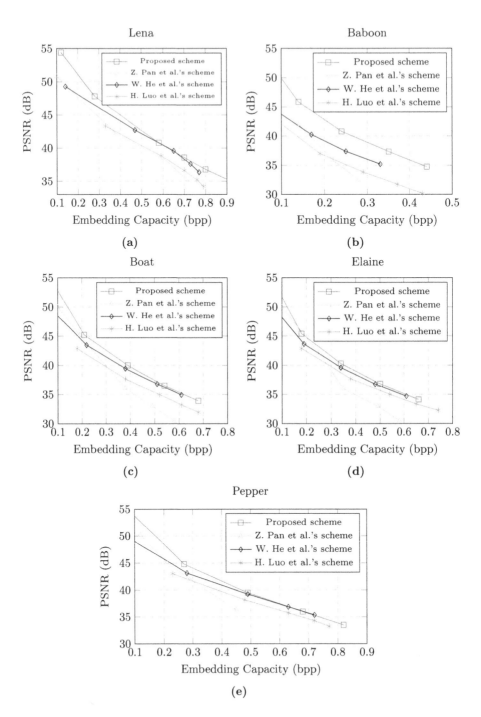

Fig. 7. Performance comparison with other schemes.

Table 1. Comparison with W. He et al.'s scheme.

Image	Scheme	EL = 1		EL = 3		EL = 5		EL = 7		EL = 9	
		EC	PSNR	EC	PSNR	EC	PSNR	EC	PSNR	EC	PSNR
Lena	Proposed	0.12	54.42	0.44	43.7	0.7	38.58	0.89	35.44	1.04	33.27
	W. He et al.	0.14	49.27	0.47	42.71	0.65	39.56	0.73	37.61	0.77	36.3
Baboon	Proposed	0.04	56	0.13	45.87	0.24	40.8	0.34	37.35	0.44	34.76
	W. He et al.	0.03	50.65	0.09	44.23	0.17	40.25	0.25	37.38	0.33	35.2
Boat	Proposed	0.06	55.54	0.21	45.22	0.39	40	0.54	36.49	0.68	33.91
	W. He et al.	0.06	50.13	0.22	43.47	0.38	39.45	0.51	36.79	0.61	34.93
Elaine	Proposed	0.05	55.67	0.18	45.41	0.34	40.29	0.5	36.79	0.66	34.12
	W. He et al.	0.06	50.21	0.19	43.64	0.34	39.59	0.48	36.74	0.61	34.69
Pepper	Proposed	0.07	55.32	0.27	44.81	0.49	39.46	0.68	35.95	0.82	33.49
	W. He et al.	0.07	49.97	0.28	43.14	0.49	39.2	0.63	36.83	0.72	35.34

5   Time Complexity Analysis

The time complexity of our algorithm is $O(n)$ for finding the reference pixel (max and min) and the algorithm proposed by W. He et al. has the highest time complexity of $O(n^2)$ since they employ sorting of pixel values.

6   Conclusions and Future Work

In this paper, we have put forward a new multilevel histogram shifting based method for RDH. The performance of the proposed scheme has been compared with many other histogram shifting based RDH techniques. The results of the comparison prove that our scheme performs better in most of the cases.

The need to communicate min and max points (which was a requirement in Ni et al.'s work) has been eliminated by using reference points which can be easily obtained at the decoding end. The proposed scheme provides high embedding capacity along with the good quality of the embedded image. At the decoding end, the exact data which was embedded at the sender's side was fully extracted, and the original cover image was restored for all the test images.

One limitation of our work is that the PSNR of the embedded image degrades for higher *EL*. One future direction would be to overcome this demerit. The proposed technique can also be further enhanced to be applied to other types of media, such as audio and video.

References

1. Kumar, C., Singh, A.K., Kumar, P.: A recent survey on image watermarking techniques and its application in e-governance. Multimed. Tools Appl. **77**(3), 3597–3622 (2018)
2. Islam, S., Das, A., Gupta, S., Gupta, P.: Data hiding in medical images. J. Comput. **9**(3) (2014). https://doi.org/10.4304/jcp.9.3.513-518

3. Liu, Y., Qu, X., Xin, G.: A ROI-based reversible data hiding scheme in encrypted medical images. J. Vis. Commun. Image Represent. **39**, 51–57 (2016)
4. Barton, J.M.: Method and apparatus for embedding authentication information within digital data, 8 July 1997. US Patent 5,646,997
5. Prathap, I., Natarajan, V., Anitha, R.: Hybrid robust watermarking for color images. Comput. Electr. Eng. **40**(3), 920–930 (2014). https://doi.org/10.1016/j.compeleceng.2014.01.006
6. Parah, S.A., Ahad, F., Sheikh, J.A., Bhat, G.M.: Hiding clinical information in medical images: a new high capacity and reversible data hiding technique. J. Biomed. Inform. **66**, 214–230 (2017)
7. Tian, J.: Reversible data embedding using a difference expansion. IEEE Trans. Circuits Syst. Video Technol. **13**(8), 890–896 (2003)
8. Peng, F., Li, X., Yang, B.: Improved PVO-based reversible data hiding. Digit. Sig. Process. **25**, 255–265 (2014). https://doi.org/10.1016/j.dsp.2013.11.002
9. Qu, X., Kim, H.J.: Pixel-based pixel value ordering predictor for high-fidelity reversible data hiding. Sig. Process. **111**, 249–260 (2015). https://doi.org/10.1016/j.sigpro.2015.01.002
10. Ni, Z., Shi, Y., Ansari, N., Su, W.: Reversible data hiding. IEEE Trans. Circuits Syst. Video Technol. **16**, 354–362 (2006)
11. Lee, S.K., Suh, Y.H., Ho, Y.S.: Reversiblee image authentication based on watermarking. In: 2006 IEEE International Conference on Multimedia and Expo, pp. 1321–1324. IEEE (2006)
12. Tai, W.L., Yeh, C.M., Chang, C.C.: Reversible data hiding based on histogram modification of pixel differences. IEEE Trans. Circuits Syst. Video Technol. **19**(6), 906–910 (2009). https://doi.org/10.1109/tcsvt.2009.2017409
13. Pan, Z., Hu, S., Ma, X., Wang, L.: Reversible data hiding based on local histogram shifting with multilayer embedding. J. Vis. Commun. Image Represent. **31**, 64–74 (2015). https://doi.org/10.1016/j.jvcir.2015.05.005
14. Zhao, Z., Luo, H., Lu, Z.M., Pan, J.S.: Reversible data hiding based on multilevel histogram modification and sequential recovery. AEU - Int. J. Electron. Commun. **65**(10), 814–826 (2011)
15. Fu, D.S., Jing, Z.J., Zhao, S.G., Fan, J.: Reversible data hiding based on prediction-error histogram shifting and EMD mechanism. AEU - Int. J. Electron. Commun. **68**(10), 933–943 (2014). https://doi.org/10.1016/j.aeue.2014.04.015
16. He, W., Xiong, G., Zhou, K., Cai, J.: Reversible data hiding based on multilevel histogram modification and pixel value grouping. J. Vis. Commun. Image Represent. **40**, 459–469 (2016)
17. Luo, H., Yu, F.X., Chen, H., Huang, Z.L., Li, H., Wang, P.H.: Reversible data hiding based on block median preservation. Inf. Sci. **181**(2), 308–328 (2011)

Miscellaneous Mix

Anti-forensics of a NAD-JPEG Detection Scheme Using Estimation of DC Coefficients

Arkaprava Bhaduri Mandal$^{(\boxtimes)}$ and Tanmoy Kanti Das

Department of Computer Applications,
National Institute of Technology, Raipur,
G.E. Road, Raipur 492010, Chhattisgarh, India
{abmandal.phd2017.ca,tkdas.mca}@nitrr.ac.in

Abstract. Bianchi et al. proposed a method to detect the non-aligned double JPEG (NAD-JPEG) compression using the presence of distortions in the Integer Periodicity Map (IPM) of DC coefficients of any JPEG image. However, we found that the IPM can be easily altered without affecting the visual quality of an image. In this paper, we propose a new anti-forensics scheme that alters the IPM to deceive the Bianchi et al. scheme. In our proposed method, a statistical model of the DC coefficients from singly compressed JPEG image is used to generate an estimated image which is free from quantization artifacts that are present in the IPM. The estimated image is subjected to NAD-JPEG compression. It was found that the DC values of NAD-JPEG image are no longer be the multiples of the corresponding primary quantization step size q_1. As a result, the DCT coefficients do not cluster around the lattice related to the q_1 and the IPM of the double JPEG compressed image seems to be the IPM of a singly compressed JPEG image. Experimental results show the effectiveness of the proposed anti-forensics scheme as the accuracy of the said forensics method get reduced to less than 50% in case of anti-forensically modified images.

Keywords: Double JPEG compression detection · Anti-forensics · Approximation of DC coefficients

1 Introduction

Creation and distribution of digital images became very easy after the introduction of social media in the last decade. Some of these images are found to be forged and used to create social and financial disturbances. Automatic detection of forged images was an issue that required immediate attention. Consequently, many detection schemes [14, 21, 22] are currently available in the existing literature and some of them even got deployed in the live systems [7]. These schemes

This work is supported by Ministry of Electronics and Information Technology, Govt. of India; grant no "12(1)/2017-CSRD".

may work as expected when the forgers are seemingly unaware of the basic image processing and forensics techniques. However, if the forgers are technically qualified and possess advanced knowledge of signal and image processing, they may be able to conceal their footprints without being caught. Thus, there is an urgent need to analyze each of the available forensics schemes from security and robustness perspective. Here, we propose a counter forensics scheme to analyze the robustness of any forensics scheme which is dependent on the statistical property of the DC coefficients for the detection of prior JPEG compression.

Most of the existing forensics techniques for detection of prior JPEG compression work with AC components of DCT coefficients and some schemes even work in the spatial domain. One such scheme was proposed in [6] by Fan et al. in 2003. They have used the presence of blocking artifact to determine whether an image underwent JPEG compression previously or not. They have also developed techniques to estimate the quantization table if an image found to be JPEG compressed previously. A counter forensics method to evade the detection by Fan et al. scheme was proposed in [18]. Stamm et al. identified the changes (a.k.a. distortion) occurred in the distribution of DCT coefficients of a JPEG image due to compression and a method to remove those distortions was proposed to highlight the weakness of the Fan et al. forensics scheme.

A generic counter forensics scheme, which can neutralize several distortions, has been proposed in [5]. It consists of four major steps having three distinct processes. At first, the input image J is subjected to a total variation based *deblocking* procedure in the spatial domain to remove the blocking artifacts that were produced by JPEG compression. The deblocked image J_B is further subjected to a DCT *histogram smoothing* to remove the discontinuities in the DCT histogram to generate J_{BS}. Though the quantization artifacts got removed in the last step, some additional noise has also been introduced in the generated image. Thus to remove the noise, total variation based deblocking procedure is used again on the J_{BS} to get J_{BSB}. Finally, *decalibration* operation is used on J_{BSB} to produce the attacked image J'. An improvised version of Fan et al. scheme has been proposed in [17].

It is well known that any image processing operation leaves behind a trail of signatures on the image and counter forensics schemes are not an exception. Lai et al. [9] was able to identify the traces left behind by Stamm et al. [18] counter forensics scheme which lead to the development of more robust forensics schemes. They have used the presence of a high number of zero-valued DCT coefficients in any JPEG image for detection of prior JPEG compression. In a similar direction, they have also used the calibrated feature to identify the traces left behind by JPEG compression. A generic anti-forensics scheme to evade detection by any forensics scheme that utilizes the presence of distortions in AC coefficients has been presented in [4].

The presence of signatures related to double JPEG compression in an image is the clearest indication that the image underwent some kind of manipulation. Thus, the detection of double JPEG compression received lots of attention in recent times [12,13,15,19]. Lukáš et al. [11] used the presence of double peak and missing values in the DCT coefficients to determine whether an image subjected to double JPEG compression or not. In a similar direction, Huang et al. [8] proposed a method to detect the double JPEG compression by comparing the number of different DCT coefficients between two successive compressions of the same image. An anti-forensics technique to evade the detection by the said method has been proposed in [10]. Note that, the use of anti-forensics method may also introduce unwanted signals in an image which may reveal the maliciousness of the anti-forensically modified image. Thus, a forger must balance three conflicting requirements, i.e. balance the tradeoffs between concealability-rate-distortion in any anti-forensics of JPEG compression to remain undetectable [2].

In this paper, we study a well-known algorithm for double JPEG compression detection from security and robustness perspective. Most of the existing forensics schemes assume that the forgers neither possess the knowledge of signal and image processing nor aware of the existence of forensics (or anti-forensics) schemes. Here we adopt the principles from cryptography and assume that the forgers are aware of the algorithmic aspects of forensic detection methods. It is well known that the integer periodicity of DCT coefficients exhibit different characteristics when the underlying image is subjected to single or double JPEG compression. This property was subtly used by Bianchi et al. in their detection scheme. However, we could show that the integer periodicity is not unique and it can be modified without much loss in visual quality of an image. In the following section, we propose a method through which one can change the integer periodicity of a JPEG image without any significant loss in image quality and evade the detection by Bianchi et al. scheme. Our analysis raises the serious question regarding the forensics paradigm based on statistical distortion.

The remainder of this paper is organized as follows. Section 2 briefly reviews the existing NAD-JPEG detection scheme proposed by Bianchi et al. [1] for forensics analysis. The proposed anti-forensics scheme along with the algorithm is illustrated in Sect. 3. Section 4 presents the analysis of the experimental results to evaluate the efficacy of our proposed algorithm. Finally, the concluding remarks are drawn in Sect. 5.

2   NAD-JPEG Detection Scheme of [1]

Nowadays, JPEG is by far the most popular image compression format used to store the captured image and any post-processing of these images may give rise to the double JPEG compression. Majority of these double compression cases are NAD-JPEG where blocking grid of the second compression is not aligned to the corresponding grid of the first compression. It is well understood that the existence of a NAD-JPEG points to a situation where the authenticity of the image can be seriously questioned. One of the popular schemes to detect NAD-JPEG compression was proposed in [1] where authors studied the statistical properties of DCT coefficients from original, singly and doubly compressed JPEG images. Let us denote the original uncompressed image in the spatial domain as I^0 and the corresponding singly compressed JPEG image as I^1 in the spatial domain. Thus I^1 can be expressed as

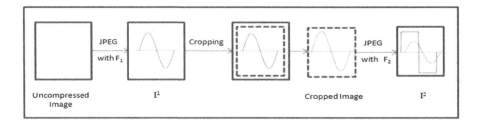

Fig. 1. Block diagram of a typical forging process.

$$I^1 = D^{-1}(Q_{F_1}^{-1}(Q_{F_1}(D(I^0)))) + E_1 \qquad (1)$$

Here, $D(.), D^{-1}(.)$ represent the process of block-based discrete cosine transform and inverse discrete cosine transform respectively. Similarly, $Q(.), Q^{-1}(.)$ represent the quantization and de-quantization process respectively. E_1 is the error introduced by rounding and truncation of pixel values to nearest 8-bit integers. Now we can express the doubly compressed JPEG image as

$$\begin{aligned} I^2 &= D^{-1}(Q_{F_2}^{-1}(Q_{F_2}(D(S_{y,x}(I^1))))) + E_2 \\ &= D^{-1}(Q_{F_2}^{-1}(Q_{F_2}(D(S_{y,x}(D^{-1}(Q_{F_1}^{-1}(Q_{F_1}(D(I^0)))) \\ &\quad + E_1))))) + E_2 \end{aligned} \qquad (2)$$

Here $S_{y,x}(.)$ denotes the process of grid shifting by y rows and x columns. If the grid is aligned with the previous compression then we have the values of x, y as multiples of 8, including zero. All other values of y, x lead to the creation of a non-aligned double JPEG compressed image.

If we consider only the DC coefficients from each block of the image I^2, then the DC coefficients will cluster around two different lattices corresponding to quantization step size q_1, q_2. Here, quantization step size q_1 (q_2) corresponds to quality factor $F_1(F_2)$ of first (second) JPEG compression. The basic idea behind the Bianchi et al. [1] forensics algorithm is that of detecting the presence of these clusters for all possible grid shifts using the concept of integer periodicity map (IPM).

Let us now apply grid shift $S_{i,j}(.)$ on (I^2) in the spatial domain and perform a block-based DCT afterward. Now three possible scenarios arise : (a) the grid is completely aligned with the grid of the second compression, i.e., $i = j = 0$ (b) grid is completely aligned with the grid of the first compression, i.e., $i = y, j = x$ (c) all other cases. The periodicity of DCT coefficients will be different for three different cases and let us now concentrate only on the DC coefficients for further analysis. The clustering of DC coefficients around the lattice can be measured by the periodicity of the computed histogram of DC coefficients. Bianchi et al. employed the Fourier transform to measure the periodicity of the histogram at frequencies which is reciprocal of quantization step size q and the values are given by

$$\nu_{ij}(q) \triangleq \sum_l \eta_{ij}(l)e^{-j\frac{2\pi l}{q}}, q \in \mathbb{N} \tag{3}$$

where η_{ij} is the histogram of DC coefficients when the grid shift applied to I^2 is (i,j).

When the image I^2 is already a NAD-JPEG image having grid shifted by (y,x), the absolute values of $\nu_{00}(q_2)$ and $\nu_{yx}(q_1)$ should be considerably higher than other values. Here q_1 and q_2 is the quantization step size of DC coefficients in first and second JPEG compression respectively. In the absence of NAD-JPEG, only one peak will be observed at $\nu_{00}(q_2)$. These observations lead to the development of IPM to analyze the characteristics of $\nu_{ij}(q)$ and the IPM for quantization step size q is defined as

$$\mu_{ij}(q) \triangleq \frac{|\nu_{ij}(q)|}{\sum_{i'j'}|\nu_{i'j'}(q)|}, 0 \le i, i' \le 7, \ 0 \le j, j' \le 7 \tag{4}$$

It is quite obvious that the magnitude of $\mu_{00}(q_2)$ and $\mu_{yx}(q_1)$ will be substantially higher than any other values of $\mu_{ij}(q)$ in the presence of NAD-JPEG. Presence of peak can be measured from the min-entropy of $\mu_{ij}(q)$ as the presence of a peak is associated with low min-entropy, for e.g., if min-entropy $H_\infty(q)$ is less than threshold T_1, it indicates the presence of a peak. However, the value of q_1 is not available and we need to check all possible values of q to find out the value of q_1. In fact, any value of $q(\ne q_2)$ indicating the presence of a peak is assumed as the value of q_1.

The previous strategy for identification of NAD-JPEG is effective only when the quantization step size q_1 and q_2 is different. However, when $q = q_1 = q_2$ it may not be possible to identify the presence of first JPEG compression clearly due to the presence of two peaks. Even visual inspection of IPM may fail in certain cases. Authors overcame this problem by exploiting the property of $\mu_{ij}(q_2)$. It was observed that the $\mu_{ij}(q_2)$ is almost symmetric with respect to the point $\mu_{44}(q)$. This observation leads to the development of differential IPM or DIPM which is defined as follows.

$$\mu'_{ij}(q) \triangleq \frac{max(\mu_{ij}(q) - \Pi(\mu_{ij}(q)),0)}{\mathcal{K}} \tag{5}$$

Here $\Pi(\mu_{ij}(q)$ is the predicted value of μ_{ij} using the symmetric property of IPM. The $\mathcal{K}$ is constant such that the sum of DIPM is equal to 1. If the min-entropy of DIPM is less than the threshold, i.e., $H'_\infty(q) < T_2$, then we are confirmed about the presence of a peak. The NAD-JPEG Detection Algorithm considers three following scenarios in the detection process: (i) presence of NAD-JPEG where $q_1 \ne q_2$, (ii) presence of NAD-JPEG where $q_1 = q_2$, (iii) absence of NAD-JPEG. Here, the term absence means that the image is either singly JPEG compressed or doubly compressed with aligned grids. The pseudo code of the detection algorithm is as follows.

Algorithm 1. NAD-JPEG Detection Algorithm

Input: A JPEG image I^2

1: **for** $(i = 0; i \leq 7; i + +)$ **do**
2:    **for** $(j = 0; j \leq 7; j + +)$ **do**
3:        Compute DCT as $D(S_{i,j}(I^2))$.
4:        Compute the histogram η_{ij} of DC coefficients generated in the last step.
5:        **for** $(q = q_{min}; q \leq q_{max}; q + +)$ **do**
6:            Compute $\nu_{ij}(q)$.
7:        **end for**
8:    **end for**
9: **end for**

10: **for** $(q = q_{min}; q \leq q_{max}; q + +)$ **do**
11:    **for** $(i = 0; i \leq 7; i + +)$ **do**
12:        **for** $(j = 0; j \leq 7; j + +)$ **do**
13:            Compute $\mu_{ij}(q)$.
14:            **if** $q = q_2$ **then**
15:                Compute $\mu'_{ij}(q)$.
16:            **end if**
17:        **end for**
18:    **end for**
19:    Compute $H_\infty(q)$.
20:    **if** $(q = q_2)$ **then**
21:        Compute $H'_\infty(q)$.
22:    **end if**
23: **end for**

24: Select
25:    $H_\infty = min_q H_\infty(q)$.
26:    $q_1 = arg\ min_q H_\infty(q)$.
27:    $(y, x) = arg\ max_{i,j} \mu_{ij}(q_1)$, such that $(y, x) \neq (0, 0)$.

28: **if** $H_\infty < T_1$ **then**
29:    return NAD-JPEG, q_1, (y, x).
30: **else if** $H'_\infty(q_2) < T_2$ **then**
31:    return NAD-JPEG,q_2,$(y, x) = arg\ max_{(i,j)} \mu'_{ij}(q_2)$.
32: **else**
33:    return Non-NAD-JPEG.
34: **end if**

---

3   Proposed Anti-forensics Method

The success of the detection algorithm 1 depends on the preservation of the exact statistical nature of DCT values of both I^1 and I^2. Stamm et al. [18] demonstrated that it is not difficult to alter the distribution of AC coefficients by adding noise in the DCT domain of a JPEG image to fool the forensics detectors. However, they claimed that there is no good model to estimate the DC coefficients. Consequently, it is difficult to alter the statistical nature of

Original Image   Jpeg Image(F_1=54%)

Fig. 2. Source images (Uncompressed and Singly compressed JPEG)

Forged Image (F_2=72%)   Attacked Image (F_2=72%)

Fig. 3. Target images (Doubly compressed JPEG with F_1=54%)

DC coefficients. Thus, random noise was added to alter the nature of the DC coefficients in the first block of Fig. 4. Specifically, we randomly modify each value of the DC coefficients from the singly compressed JPEG image I^1 by a range of $\pm2\%$. Consequently, the periodic nature of DC coefficients gets disturbed. Hence, the usual statistical nature of DC coefficients of the doubly compressed JPEG image I^2 is also gets perturbed causing the values of H_∞ and H'_∞ to change in a specific way and the Algorithm 1 is unable to detect NAD-JPEG in many instances.

The reliability of any forensics algorithm depends on how well it can withstand this type of intentional modifications of an image by forgers to conceal their footprints. From the forger's point of view, the attack is considered successful if the forensics algorithm is unable to properly classify most of the forged images. The term *attack* is used to mean the application of anti-forensics techniques on a forged image to fool the forensics detectors. Let us now present the effect of random noise addition over IPM.

3.1 Effect of Random Noise Addition on IPM

The usual motivation of random noise addition is to generate a double compressed image which will behave like a singly compressed JPEG image causing any double JPEG compression detection algorithm to fail. Here, the presence of a peak in any IPM is used for detection of double JPEG compression. Equation 6

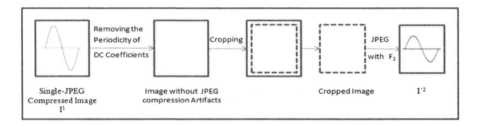

Fig. 4. Block diagram of anti-forensics algorithm

presents an IPM from a forged image. It can be observed that a peak is present at a location (6,6) which clearly identify the image as a NAD-JPEG image. Moreover, the location of a peak has a direct relation with the amount of cropping. Corresponding IPM generated by random noise addition using the framework is presented in Eq. 7. After random noise addition, the peak is present at the same location but the peak is more subtle due to the reduction in its magnitude. In fact, any further increase in the strength of noise removes the peak. However, the image quality degrades to an unacceptable level. Thus, the strategy to disturb the periodicity of DC coefficients may be able to defeat the NAD-JPEG detection but we require an algorithm to change the DC coefficients without affecting the visual quality of the resultant image.

$$IPM_f = \begin{bmatrix} 0.017 & 0.025 & 0.025 & 0.004 & 0.017 & 0.018 & 0.008 & 0.026 \\ 0.030 & 0.030 & 0.005 & 0.013 & 0.007 & 0.022 & 0.012 & 0.038 \\ 0.027 & 0.004 & 0.006 & 0.011 & 0.018 & 0.019 & 0.023 & 0.016 \\ 0.023 & 0.009 & 0.012 & 0.025 & 0.014 & 0.008 & 0.018 & 0.011 \\ 0.007 & 0.017 & 0.016 & 0.019 & 0.025 & 0.021 & 0.014 & 0.014 \\ 0.013 & 0.012 & 0.005 & 0.026 & 0.002 & \mathbf{0.710} & 0.029 & 0.030 \\ 0.015 & 0.015 & 0.020 & 0.018 & 0.029 & 0.012 & 0.016 & 0.023 \\ 0.004 & 0.004 & 0.013 & 0.026 & 0.018 & 0.025 & 0.025 & 0.025 \end{bmatrix} \quad (6)$$

$$IPM_r = \begin{bmatrix} 0.019 & 0.036 & 0.019 & 0.012 & 0.007 & 0.016 & 0.010 & 0.012 \\ 0.008 & 0.019 & 0.017 & 0.006 & 0.010 & 0.018 & 0.009 & 0.012 \\ 0.009 & 0.020 & 0.012 & 0.006 & 0.016 & 0.008 & 0.027 & 0.025 \\ 0.014 & 0.006 & 0.018 & 0.015 & 0.013 & 0.011 & 0.007 & 0.021 \\ 0.009 & 0.007 & 0.011 & 0.004 & 0.013 & 0.021 & 0.020 & 0.019 \\ 0.010 & 0.014 & 0.003 & 0.009 & 0.018 & \mathbf{0.115} & 0.008 & 0.019 \\ 0.015 & 0.015 & 0.012 & 0.019 & 0.018 & 0.009 & 0.016 & 0.013 \\ 0.011 & 0.026 & 0.027 & 0.018 & 0.017 & 0.009 & 0.011 & 0.013 \end{bmatrix} \quad (7)$$

3.2 DC Estimation Algorithm

The basic idea behind the detection algorithm proposed in [1] is the presence of periodicity in the DC coefficients of the JPEG image. If one can destroy the periodicity from a JPEG image without affecting the image quality or other

statistical properties of the DC coefficients, it would be impossible for the said
detection scheme to differentiate between a singly compressed and doubly compressed image. Random noise addition can remove the periodicity successfully
but image quality gets affected as pointed out earlier. To overcome this, we here
introduce a DC estimation algorithm which employs a sliding window technique
to model the DC coefficients. It was reported earlier that there is an inter-
relationship among the DC coefficients of neighboring blocks but the relationships are not well understood [20]. Proposed approximation process preserves the
inter-relationships among the neighboring DC coefficients to maintain the statistical and visual quality of the image. In this paper, we propose an approximation
method based on the "surface fitting" to model the DC coefficients. The model
establishes a relationship among neighboring DC coefficients and the model can
be used to estimate the DC coefficients of a particular location. Basically a window Ψ^b consists of all the neighboring DC coefficients of block b including the
DC coefficient of b itself. Let us first describe the process using a specific window
Ψ^b. Normally, the top left value of the window consists the DC coefficient whose
value we want to estimate, i.e. ψ^b, the DC coefficient of block b in this example.

To build the approximation model, we use a polynomial regression method
of two variables. Here, h, w are two independent variables indicating the location
of cells in a window and the value of the DC coefficient $\psi^b_{h,w}$ is the dependent
variable. One such typical model can be described as

$$\psi^b_{h,w} = \sum_{r=0}^{n}\sum_{c=0}^{n} \beta_{rc}.h^r.w^c \mid (r+c) \leq n \tag{8}$$

Here, β_{rc} is a constant term. A more generalized version of the Eq. 8 is given
below. Here, the degree of the polynomial is maximum of m, n.

$$\psi^b_{h,w} = \sum_{r=0}^{m}\sum_{c=0}^{n} \beta_{rc}.h^r.w^c \mid (r+c) \leq max(m,n) \tag{9}$$

This is also termed as response surface and any point on this surface basically
represent a DC coefficient which is an approximate value. These values do not
maintain the periodicity of DC coefficients w.r.t. the quantization step size. For
any window, the Eq. 9 can be represented as the Eq. 10 when $m = 3$ and $n = 4$.
In all our experiments the Eq. 10 is used for the approximation as these values
are producing a good approximation of DC coefficients. However, one can use
other values of m and n if they produce better approximation.

$$\begin{aligned}
\psi^b_{h,w} = {} & \beta_{00} + \beta_{10} * h + \beta_{01} * w + \beta_{20} * h^2 \\
& + \beta_{11} * h * w + \beta_{02} * w^2 + \beta_{30} * h^3 \\
& + \beta_{21} * h^2 * w + \beta_{12} * h * w^2 + \beta_{03} * w^3 \\
& + \beta_{31} * h^3 * w + \beta_{22} * h^2 * w^2 + \beta_{13} * h * w^3 \\
& + \beta_{04} * w^4.
\end{aligned} \tag{10}$$

Computing the coefficient values using the Ψ^b (refer Eq. 11), and by substituting the coefficients in Eq. 10, we obtain the Eq. 12. We have used the equation 12 to compute the approximated value of $\psi_{1,1}^b$, and the resultant $\bar{\Psi}^b$ is presented in Eq. 13. One can observe that all the values of Ψ^b are multiples of 11 but the approximated value $\psi_{1,1}^{\prime b} = 367$, is no longer a multiple of 11. Thus the periodicity of the DC coefficients are broken as expected.

$$\Psi^b = \begin{bmatrix} \mathbf{363} & 66 & 143 & 220 & -495 \\ 396 & 462 & 99 & 297 & -473 \\ 715 & 638 & 385 & 330 & -165 \\ 990 & 814 & 506 & 110 & -550 \\ 935 & 836 & 440 & 110 & 198 \end{bmatrix} \tag{11}$$

$$\begin{aligned} \psi_{h,w}^{\prime b} = \; & 1828 - 2276 * h - 585 * w + 729.9 * h^2 \\ & + 1679 * h * w - 587.7 * w^2 - 77.37 * h^3 \\ & - 299 * h^2 * w - 375.2 * h * w^2 + 290.7 * w^3 \\ & + 26.03 * h^3 * w + 13.53 * h^2 * w^2 + 34.74 * h * w^3 \\ & - 34.83 * w^4. \end{aligned} \tag{12}$$

$$\bar{\Psi}^b = \begin{bmatrix} \mathbf{367} & 66 & 143 & 220 & -495 \\ 396 & 462 & 99 & 297 & -473 \\ 715 & 638 & 385 & 330 & -165 \\ 990 & 814 & 506 & 110 & -550 \\ 935 & 836 & 440 & 110 & 198 \end{bmatrix} \tag{13}$$

The algorithm used to build the model is as follows.

Algorithm 2. DC Estimation Algorithm

Input: A matrix Ψ (a.k.a window) of de-quantized DC coefficients having size $\gamma \times \gamma$.
Output: Approximated DC coefficient $\psi_{k,k}^{\prime b}$, where $k = 1$.

1: Build a model using equation 9 from Ψ.
2: Estimate $\psi_{k,k}^{\prime b}$ using the model. Here, $k = 1$.

In normal circumstances the estimated DC coefficients $\psi_{k,k}^{\prime b}$ should not differ from its original value $\psi_{k,k}^b$ by a great extent. However, due to the nature of DC coefficients, the constructed model may not be perfect in very few cases. To maintain the visual quality in those cases, we restrict the difference between original value and estimated value within a range of $\pm 5\%$ of the original values.

$$IPM_a = \begin{bmatrix} 0.010 & 0.011 & 0.004 & 0.020 & 0.004 & 0.012 & 0.017 & 0.018 \\ 0.017 & 0.026 & 0.016 & 0.026 & 0.008 & 0.020 & 0.006 & 0.015 \\ 0.005 & 0.016 & 0.007 & 0.008 & 0.009 & 0.031 & 0.023 & 0.007 \\ 0.017 & 0.011 & 0.016 & 0.032 & 0.001 & 0.010 & 0.033 & 0.024 \\ 0.025 & 0.010 & 0.028 & 0.020 & 0.027 & 0.006 & 0.007 & 0.010 \\ 0.011 & 0.010 & 0.021 & 0.002 & 0.042 & \mathbf{0.006} & 0.018 & 0.008 \\ 0.026 & 0.013 & 0.009 & 0.030 & 0.021 & 0.024 & 0.024 & 0.020 \\ 0.004 & 0.011 & 0.006 & 0.019 & 0.011 & 0.025 & 0.012 & 0.010 \end{bmatrix} \tag{14}$$

Any color JPEG image consists of three different coefficient matrix for three different color components, namely Y, C_b, C_r. Each of these components is having its own quantization table. Consequently, we have to approximate DC coefficients of three different coefficient matrix. The entire process is presented in the Algorithm 3 and the effectiveness of the proposed algorithm is visible from the IPM presented in Eq. 14. The said IPM is generated from the same image that has been used to generate the IPMs in Eqs. 6 and 7. It is quite clear that the nature of the IPM is uniform and the position (6,6) of the IPM no longer represents the peak. Note that, the proposed anti-forensics technique removes the clustering of DC coefficients around the primary quantization step size which ensures an uniform IPM as visible in Eq. 14. Consequently, the detector proposed by Bianchi et al. fails to detect the counter forensically modified NAD-JPEG image as a forged image.

Algorithm 3. NAD-JPEG Anti-Forensics Algorithm

Input: Singly compressed JPEG image I^1
Output: Anti-forensically modified doubly compressed JPEG image I'^2

1: **for each** channel $\lambda \in \{Y, Cb, Cr\}$ **do**
2:    Read the dequantizaed DC coefficients of I^1_λ to matrix $\mathcal{D}$ having size $u \times v$.
3:    **for** $i = 1$ to $(u - \gamma + 1)$ **do**
4:      **for** $j = 1$ to $(v - \gamma + 1)$ **do**
5:        Create a window Ψ from the neighborhood of $\mathcal{D}_{i,j}$.
6:        Compute approximated $\mathcal{D}'_{i,j}$ by algorithm 2 using Ψ.
7:      **end for**
8:    **end for**
9:    Compute rest of the $\mathcal{D}'_{i,j}$ as $\mathcal{D}'_{i,j} = \mathcal{D}_{i,j}(1 + p)$,
      where p is random value between -0.05 to 0.05.

10:    Replace the DC coefficients of I^1_λ by $\mathcal{D}'_{i,j}$ to get I'^1_λ.
11: **end for**
12: Crop the image I'^1 randomly to get a non-aligned image.
13: Re-compress the cropped image with quality factor F_2 to yield I'^2.

---

4   Experimental Results

Validation of our proposed anti-forensics method is carried out using 500 randomly selected color images from UCID-v2 [16] image dataset.

Table 1. Detection accuracy (%) of [1] for forged images

F₁	F₂					
	54	63	72	81	91	96
54	98.0	99.0	99.5	99.5	97.5	96.0
63		97.5	99.0	99.5	97.5	96.0
72			97.0	99.5	97.5	96.0
81				89.0	97.5	96.0
91					86.5	96.0

Table 2. Accuracy (%) of detector [1] for images (512 × 384) attacked by proposed model

F₁	F₂					
	54	63	72	81	91	96
54	0	1	3	7	40	46
63		0	0	2	20	32
72			0	0	24	25
81				4	12	11
91					2	6

Table 3. Average PSNR (in dB) of attacked images w.r.t. forged images (512 × 384)

F₁	F₂					
	54	63	72	81	91	96
54	37.12	37.48	37.91	38.54	39.54	40.36
63		37.41	37.82	38.42	39.42	40.26
72			37.82	38.42	39.41	40.28
81				38.41	39.38	40.26
91					39.31	40.17

UCID dataset comprises 1338 uncompressed color images having size 512 × 384 and contain a wide variety of subjects. To simulate the NAD-JPEG compression, i.e. the forging process, each uncompressed image of the dataset has been initially JPEG compressed by a quality factor $F_1 \in \{54, 63, 72, 81, 91\}$. These quality factors have been considered by Bianchi et al. [1] also. Thus, we have 2500 singly compressed JPEG image in our dataset. These images are further subjected to decompression, cropping and re-compression using a JPEG quality factor $F_2 \in \{54, 63, 72, 81, 91, 96\}$. A block diagram of the said process is presented in the Fig. 1. After the second JPEG compression, 15,000 NAD-JPEG images are available in our dataset. These images have been subjected to the detection process of Bianchi et al. and the result is presented in the Table 1.

Note that, the results are reported for $F_2 \geq F_1$ as the detection algorithm 1 is meant for only those cases where $F_2 \geq F_1$. It is apparent from the results that the accuracy of the detection process is quite high if no anti-forensics algorithm is used to deceive the detector.

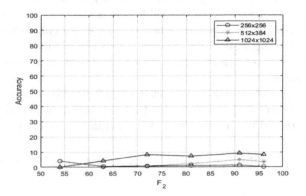

Fig. 5. Accuracy (%) of q_1 estimation.

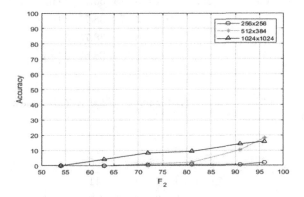

Fig. 6. Accuracy (%) of grid shift estimation.

Proposed anti-forensics technique expects a singly compressed JPEG image as an input and produces a non-aligned doubly compressed JPEG image that posses the statistical properties of a singly compressed JPEG image. Here, by statistical properties we mean the statistical properties of DC coefficients only. The proposed technique first removes the statistical artifacts from the singly compressed JPEG image by erasing the periodicity of DC coefficients present in that JPEG image. Afterward, it follows the path described by Bianchi et al. [1] to produce a NAD-JPEG image I'^2. The entire process is presented in the Fig. 4. It is obvious that I'^2 would not bear any signature of the first compression. Consequently, I'^2 would behave like a singly compressed JPEG image if we analyze the periodicity of DC coefficients retrieved from the anti-forensically modified image

I'^2. Thus, we expect detection algorithm 1 would be unable to decide about the nature of I'^2. For verification, we produce 15,000 attacked images with different quality factors $F_2 \in \{54, 63, 72, 81, 91, 96\}$ from the 2500 singly compressed JPEG images already present in our dataset. All these attacked images are subjected to detection algorithm 1 and the accuracy of the detector against the attacked images are presented in the Table 2. It is obvious that anti-forensics is able to deceive the detection process when $F_2 - F_1 < 30$. The detection accuracy improves with the increase in the difference between F_1 and F_2. However, the detection process never achieves an accuracy better than a random two-class classification process.

Further analysis of those attacked images which have been detected as NAD-JPEG images is carried out to determine the accuracy of estimated quantization step size and grid shift. The results are reported in Figs. 5 and 6.

Table 4. Average PSNR (in dB) of attacked images w.r.t. forged images (256 × 256)

F_1	F_2					
	54	63	72	81	91	96
54	36.45	36.78	37.22	37.85	38.87	39.70
63		36.73	37.13	37.75	38.78	39.61
72			37.15	37.75	38.77	39.62
81				37.73	38.75	39.61
91					38.67	39.53

Table 5. Accuracy (%) of detector [1] for images (256 × 256) attacked by proposed model the table

F_1	F_2					
	54	63	72	81	91	96
54	4	0	1	3	4	11
63		1	0	2	1	8
72			2	0	4	5
81				1	2	1
91					7	2

Another important aspect is the quality of the images produced by the proposed anti-forensics technique. If the quality of the attacked images is high, then only the proposed anti-forensics scheme will have any significance. We present the average PSNR of the attacked images with respect to the corresponding forged images in the Table 3. Note that, the overall PSNR observed among 45,000 attacked images is more than 36dB which demonstrates the effectiveness of our algorithm to produce high quality attacked images. A set of such images are presented in Figs. 2 and 3. Validation of the proposed anti-forensics method on images having size 256×256 also carried out using 500 images initially selected from the UCID-V2 dataset. The central portion of these images is cropped to produce 500 images having size 256×256. The same process as described above is followed to produce $15,000$ forged and attacked images. Results regarding the detection process against these images are available in the Tables 4 and 5. A similar process has been followed on 500 randomly selected images from RAISE dataset [3] to create a set of forged and attacked images of size 1024×1024 and the corresponding results are reported in the Tables 6 and 7.

Table 6. Average PSNR (in dB) of attacked images w.r.t. forged images (1024×1024)

F_1	F_2					
	54	63	72	81	91	96
54	39.00	39.38	39.82	40.33	40.94	41.44
63		39.30	39.59	40.14	40.74	41.25
72			39.76	40.24	40.82	41.32
81				40.32	40.85	41.32
91					40.87	41.32

Table 7. Accuracy (%) of detector [1] for images (1024×1024) attacked by proposed model

F_1	F_2					
	54	63	72	81	91	96
54	0	8	17	25	29	25
63		0	8	8	25	29
72			0	4	8	4
81				0	8	13
91					0	8

5   Conclusion

Double JPEG compression is one of the most prominent telltale sign of maliciousness of an image. Consequently, detection of double JPEG compression received a lot of attention from the researchers and several double JPEG compression detection schemes have been published in recent times. In this paper, we have concentrated on one such scheme [1] which has been proposed to detect non-aligned double JPEG compression using statistical properties of DC coefficients of an image. We have demonstrated that the statistical properties of the DC coefficients can be altered without affecting the image quality and the resultant image can evade the said NAD-JPEC detection process. The proposed anti-forensics method can be extended to defeat any double JPEG compression detection scheme that relies on the statistical properties of DC coefficients. Thus, the presented anti-forensics method cast serious doubt regarding the efficacy of double JPEG compression detection schemes when the suspect image is altered using any anti-forensics method.

References

1. Bianchi, T., Piva, A.: Detection of nonaligned double JPEG compression based on integer periodicity maps. IEEE Trans. Inf. Forensics Secur. **7**(2), 842–848 (2012). https://doi.org/10.1109/TIFS.2011.2170836
2. Chu, X., Stamm, M.C., Chen, Y., Liu, K.J.R.: On antiforensic concealability with rate-distortion tradeoff. IEEE Trans. Image Process. **24**(3), 1087–1100 (2015)
3. Dang-Nguyen, D.T., Pasquini, C., Conotter, V., Boato, G.: RAISE: a raw images dataset for digital image forensics. In: Proceedings of the 6th ACM Multimedia Systems Conference, MMSys 2015, pp. 219–224. ACM, New York (2015). https://doi.org/10.1145/2713168.2713194
4. Das, T.K.: Anti-forensics of JPEG compression detection schemes using approximation of DCT coefficients. Multimed. Tools Appl. **77**(24), 31835–31854 (2018). https://doi.org/10.1007/s11042-018-6170-7
5. Fan, W., Wang, K., Cayre, F., Xiong, Z.: JPEG anti-forensics with improved tradeoff between forensic undetectability and image quality. IEEE Trans. Inf. Forensics Secur. **9**(8), 1211–1226 (2014)
6. Fan, Z., de Queiroz, R.L.: Identification of bitmap compression history: JPEG detection and quantizer estimation. IEEE Trans. Image Process. **12**(2), 230–235 (2003)
7. Farid, H.: A survey of image forgery detection. IEEE Signal Process. Mag. **2**(26), 16–25 (2009)
8. Huang, F., Huang, J., Shi, Y.Q.: Detecting double JPEG compression with the same quantization matrix. IEEE Trans. Inf. Forensics Secur. **5**(4), 848–856 (2010)
9. Lai, S.Y., Böhme, R.: Countering counter-forensics: the case of JPEG compression. In: Filler, T., Pevný, T., Craver, S., Ker, A. (eds.) IH 2011. LNCS, vol. 6958, pp. 285–298. Springer, Heidelberg (2011). https://doi.org/10.1007/978-3-642-24178-9_20
10. Li, H., Luo, W., Huang, J.: Anti-forensics of double JPEG compression with the same quantization matrix. Multimed. Tools Appl. **74**(17), 6729–6744 (2015)
11. Lukáš, J., Fridrich, J.: Estimation of primary quantization matrix in double compressed JPEG images. In: Proceedings of DFRWS (2003)
12. Luo, W., Huang, J., Qui, G.: JPEG error analysis and its applications to digital image forensics. IEEE Trans. Inf. Forensics Secur. **5**(3), 480–491 (2010)
13. Milani, S., Tagliasacchi, M., Tubaro, S.: Discriminating multiple jpeg compression using first digit features. In: 2012 IEEE International Conference on Acoustics, Speech and Signal Processing (ICASSP), pp. 2253–2256, March 2012
14. Niu, Y., Li, X., Zhao, Y., Ni, R.: An enhanced approach for detecting double JPEG compression with the same quantization matrix. Sig. Process.: Image Commun. **76**, 89–96 (2019)

15. Pevny, T., Fridrich, J.: Detection of double-compression in JPEG images for applications in steganography. IEEE Trans. Inf. Forensics Secur. **3**(2), 247–258 (2008)
16. Schaefer, G., Stich, M.: UCID: an uncompressed color image database. In: Yeung, M.M., Lienhart, R.W., Li, C.S. (eds.) Storage and Retrieval Methods and Applications for Multimedia 2004, vol. 5307, pp. 472–480, December 2003. https://doi.org/10.1117/12.525375
17. Singh, G., Singh, K.: Improved JPEG anti-forensics with better image visual quality and forensic undetectability. Forensic Sci. Int. **277** (2017). https://doi.org/10.1016/j.forsciint.2017.06.003
18. Stamm, M.C., Tjoa, S.K., Lin, W.S., Liu, K.J.R.: Anti-forensics of JPEG compression. In: 2010 IEEE International Conference on Acoustics, Speech and Signal Processing, pp. 1694–1697, March 2010. https://doi.org/10.1109/ICASSP.2010.5495491
19. Taimori, A., Razzazi, F., Behrad, A., Ahmadi, A., Babaie-Zadeh, M.: Quantization-unaware double JPEG compression detection. J. Math. Imaging Vis. **54**(3), 269–286 (2016)
20. Uehara, T., Safavi-Naini, R., Ogunbona, P.: Recovering DC coefficients in block-based DCT. IEEE Trans. Image Process. **15**(11), 3592–3596 (2006). https://doi.org/10.1109/TIP.2006.881939
21. Wei, H., Yao, H., Qin, C., Tang, Z.: Automatic forgery localization via artifacts analysis of JPEG and resampling. In: Yang, C.-N., Peng, S.-L., Jain, L.C. (eds.) SICBS 2018. AISC, vol. 895, pp. 221–234. Springer, Cham (2020). https://doi.org/10.1007/978-3-030-16946-6_18
22. Xue, F., Lu, W., Ye, Z., Liu, H.: JPEG image tampering localization based on normalized gray level co-occurrence matrix. Multimed. Tools Appl. **78**(8), 9895–9918 (2019). https://doi.org/10.1007/s11042-018-6611-3

Differential Attack Graph-Based Approach for Assessing Change in the Network Attack Surface

Ghanshyam S. Bopche[1,2]([envelope]) [iD], Gopal N. Rai[3] [iD], B. Ramchandra Reddy[1] [iD], and B. M. Mehtre[2] [iD]

[1] Madanapalle Institute of Technology and Science (MITS), Madanapalle, Andhra Pradesh, India
ghanshyambopche.mca@gmail.com, brcreddy.mtech@gmail.com
[2] Centre of Excellence in Cyber Security, IDRBT, Hyderabad, India
mehtre@gmail.com
[3] Collins Aerospace, Hyderabad, India
gopalnrai@gmail.com
https://www.mits.ac.in/,
http://www.idrbt.ac.in,
https://www.rockwellcollins.com/

Abstract. Assessing change in an attack surface of dynamic computer networks is a formidable challenge. Researchers have previously looked into the problem of measuring network risk and used an attack graph (AG) for network hardening. However, such AG-based approaches do not consider the likely variations in the attack surface. Further, even though it is possible to generate attack graphs for a realistic network efficiently, resulting graphs poses a severe challenge to human comprehension. To overcome such problems, in this paper, we present a differential attack graph-based change detection technique. We proposed a change distribution matrix-based technique to discern differences in the network attack surface. Our method not only detects the degree of change in the network attack surface but also finds the root causes in a time-efficient manner. We use a synthetic network to illustrate the approach and perform a set of simulations to evaluate the performance. Experimental results show that our technique is capable of assessing changes in the attack surface, and thus can be used in practice for network hardening.

Keywords: Network security · Multistage attacks · Attack surface · Attack graph · Security metric · Change distribution

1 Introduction

In order management and control of network security, early detection of critical events is fundamental to the capability building like an early warning system. Today's computer networks are dynamic and undergoing continuous evolution

© Springer Nature Switzerland AG 2019
D. Garg et al. (Eds.): ICISS 2019, LNCS 11952, pp. 324–344, 2019.
https://doi.org/10.1007/978-3-030-36945-3_18

in terms of complexity and size. Accordingly, the network attack surface is also under constant change. The attack surface [21,22] of a computer network is the subset of system or network configurations and vulnerabilities (disclosed vulnerabilities in particular) that an adversary can exploit to compromise the mission-critical resources [38]. Assessing the degree of change in the network attack surface and pinpointing the responsible root causes is of the utmost importance for proactive network hardening.

In this paper, we focus on the temporal aspects of the exploitable vulnerabilities and vulnerable service connectivities. The inherent difficulty in assessing the change in the network attack surface [21,22] over the predetermined sampling interval of Δt and pinpointing the hidden root causes has motivated our work. To the best of our knowledge, so far, there is no work on assessing the temporal variation in the network attack surface. In this respect, our work is significant as it deals with the variation in the attack surface while monitoring network security performance.

Significant contributions of this paper are as follows. First, we establish the notion of the network attack surface to capture the group of network resources likely to be used by an adversary during network intrusion. For a given network, a pair of exploit-dependency attack graphs (i.e., $\langle G_1, G_2 \rangle$, generated apart in time by sampling interval Δt) successfully captures the network attack surface and temporal changes in it. Second, we employed an error-correcting graph matching based technique [36] to measure the degree of change in the attack surface. Third, we proposed a change distribution matrix-based technique to determine the newly introduced exploits and their enabling conditions. Finally, we performed several experiments to validate the proposed method. Experimental results show that the proposed technique can successfully access the degree of variation in the network attack surface. Further, it identifies meaningful changes and pinpoints hidden root causes.

2   Prior Works

Today's computer network plays an important role as it binds all the information assets together and provides a means of operational transactions where different entities can participate, exchange information, and carry out operations over the information by making use of specific ports, protocols, and services provided by the network. It may create the possibilities of exposure to mission-critical information. Proactive identification of all the potential threats to the mission-critical network resources using an attack graph (a well-known graphical network security model) is a widely recognized research area. Kaynar [16] provides a systematic study of the various tools and techniques available for the attack graph generation. Even though several tools, e.g., MulVAL [32], NetSPA [14], Cauldron [15], etc. efficiently generates attack graph for practical networks, generated graphs are complex and incomprehensible to human. The manual analysis of such graphs is impractical and makes it difficult for the process of network hardening. Several graph analysis techniques have been proposed in the literature to extract the security-relevant information. The primary goal of the attack graph analysis is to predict future attacks [10], determine the optimal set of exploits, and initial conditions [18,34] for efficient network immunization, and access the risk posed by an adversary to the critical enterprise resources [1,9]. Further, the number of metrics [13,27] proposed to measure security strength of network configuration.

While the above stated AG-based approaches provide network hardening solutions, they are not useful in the context of the dynamic attack surface. Previously proposed AG-based metrics [12,13,28,30,33,37,38], etc. are too coarse to be useful for security management. In other words, the network administrator wants to know which network or security-related events are accountable for the increase in the attack surface. To conclude, existing AG-based approaches unable to alert about compelling events, do not provide any knowledge about where in the attack surface changes has been occurred, and what are the root causes.

Outside attack graph literature, several graph distance metrics have been proposed to compare graphs for similarity. Essentially, the graphs in a pair $\langle G_1, G_2 \rangle$ considered to be matching if there is a graph isomorphism among them [2]. Showbridge et al. [36] used edit distance based on the error-correcting graph matching to monitor the performance of telecommunication networks. To pinpoint the essential variations and unknown abnormal activities in the network, Liao and Striegel [20] used a graph differential anomaly visualization. Advanced metrics such as Tabu [19], RASCAL [35], and DeltaCon [17] have been used largely to examine the chemical graphs for their similarity or dissimilarity. Ning et al. [25] used an error-correcting graph/subgraph isomorphism to learn about the adversarial attack strategies. In our previous works [3,4], we have used graph edit distance [24] and maximum common subgraph [5] to study the effect of changes in the network topology and security factors on to the attack surface. Upon observing the significant variation in the attack surface, the administrator needs to closely inspect the current attack graph (in a pair $\langle G_1, G_2 \rangle$) to find out the root causes accountable for the change. However, the generated attack graph for a reasonable size network poses a severe challenge for human comprehension. To conclude, neither of the previously proposed AG-based approaches provides the knowledge about "how much change occurred in the network attack surface?", "wherein the attack surface change has occurred?" and "what are the root causes for such change?".

By observing the shortcoming of the state of the art metrics described in the literature, we conclude that there should be metrics which not only capture the temporal variations in the network attack surface but guide administrator in identifying or pinpointing the root causes. To bridge the gap, we propose to apply the notion error-correcting graph matching [36] to assess the degree of variations in the network attack surface by measuring the distance between consecutive attack graphs generated over an arbitrary sampling interval Δt. For a given network, the generated exploit-dependency attack graph captures the underlying attack surface in terms of exploitable technical vulnerabilities and vulnerable service connectivities [38].

3   Design Motivation: An Example Scenario

To develop insight about the problem we propose to solve, we consider a Test Network shown in Fig. 1. Here, $Host_1$, $Host_2$ and $Host_3$ constitute the internal network. Host Ha is the anonymous malicious user, and her objective is to become superuser of the $Host_3$. Here, our main concern is "whether an adversary can acquire administrative privileges on $Host_3$?" Firewalls are set up to acknowledge all outbound connections, but blocks inbound connection requests to $Host_0$ only. Hosts internal to the network are allowed to assess available services via designated ports described by the access control policies shown in Table 1. We believe each host in the test network has one or more well-known vulnerabilities indexed by CVE number [7], as tabulated in Table 2.

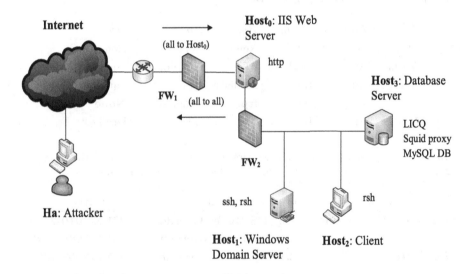

Fig. 1. A test network

Table 1. Connectivity-limiting firewall rules for the Test Network at time t

Host	Attacker	$Host_0$	$Host_1$	$Host_2$	$Host_3$
Attacker	localhost	All	None	None	None
$Host_0$	All	localhost	All	All	Squid, LICQ
$Host_1$	All	IIS	localhost	All	Squid, LICQ
$Host_2$	All	IIS	All	localhost	Squid, LICQ
$Host_3$	All	IIS	All	All	localhost

Table 2. Services and vulnerability description of the Test Network at time t

Host	Services	Ports	Vulnerabilities	CVE
$Host_0$	IIS Web Service	80	IIS Buffer Overflow	CVE-2010-2370
$Host_1$	ssh	22	ssh buffer overflow	CVE-2002-1359
	rsh	514	rsh login	CVE-1999-0180
$Host_2$	rsh	514	rsh login	CVE-1999-0180
$Host_3$	LICQ	5190	LICQ-remote-to-user	CVE-2001-0439
	Squid proxy	80	squid-port-scan	CVE-2001-1030
	MySQL DB	3306	local-setuid-bof	CVE-2006-3368

Table 3. Firewall rules for the Test Network at time $(t + \Delta t)$. Highlighted entries represent change in Firewall policies over Δt.

Host	Attacker	$Host_0$	$Host_1$	$Host_2$	$Host_3$
Attacker	localhost	All	None	None	None
$Host_0$	All	localhost	All	**Netbios-ssn**	Squid, LICQ
$Host_1$	All	IIS	localhost	**None**	Squid, LICQ
$Host_2$	All	IIS	**ftp, rsh**	localhost	**None**
$Host_3$	All	IIS	All	All	localhost

Table 4. Services and vulnerability description of the Test Network at time $(t + \Delta t)$. Highlighted entries represent newly introduced services and vulnerabilities.

Host	Services	Ports	Vulnerabilities	CVE IDs
$Host_0$	**IIS Web Service**	**80**	**IIS Buffer Overflow**	**CVE-2010-2730**
	ftp	**21**	**ftp buffer overflow**	**CVE-2009-3023**
$Host_1$	**ftp**	**21**	**ftp rhost overwrite**	**CVE-2008-1396**
	rsh	514	rsh login	CVE-1999-0180
$Host_2$	**Netbios-ssn**	**139**	**Netbios-ssn nullsession**	**CVE-2003-0661**
	rsh	514	rsh login	CVE-1999-0180
$Host_3$	LICQ	5190	LICQ-remote-to-user	CVE-2001-0439
	Squid proxy	80	squid-port-scan	CVE-2001-1030
	MySQL DB	3306	local-setuid-bof	CVE-2006-3368

As our example network is dynamic, we expect certain changes in the form of change in the service connectivity, the introduction of the vulnerable services, disclosure of new vulnerabilities, etc. Such changes in the network configuration highlighted in Tables 3 and 4. As there is a change in the network topology factors and security factors as well, there is a notable change in the network attack surface. Goal-oriented exploit-dependency attack graph for this network configuration at time $t + \Delta t$ is shown in the Fig. 2(b). Here Δt is an arbitrary sampling interval. The decision of the Δt selection needs to be done precisely, and it depends on the expertise of the security analyst [4].

A goal-oriented exploit-dependency attack graph [29,39] of the test network at time t is shown in Fig. 2(a). Here, the attack graph has two kinds of vertices, namely, exploits and conditions, and it shows all the attack paths available to an adversary. The generated exploit-dependency attack graphs are goal-oriented, finite, and contain neither multiple edges nor loop. We have slightly customized MulVAL [32] so that it constructs attack graphs with uniquely labeled nodes. Automatic generation of the exploit-dependency attack graphs [29,31,32] is beyond the scope of this article.

Quick identification of variations in the attack surface and hidden root causes is crucial to the prevention of future attacks. The critical observation is that the test network at different instants of time (here, t and $t + \Delta t$) has the same value of the previously proposed attack graph-based metrics. However, the underlying attack surface is different. The remainder of this paper deal with an issue of measurement of variations in the attack surface. Further, we are interested in pinpointing the root causes.

Understanding the temporal differences between successive attack graphs generated apart in time by sampling interval of Δt is usually the first important step towards finding a change in the attack surface of dynamic networks. The change detection in the attack surface, which is the main focus of this paper is defined as follows:

Definition 1 (Attack Surface Change Detection).
Given: a sequence of goal-oriented exploit-dependency attack graphs generated apart in time by sampling interval Δt.
Find:

1. *the degree of variation in the network attack surface over Δt, as well as*
2. *the root causes accountable for the variation in the attack surface.*

4 Network Attack Surface: A Formal Model

In this section, first, we establish the notion of the network attack surface ($\mathcal{N\!AS}$). Next, we show how the exploit-dependency attack graph [39] ideally captures the $\mathcal{N\!AS}$ and dynamics in it.

4.1 Notion of the Network Attack Surface

Wang et al. [38] were the first who applied the notion of attack surface to the entire computer network. The author's primary focus was on interfaces like remotely exploitable services. According to Cybenco et al. [8], $\mathcal{N\!AS}$ consists of exploitable technical vulnerabilities and vulnerable network configurations. We borrowed the idea of the network attack surface from Cybenko et al. [8].

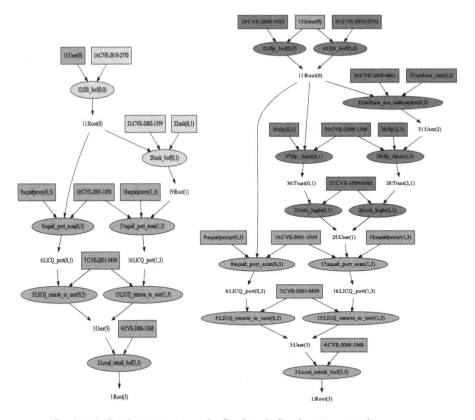

a: G_1- Attack Graph at time t b: G_2- Attack Graph at time $t + \Delta t$

Fig. 2. Differential attack graphs visualization at the node level. Here, each *initial condition* is shown by a box, *exploit* by an oval, and *postcondition* by a plain text. Pink colored nodes: appeared only in G_2; Cyan colored nodes: appeared in both the attack graphs G_1 and G_2; Green colored nodes: appeared only in G_1. (Color figure online)

Let $\mathcal{N} = \{h_0, h_1, h_2, \ldots, h_n\}$ be a finite set of hosts in a network that can be a potential target for an adversary. Here host h_0 is the attacking host from where an adversary can launch multistage attacks. Mainly, the security configuration of a given network $\mathcal{N}$ comprise of two facts as follows:

1. A finite set of services $\mathcal{S}$ and related vulnerabilities.
2. Service connectivity relation among the hosts.

Let $\mathcal{S} = \bigcup_{i=1}^{n} S_i$ be a finite set of services accessible over the network $\mathcal{N}$. Here $S_i \in \mathcal{S}$ represents the set of services running over the host h_i. Let $\mathcal{C} = \bigcup_{i=1}^{n} C_i$ be a finite set of service connectivity relation, where $C_i \in \mathcal{C}$ is the set of service connectivity relations from host $h_i \in \mathcal{N}$.

Let $Conf(\mathcal{N})$ represents the security configuration of the network $\mathcal{N}$. Each machine in $\mathcal{N}$ hosts critical services, vulnerable to one or more exploits. Let $V = \bigcup_{i=1}^{m} V_i$ be a set of vulnerabilities in the network $\mathcal{N}$, where m indicates the total number of disclosed technical vulnerabilities in the $\mathcal{N}$. Each $V_i \in V$ is related with the single service on a single host. Let $VN_i = \{vn_{i,1}, vn_{i,2}, \ldots, vn_{i,p}\}$ be a set of exploitable vulnerabilities in the host $h_i \in \mathcal{N}$. The total number of exploitable vulnerabilities in $\mathcal{N}$ is represented by the set $VN = \bigcup_{i=1}^{n} VN_i$ and $VN \subseteq V$. For the set of vulnerabilities which can be exploited remotely, we need to look at service connectivity between the pair of hosts $\langle h_i, h_j \rangle$.

Let $\mathcal{C}' = \bigcup_{i=1}^{n} C_i'$ be the set of vulnerable service connectivity relations in $\mathcal{N}$ and $\mathcal{C}' \subseteq \mathcal{C}$. Let $VN' \subseteq VN$ be the set of vulnerabilities likely to be incrementally exploited to reach and compromise the target. Moreover, let $\mathcal{C}'_v \subseteq \mathcal{C}'$ be the set of service connectivities that can be used during the multistage attack. Contribution mentioned above of VN' and $\mathcal{C}'_v$ indicates their possibility of being used by an adversary during the incremental network compromise. In conclusion, the network attack surface ($\mathcal{NAS}$) is a subset of network configuration (vulnerable service connectivities) and well-known technical vulnerabilities that an adversary can exploit to reach and compromise the target. With the notion of the $\mathcal{NAS}$ discussed above, we define $\mathcal{NAS}$ as follows:

Definition 2 (Network Attack Surface). *Given a set of vulnerable service connectivities $\mathcal{C}'_v \subseteq \mathcal{C}'$, and a set of exploitable technical vulnerabilities $VN' \subseteq VN$ that can be used by an adversary to incrementally compromise the network $\mathcal{N}$, the network attack surface ($\mathcal{NAS}$) is the set, where $\mathcal{NAS} = \{\mathcal{C}'_v \cup VN'\}$.*

4.2 Model to Capture the Network Attack Surface ($\mathcal{NAS}$)

Mainly, an exploit-dependency attack graph [39] portray exploits and their respective enabling conditions, e.g. the presence of exploitable vulnerabilities, vulnerable service connectivities, etc. The graph constitutes two types of edges, namely, *require edge* and *imply edge*. Essentially, *require edge* is a directed edge from the security condition (i.e., either initial condition or postcondition) to an exploit and it captures the conjunctive nature of conditions to activate the exploit [11]. However, an *imply edge* is a directed edge from the exploit to a postcondition. As the *require edge* captures the detail about the network resource involvement (e.g., vulnerable services, service connectivities, etc.), the notion of an attack surface for a given network is perfectly captured by the attack graph.

We portray the network attack surface, i.e., $\mathcal{NAS}(Conf(\mathcal{N}))$ by means of an exploit-dependency attack graph $G(\mathcal{E} \cup \mathcal{I}, R_r \cup R_i)$ [39]. Here, $\mathcal{E}$ is a set of exploits, $\mathcal{I}$ a set of conditions (both initial conditions and postconditions). Accordingly, we can determine the variation in the network attack surface by computing distance between a pair of exploit-dependency attack graphs generated over the sampling interval of Δt across multiple timelines. In doing so, we can identify the important network topology and security factor, which are accountable for the variation in the $\mathcal{NAS}$.

4.3   Dealing with Variations in the Network Attack Surface ($\mathcal{NAS}$)

Today's computer networks are undergoing a continuous change in terms of their size and complexity. Such a shift in a network configuration is as a result of the enumeration of several actions taken by the network administrator as a part of network maintenance and security hardening. Furthermore, there will be a change in the network attack surface due to events which are not under the administrative control. A partial list of such network dynamics that lead to a significant variation in the network attack surface compiled as follows:

– Change in the network configuration due to routine network maintenance activities such as:
  • Installation/removal of network devices such as workstations, servers, routers, firewalls, IDPS, etc.
  • Installation and uninstallation of softwares and services.
  • Reconfiguration of access control policies.
– Users increased flexibility in installing and configuring software, and services.
– Misconfiguration of software/hardware devices.
– Failure of security devices such as firewall, IDPS, etc.
– Application of security countermeasures, e.g., patching of vulnerabilities.
– Discovery of new vulnerabilities.

Let M be the list of all plausible events that results in a notable variation in the network attack surface. Post application of the action set M, the initial network configuration $Conf(\mathcal{N})$ changes. Let $Conf(\mathcal{N}) \oplus M$ be the resulting configuration and $\mathcal{NAS}(Conf(\mathcal{N} \oplus M))$ be the resulting network attack surface. Such variations in $\mathcal{NAS}$ over Δt can be captured by an exploit-dependency attack graph generated at time $t + \Delta t$.

5   Assessing Change in the Network Attack Surface

We are particularly interested in three problems. First, "how much change has occurred in the attack surface over Δt as a result of network dynamics?". Second, "what are the newly introduced changes in the attack surface?". Third, "what are the root causes?". The first can be answered by applying the concept of error-correcting graph matching (ecgm) [5,23] for a pair of successive attack graphs $\langle G_i, G_j \rangle$ generated over a sampling interval Δt. Whereas the latter two will can be answered with the help of the change distribution matrix.

5.1   Error-Correcting Graph Matching (ecgm)

Before discussing the concept of error-correcting graph matching (ecgm), an attack graph representation of the network attack surface $\mathcal{NAS}$ must be defined. Only the issues associated with dynamic changes in the network attack surface are considered here.

Definition 3. *A labelled exploit-dependency attack graph G is a three-tuple $G = (V, E, \rho)$, where*

- *V is a finite set of vertices, i.e., $V = \mathcal{E} \cup \mathcal{I}$.*
- *$E \subseteq V \times V$ is a set of Edges, i.e., $E = R_r \cup R_i$*
- *$\rho : V \to L_V$ is a function assigning labels to the vertices*

In this definition, $\mathcal{E}$ is a set of exploits, $\mathcal{I}$ a set of conditions (both initial conditions and postconditions), $R_r \subset (\mathcal{I} \times \mathcal{E})$ is a require relation, $R_i \subset (\mathcal{E} \times \mathcal{I})$ is an imply relation, L_V is the set of symbolic labels uniquely identifying each node in the attack graph G, and ρ is a function assigning unique labels to the vertices.

In general, *ecgm* measures the difference between the two input graphs by determining the least cost sequence of edit operations required to transform one graph into the other. To successfully use *ecgm*, we only consider the edit operation in terms of the deletion of *require edges*. It is because, *require edge* is the only attack graph construct, which thoroughly describes the contribution of network resources to the changing network attack surface. The algorithm 1 detects such newly introduced *require edges* in the attack graph G_2 generated at time $t + \Delta t$.

Algorithm 1. *findEdges*: Find the newly introduced *require edges* in an Exploit-dependency Attack Graph G_2

    Input:
    $\langle G_1, G_2 \rangle \to$ a pair of goal-oriented exploit-dependency attack graphs generated over the sampling interval Δt
    Output:
    $NewInit \subset V_2 \backslash V_1 \to$ set of newly introduced initial conditions
    $NewRequireEdge \subset E_2 \backslash E_1 \to$ set of newly introduced require edges
1: $\langle V_1, E_1 \rangle \leftarrow G_1$
2: $\langle V_2, E_2 \rangle \leftarrow G_2$
3: $G_3 \langle V_3, E_3 \rangle \leftarrow G_2 \backslash G_1$
4: **if** $(G_2 \backslash G_1 = \phi)$ **then**
5:     Print: "No change in the network attack surface over Δt "
6: **else**
7:     **for all** $u \in V_3$ **do**
8:         **if** $(indegree(u) == 0)$ **then**
9:             $NewInit \leftarrow u$
10:         **end if**
11:     **end for**
12:     **for all** $u \in NewInit$ **do**
13:         **if** $(u == i)$ for one or more $(i, j) \in E_3$ **then**
14:             $NewRequireEdge \leftarrow (i, j)$
15:         **end if**
16:     **end for**
17: **end if**

Definition 4 (Edit Operation). *Given the exploit-dependency attack graph*
$G_2 = (V_2, E_2, \rho)$ *generated at time (t + Δt), define an edit operation δ on G_2 as*
follows:
$(e \rightarrow \$)$: *deleting the newly introduced require edge e from G_2. This represents*
removing dependency between the initial condition and exploit.

From a hardening perspective, analysts are interested only in newly introduced vulnerabilities and configuration changes that lead to an increase in attack
surface. Therefore, unlike [36], we applied the *ecgm* procedure to the attack graph
pair $\langle mcs(G_1, G_2), G_2 \rangle$. Here $mcs(G_1, G_2)$ represents the portion of the attack
graph G_1 (or attack surface) which is invariant over time Δt. The persistence
of $mcs(G_1, G_2)$ over Δt is due to the constraints like- unavailability of vulnerability patches, limited hardening budget, etc. Therefore, the analyst's goal is to
identify all the newly introduced vulnerabilities, enabling conditions, and then
patch/fix them, so that graph G_2 reduces to $mcs(G_1, G_2)$.

Definition 5. *Given an attack graph $G_2 = (V_2, E_2, \rho)$ at time $t + \Delta t$ and a*
sequence of edit operation $\Delta = (\delta_1, \delta_2, \ldots, \delta_k), k \geq 1$, the edited attack graph
$\Delta(G)$ *becomes* $\Delta(G) = \delta_k(\ldots \delta_2(\delta_1(G_2)) \ldots) = mcs(G_1, G_2) = (V_\delta, E_\delta, \rho)$ *where:*

- $V_\delta \subseteq V_2$
- $E_\delta \subseteq E_2$

Note that the removal of each *require edge* δ_i is assigned a cost $C(\delta_i)$, then
the total cost associated with the sequence of edit operations Δ is

$$C(\Delta) = \sum_{i=1}^{k} C(\delta_i) \tag{1}$$

In practice, an exploit is prevented from execution by disabling any one of the
initial enabling conditions. But, here we consider the removal of all the *require*
edges of all the newly introduced exploits in G_2. It is because our goal is to
assess the degree of change in the attack surface and pinpoint the root causes as
well.

If the cost associated with the removal of each of the newly introduced *require*
edge is 1, then the edit sequence cost becomes the difference between the total
number of *require edges* in attack graph G_2 and all the *require edges* that are in
common to both G_1 and G_2.

Definition 6 (Degree of variation in the network attack surface).
Let the attack graph for the enterprise network operating at time t is $G_1 =$
(V_1, E_1, ρ), *and let* $G_2 = (V_2, E_2, \rho)$ *be the attack graph for the same network at*
time t', where $t' = (t + \Delta t)$. The distance $d(mcs(G_1, G_2), G_2)$ is given by:

$$d(mcs(G_1, G_2), G_2) = |require\ edges(G_2)| - |require\ edges(mcs(G_1, G_2))| \tag{2}$$

where the cost function for edit operation δ is

$$C(\delta) = \begin{cases} 1 & ; \delta = (e \rightarrow \$) \\ 0 & ; otherwise \end{cases}$$

The edit distance d, as a measure of the change in network attack surface, increases with increasing degree of change experienced by the network over time Δt. The edit distance d is bounded below by $d = 0$ when there is no change in the attack surface, and above by $d = |require\ edges(G_2)|$, when the network attack surface is entirely different.

5.2 Pinpointing the Root Causes

Since each network event (as discussed in Sect. 4.3) can cause changes in the attack surface, our next objective is to pinpoint such events. For the attack graph pair $\langle G_1, G_2 \rangle$ shown in Fig. 2, the edit distance d has indicated significantly different attack surface.

To portray newly introduced changes in G_2, we present a change distribution matrix C, as shown in Fig. 3. It shows newly introduced changes in the attack surface, which is not clear even with the powerful attack graph visualization. The rows and columns of C represent initial conditions and exploits in the attack graph G_2, respectively. The existence of *require edge* deleted from G_2 is represented in the matrix $C = [c_{ij}]$ by the corresponding row-column entry $c_{ij} = 1$. Here, i and j are the respective condition and exploit of the deleted *require edge*. C with non-zero entry $c_{ij} = (-1)$ represents the set of *require edges* that are stable over time Δt. Whereas, an entry $c_{ij} = 0$ record edges that are not present in G_2. Essentially, C is a sparse matrix because of the unidirectional edges in the exploit-dependency attack graph.

Initial Conditions ↓   Exploits →

	2	5	8	12	15	17	23	26	29	32	35	37	40
4	-1	0	0	0	0	0	0	0	0	0	0	0	0
7	0	-1	0	0	-1	0	0	0	0	0	0	0	0
9	0	0	-1	0	0	0	0	0	0	0	0	0	0
10	0	0	-1	0	0	-1	0	0	0	0	0	0	0
13	0	0	0	0	0	0	1	0	0	0	0	0	1
18	0	0	0	0	0	-1	0	0	0	0	0	0	0
24	0	0	0	0	0	0	1	0	0	0	0	0	0
27	0	0	0	0	0	0	0	1	0	0	1	0	0
30	0	0	0	0	0	0	0	0	1	0	0	0	0
33	0	0	0	0	0	0	0	0	0	1	0	0	0
34	0	0	0	0	0	0	0	0	0	1	0	0	0
38	0	0	0	0	0	0	0	0	0	0	0	1	0
39	0	0	0	0	0	0	0	0	1	0	0	1	0
41	0	0	0	0	0	0	0	0	0	0	0	0	1

Fig. 3. Change distribution matrix C

Definition 7 (Change Distribution Matrix).   *The change distribution matrix $C = [c_{ij}]$ is $|V_p| \times |V_q|$ matrix that describes the change in the network attack surface in terms of newly introduced exploits and associated initial conditions, where*

– $V_p, V_q \subset V_2$ *and*

$$c_{ij} = \begin{cases} 1 & ; e(i,j) \in R_{r'}, R_{r'} \subset R_r \subset E_2 \\ -1 & ; e(i,j) \in R_{r''}, R_{r''} \subset R_r \subset E_2 \\ 0 & ; otherwise \end{cases}$$

In this definition, the matrix $C = [c_{ij}]_{p \times q}$ is a set of p initial conditions and q exploits arranged in a rectangular array of p rows and q columns. $R_{r'}$ is the set of newly introduced *require edges* between initial conditions and exploits in an attack graph G_2. $R_{r'}$ does not constitute *require edges* which starts from the postcondition. Whereas, $R_{r''}$ represents the set of *require edges* that are stable over Δt.

Initial Conditions ↓	2	5	8	12	15	17	23	26	29	32	35	37	40	Sum
4	0	0	0	0	0	0	0	0	0	0	0	0	0	0
7	0	0	0	0	0	0	0	0	0	0	0	0	0	0
9	0	0	0	0	0	0	0	0	0	0	0	0	0	0
10	0	0	0	0	0	0	0	0	0	0	0	0	0	0
13	0	0	0	0	0	0	0	0	0	0	0	0	1	1
14	0	0	0	0	0	0	0	0	0	0	0	0	0	0
18	0	0	0	0	0	0	0	0	0	0	0	0	0	0
24	0	0	0	0	0	0	1	0	0	0	0	0	0	1
27	0	0	0	0	0	0	0	1	0	0	1	0	0	2
30	0	0	0	0	0	0	0	0	1	0	0	0	0	1
33	0	0	0	0	0	0	0	0	0	1	0	0	0	1
34	0	0	0	0	0	0	0	0	0	1	0	0	0	1
38	0	0	0	0	0	0	0	0	0	0	0	1	0	1
39	0	0	0	0	0	0	0	0	1	0	0	1	0	2
41	0	0	0	0	0	0	0	0	0	0	0	0	1	1
Sum	0	0	0	0	0	0	2	1	2	2	1	2	2	

Exploits →

Fig. 4. Reduced change distribution matrix C_R

The heat map corresponding to the matrix C is shown by Fig. 5(a). It provides a quick overview of the security configuration of the managed network. Since the security analyst is interested only in newly introduced changes, we reduced the original matrix C to the matrix C_R, as shown in Fig. 4. Such a reduced matrix C_R and respective heat map in Fig. 5(b) shows the concise representation of the newly introduced changes in the network attack surface.

The rows and columns of the matrix C_R can be placed in any order, without affecting the "require relationship" between initial conditions and exploits. But the ordering that capture similarly connected attack graph elements is desirable. In particular, we seek an order that tends to cluster non-zero matrix elements. It allows us to treat such clusters of similarly connected elements as a single unit as we analyze matrix C_R. We, therefore, performed clustering operations to reorder C_R so that the block of similarly connected *require edges* emerge.

The clustering of rows and columns reveals security-relevant information, making essential features apparent for network hardening. Clustering re-arranges the rows and columns of the matrix C_R to form homogeneous groups. In this way, patterns of similar "require relationship" in G_2 are clear, and groups considered as a single unit. For the clustered matrix, we retain the ordering induced by clustering, so that patterns in the attack graph structure are still apparent. The employed clustering technique is fully automatic, is free of the parameter, and having quadratic time complexity in the size of change distribution matrix C_R.

5.3   Observations

Careful analysis of the clustered change distribution matrix reveals the newly introduced changes in the network attack surface. Security analysts make network hardening decisions based on the top initial conditions that contribute most to the attack surface. To extract security-relevant information, we have performed clustering operations over C_R as follows:

1. **Column-wise Clustering**

   Figure 6(b) shows the matrix C_R after column clustering. The essence of such clustering is that it provides knowledge of the initial conditions that enable two or more exploits. Initial conditions, e.g., 27, and 39, are responsible for the successful execution of two exploits each. If anyone of the above two vulnerabilities, i.e., $CVE - 1999 - 0180$ and $CVE - 2008 - 1396$ is patched, then the majority of the attack paths can be removed and hence the attack opportunities available to an adversary. Knowledge of such initial conditions that covers a large number of exploits can be used for efficient network hardening in a resource-constrained environment.

2. **Row-wise Clustering**

   Figure 6(c) shows the matrix C_R after row clustering. The goal is to distinguish between stable and newly introduced exploits. From Fig. 6(c), it is clear

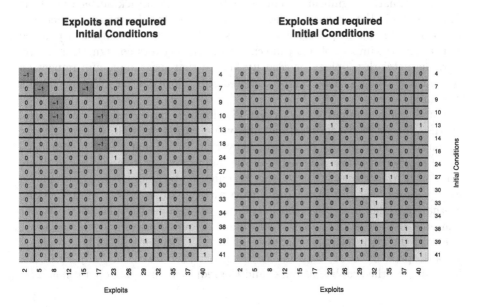

a: Unclustered change distribution matrix C

b: Unclustered change distribution matrix C_R

Fig. 5. Each red block with non-zero entry 1 corresponds to the newly introduced *require edge*. Whereas, each gray block with the non-zero entry (−1) corresponds to the *require edges* that are stable over time Δt. (Color figure online)

that exploit 26, and 35 are stable over time. In an attack graph G_1, exploits 26, and 35 are dormant. In other words, associated vulnerabilities were not exploitable at time t due to the unavailability of one or more initial conditions. Due to the change in the network topology and security factors over Δt, these exploits are activated and become the part of the attack graph G_2. Stable exploits can be easily identified as there is only one *require edge* for them. Whereas, as shown in Fig. 6(c), exploits 23, 29, 32, 37, and 40 are newly introduced exploits. We successfully identified the conserved vulnerability clusters in a dynamic network over time. Proactive detection of such newly introduced exploits alerts, security assessor about the possible intrusion.

3. **Total Clustering (Row-wise Clustering followed by Column-wise Clustering or vice versa)**

   Finally, we have performed a total clustering of over C_R, as shown in Fig. 6(d). The intuition behind such clustering is that it provides knowledge about the portion of the attack surface that suffered maximum change. It shows top k nodes, both initial conditions, and exploits that have maximum impact on the attack surface. As the vulnerability remediation is resource and time consuming, it is crucial to identify the newest and largest problems and remediate those first.

We have shown how our proposed change detection technique can succinctly summarize significant changes in the network attack surface resulting from changes in the network (or host) configuration. In other words, our change detection technique helps security analysts in doing what-if analysis of planned changes and the impact of real-time changes in the network configuration. Moreover, the network topology or security factors that have maximum impact on the network attack surface can be detected and prioritized for efficient network hardening.

Our implementation of the change distribution matrix uses Python sparse matrices for internal computations and visualization, as well. Essentially, the computational complexity of operations over the sparse matrices is proportional to the number of nonzero elements in the matrix (in our case number of newly introduced *require edges*). Our change distribution technique is fully automatic, uses quadratic memory in the order of vertices to store the C_R matrix. As an alternative to the change distribution matrix, one can use the adjacency list. The adjacency list keeps all the newly introduced required edges and uses no space to record the edges that are not present in G_2. Therefore, there is a trade-off (in both space and time) between change distribution matrix and adjacency list, depending on the graph sparseness and the required clustering operations [26].

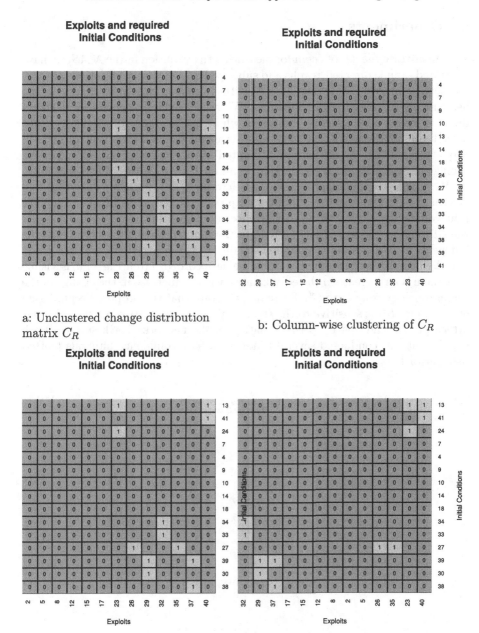

a: Unclustered change distribution matrix C_R

b: Column-wise clustering of C_R

c: Row-wise clustering of C_R

d: Total clustering of C_R

Fig. 6. Clustering operations over change distribution matrix C_R

6   Experiments

To demonstrate the use of *ecgm* for measuring the variation in the $\mathcal{NAS}$, we have generated sample directed graphs and subjected it to arbitrary variations to show an increase in graph edit distance (d) with increasing degree of change in the network topology and security factors. We have randomly generated arbitrary directed graph G containing 100 nodes where the average edge density is not more than 3. In practice, the maximum edges incident on each type of node in exploit-dependency attack graphs is limited by a constant k [4]. Graphs with average edge density 3 were generated to mimic the properties of attack graphs.

We model the dynamic behavior of digraph G by randomly inserting and deleting vertices to form the modified graph G', subject to an input probability that vertices should be changed. The effect of change in the graph topology on the edit distance d shown in Fig. 7. Here the input probability of change is the independent variable being manipulated during the experiment, and the graph edit distance is the dependent variable being recorded. From Fig. 7, it is visible that there is an increase in the edit distance with an increase in the change in the graph topology from G to G'. Therefore, we state that the proposed ecgm-based edit distance (d) is sensitive to the structural differences between a pair of input attack graphs and hence, to the variation in the network attack surface. Each experiment was conducted several times, with 99% confidence intervals plotted using error bars.

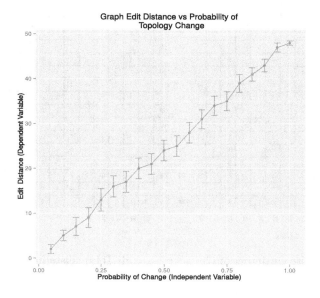

Fig. 7. Graph edit distance vs. Probability of graph topology change.

Computational time for Edit Distance

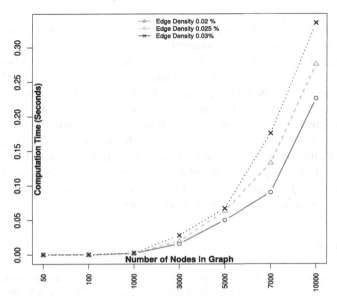

Fig. 8. Computation time for edit distance under different edge densities.

Because of the unavailability of benchmark data sets in the attack graph domain, we made use of synthetic data sets to find out the computational complexity of the proposed ecgm-based technique. The test is conducted to confirm whether the results obtained for a small hypothetical network can be generalized to large enterprise networks. We have generated two synthetic data sets that constitute normally-distributed random edges with an average edge density of 0.02%. In particular, we made use of the Fan Chung algorithm [6] to create such data sets. For each synthetic data set with average edge density 0.02%, we have a graph series (S). Each graph in a sequence consists of 50, 100, 1000, 3000, 5000, 7000, and 10000 nodes. Another series S' is generated as a counterpart subjected to random variations (with input probability of change: 0.05%) to show an increase in the edit distance d, for evaluation of *ecgm* computation times. The above experiment is replicated average edge density, such as 0.025% and 0.03%.

To assess the computational complexity of ecgm-based edit distance, we use both the series S and S'. We have chosen the first graph, G_1 from S, comprising 50 unique nodes. Another graph G'_1 from S' with the same number of nodes (as in G_1) but few with different label representation chosen. These two graphs G_1 and G'_1 are evaluated for edit distance. The preceding procedure replicated for all other graphs in a series S. As depicted in Fig. 8, the effect of higher edge densities on the computation time of edit distance is apparent. It exhibits higher computational times required for graphs with higher edge densities.

7 Conclusions

We have presented a differential attack graph-based change detection technique to assess changes in the attack surface of dynamic computer networks. An error-correcting graph matching (ecgm) based similarity measure is employed to identify the degree of change in the attack surface. Further, we introduced a change distribution matrix-based technique in the context of exploit-dependency attack graphs, so that the portion (or region) of the attack graph that suffered change inferred quickly. The newly introduced changes then grouped to facilitate efficient network hardening. Such a change distribution technique can help make the attack graph more understandable and useful. We explored the viability and efficacy of the proposed method and showed that our approach is capable of assessing change in the attack surface at the level of initial conditions, and hence can be used in practice for network hardening.

References

1. Bhattacharya, P., Ghosh, S.K.: Analytical framework for measuring network security using exploit dependency graph. IET Inf. Secur. **6**(4), 264–270 (2012)
2. Bondy, J.A., Murty, U.S.R., et al.: Graph Theory with Applications, vol. 290. Macmillan, London (1976)
3. Bopche, G.S., Mehtre, B.M.: Extending attack graph-based metrics for enterprise network security management. In: Nagar, A., Mohapatra, D.P., Chaki, N. (eds.) Proceedings of 3rd International Conference on Advanced Computing, Networking and Informatics. SIST, vol. 44, pp. 315–325. Springer, New Delhi (2016). https://doi.org/10.1007/978-81-322-2529-4_33
4. Bopche, G.S., Mehtre, B.M.: Graph similarity metrics for assessing temporal changes in attack surface of dynamic networks. Comput. Secur. **64**, 16–43 (2017)
5. Bunke, H., Shearer, K.: A graph distance metric based on the maximal common subgraph. Pattern Recogn. Lett. **19**(3–4), 255–259 (1998)
6. Chung, F., Lu, L.: Connected components in random graphs with given expected degree sequences. Ann. Comb. **6**(2), 125–145 (2002)
7. CVE: Common vulnerabilities and exposures. https://cve.mitre.org/
8. Cybenko, G., Jajodia, S., Wellman, M.P., Liu, P.: Adversarial and uncertain reasoning for adaptive cyber defense: building the scientific foundation. In: Prakash, A., Shyamasundar, R. (eds.) ICISS 2014. LNCS, vol. 8880, pp. 1–8. Springer, Cham (2014). https://doi.org/10.1007/978-3-319-13841-1_1
9. Dai, F., Hu, Y., Zheng, K., Wu, B.: Exploring risk flow attack graph for security risk assessment. IET Inf. Secur. **9**(6), 344–353 (2015)
10. GhasemiGol, M., Ghaemi-Bafghi, A., Takabi, H.: A comprehensive approach for network attack forecasting. Comput. Secur. **58**, 83–105 (2016)
11. Ghosh, N., Chokshi, I., Sarkar, M., Ghosh, S.K., Kaushik, A.K., Das, S.K.: NetSecuritas: an integrated attack graph-based security assessment tool for enterprise networks. In: Proceedings of the International Conference on Distributed Computing and Networking, p. 30. ACM (2015)
12. Huang, Z.: Human-centric training and assessment for cyber situation awareness. Ph.D. thesis, University of Delaware (2015)

13. Idika, N., Bhargava, B.: Extending attack graph-based security metrics and aggregating their application. IEEE Trans. Dependable Secure Comput. **9**(1), 75–85 (2012)
14. Ingols, K., Chu, M., Lippmann, R., Webster, S., Boyer, S.: Modeling modern network attacks and countermeasures using attack graphs. In: 2009 Annual Computer Security Applications Conference, pp. 117–126. IEEE (2009)
15. Jajodia, S., Noel, S., Kalapa, P., Albanese, M., Williams, J.: Cauldron-mission-centric cyber situational awareness with defense in depth (2011)
16. Kaynar, K.: A taxonomy for attack graph generation and usage in network security. J. Inf. Secur. Appl. **29**, 27–56 (2016)
17. Koutra, D., Vogelstein, J.T., Faloutsos, C.: DELTACON: a principled massive-graph similarity function. In: Proceedings of the 2013 SIAM International Conference on Data Mining, pp. 162–170. SIAM (2013)
18. Kundu, A., Ghosh, S.K.: A multi-objective search strategy to select optimal network hardening measures. Int. J. Decis. Support Syst. **1**(1), 130–148 (2015)
19. Kvasnicka, V., Pospichal, J.: Fast evaluation of chemical distance by tabu search algorithm. J. Chem. Inf. Comput. Sci. **34**(5), 1109–1112 (1994)
20. Liao, Q., Striegel, A.: Intelligent network management using graph differential anomaly visualization. In: 2012 IEEE Network Operations and Management Symposium, pp. 1008–1014. IEEE (2012)
21. Manadhata, P., Wing, J.: Measuring a system's attack surface. Technical report CMU-CS-04-102, January 2004
22. Manadhata, P., Wing, J.: An attack surface metric. IEEE Trans. Softw. Eng. **37**(3), 371–386 (2011)
23. Messmer, B.: Efficient graph matching algorithms for preprocessed model graphs (1996)
24. Messmer, B., Bunke, H.: A new algorithm for error-tolerant subgraph isomorphism detection. IEEE Trans. Pattern Anal. Mach. Intell. **20**(5), 493–504 (1998)
25. Ning, P., Xu, D.: Learning attack strategies from intrusion alerts. In: Proceedings of the 10th ACM Conference on Computer and Communications Security, pp. 200–209. ACM (2003)
26. Noel, S., Jajodia, S.: Understanding complex network attack graphs through clustered adjacency matrices. In: 21st Annual Computer Security Applications Conference, ACSAC 2005, pp. 10-pp. IEEE (2005)
27. Noel, S., Jajodia, S.: Metrics suite for network attack graph analytics. In: CISR 2014, pp. 5–8 (2014)
28. Noel, S., Jajodia, S.: A suite of metrics for network attack graph analytics. In: Wang, L., Jajodia, S., Singhal, A. (eds.) Network Security Metrics, pp. 141–176. Springer, Cham (2017). https://doi.org/10.1007/978-3-319-66505-4_7
29. Noel, S., Jajodia, S., O'Berry, B., Jacobs, M.: Efficient minimum-cost network hardening via exploit dependency graphs. In: Proceedings of 19th Annual Computer Security Applications Conference, pp. 86–95. IEEE (2003)
30. Noel, S., Wang, L., Singhal, A., Jajodia, S.: Measuring security risk of networks using attack graphs. IJNGC **1**, 135–147 (2010)
31. Ou, X., Boyer, W.F., McQueen, M.A.: A scalable approach to attack graph generation. In: Proceedings of the 13th ACM Conference on Computer and Communications Security, pp. 336–345. ACM (2006)
32. Ou, X., Govindavajhala, S., Appel, A.W.: MulVAL: a logic-based network security analyzer. In: USENIX Security Symposium, Baltimore, MD, vol. 8, pp. 113–128 (2005)

33. Pamula, J., Jajodia, S., Ammann, P., Swarup, V.: A weakest-adversary security metric for network configuration security analysis. In: Proceedings of the 2nd ACM workshop on Quality of Protection, pp. 31–38. ACM (2006)

34. Poolsappasit, N., Dewri, R., Ray, I.: Dynamic security risk management using Bayesian attack graphs. IEEE Trans. Dependable Secure Comput. **9**(1), 61–74 (2012)

35. Raymond, J.W., Gardiner, E.J., Willett, P.: RASCAL: calculation of graph similarity using maximum common edge subgraphs. Comput. J. **45**(6), 631–644 (2002)

36. Showbridge, P., Kraetzl, M., Ray, D.: Detection of abnormal change in dynamic networks. In: Proceedings of Information, Decision and Control, IDC 1999, pp. 557–562 (1999)

37. Tupper, M., Zincir-Heywood, A.N.: VEA-bility security metric: a network security analysis tool. In: 2008 Third International Conference on Availability, Reliability and Security, pp. 950–957. IEEE (2008)

38. Wang, L., Jajodia, S., Singhal, A., Cheng, P., Noel, S.: k-zero day safety: a network security metric for measuring the risk of unknown vulnerabilities. IEEE Trans. Dependable Secure Comput. **11**(1), 30–44 (2014)

39. Wang, L., Noel, S., Jajodia, S.: Minimum-cost network hardening using attack graphs. Comput. Commun. **29**(18), 3812–3824 (2006)

Author Index

Printed in the United States
By Bookmasters